HV
6529   Watkins, Ronald J.
.W38
1993   Birthright.

$22.50

DATE			

BAKER & TAYLOR BOOKS

BIRTHRIGHT

ALSO BY RONALD J. WATKINS

High Crimes and Misdemeanors
Evil Intentions

BIRTHRIGHT

MURDER, GREED, AND POWER IN THE U-HAUL FAMILY DYNASTY

RONALD J. WATKINS

WILLIAM MORROW AND COMPANY, INC.

NEW YORK

It is the policy of William Morrow and Company, Inc., and its imprints and affiliates, recognizing the importance of preserving what has been written, to print the books we publish on acid-free paper, and we exert our best efforts to that end.

Library of Congress Cataloging-in-Publication Data

Watkins, Ronald J.
    Birthright : murder, greed, and power in the U-Haul family dynasty
 / by Ronald J. Watkins.
        p.   cm.
    Includes index.
    ISBN 0-688-11255-2
    1. Murder—United States—Case studies. 2. Shoen, Leonard Samuel,
1916–   . 3. Businessmen—United States—Biography. 4. U-Haul
International—Officials and employees—Biography. 5. Shoen family.
I. Title.
HV6529.W38   1993
364.1'523'092—dc20
[B]   93-16323
                                                                CIP

Printed in the United States of America

First Edition
1 2 3 4 5 6 7 8 9 10

BOOK DESIGN BY MM DESIGN 2000 INC.

For Jo Ann

ABOUT THE BOOK

U-Haul International is one of the most recognized corporations in America. Its distinctively painted orange and white trailers and trucks are as recognizable on our highways as semitrucks. U-Haul has become such a part of America it is difficult to imagine there was ever a time when such a company did not exist. Yet in 1945, when Leonard Samuel Shoen built his first trailer, the idea of a nationwide network of one-way rental trailers and trucks was considered absurd.

In those days Americans with money paid a van line to move them, and those without it overloaded cars and sold or gave away what they could not carry. Trailers were rare and had to be purchased for the move with the hope, often futile, of reselling them at the end of the trip.

U-Haul International became a four-billion-dollar company with an annual income approaching one billion dollars, and it was, for nearly all its history, the unique creation of its founder, L. S. Shoen. It was, and is, one of the largest family-held corporations in America. Despite this, the family that owns and runs this multibillion-dollar empire has until recently shunned publicity and is largely unknown.

It was L. S. Shoen's dream to build a business empire, then have his family take over from him. U-Haul was to be his legacy. He lived to see, and bitterly regret, the realization of that dream. Sadly the story of the Shoen family and of U-Haul is a tale of greed, nepotism, and murder.

It is said that no one can know the truth of a marriage from the outside, for only the couple know themselves. It is also likely true that no one but one of its members can really know a family. This is, in large measure, an examination of an American family, and only the candid members of that family can truly know how close to the mark this book has come. However, it is also a fact that to observe from the outside can reveal a greater truth. And so it is here.

Various members of the Shoen family, their associates, and their friends participated with the project for different and sometimes not very noble motives. Some took part out of a sense of duty and deeply felt obligation. The single most remarkable revelation in this enterprise for me was the determination of members of the Shoens to protect others in the family even in the light of monstrous events and grotesque misconduct. Memories of holidays spent together, of play as children all served emotionally to temper a logical scathing condemnation of family behavior.

In May 1991 I proposed a book on the Shoen family and U-Haul to my publisher, William Morrow and Company. At the time I had never spoken with a single member of the family, nor had I formed an opinion about the family feud then being waged. After receiving a contract, I wrote letters to all the major figures in the Shoen family to solicit their assistance. Following negotiation, it was agreed that in exchange for his cooperation L. S. Shoen would share in the proceeds from this book. It was also agreed that I would have exclusive control over the work. Neither L. S. Shoen nor his representatives have seen any portion of this book prior to publication. It was expressly agreed that I would portray events and L. S. Shoen as I saw them, and if he was cast in an unfavorable light, so be it. This was a difficult request of a man accustomed to control, but L. S. Shoen entered the project with considerable dedication.

As a consequence, I was given substantial access to his private journals, family letters, taped telephone conversations, decades of home movies, and a vast trove of documents gathered over a lifetime. It was material enough for ten books, let alone one. Unfortunately L. S. Shoen's cooperation was not total, and he often ignored requests for journal entries covering crucial periods of his life or produced copies with portions excised. Some of the information obtained during interviews was not accurate in that it was inconsistent with the established facts or contrary to other, sworn statements he had made.

All this is familiar ground to writers of nonfiction, and L. S. Shoen was no worse and to some extent considerably better than other sources I have used in previous books. He demonstrated a remarkable level of candor in examining his own life and was far more merciless on himself than on any other person we discussed. Still, there were areas where he withheld or sought to mislead.

There were some sixteen pending lawsuits involving Shoen family members during the period of research, so in addition to the material provided by Mr. Shoen, more than one hundred depositions were available. They proved a wealth of information, especially from those who declined to be interviewed.

Repeated efforts were made to talk to every Shoen child. Those who refused either ignored or rejected those requests on several occasions. My thanks to Dr. Samuel Shoen, Michael Shoen, and Katrina Shoen for their participation. My thanks also to those children and others who asked not to be named.

Several key participants declined to be interviewed. They were Edward "Joe" Shoen, Mark Shoen, Suzanne Shoen Anderson, and Harry DeShong, Jr. Nevertheless, I sought out others to tell their stories as they knew them, studied their depositions, and have labored to be evenhanded and fair in their portrayals. There are anecdotes about which only the involved parties have knowledge. I would have included alternate versions, but as no interview was granted, I had no opportunity to do so.

Edward "Joe" Shoen, who was chief executive officer for U-Haul, also refused me access to the corporate archives. In fact, he personally informed me I would be arrested if I attempted to enter any portion of the U-Haul corporate offices other than the public cafeteria. As a consequence, the history of U-Haul has been re-created from public records, the private records of L. S. Shoen, and the memories of many who were there.

It should be understood that nearly every source I approached either declined to participate or insisted that his or her cooperation never be divulged. Almost to a person, sources told me that they feared reprisal if they were known to have cooperated. I was repeatedly told of U-Haul employees' being fired for having granted interviews to the police investigating the murder of Eva Shoen. My assurances of confidentiality have required that sources rarely be named in the text and that it be written in places so as to be source-neutral.

In many cases potential sources refused not only cooperation but even the lowest level of contact with me. Telephones at U-Haul were routinely monitored by staff loyal to upper management. Messages left for one person were commonly answered by someone more senior and much closer to management. I quickly switched my approach and began calling employees at their homes. Under oath Edward "Joe" Shoen testified that the company monitored employees' telephones and possibly their homes as well.* In the belief that the call was being monitored and they would be fired for having answered the telephone, some potential sources were reduced to tears simply because I had called them suggesting a meeting. More than one source told me I would be murdered for even attempting to write this book.

During most of the period of research for this work I was under subpoena by either Edward "Joe" Shoen or Mark Shoen to produce all my research material, to name my sources, and to tell everything I had uncovered regarding the murder of Eva Berg Shoen. Both waged a relentless campaign to discover my confidential sources.

---

*Deposition of Edward "Joe" Shoen, Maricopa County Superior Court, CV 88-20139, Volume III, taken December 6, 1988:

ATTORNEY: All right. I seek also to ask you about tapes. Has anybody ever had any taping done of the telephones at U-Haul or at the residences or on the private lines or U-Haul lines of any employees, to your knowledge?
EDWARD "JOE" SHOEN: Yes.
Q: And in the last two years to what extent was this taping done and by whom?
A: Taping is a regular procedure there.
Q: But who did it?
A: We have a whole department that does that, and I don't know . . .
Q: And the name of that department is called what?
A: Something like sales monitoring or something of that nature . . .
Q: Do they tape your phone, too?
A: No, usually they give me tapes. . . .

I retained the services of my friend Guy Bradley Price, who served as my legal counsel.

In December 1991 the federal court in Phoenix ruled I was protected by the state's media shield law, but three months later, following an adverse ruling by an Arizona court of appeals concerning another writer, my protective order was lifted. The federal court refused my request for a stay of the deposition while a renewed motion was prepared, and I was compelled to appear. At that two-and-a-half-hour deposition I invoked my First Amendment right to refuse to answer any question concerning sources 116 times. The U-Haul lawyers took me before the federal judge and argued that I be sanctioned—i.e., jailed—until I answered.

The American Association of Publishers filed an amicus brief on my behalf, as did the Authors Guild, the PEN American Center, the Society of Authors' Representatives, and the Arizona Chapter of the American Civil Liberties Union.

Armed with this ammunition, my attorney persuaded the federal court to restore the protective order in most regards, based this time on my rights under the First Amendment. Unfortunately the court's subsequent interpretation of this last ruling required that I produce my tapes and notes of my interviews with L. S. Shoen and that I answer all questions put to me about anything, confidential or not, that he may have told me. When I refused, I was cited for contempt of court and fined two hundred dollars a day until I complied. I appealed the federal court's order to the Ninth Circuit. The New York law firm of Weil, Gotshal & Manges signed on board as co-counsel, pro bono. Attorney Gloria C. Phares, working with my attorney, Guy Price, prepared and submitted the Ninth Circuit briefs on my behalf. The matter was argued orally in San Francisco on December 16, 1992, and is pending at this writing.

This all served to remind me just how precarious the right to publish really is in the United States. My thanks to my publisher, William Morrow and Company, for advancing additional funds to me to make possible my defense of this work.

A note about U-Haul: As early as 1950 what is commonly referred to as U-Haul was actually three interrelated corporations, and by 1970 there were more than thirty-five. At that time a new parent corporation was organized and named Amerco. It remains the primary holding company to this day. To avoid confusion, and since it is essentially correct, I have identified the company throughout the book simply as U-Haul, though that strictly applies now to only a single, albeit the major, component of the Amerco companies.

Acknowledgments that are essential to the writer are generally skipped by the reader, but the reality is that without the help of many people this book and others like it would never be produced. I thank L. S. Shoen for his courtesy in what was nearly always a painful process. I thank his wife Carol for accepting me into her home and welcoming me. Thanks to San Miguel County Sheriff Bill Masters, Investigator Kim Pound, and Coroner Robert A. Dempsey for their professionalism and courtesies.

My thanks also to my agent, Mike Hamilburg, and his assistant, Joanie Socola, for their patience, encouragement, and assistance.

Editors can make or break any writer, and I have been blessed with one who consistently demonstrates a gentle touch and respect for the original manuscript. My deepest appreciation to Lisa Drew, who was senior editor and vice-president at William Morrow and Company when the book was contracted and who completed nearly all the editing, for her countless suggestions and criticisms that served to produce a superior work. I also thank Bob Shuman for putting up with my complaints and for always doing what he says he will when he says he will do it. A rare commodity. Thanks to him also for filling in for Lisa at the last moment when she left Morrow to join Macmillan as publisher of Lisa Drew Books. Thanks to Katherine Boyle for her courtesies and assistance.

Publicists usually receive no praise because they are assigned the book only after the acknowledgment has been written, so I wish to thank my Morrow publicist, Phyllis Heller, for the outstanding work she performed for my first two books.

I thank those personal friends who offered suggestions and encouragement throughout the process, including Steve and Lisa Tufts, Allen Reed, and Phil MacDonnell. Special thanks to Mike Murphy for his time and effort.

While it is possible to read every document, to examine every nook and cranny personally, it would slow the process and increase the risk of overloading the narrative with minutiae. For that and for her suggestions and criticisms I have always relied upon my wife. While other writers have research teams, I have Jo Ann. Once again she served as my research assistant and spent untold hours on the most boring material imaginable, plucking from it nuggets that served to explain seeming mysteries based on other material and directed my inquiry into new, meaningful areas. She is my biggest fan and my closest friend, and I thank her from the bottom of my heart for her devotion and assistance.

In this work are attributed and unattributed statements of members of the Shoen family, of current and former employees of U-Haul, which name individuals they suspect or believe are responsible for or are implicated in the murder of Eva Berg Shoen. It must be kept in mind that no one has officially been publicly linked to the murder nor has anyone been arrested or charged. These statements are offered not as evidence of the guilt of those named but rather to show the states of mind of the speakers, that is, their emotional attitudes. It must be assumed that each person whose name is mentioned as a possible suspect is innocent of involvement.

Finally, a word about the Shoen family. Some of the most decent and honorable people I have ever met are Shoens, and some of the biggest scoundrels I have known belong to the family as well. Lest we judge them too harshly, bear in mind the statement of one of the children: "It's all about money. Look at your own family. Imagine a billion dollars thrown on them. Imagine the consequences that would have."

—Ronald J. Watkins
Phoenix

THE FAMILY

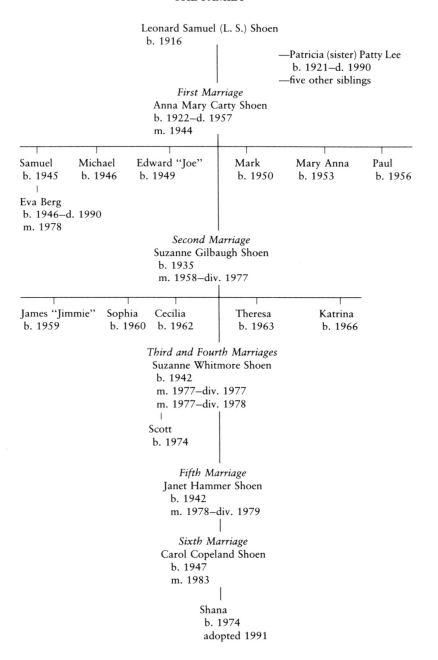

Leonard Samuel (L. S.) Shoen
b. 1916

—Patricia (sister) Patty Lee
b. 1921–d. 1990
—five other siblings

First Marriage
Anna Mary Carty Shoen
b. 1922–d. 1957
m. 1944

Samuel	Michael	Edward "Joe"	Mark	Mary Anna	Paul
b. 1945	b. 1946	b. 1949	b. 1950	b. 1953	b. 1956

Eva Berg
b. 1946–d. 1990
m. 1978

Second Marriage
Suzanne Gilbaugh Shoen
b. 1935
m. 1958–div. 1977

James "Jimmie"	Sophia	Cecilia	Theresa	Katrina
b. 1959	b. 1960	b. 1962	b. 1963	b. 1966

Third and Fourth Marriages
Suzanne Whitmore Shoen
b. 1942
m. 1977–div. 1977
m. 1977–div. 1978

Scott
b. 1974

Fifth Marriage
Janet Hammer Shoen
b. 1942
m. 1978–div. 1979

Sixth Marriage
Carol Copeland Shoen
b. 1947
m. 1983

Shana
b. 1974
adopted 1991

CONTENTS

17

How sharper than a serpent's tooth it is
To have a thankless child!

—William Shakespeare, *King Lear*

No man should give away his wealth or power until he
dies. No way! No way!

—L. S. Shoen, founder of U-Haul

I have supped with an alleged devil and dined with a
maniac and all the while I have loved these same people.

—Katrina Shoen, writing of her father and brother Joe

TELLURIDE

In late summer in Telluride, Colorado, the night wind rustles through the aspen, and there is a soft whisper as it moves across the face of the mountains. The scent is a gentle fragrance, free of all trace of human presence.

On the approach highway, State 145, winding through the mountains just three miles from the Telluride turnoff, are the Ski Ranch estates. While it is not the most exclusive in the area, it is an enclave for the well-off, those who desire and can afford privacy. The houses are spaced far apart on Lawson Hill, and the graveled roads snake back and forth, concealing most houses from one another.

On Sunday evening, August 5, 1990, Dr. Samuel Shoen had unexpectedly driven to his other residence in Paradise Valley, Arizona, to prepare himself for the next phase of the seemingly unending struggle for control of the multibillion-dollar corporation owned by the family into which he had been born. Left alone in their half-million-dollar log cabin, his forty-four-year-old wife, Norwegian-born Eva Berg Shoen, sat with their two children, Bente and Esben, and the ten-year-old daughter of a friend who was spending the night.

Windows are popular in Telluride because people love the outdoors. They are left uncovered even at night, and light streams from them into the darkness like searchlights. At a distance the windows are bright jewels in a black sea.

Eva raised saluki dogs, and they were outside in the large fenced yard. Normally quiet, they were uneasy this night, and Eva could not silence them. Usually obedient and quiet, the dogs became agitated at unpredictable intervals. It lasted a night or two, then went away, only to return a week or so later.

This night she brought them into the house, but they immediately ran to the windows and barked uncontrollably. Finally Eva gave up trying to quiet them and put them in a basement room designed for their keep. There the animals piled together and in the comfort of the pack lapsed into watchless sleep.

Eva put the children to bed in their ground-floor room, then went upstairs to her bedroom and turned out the lights. Slowly the house quieted as she fell asleep, alone with the sound of the wind outside for comfort. It was, she often said, much like her native Norway.

After midnight men entered the silent house and softly crept through the living room, then up the wooden stairs. They moved across the landing, into the bedroom, where they seized the sleeping Eva. As the men fought to hold her down, she struggled violently against her attackers. She was a slender but very fit woman and was specially trained to protect herself in case of this very possibility.

Eva fought without making a sound. A cry might have awakened the children and placed them in mortal danger. Silently she extended to her children this last measure of a mother's protection. She struggled furiously, bruising herself in her effort to escape.

But it was to no good end. The attack was unrelenting, and she was no match for the men. Once they had her under control, there was no attempt at rape, nor was there a robbery of any kind. Everything of value in the house was left untouched. The men had come to take something else.

At close range a single shot from a .25 caliber handgun was fired into her back. She was carried, or dragged herself, to the top of the stairs. Then her killers fled as quietly as they had entered. She lay there with her legs draped down the steps and her upper body on the landing as her heart beat, then slowed, and the life drained from her. After a few moments she was dead.

Early in the morning ten-year-old Bente awoke alone and turned on the television. She let the dogs upstairs, and they romped as usual. Her mother should have been up to make breakfast but uncharacteristically remained upstairs. At seven-thirty Bente watched one of the dogs perform a trick and decided to awaken her mother to tell her about it. As she reached the top of the stairs, she saw her mother's lifeless, pale body and began to scream.

San Miguel County Sheriff William "Bill" Masters hoped it was a mistake when he received the telephone call because this was one of those perfect Colorado Rocky Mountain summer mornings. Just back from a trip east he was not ready for trouble. He located the Shoen house only with difficulty and was greeted by the lay coroner, a local real estate agent. "I think she's really dead," the coroner said. "Jeanne's inside."

Jeanne Josie was a neighbor, a friend of the family, who took the children in after they discovered their mother's body. She met Masters by the door. "She's dead. I think she fell," she told the sheriff.

Masters told them both to leave the house while he checked the body.

At the top of the stairs Eva did not look to him as if she had fallen. Blood covered the sheet in which she was partially wrapped, and the bedroom was soaked in blood. On the floor the sun caught the glint of metal. Masters bent over and stared at the .25 caliber shell casing.

In his ten years as sheriff this was his first murder.

Investigator Kim Pound arrived a few minutes later, and Masters sent him down the street to interview the children at Jeanne's. There Pound heard an incredible story as the youngsters maturely told him of corporate boardroom brawls, endless lawsuits, threats, and accusations. This quiet family, he learned, was vastly rich and engaged in a violent, relentless dispute for control of the family wealth. He called the police in Arizona to confirm what the children said. Before Pound left to brief the sheriff, eight-year-old Esben took his sleeve and asked in his child's trusting voice, "You will find who killed my mom, won't you?"

When Masters's deputy told him what he had learned, the sheriff was incredulous. Could a family feud have led to this? It seemed impossible to believe. And for a time it was impossible to believe as his tiny office explored the other more traditional and local leads. But within weeks the search led Masters and Pound out of the mountains of Colorado, across the alien landscape of the Navajo Nation, down into the metropolis of Phoenix. Because it was from there, the investigation told them, the murder of Eva Berg Shoen had emanated.

The Shoen family was severed into two competing camps that were struggling for control of a multibillion-dollar enterprise. More than a dozen lawsuits had been filed, and the feud had been prominently featured in national magazines. There had been fistfights and death threats. It had been brother against brother, son against father, for years. And now this.

To those who knew her best, and knew the family into which she had married, there was little doubt who had caused her death or why Eva Shoen had been murdered. Others refused to think that her death could have anything to do with the family struggle.

Understanding what happened that summer of 1990 requires a journey that begins a lifetime earlier, in a peaceful valley of Oregon, in a nation that exists today only in memory.

CHAPTER ONE

AVOIDING THE TRAP

W hen the end of summer comes to the Willamette Valley of western Oregon, the groves are ripe and ready for harvest. So it is today; so it was in 1932. Locals and migrant workers gathered in the rich valley to harvest berries, cherries, plums, hops, and, in the fall, apples. In the years of the Great Depression the temperate climate drew the hopeful for hundreds of miles. Bounty could be plucked from the bushes and trees, and farmers paid hard cash for bushel baskets of fruit.

The America of 1932 was a poorer nation, a more rural country with a less educated population and fewer certainties. There was no national unemployment system, no economic umbrella against want save charity. It was the fear of want and deprivation that brought these workers to the splendor of this valley.

The work was demanding, but such were the times that entire families joined in. A few lived in makeshift housing on the farms where they worked, but large numbers camped beside their Model-T Fords or pickup trucks. When the harvest was good, they labored to exhaustion in the long summer hours; when it was not, they did without. These were people who had come here of necessity—decent, hardworking people leading, if not a hand-to-mouth existence, at least a season-to-season one. They had been evicted from farms, had left family and friends in search of a better life.

One of the families working the crops was that of Samuel Joseph Shoen, his wife, Sophia, and their seven children. There was, on the surface, little to distinguish the Shoens from other migrant workers. But life had not always been like this for them.

Twenty-four-year-old Samuel had been working the harvest outside Bismarck, North Dakota, when he met eighteen-year-old Sophia. Following a whirlwind courtship driven by the knowledge that Samuel would soon be moving on, the couple were married. Their first child, a daughter, followed a respectable time later, and in 1916, on Leap Year's Day, their second child was born and named Leonard Samuel Shoen.

In 1923 Samuel Shoen made the decision to try his fortune out west and moved the family by car to the hamlet of Shedd, Oregon, with a population of four hundred. With his savings of seven hundred dollars he bought the confectionery store and became a local businessman. Over the next few years he acquired the general store, the soda fountain, a lumberyard, and a service station from which he also sold cars.

His children were the best known in town and the most spoiled. Leonard Samuel, called in later years both Lenny and Sam but ultimately simply L.S., was known for his stubbornness and was nicknamed Stub by his parents. He demonstrated an early interest in the family enterprises, an interest his father encouraged. Even in strange stores the boy wandered behind the counter to look, as if there by right. The family prospered, and there was no reason for this not to have been Samuel's life course. But in the first of what proved to be a string of many strategic errors in business judgment, Samuel abruptly sold his businesses in 1928 and with the proceeds bought a red dirt farm near Turner, Oregon—a farm with a three-thousand-dollar mortgage.

During that first year agricultural prices plummeted, and it was quickly apparent there would be no money for interest payments, let alone for the debt itself. The oldest boys and their father hired themselves out pitching hay, working twelve hours a day. L.S. worked so hard that at night he lacked the strength to eat his supper.

There was not enough money to pay the interest the first year so the payment was rescheduled and the summer L.S. was fourteen the family went to the fields. The labor of a migrant worker was demanding. Hands were cut and chafed from the picking, stained from overripe berries, and backs ached from the effort. Five years L.S.'s junior was sister Patricia, called Tootsie by the family when she was a child and Patty Lee when she was grown. L.S. was her favorite, and she worked beside him during the days.

These long months picking the harvest could have been an unpleasant time, but Samuel was a persistent optimist and a consummate teacher. This period of working as laborers in the orchards, he explained to his children, was only temporary. Life was the way it was described in the Bible: Seven years of bad were always followed by seven of good. Someday he would be a millionaire, and they would have the luxuries of life. In the Oregon summer nights L.S.'s face was lit by the fire as he sat beside his father, listening to his promises and dreams, believing it would be so.

When the harvest was over, the Shoens returned to their farm in Turner and L.S. went back to school. The demands for money were such that he took any job he could for pay and more often than not attended high school only two or three days a week. One winter he left school entirely to cut cordwood and as a result, though he was quick and studious, he was barely able to graduate the spring he turned seventeen in 1933.

It was the custom in this region to marry soon after high school graduation. L.S. believed marriage was a trap he wished to avoid. He vowed he would remain single and never have any children.

Circumstances presented an unexpected opportunity when Samuel's brother died, leaving Samuel a small inheritance. While the rest of the family remained on the farm, Samuel and L.S. traveled to Portland, where they enrolled in barber school. Samuel found it impossible to get work for his keep. The industrious L.S. had little trouble, on the other hand, and he found a job sweeping out a small downtown hotel in exchange for a room for the two of them. At a nearby restaurant he worked nights washing dishes, often until 4:00 A.M., in exchange for their meals. During days he attended barber school.

L.S. carefully saved, actually pennies, since he would need a barber's shirt once he graduated. A young man of boundless energy and a quick intellect, L.S. walked miles about the city. He loved to dance but had no extra money, so at night he hung around outside the dance halls, watching the well-dressed couples enviously and listening to the enticing rhythms of swing.

Nine months after moving to Portland, Samuel and L.S. were graduated as apprentice barbers. However, rather than practice his new profession, Samuel decided to invest what was left of his inheritance into building a small hotel near Salem, Oregon. L.S. declined to join him and landed a job in Klamath Falls, Oregon, where he intended to serve his apprenticeship before becoming a master barber.

Though only eighteen years old, L.S. believed that nothing was gained in life without sacrifice, and he was prepared to pay whatever price was required to achieve success, to become someone. He had also decided that he should enter a business, though he saw the step as temporary. He did not know a great deal about barbering, but already he could see the difference between being a barber and owning a shop. While others were satisfied to practice their skill, L.S. planned to be an entrepreneur. The desire to be a businessman, to control his own destiny, was already deeply planted.

For the next three years L.S. served his apprenticeship, and by working odd jobs, he earned twenty dollars a week. For some time he had considered his life's course. He was motivated in no small part by the economic deprivation he and his siblings had suffered as migrant workers as well as by his need to improve his standing in the community. He decided he would become a medical doctor. Doctors were respected and well paid, he reasoned, even in the worst of times.

L.S. also decided he would run a barbershop until he completed medical school. He applied to and was accepted at Oregon State University in Corvallis and near the campus located a two-chair barbershop. For two hundred dollars down and regular payments, he became the owner and within the year had paid for the shop but sold it to loan the money to his father.

L.S. located an unused barbershop in downtown Corvallis, which he rented for five dollars a week. In Albany he opened a three-chair shop in the St. Francis Hotel, and in both Albany and Corvallis he operated beauty parlors. His sister Patty Lee finished beauty school and was put to work managing a parlor for him.

With sharp clothes, a pencil-thin mustache, a new car, and money in his pocket, L.S. quickly earned a campus reputation as a party man, and it was a reputation he relished. But with the start of the Second World War he immediately lost his barbers and many of his customers. Almost overnight he had to close his once-thriving shops and by his senior year was forced to support himself by cutting hair in his room.

L.S. entered medical school at the University of Oregon in Portland and decided psychiatry would be his specialty.

Camp Adair had been built outside Portland, and L.S. acquired the concessions for both the barber and beauty shops and arranged for his parents to manage the new business. Later he procured the same arrangements which his father also managed at Hanford, Washington, where the atomic engineers' works were built.

Though he intended to become a doctor, L.S. gave considerable thought to success in business. While most people were content to hold steady jobs, many dreamed of starting businesses and striking it rich. Lots of people, L.S. believed, had good ideas. Many possessed the talent and drive to see their ideas through to success. The difference between him and others, he concluded, was in his willingness to take a risk. And that was the key to success. Americans were afraid of failure, he decided, and that was why the vast majority led narrow lives and settled into jobs that they didn't like but that were secure and paid the bills.

L. S. Shoen was a fit, stout man of above-average height who wore his hair slicked down. With a Mercury convertible and a houseboat on the Willamette River, he acquired the same reputation in medical school he had enjoyed for a time in college. For reasons of ego he worked hard at creating the illusion that balancing a rich social life, receiving good grades, and running his businesses was easy.

As always L.S. was filled with energy, and even after attending classes, and dancing until after midnight, he studied until 4:00 A.M. Generous with his money and flamboyant in manner, he could not help incurring the hostility of some students and professors. Arrogance also came easily to the sharp-dressing L.S., and it created enmity toward him.

L.S.'s reputation existed not just in medical school but even within his own family, where he achieved and exercised a surprising level of control. The greatest responsibility had always fallen to him as the oldest boy, and twice as an adult he had provided his father with a livelihood. If it was possible to become a legend in one's own family, L.S. was on his way to achieving that status. Patty Lee, for one, worshiped her older brother. She enrolled in nearby Marylhurst College, introduced him to her classmates and L.S. routinely attended college dances with them.

To avoid being drafted, he enrolled in the Navy's cadet program and attended classes in uniform. After graduation he planned to enter the service as a psychiatrist. In 1943 L.S. had his life planned.

One Friday evening L.S. was attending a dance with his sister Patty Lee and a few of her friends. L.S. was resplendent in a new tuxedo, matching topcoat, and hat. With his sister was Anna Mary Carty, student body president and recently queen of the ball. She had been raised on her family's farm in nearby Ridgefield, Washington. The dashing L.S. approached her table and asked her to dance.

Anna Mary was soon one of L.S.'s steady girls. After graduation she roomed with Patty Lee Shoen in Portland, where L.S. continued seeing her. Patty Lee and Anna Mary were fast friends, but L.S.'s sister did not consider the farmer's daughter good enough for her brother. She told L.S. she believed her roommate had her sights on him, and L.S. laughed with that full, rich, distinctive Shoen roar, proclaiming with bravado that no woman would catch him; he had been dodging that trap for years.

But of all the women he dated, Anna Mary was the most appealing, and in moments of reflection he realized this was a woman he could marry. Still, he had heard her heart beating erratically and had taken her to consult with a specialist who told him that Anna Mary suffered from tetralogy of Fallot, an extremely serious condition that would result in her premature death. As a consequence, L.S. ruled out any thought of marrying her.

There was an element of coldness in this decision not to marry the woman he loved. When others might be caught up in the emotion of a moment, L.S. could step back and analyze a decision as if he were balancing his bank account. He had a well-above-average intelligence, which had always served him well. He believed it was possible not to be driven by emotion, but rather to make all decisions through logic and self-interest. However, despite his intellectual reservations, L.S. bought Anna Mary a diamond ring. Unable to give it to her, he hid it in a drawer.

The first month of his senior year at medical school L.S. was seated in a lab when he answered "present" for an absent friend. This was a common practice, but L.S. was not just any student, and he had picked the wrong professor. This one declared that L.S. was a "smart aleck" and needed punishment. The pettiness of the infraction was offset by L.S.'s conspicuous behavior. Others on the school's staff agreed, and to his disbelief, he was expelled from medical school.

L.S.'s plans, which he had carefully nurtured, were destroyed in that moment. He believed that resentment over his flamboyant affluent life-style contributed to his expulsion as much as any misconduct on his part, but there was more to it than that. The previous spring he had taken the three-hour oral exam given all students about to enter the senior year. Informed he had failed, he dismissed the exercise as "a farce." While he had been so busy creating the illusion of the successful student, he had neglected his studies.

L.S. was plunged into a deep depression. Since he was no longer enrolled in college, he was immediately inducted into the Navy, not as an officer doctor but as an enlisted recruit. In this black period, of all his college friends, only Anna Mary regarded him with unchanged respect. In a spontaneous act, and still in depression, L.S. proposed to her during a week's leave, presenting her with the ring he had hidden for so many months. Anna Mary told him that she had always wanted to marry him and had prayed for the day when he would ask her.

Patty Lee argued relentlessly that L.S. was making a terrible mistake. L.S. was vulnerable, she said; his life was in ruins. He couldn't let this woman take advantage of him. But L.S. persisted, and on February 4, 1944, the lovely Anna Mary Carty and Leonard Samuel Shoen went to St. Lawrence Catholic Church in Portland to be married. He had little religious training, as his father had been a Protestant and his mother a Catholic, but his mother had seen that he was christened. Anna Mary had made it clear theirs would be a Catholic marriage, and he did not object.

When the priest asked if there was any reason why this couple should not be joined in matrimony, Patty Lee shot to her feet and ranted against Anna Mary. Shouting through her tears so everyone could hear, she begged her brother not to go through with the marriage. Anna Mary, she insisted, was taking advantage of her brother. L.S. didn't really love her; he was doing this only because he was vulnerable. The marriage had to be stopped, and she was going to object until it was.

Those in attendance were shocked by the outburst. There were those present who knew how strongly Patty Lee felt, but they had never expected this. Patty Lee continued ranting without letup and finally was physically pulled from the church. When the buzz created by this outburst trailed off, the ceremony resumed, and in moments L.S. and Anna Mary were married.

CHAPTER TWO

TELL IT TO A. M. CARTY

Following their wedding the newlyweds spent a night together before L.S. returned to training. Within weeks, and before his bride could join him, he was diagnosed with rheumatic fever and transferred to a naval hospital in Corona, California. Anna Mary found a small apartment in Los Angeles, thirty-five miles from the hospital. Though she had been cautioned to have no children, by May Anna Mary was pregnant; Catholic marriages in 1944 produced children early and often.

After several months, though still hospitalized, L.S. was well enough to be up and about. He was trained as a Hospital Apprentice First Class and joined the doctors in their rounds, even covering for them when they were unavailable. In February 1945, Anna Mary gave birth to a son whom the couple named for L.S.'s father, Samuel.

There was a hole in the cyclone fence surrounding the hospital, and L.S. took unauthorized leave by slipping through it. He wanted his wife and son at hand and located a used trailer in a backyard. He then faced the question of moving his household without paying for a moving van.

There were car trailers, but they were few in number. Service stations or welding shops built them with the running gear from cars or trucks, and they sold for seventy-five to one hundred dollars. A service station might keep a "junker" trailer around for a day's rental at two dollars, but there was more money to be made by simply selling it and building another.

L.S. rented one and moved his family, but an idea had formed in his restless mind. That night in his journal he wrote, "I am intrigued by the business potential of this idea especially from the standpoint of one-way rentals." L.S. had begun a journal in 1941, at first jotting down the day's events but over the years adding more and more detail. He had read once that all great men kept a journal, and L.S. intended to be great.

Though his family was now living nearby, L.S. was still technically hospitalized. He could sneak off for a few hours in the evening, but his days were largely free—and boring. Lying there in his bed, with paper and pen, he became consumed with the idea of rental trailers. As he put his mind to the matter, it occurred to him that the real money to be made would be in establishing nationwide rental locations and renting trailers for one-way moves. He worked feverishly on his scheme and finally concluded that it was possible for fifty Americans routinely to require the use of one trailer. One trailer to service every fifty Americans equaled about three million, and at two dollars a day, the figure was mind-boggling.

He even had a name for his new company: U-Haul.

The war ended that summer, and now fully recovered, L.S. was discharged from the Navy. He stayed with a relative in Los Angeles while he called on the trailer rental businesses to see what he could learn. He was surprised at their lack of vision. There would be no competition here.

After a few days he packed up his family and returned to Portland, where he discovered the Internal Revenue Service had held his businesses liable for all the withholding taxes his father had not collected from his employees during the war. As a consequence, L.S. was left with four thousand in cash and about one thousand dollars in barber and beauty equipment he could sell from his now-closed military shops and the one in Hanford.

This was hardly the amount of capital he had planned on to start a national chain of rental centers. With five thousand dollars he could put a down payment on a house and furnish it. He could find a job paying three hundred dollars a month and climb onto the treadmill of middle-class America. He could risk the money, lose it, and have nothing with which to support his family.

Or just maybe he could risk it and succeed.

There was no doubt in his mind what he would do. During the next months the Shoens and their baby lived with relatives because L.S. had no money to spend. The five thousand dollars were for investment.

Within two weeks of returning to Portland, L.S. had bought a junker and put it up for rent. On the wooden sides he carefully painted "U-Haul Co.—Rental Trailers—$2.00 per day."

There were four key innovations that were essential to the eventual success of U-Haul. Within days L.S. had discerned two of them. First, he needed a location for his trailers since he lacked the capital to rent or buy suitable land. Service stations were the solution though the first one turned him down flat, and it was only after several tries that he persuaded a Mobil station to take a trailer. U-Haul was in business.

Each station's share of the fee of 80 cents compared with $1.20 for L.S. just wasn't enough money to tempt an operation that made more pumping gasoline and even more from repairing cars. The trailers had a decidedly haphazard look to them, and service station managers were reluctant to put them on their lots. One manager, Jack Adair, turned L.S. down twice before reluctantly agreeing to take his trailers. While L.S. had been busy presenting an image of success to Adair, the service station manager had not been taken in since each U-Haul hitch was of a different design. But L.S. was an aggressive, tenacious salesman, and as quickly as he acquired trailers, he found stations to locate them.

Since his would be a nationwide company with a standard look, he began marking the trailers all alike. He realized at once that both sitting at a station and moving on a highway, each trailer was a billboard advertising the company. On it he included its name, the rental fee, and soon the telephone number. His second realization had been that advertising was a major expense and the nature of his enterprise had built-in billboards.

Within six months L.S. had spent all his money and placed twenty trailers into use. The haphazardly constructed junkers could not take the abuse to which renters subjected them, and the postwar retreaded tires blew out with depressing frequency. Frames separated; sidings collapsed; trailers came unhitched. L.S. had a steady income, but it all went to service the trailers. He had no capital for further expansion and no real assets against which a bank would lend money. The business was a bust.

L.S. decided to start over and this time to build his own trailers, high-quality trailers, requiring little servicing, which could turn a long-term profit. Anna Mary's father, Bill, offered to let the couple move in with him on the Carty farm and agreed to make his garage available for construction.

L.S. found he could do everything himself except weld the frames. In a pattern that was repeated again and again, L.S. threw himself into learning to weld. The voltage was wrong at the Carty farm, so Bill arranged to have a 220-volt line run to the garage. L.S. read books, bought what he needed, and welded his first frame. His technique was so poor he simply piled the welding rods into the joints until the frame couldn't possibly fall apart. It wasn't pretty, but it worked.

Both to catch the public's eye and for safety's sake, L.S. painted the trailers orange. Anna Mary's eighteen-year-old brother Hap Carty, home on a two-week leave, helped assemble those first U-Haul–built trailers. Then, on his own, L.S. assembled another ten in two months. While doing this, he signed up rental agents across the river to Vancouver, Washington, and from there to Seattle. By the summer of 1946 U-Haul had a fleet of seventy trailers.

When L.S. approached a service station, he claimed to be representing a new company that was big in California, and he never acknowledged he was the owner. To add to the lie of size, and from size to suggest success, L.S. numbered his trailers creatively. The first ten were numbered 101 to 110. The second ten were numbered 211 to 220, the next ten 321 to 330, and so on.

L.S. moved back to Portland, where he rented a service station with a construction bay. A crude house in the rear was thrown into the deal. L.S. had no living money, so Anna Mary, well pregnant with their second child, set up housekeeping with apple boxes for chairs, an oil heater, and a borrowed bed. This became U-Haul headquarters.

Each week L.S. went on the road to collect his fees and service the trailers in his overalls. He worked U-Haul as an obsession. He had one employee to run the station and work on building trailers with him, and by the end of the year a hundred trailers were in use.

But this was still a sideline, one that intrigued him, yes, but not the primary interest of his professional life. He wanted to be a doctor but his efforts to return to medical school were as unsuccessful as he had feared.

When a customer wanted to rent a trailer for a one-way haul to Los Angeles, L.S. gave him his best trailer, the only one with new tires, for twenty-five dollars, called his relation, and asked if he would accept delivery. The morning after it reached Los Angeles, it was stolen from the yard and never seen again.

A few months later L.S. dispatched a second trailer to Los Angeles, and this time he drove down to recruit an agent. After refusals at every gas station he piqued one man's interest, but the owner only wanted to sign up with a major company. "What sort of backing do you have?" he asked.

L.S. considered that. His answer must make the right impression. "Do you think a hundred thousand is sufficient backing?" he asked rhetorically, then signed the agent.

On his return to Portland, he picked up an agent in Oakland. U-Haul now had rental agents from Seattle to Los Angeles. In California U-Haul was presented as a big operation out of Washington and Oregon. In Washington it was a big operation in Oregon and California. Since it was no longer possible for L.S. personally to call on his agents each Monday, they were required to file a report along with the proceeds. He and Anna Mary devoted considerable effort to the necessary paper work. Each week L.S. mailed a new report form with the self-addressed stamped "Mail on Monday" envelope, so he struck on the idea of including an agency bulletin. In time these grew in length and complexity until eventually they became L.S.'s discourses on the meaning of life as well as the efficacy of the work ethic.

With a network of twenty rental agents along the West Coast L.S. took to the road for two and three weeks at a time; to hold down expenses, he slept in the backseat of his car. He ate an unvarying diet of the cheapest hamburgers he could find, wolfing down his food so as not to waste a single second of work time.

Whenever possible, he drove all night, and it was not unusual for him to pick up a hitchhiker and have him drive while L.S. slept in the rear. He arrived at a service station in soiled overalls with a chest of tools and was simply called the trailer man.

In 1947 L.S. bought a lot in Portland for the construction of trailers and in 1948 decided he was ready to go nationwide. He struck on a novel, and daring, plan. He advertised one-way rentals "anywhere." The fact that no agents existed anywhere but on the West Coast was of no concern. A prospective customer was told he could have the trailer for half price. All he had to do was locate a service station owner who might like to be an agent, leave the trailer with the paper work, and tell L.S. where the trailer was. It worked surprisingly well. Several trailers were lost, but by late that year U-Haul had a fleet of two hundred and rental agents scattered nationwide.

But U-Haul had struck a wall in expansion. To be a real success, it had to be everywhere, not scattered about. It had to become synonymous with self-moving. L.S. had no means of finance to obtain the number of trailers he needed, and at his current rate, it would take decades to build them. Though he approached bankers, none would consider risking the kind of money he needed. In Washington, Oregon, and California he organized corporations and for a time attempted to obtain capital by selling shares. But altogether he was able to raise no more than thirty thousand dollars.

L.S. hit the road, driving nationwide. His custom was simply to drop by a rental agent unannounced. If he did not find the operation satisfactory, he exploded in a torrent of profanity that became legendary. He closed agents who were not working out, recruited others, collected rental fees, hunted down stolen trailers, and repaired others in the dead of night. If trailers were kept in a locked compound, he climbed over the fence and repaired them by flashlight. One night in New Orleans the local police arrested him for burglary, and the startled rental agent was dragged down to the station to identify L.S. as the trailer man.

He was hounded by trivial questions and complaints as he made his rounds. There was a system in place to take care of these—the "Mail on Monday" to communicate with the Portland office and the agency bulletin or a letter for the reply—but when agents had a U-Haul representative at hand, they thought they should get solutions at once.

So L.S. created a mythical boss, A. M. Carty. He represented that he worked for this Carty, who made policy decisions and solved local problems. "I have to check with A. M. Carty" was his standard response. Once he was home in Portland, Anna Mary Shoen, née Carty, wrote back the answer.

By 1951 L.S. had given up any thought of returning to medical school. With a growing family and the demands of his business—and with every medical school refusing to accept him—he reluctantly gave up his dream. He still wanted a professional degree and already could see he needed to understand law better, so he enrolled in the Northwestern College of Law (later Lewis and Clark College) night program in Portland, using his veteran's benefits. It seemed foolish not to take advantage of the money.

Two instructors, both local lawyers, impressed him. These men were peers and knew L.S. was running his own company.

Though L.S. had quickly grasped the need for quality in his trailers and the competitive advantage his trailers gave him as moving billboards, every attempt he had made to obtain financing had been a failure. Steady growth was possible if he continued as he was, but it would take decades to establish the network he had in mind. This had never been more apparent than during those long drives on the road when he had passed up many possible rental agent locations because he lacked enough trailers. At any time a well-financed national company might seize his idea and run U-Haul out of business.

L.S. no longer recalls if it was he or Anna Mary who came up with the brilliant solution that had evaded him for six years and was the third key innovation which led to the long-term success of U-Haul. Family tradition says it was Anna Mary. According to the story, she was reading a history that discussed the westward expansion of the United States. The railroads, she read, had faced a similar problem—they needed far more boxcars than they could finance—and solved the problem by finding investors who would organize to purchase fleets of boxcars. These cars would be the separate property of the fleet owners, who would give the railroad use of the cars in exchange for a percentage of each car's earnings.

Within days he had drawn up a comprehensive program for fleet ownership. Fleet owners ran no risk since they invested only the money it cost to produce the trailers, which were the collateral that guaranteed their investment. U-Haul assumed all costs, including insurance, maintenance, and distribution. Each month fleet owners received the record of rentals for their trailers. The rate of return was about 20 percent a year for the rental life of the trailer, which L.S. computed to be twenty to thirty years. It was a gold mine for investors and found money for U-Haul. The trailers cost nothing for him to build, and he could acquire them as fast as investors and rental agents could be located. On a strictly dollars-and-cents basis this was very expensive financing since fleet trailers would return less money to the company; but no other financing was available, and this allowed rapid national expansion.

L.S. took his written proposal to his law professors. The men were enthusiastic and stunned L.S. when each committed fifteen thousand dollars that night. Even more important, they told friends, and within weeks the first fleet cooperative was organized with more capital than L.S. had ever seen before. His trailer-manufacturing facility was quickly expanded but even then was strained to capacity to meet the demand. Almost overnight U-Haul went from two hundred trailers to one thousand. Then it doubled, and shortly thereafter it tripled. Suddenly U-Haul was everywhere, and capital was no longer a problem.

But one of his law school instructors put his finger on the future that evening at night school as he held L.S.'s fleet proposal. His words were prophetic. "Sam," he said to L.S., "your problem now is going to be the management of greed."

CHAPTER THREE

FIRE, FIRE, AIM, FIRE, FIRE

Duuring these years of exertion life had not been easy for Anna Mary. In 1945 there had been her first son, Samuel, followed only sixteen months later by Michael, then Edward Joseph, called Joe, and, in 1950, Mark. While L.S. was still struggling with U-Haul, he looked, typically, for cheap housing for his family. He spotted a house framed with a roof and outside walls, part of a subdivision that had failed. He bought a lot on East Moorland Street in Portland, moved the house, and set about finishing it. Inside, he stored extra tires and trailer gear. Because he was on the road so often and consumed with business when he wasn't, the remodeling took a long time. From the exterior the house was acceptable, but inside, Anna Mary lived surrounded by two-by-fours and open wiring, dust, and the inconvenience of construction. She was required to live on two hundred dollars a month. When the new fleet finance arrangement was in place, the money increased dramatically, and L.S. moved the family to an upper-middle-class neighborhood on SE Thirty-fourth Street in Portland.

L.S. owed a great debt to his wife and the Carty family. It had been Bill Carty, after all, who gave his family a place to stay and made his farm available to build the first trailers. When young Hap Carty was discharged from the service, he went to work for L.S. at the Portland service station in charge of trailer construction.

Despite being both headstrong and a know-it-all, Hap did good work and showed early loyalty to U-Haul.

The four boys were a handful for their mother. When Mark was six months old, he suffered an attack of encephalitis and was bedridden with a high fever for weeks. Joe was the happiest of the boys, full of laughter and joy. He had a spring-supported baby seat and was constantly bouncing up and down in it, giggling. L.S. held Joe on his lap and commented repeatedly to his wife that he was the spitting image of Anna Mary's brother James Carty.

The four Shoen boys were an active and aggressive bunch. Both Sam and Mike played Little League. Joe grew into a quiet child with a steady disposition but a secretive personality. Mark was hot-tempered but sensitive, and his feelings were the most easily hurt. The boys were Cub Scouts, and Anna Mary was den mother three years in a row. The family went to the Carty farm regularly, and while L.S. and Anna Mary talked to her parents, the boys had the run of the place, riding horses, playing cowboys and Indians, prowling everywhere, and setting off firecrackers on the Fourth of July.

In 1953 Anna Mary gave birth to a daughter the couple named Mary Anna. Though none of her pregnancies had been difficult, her doctor monitored her condition closely since each was potentially life-threatening. Ten years before, L.S. had been told Anna Mary's condition would result in early death. He understood that any of her pregnancies could be fatal, yet he never took her to a heart institute or had a specialist examine her. In fact, a medical procedure that might have cured Anna Mary's condition had been developed, but neither she nor L.S. learned of it.

The year Mary Anna was born L.S. began giving stock in U-Haul to his children. Typically he made the arrangements himself rather than waste money on a lawyer. "Had L.S. spent five hundred dollars for a lawyer in 1950," Michael Zivian, a later associate, said, "none of the rest would have followed." L.S. paid no dividends and voted the stock for his minor children. The amounts he gave them did not constitute a majority and cost him nothing. "I don't know what they're going to do with the stock," he wrote, "or whether it will be worth anything..." but he continued giving it at the rate permitted by the gift tax exemptions, and once he had started down this road he considered himself committed to it.

It was not necessary that he give his children voting shares to present them with the future wealth of the company. Other types of shares would accomplish that, or even voting trusts, but he did not know about them. Much of his childhood had been marked by poverty, and he was building U-Haul in part to secure the future of his children and their children. He would earn his living from the company, but his children would own it as a right of birth. U-Haul was as much for them as for Anna Mary and him.

In 1955 L.S. was graduated from Northwestern College of Law at the top of his class and then passed the bar. The company had suffered, he believed, while he had attended school, but now he was prepared to make it what he had envisioned ten years before while in the naval hospital in Corona.

In evaluating the success of U-Haul, L.S. concluded that his timing could not have been better. Before the Second World War the American highway system was largely inadequate to en- courage moving. Cars were underpowered to pull a trailer, and the bumpers too insubstantial for hitching. All these draw- backs ended after 1945. Congress invested billions in a national highway system; cars increased in horsepower; bumpers were strengthened.

In its first two years the new fleet investment financing system produced two million dollars, and by 1955 it was delivering capital at the rate of two hundred thousand dollars a month. There were more than two hundred separate fleets in the system, and U-Haul was manufacturing trailers at the rate of six hundred a month. L.S. had ten thousand trailers on the road.

After L.S. had passed the bar, the Shoens left the five children with Anna Mary's family and took an extended two-month car trip across the nation, combining business with pleasure. The or- ganization could no longer be managed by L.S. out of Portland, so he hired regional supervisors who would report directly to him.

One associate from this time remembers the road trip was not in any way luxurious. He told of L.S.'s ordering a single plate of food from which L.S. and his wife both ate, fighting over every bite. Perhaps the story is apocryphal, but L.S. lived as cheaply on the road with his wife as he did alone.

L.S. was now a vigorous, full-bodied man, slightly overweight. In his mid-thirties he already appeared middle-aged. His hair was retreating, and by the time he was forty he was on his way to acquiring the distinctive Shoen bald scalp. He was a talker who rarely took the time to listen unless he was engrossed in learning something. He argued a subject from every angle, sometimes talking himself into corners. He was an aggressive, headstrong man people tended to like or dislike immediately, though he always remained intriguing. A longtime competitor and former friend once acknowledged that while L.S. often was a real son of a bitch, the man "liked the way his mind worked" and still talked to him regularly.

As for the business, L.S. ran U-Haul with an iron hand. No one knew it as he did, and he managed every aspect of the company. He demanded things be done his way and fired those who dissented, developing an increasingly controlling personality.

Anna Mary complained of his long absences, but L.S. was a driven man, convinced the company would fail if he did not devote all his energy to it. Preoccupied with business even when he was not on the road, he could hardly have been called a family man, and it was Anna Mary who made their house a home.

By this time Anna Mary was showing the long-term effects of her heart condition and repeated pregnancies. Her lungs received insufficient blood, and she had developed a slightly wasted look. But she was so full of life, so carefully attired, and so optimistic that her condition was not recognized. She was gracious, a lady, a favorite of college sorority sisters and the congregation of the Holy Family Catholic Church.

L.S. had watched his wife cope with the house, the children, and the business and still find time for college and church. He had also observed her constant optimism in the face of adversity. The result was to give him a deep respect for her Catholicism. It appeared to him that she drew her strength from her church, and though his own religious education had been nil, he developed an admiration for Catholicism that for a time overcame his natural inclination to agnosticism.

The Shoens no longer suffered any form of economic deprivation and though L.S. was fond of saying that he risked every dime he had every day, there was more than enough money to support his family. U-Haul was a million-dollar concern, a veritable cash cow, as others later noted, though not without its ups and downs. The home office in Portland employed forty people, and gradually L.S. discarded his penny-pinching ways with the household.

Across the street from the Shoens lived the Gilbaughs, James and Lillian. James's father had founded the Portland Casket Company and built it into the premier provider in the region. When he died, James's mother assumed financial control of the company, which was managed by her three sons and daughter. James was the president and head of marketing. Though the Gilbaughs were a few years older than L.S., they became fast friends. L.S. in particular had a close friendship with Lillian, whom he viewed as a combination mother figure and older sister since she was only five years older than he. The Gilbaughs sat for the Shoen children, a natural extension of the friendship between their youngest son and Sam, who were the same age and were regular playmates. The oldest Gilbaugh child, Suzanne, was a striking young woman who was attending college at nearby Oregon State College.

In June 1956 Anna Mary gave birth to the Shoens' sixth child, a son the couple named Paul. L.S. had returned from an extended trip barely in time to take her to the hospital. The day after the delivery Anna Mary gave her husband hell for his absences, but the following week he was back on the road.

On October 19, at home in Portland, L.S. and Anna Mary retired early. About midnight the telephone rang, and she awoke from a deep sleep to answer it. When she fell back to sleep, Anna Mary's breathing was labored. L.S. awoke to sounds of his wife struggling to stay alive and soon she lapsed into a coma from which he could not awaken her. L.S. laid her on her back and moved her arms in what was then the accepted technique for artificial respiration. It had no effect. He called the family doctor only to discover Anna Mary's heart had stopped beating entirely while he was telephoning. Desperate, L.S. began pounding her chest, over and over, willing the heart to resume beating. And shortly it did. By the time the doctor arrived she was breathing and soon regained consciousness. The doctor placed her in the hospital, where she remained for three more days.

For several years L.S. had forgotten Anna Mary's frail state of health. With six healthy children and in the face of his wife's constant good cheer, it had been easy to dismiss her chronic condition. When she returned home, the family doctor met with the pair to persuade them to continue a normal life. L.S. canceled his road trips and for the next few months worked from the corporate office and went home each night. When it seemed that life was as it had been, he returned to the road and the building of his company.

During this time L.S. determined the final element for the success of U-Haul because it became necessary to dispose of the older trailers. L.S. had given the matter considerable thought and decided that selling the trailers would be a catastrophe. He ordered instead that they be dismantled. What could be used again was, and what could not was discarded.

Considering the large number of trailers and the limited security at most service stations, very few trailers were actually stolen. L.S. concluded this was because there was nowhere to sell them. Though they were not as distinctive in shape as they eventually became, U-Haul trailers had their own look. Even when they were painted another color, they were easily spotted, especially by alert U-Haul employees. If L.S. sold them, there would be U-Haul trailers with new coats of paint everywhere. How could his employees possibly tell the used trailers from those stolen and sold to a rival? As long as U-Haul created no aftermarket, the low theft rate would continue. In addition, potential competitors would be denied an easy source of trailers. So trailers were dismantled.

This was a typical decision for L.S. He early grew accustomed to looking at least ten years ahead and pointing his company in the direction he had selected. He rarely took the time to explain to subordinates what he had in mind. Instead he gave the orders, and the company lurched toward his goals. It was not unusual for him to overstep himself or improperly to identify a target. "Fire, fire, aim, fire, fire" was how one associate described it. When misdirection occurred, L.S. made a "180 turn," an expression that peppered his conversation. He prided himself in his ability to turn the company on a dime. This hit-or-miss approach, however, was disconcerting for his employees, and L.S. quickly assumed the reputation as an eccentric, a role he relished.

One of the original regional managers, John Fowler, joined U-Haul at this time and opened up the Midwest for the company. Throughout his career he reported directly to L.S., a boss he found both fascinating and frustrating. L.S. changed his mind too often and switched direction too quickly for Fowler's taste, but he was also eminently fair.

L.S.'s commitment to U-Haul could be disturbing on occasion. In the mid-1950s, when U-Haul was still in Portland, L.S. summoned the half dozen senior men who ran the company for a three-day seminar. Rather than pay for an extra night's lodging he had booked them on overnight return flights. But when they arrived at the airport, it was socked in with fog. Two of the men expressed reservations about going up despite L.S.'s assurance that the pilots there did it all the time. Then Fowler joked that it would be a shame for all of U-Haul's upper management to be killed in a single plane wreck. L.S. considered the thought, then said, "And after all that work we put in the past three days, too." The men were shocked, and when L.S. realized they were just joking, he hastily added unconvincingly, "Just kidding."

Then, in late April 1957, L.S. returned from another extended trip to the East. Only that week Anna Mary had finished rewriting the constitution for the Holy Family Mothers' Club. The day after L.S. arrived the couple attended the funeral of a friend who had committed suicide, and Anna Mary spoke philosophically of death as they left the cemetery. That Thursday they attended Mark's first communion and then went to dinner with their friends and neighbors the Gilbaughs, as they had so many times before.

The next morning over breakfast with the children L.S. told

Anna Mary that it looked as though U-Haul was really going to be a lasting success. "Life is just going too well," he added negatively; "it can't last."

Anna Mary chastised her husband and told him not to think like that. "This is the way God wants it to be," she said, "and you should enjoy it." L.S. wanted to believe her, but his experience had always been that periods of good were inevitably followed by equal periods of bad. Life was, he had been taught, much as described in the Old Testament.

That night Anna Mary, who had had an especially demanding day preparing for a Scouting function, was exhausted and untypically irritable. At about 2:00 A.M. L.S. awakened to use the bathroom. When he slipped into bed, Anna Mary said, "Oh, my God, Sam, you frightened me!" L.S. returned to sleep but soon realized that his wife had lapsed into a coma. He shook her, but she did not stir, and very quickly thereafter her heart stopped beating. L.S. pulled Anna Mary to the floor and administered resuscitation. Still her heart would not start. He tried again. No success.

L.S. ran to awaken Sam and Mike, ordering them to call a priest and the family doctor. Sam went to the hallway telephone and through the door saw his mother lying on the floor. L.S. was beating on Anna Mary's chest over and over. Her heart would not beat. The doctor soon arrived and administered a heart stimulant. L.S. continued resuscitation but with no success.

When the priest arrived, Sam escorted him upstairs and watched as he gave the last rites of the church. Anna Mary did not awaken and was soon dead. Mary Anna, Joe, Mark, and the baby, Paul, all slept through the trauma.

Sam was twelve years old that night. Until the year before, when his mother had been hospitalized, he had never realized she was ill, and until now he had not known that she had a terminal medical condition. The priest spoke to Sam and his stunned brother Mike, while two ambulance attendants went up the stairs, and a few moments later the boys watched as their mother's body was carried out on a stretcher.

Sam was emotionally numb. Everything that had happened since his father had first shouted at him to get out of bed had been unreal. He still could not accept the fact that his mother was dead.

L.S., who was visibly shaken and was coping only with great effort, told the boys, "This was God's will."

Mike gazed off, avoiding his father's eyes, and stared at a light bulb. *That's it for you, God,* he thought forcefully. L.S. had been the provider, but Anna Mary had been the emotional sustenance. Mike knew in the moment he realized that his mother was dead that the love in the family had died with her.

The other children woke up at their usual hour, and L.S. quietly told them that the mother who had tucked them into bed the night before was gone.

Anna Mary's death was a tragedy not only for the six children but also for her husband. Two days later, before she was buried, L.S. sat down to write his children a letter. He wanted them to know later of his feelings at the time, and he wished to memorialize the events for them while they were fresh. He wrote: "The purpose of this letter is to tell you something about your mother. Time will dull the memory of all of us, including you older boys. Paul will not be able to remember her at all, and Mary Anna will be unlikely to recollect much about her. Your mother's influence will undoubtedly leave its mark on Sammy, Mike, Joe, and Mark. Her influence has left an indelible imprint on me.... If ever a saint lived, she was one."

He went on to describe her life, how they met, and her contribution to U-Haul. "No matter where I would take her, or what the circumstances, she was always an asset and complement to me. Her loyalty was unfailing, sincere and convincing. I can say that we never had a fight.... Her sacrifices she made for me while the business grew, while I attended night law school, and while I directed a nationwide business were too many to relate here...."

He then told of her heart condition and the circumstances of her death. He concluded: "I will try to give you some of the love that you would have had. I will try to impart to you the Catholic faith that she would have given you. As you grow older and read this, please help me. God love her and you, L. S. S."

On May 7, 1957, Anna Mary was buried at St. Mary's Cemetery near the Carty farm following high mass at Holy Family Catholic Church. Her sons Sam and Mike served as altar boys at the packed service. L.S. added two postscripts to his letter to tell his youngest children about the funeral, then put it away to give them later.

He had exaggerated Anna Mary's role in the success of U-Haul, as he did again and again in the years to follow. He did it for what he believed were the best of reasons. He wanted his children to think well of their mother and understand the part she had played in what was to be their fortune. In fact, her role was less than he would attribute to her, but in another way it had been more. A wife who nags, one who will not sacrifice or bear long absences can make it impossible for an entrepreneur trying to build a company. Her contribution had been primarily that of the good mother and the dutiful mate, roles expected of a woman with her background at that time. If she had not built U-Haul, she had unconditionally supported its founder, a contribution even greater than the one he described for their children.

L.S. developed a mythology for Anna Mary. For her children she was to assume heroic and perfect proportions. L.S. fed this mythology to preserve her memory, and perhaps in light of the turns his personal life took, his marriage to her and those early years were indeed his happiest and deserving of the legendary status he gave them. In time he came to consider their wedding day the happiest of his life.

There are few life-altering experiences, and the premature death of a mother and wife is surely one of them. L.S. could not have imagined the profound and tragic consequences of this early death or for how many years those consequences would be felt.

There is in that letter to his children more than praise for the deceased wife. There is also guilt.

L.S. told his children, and others in the decades to follow, that theirs had been a happy, a nearly perfect marriage. But thirteen months before her death, barely six months prior to her first heart attack, Anna Mary wrote her husband a special delivery letter, its urgency apparent in the last paragraph: "That's all I know on that—We are fine here. Supposed to be 70–75 degrees today— lasting through Sunday. Wish I'd hear a squeak from you as to when, if ever, I'll see you again. All my love Anna Mary."

L.S. was forty-one years of age. He had not been a man to be tied to one woman when he had been in college, and he was never an easy man to live with. It is understandable, perhaps inevitable that strain existed between them.

Anna Mary had expressed again and again her disapproval of his long absences, and he had ignored her. L.S. understood the inevitability of her dying, but had he contributed to its coming prematurely? How did he feel about the six children he had played a role in bringing into their marriage, children whose births he knew were life-threatening? What of the strain he had brought to the relationship?

There was clearly guilt over Anna Mary, but she was dead. Even more, there was guilt over the children, now motherless.

The measure of that guilt is taken in his behavior during the coming years. While Sam and Mike continued to have the same father they had always known, the younger children, especially Joe and Mark, were reared by a very different man, one driven to make amends. And in those different upbringings was to come tragedy of an even greater magnitude than that of the death of Anna Mary at age thirty-four.

CHAPTER FOUR

THE BITCH

Following their mother's funeral, L.S. sent the four oldest boys and Mary Anna to stay at the Carty farm while he remained in Portland with the infant, Paul. L.S. was numb with grief, and he could scarcely bear to see his children because they reminded him of their mother. "I know now how much I loved her," he wrote, "and how much she meant to me.... The loss is indescribable."

To L.S.'s great relief it seemed that the children had not been overly affected by Anna Mary's death, and in his own distress he clung to that illusion. Perhaps it made it easier to leave the oldest on the farm, and it surely assuaged his own guilt. Around the corner from his house he spent at least an hour each day talking to Lillian Gilbaugh.

Bill Carty assumed the role of surrogate father to the boys. He had Sam and Mike accompany him for long hours as he worked the land, and he took the opportunity to teach them honesty and responsibility. Carty maintained the farm as if it were a park, but he never hesitated to remind the boys that God was the architect. It was Carty's duty to maintain His work.

Along the river were the remains of a long-abandoned steamboat, and Indian artifacts could be found everywhere. The farmhouse was ruggedly constructed of beams and was rich with the aroma of old wood and home cooking. Shotguns hung on the wall along with an antique pistol, and outside sat an old buggy that had been used by Carty's father in the Wyoming gold rush. There was a sense of history and drama about the place. Of all the boys, Mike liked the farm best, and the summer of 1957 he formed a lasting bond with it.

Back in Portland, James Carty, Anna Mary's ill-tempered brother, was spreading the word that L.S. had murdered Anna Mary. The family, seeing L.S.'s obvious grief, dismissed the thought. There had been bruises on her body caused by L.S.'s vigorous efforts to revive her, but James gave these an ominous interpretation. In addition, he pointed out, his sister had been buried without an autopsy. Family members dismissed these arguments as irrelevant since Anna Mary's heart condition was common knowledge, but James Carty persisted in his allegations.

After roaming the country as a hobo, James Carty had graduated from college, then put himself through law school. L.S. employed him for a short while but was quickly forced to fire his combative brother-in-law. L.S. believed that James was still angry over that experience and that his allegations were just another sign of the dark side of his brother-in-law's personality.

Mike was not the only one who realized that much of the love had left the family with Anna Mary gone. L.S. could be very critical of himself in many regards, and he knew that he was not as outgoing and demonstratively loving as he should be. "I must learn to be cheerful and have faith," he wrote, worried that his grief would have an adverse effect on the children. A few days later, after a visit with the oldest boys, he wrote, "Tried to be kind and loving to the children."

But it was not easy for him to overcome the emotional distance that often marked his family contacts.

L.S. already served on the advisory board for Marylhurst College and pledged that he would establish a scholarship in his wife's name and build a shrine to the Virgin Mary on the campus. The nuns were especially sympathetic to the plight of a wealthy widower in his early forties with six children. One month after Anna Mary's death he attended the Marylhurst commencement and was introduced to the graduating seniors by the nuns.

L.S. was having great difficulty in finding an acceptable living arrangement for his family. He hired two or three housekeepers in the weeks following the funeral, but none was right, and each was quickly fired. The children remained primarily on the Carty farm, where L.S. visited them, but he also brought them into town to stay with him for days at a time. He occasionally took Sam and Mike with him to the office.

By June L.S. had turned to the legal complications created by his wife's untimely death. He and Anna Mary had given shares in U-Haul to the children. At the time of Anna Mary's death he and she shared equally in the majority of the undistributed stock. Oregon law prescribed that because she had died without a will, half her shares were to go to L.S. and the other half to be divided equally among the children. The effect was to increase significantly the children's ownership in the company. The four oldest sons each held just under 11 percent, while Mary Anna and Paul had 9 percent. L.S. had become a minority stockholder in his own company. Since he voted their stock for the children, however, this did not present a problem.

L.S. abruptly decided to take a trip to Europe. This was a surprising event since his children had no real home and L.S.'s attempts to find a housekeeper were conspicuously unsuccessful.

He first tried to join the graduating seniors from Marylhurst on their annual European trip but found there was no room for him. He picked up Sam and Mike from the Carty farm on June 22 and drove with the boys cross country stopping along the way to check U-Haul operations and visit relatives. On the East Coast he left the boys with Hap Carty, who was working at the trailer construction plant in Willow Grove, Pennsylvania, then took a plane to London.

Just weeks following his wife's death L.S. wrote in private, "The virtue of purity has been no strain for me since Anna Mary's death. This is revealing." On the twelve-hour transatlantic flight he noted there were "no female interests" on the plane.

In Portland he was the grieving husband in a period of mourning. Free abroad from social conventions, he was a man on the make just two months after Anna Mary's death. He did not appear troubled by the hypocrisy in his behavior.

He spent three days seeing London in the company of a young

woman he met after he arrived, but he soon decided to crash the Marylhurst tour en route and promptly flew to Rome, where he took a room at their hotel. The young women were sympathetic to this well-known widower and welcomed his presence. "Look, girls," he announced loudly at intervals, "I'm the only available man until you get home." He was greeted with peals of laughter.

L.S. was drinking and eating so much he chastised himself in private but continued to do it nonetheless. He devoted himself to the pretty young women and "pitched" them hard. Soon he was focusing on one woman who attracted him considerably. He talked his way onto the tour and thereafter spent nearly all the remaining three weeks with her. He agonized over this, not for seeing a woman during the conventional mourning period but over his inability to control his emotions.

"I am in a real state of mental confusion," he wrote, "the same as prior to my marriage I guess. I get all involved about nothing with some woman. . . . So what am I going to do?" Several times he attempted to focus attention on others on the tour, but he kept returning to the same young woman. When the tour ended in Paris, he flew alone to London and, perhaps with an eye to ending this infatuation, looked up the other woman he had seen three weeks earlier.

On the flight across the Atlantic he passed the time with a female passenger. It was clear by now what he was really up to, clear even to L.S. "[S]he is too young and not smart enough for me," he wrote of her.

That first night in Portland L.S. gathered a group of young men and women and had a party until the following afternoon. This became so frequent and conspicuous an occurrence that Anna Mary's mother gave her son-in-law a tongue-lashing for his unseemly conduct. He was showing her recently deceased daughter no respect at all. The lecture had little effect. Though he tempered his behavior somewhat, it remained essentially unchanged.

His actions in the short months since his wife's death raised a serious question as to how much L.S. had actually loved Anna Mary. He resembled more a man let out of prison than one experiencing a tragic personal loss. A mourning period of one year was normal for the loss of a spouse, one of six months was the absolute shortest that could be socially reconciled, but within eight *weeks* L.S. was chasing women with no regard for its impact on his family or his reputation.

L.S. had options in his personal life. He could step back from the hands-on, day-to-day management of U-Haul and devote more time to his children. It would have slowed the growth of the company but would have represented a real commitment to his family and was well within his means. In part, his difficulty with housekeepers was caused by his absences. The women were simply thrown into a demanding situation with little meaningful support. A commitment on his part to parenting would have made it possible to find and keep a competent housekeeper. L.S. could also have waited a respectable period and resumed dating with the anticipation that in the process he would find an appropriate wife and stepmother. But he had already rejected this approach.

At the end of summer still another housekeeper quit. She told him about his children's problems, and L.S. comprehended in part what she had said, for he wrote, "I think I understand why she quit. Apparently whoever runs this place will have to be the mother."

One day not long afterward Mike went into his parents' bedroom and asked his father what he was doing at the desk. In a drawer Mike could see thirty-odd files through which L.S. was slowly working his way. Each file bore the name of a woman, some familiar to the young boy. L.S. explained that he had opened a file on likely prospects for a new wife. He had listed the attributes he wanted and was ranking the women accordingly. Mike found this disconcerting and did not speak of it again.

Paramount in L.S.'s mind was that his new wife be a good Catholic. He had concluded that Anna Mary's Catholicism had caused her to be the woman she was. There were, he believed, many such women. All he had to do was select from the number of Catholic women listed in his growing files. This meant he could focus on the attributes he found personally appealing.

L.S. hired more housekeepers but without success. In the absence of their mother and with so many relatives making excuses and lavishing attention, Joe and Mark had become unruly. Joe's pleasant nature had vanished, and when one housekeeper briefed her replacement, she cautioned, "Watch out for Joe. He's sneaky."

Their father certainly was not of a disposition to discipline them in spite of the fact that six children all in one place were more than he could handle. L.S. tried grandmotherly housekeepers and teenage girls, but no one succeeded until he hired an attractive young German immigrant named Marianne Lieber. Lieber was unable to have children of her own and brought to the house her instinctive love of children. She kept the house with German precision, and L.S. was so impressed he resumed entertaining at home.

Lieber was aware of his need for a wife and mother, and within a few weeks she told L.S. that she would stay in her present position for a few months but thereafter would remain on only as his wife. Lieber was a handsome woman and a natural mother. His children had formed an immediate bond with her, which lifted a burden from him. But L.S. was put off by the frankness of her proposition, despite his own calculated hunt for a wife and beyond that, he thought it unseemly for a man of his station to marry his housekeeper.

Just twenty-six years out of the orchards and L.S. was searching for a woman of standing, not an immigrant looking for a ready-made family and wealthy husband.

In Lillian Gilbaugh's living room was a prominent photograph of her oldest daughter, Suzanne. Suzanne, who had completed her studies in science at Oregon State College and taken a job with the State Board of Health, was currently attending the University of North Carolina and earning a master's degree in public health. Family lore says that one day L.S. pointed to the photograph and announced to Lillian that he was going to marry Suzanne, a woman he had yet to meet, but considering the determined search in which he was engaged, that may very well have been the way he went about it.

L.S. later claimed that Lillian promoted her daughter to become his second wife. She spoke enthusiastically of Suzanne, who was nearly twenty years younger than L.S. Lillian had a quick wit and a sharp intellect. She was also well known for her cooking skills and housekeeping. On the basis of Lillian's performance, one could assume her daughter would be an able homemaker and mother.

In time the physical and personality differences between Suzanne and Anna Mary were so prominent they masked the initial similarities. Anna Mary had been a slight woman, Suzanne was taller, with a rich, buxom figure, but beyond that their appearance was very much the same. They had auburn hair, slightly prominent noses, and mild overbites. Also, both were Catholic.

In December 1957 Suzanne Gilbaugh was flying home for Christmas from graduate school. L.S. was working his East Coast operations and arranged to meet Suzanne at the Washington, D.C., airport, then accompany her on the flight west. He found Suzanne an especially beautiful young woman, and he was surprised by her intense sexual magnetism. He made his interest in her apparent and, as he put it, "came on strong."

After Christmas Suzanne returned to UNC, and L.S. continued dating his way through his files, carefully recording his scores. Most of the prospects were in their early twenties, and several were students at Marylhurst College.

Suzanne returned to Portland that spring, one year after the death of Anna Mary, and L.S. aggressively pursued her, often double-dating with her parents. Suzanne drove throughout Oregon for her job with the State Board of Health, and L.S. made it a practice to follow her in his car as he called on rental agents. He would meet her for lunch and, if she was away overnight, would take her to dinner. Jack Adair, one of U-Haul's earliest rental agents, had never seen such tenacity on the part of any man in pursuit of a woman. He noticed something peculiar about the usually hyperactive L.S. Just before he was to see Suzanne, he would make a conscious effort to calm himself down, to reduce his natural exuberance and present a staid demeanor.

There was almost nothing L.S. wasn't prepared to do to impress the young woman. When Suzanne expressed a liking for a beach house in the exclusive Gearhart area, a house she had seen since she was a child, L.S. bought it and started spending weekends there with Suzanne and her parents.

L.S. was not alone in his attention to the attractive Suzanne. For most of that summer of 1958 she was dating another, younger man, and L.S. was intensely jealous. He tried to occupy all of her time, but she still managed to see his rival.

Their relationship was anything but stable. L.S. was on an emotional roller coaster. Again and again he promised himself he would stop seeing this young woman, that he would get out of "this affair," but each time he called her again. They fought, then made up. Suzanne talked about marrying him, only to dismiss the idea the next day. Then they fought and reconciled again. L.S. found it confusing and recalled the even-tempered Anna Mary with affection.

Though Marianne Lieber had done everything she could to make herself desirable as a wife and mother, L.S. could not get over his aversion to marrying his housekeeper and the anticipated public disapproval. He was intoxicated with Suzanne, and it was apparent by now that L.S. would not marry her. Lieber left his employ that summer and took with her the order and love she had brought to his home. Sam and Mike stayed in touch with her for years.

Her departure created a crisis for L.S. as once again he could find no satisfactory replacement. But at last he had come upon what he believed would be a permanent solution to his problem.

L.S. experienced a heightened sexual reaction to Suzanne he had not ever had with Anna Mary, and by the end of the summer their relationship had entered a new plane when he persuaded Suzanne to stop seeing his rival. At night in the beach house, while Jim and Lillian Gilbaugh slept, Suzanne joined L.S. in his bedroom. He found sex with her all-consuming. She was not shy or reluctant, and her appetite was as robust as his own. The more he had of her, the more he desired. His lust for his neighbor's daughter blinded him to the reality that he did not know if they were compatible, in the face of strong indications that they were not.

When L.S. again spoke of marriage, Suzanne appeared to agree but refused to make definite plans. L.S. was concerned the Gilbaughs would learn of their sexual relationship and was even more fearful Suzanne would become pregnant. By the end of August he wrote, "I've decided to get married again," and was pressing Suzanne aggressively for an immediate wedding date. The day after she at last agreed to marry him he expressed surprise that she was actually still talking about it. "This time," he wrote, "she apparently means it for she had me tell her parents and family today."

In the end they married a week after they became engaged, the same period L.S. had given Anna Mary. There was no war emergency, only L.S.'s desire to have Suzanne spend every night in his bed. When Lillian learned of the imminent wedding date, she called L.S. at his home early one morning to voice her vigorous disapproval, but it changed nothing. Nor did the disapproval of every adult member of his own family.

During that short week L.S. drove with Suzanne to the Carty farm to visit Sam and Mike. As the just-engaged couple pulled up in a new Cadillac convertible, the boys rushed out, excited to see the car. L.S. piled the boys into the backseat for a ride with him and Suzanne, and as they were driving, L.S. announced with a grin, "You know, I'm going to marry Suzanne, and I want you to treat her right." Neither Sam nor Mike had had any idea their father was preparing to remarry. Mike had a clear recollection of the few times he had been with Suzanne, and he could tell she had no genuine interest in them. But L.S. was waiting for an answer. Finally Mike said, "Dad, it's not going to be easy, but you'll get no trouble from me." Sam agreed. They were L.S.'s dutiful sons and would do as they were told.

The boys were in for another shock as well. L.S. informed them he had decided to send them to boarding school in Oakland, California. They would be leaving after the wedding later that week.

Four days before the wedding L.S. told Sam and Mike to pack away their mother's personal items and clean out the master bedroom so he could have it painted. He and Suzanne had bought a new bedroom set that would be installed in time for that Saturday's wedding. In his enthusiasm L.S. gave no consideration to the effect these sudden plans were having on the children. Packing away their mother's belongings was like losing her all over again. But the boys did as they were told.

The morning of his second marriage L.S. lay alone in his bed until eleven. He knew that he was not doing the right thing. He knew he had been wrong to press Suzanne to marry right away since neither of them had had enough opportunity for reflection. How was this really any different from the infatuation he had experienced with the college senior during his European trip the previous summer? Only two weeks earlier he had written of his own inner confusion over Suzanne, mentioning her beauty and saying nothing of love.

Later that day, September 6, 1958, a very tense forty-two-year-old L.S. and the stunning twenty-three-year-old Suzanne Gilbaugh were married in a wedding still lavish despite the speed with which it had been arranged.

The following day the newlyweds took Sam and Mike to the train station in Portland and saw them off to the Christian Brothers St. Mary's boarding school in Oakland, California. Sam would be entering his eighth-grade year, and Mike his seventh.

L.S. and Suzanne departed on their honeymoon shortly thereafter. L.S. was scheduled to attend a conference in San Francisco, and as usual he would mix business with pleasure. The newlyweds drove down the Oregon and California coasts, L.S. stopping along the way to conduct business and display with pride his stunning and so youthful wife. L.S. wrote candidly in private that he was spending the time to "get acquainted" with her.

But within three days he was calling himself "Stupe" for having married Suzanne. In his view his bride was not at all like Anna Mary. For one thing he believed her Catholicism was shallow, and for another he found her personality was not nearly as malleable as he had believed. He was at last coming to understand that Anna Mary had been the kind of wife and companion she was because of who she had been, not because of the Catholic Church.

Divorce was out of the question; Suzanne, as a divorced Catholic woman, would have had few prospects. There was nothing to do but to get on with their life together.

Sex remained as active and intoxicating as before they were married and L.S. was not disappointed, though he found he was exhausted by her demands. They stopped in Oakland to check on the boys, but rather than see them, Suzanne urged L.S. to remain in bed with her. With difficulty he persuaded her to join him and visit his sons.

At the school Sam had fitted in at once because of his athletic prowess and was quickly a star. The brothers who ran the school soon recognized Sam's potential and were urging him to consider a life in their order or as a priest. Thomas Dooley, an American physician, was at the height of his fame as "the jungle doctor of Laos" and, because he was Catholic, was held up as an example to the impressionable students. Sam told his teachers that he would rather be a doctor like Dr. Dooley and help the needy in the world. This was an acceptable career choice, and the brothers stopped urging him into the ministry.

The more introverted Mike, however, was unhappy. Many of the other students were vicious, having come from unhappy homes. His attempts at friendship were quickly rebuffed on most fronts, and except for his brother, he lived a largely solitary existence. When L.S. drove up that day, Mike could see immediately that his father was unhappy in his marriage, so he put on a brave front and did not express his reservations about the school.

Back in Portland L.S. was also putting on a show, but less than three weeks after his wedding he made reservations for Suzanne and him to attend a married couples' retreat. He wrote that he was "worried" about the marriage.

Suzanne seemed overwhelmed with her new responsibilities in a household with the four youngest children but, regardless, was pregnant by December. There had been no discussion about starting a family, and Suzanne was not opposed to having children, but L.S. was seriously concerned about her mothering instincts. Despite his misgivings, he still believed she would make an acceptable stepmother. L.S. was comfortable enough with his home situation to resume his frequent trips, but when he returned to his Portland house that winter, he was dismayed at what he found. Portland weather was damp and frequently inclement. Anna Mary had meticulously dressed the children, and he had come to take that care for granted. Suzanne's mothering was of a different quality. Joe and Mark complained vigorously about her and her mistreatment of them. Suzanne denied it. But L.S. could see for himself that his children were sent outside to play without what he considered adequate clothing, and when he complained, Suzanne wanted to argue. He had no trouble accepting what his sons told him.

L.S. had married a mother for his children. That meant in his mind a mother like the one who had borne them. But Suzanne saw her role with the children very differently. "They lived with him," she later recalled, "and I happened to be married to him. . . ."

There were changes in the children as well. With Sam and Mike away, ten-year-old Joe became the oldest child at home. From the first he took an adversarial role with his stepmother and protected the younger children from her, as he saw it. He quickly became the new "oldest son," and L.S. was pleased at the change. The taciturn Joe was demonstrating maturity beyond his years, and this gave L.S. someone in the family on whom he could depend. They must all, he thought, make the best of this mess.

During the last year of Anna Mary's life L.S. had bought a small airplane, and though he still drove on business trips, he was increasingly looking to cover his widespread enterprise by private plane. All attempts to persuade Suzanne to attend to his children as he wished were unsuccessful, so he decided on a novel solution. He would move the family to a warm climate, and if the children were not warmly dressed, it would make no difference. He selected Palm Springs, California, and that spring contracted to have a house built.

When Sam and Mike came home for that summer, they were barraged with Joe's and Mark's complaints about Suzanne and her reported mistreatment of them. They felt sorry for their younger brothers and took the stories as a cautionary tale for themselves. As a result, they avoided Suzanne and considered themselves lucky to be living away from home most of the year.

But Joe was adamant about this woman his father had brought into their world and who was destroying their lives. From then and for the next twenty-five years, he identified Suzanne simply as "the bitch."

CHAPTER FIVE

POWER OVER THE DEVIL

Twelve-year-old Sam had been startled by his father's abrupt marriage to Suzanne Gilbaugh. Her younger brother was his best friend, and he often enjoyed Lillian Gilbaugh's hospitality. The idea of his father's being married to his best friend's big sister was disconcerting. Despite this and the speed with which events had taken place, L.S. saw that his children treated his new wife with respect, but he made the transition more emotionally difficult than necessary by insisting all the children immediately call Suzanne Mom. However, there was no thought in Sam's mind that Suzanne was his mother.

Mike, just one year younger than Sam, felt much the same. For both of them the sudden change from what remained of home to boarding school had been a shock. Coming as it did at the time of their father's remarriage, it was as if Suzanne had moved in and thrown them out.

Though St. Mary's had been especially difficult for Mike, it was no joy for Sam, who would very much have preferred to remain with his brothers and sister. But as they learned more about Suzanne and experienced her personally that summer following the marriage, boarding school no longer appeared to be an exile; rather it became a sanctuary. They were not being deprived of home by attending boarding school, for home had ended with Anna Mary's death.

The new house in Palm Springs was expansive and located in

the exclusive Smoke Tree Ranch residential enclave. Sam, who was starting high school that fall, realized that his family had moved out of the middle class.

Mary Anna entered the first grade the year the Shoens relocated to Palm Springs, but her feelings toward her stepmother were already well advanced. She felt no warmth for a stepmother who routinely introduced her as her "chief cook and bottle washer." Mary Anna was seeing herself as Cinderella, complete with wicked stepmother, since it was apparent to her that Suzanne did not care for her very much.

Soon Suzanne gave birth to her first child, a son whom the couple named James, but who was called Jimmie. He was followed in quick order by Sophia in late 1960, Cecilia in early 1962, and Theresa in 1963. Though Suzanne complained to friends that she was weary of being constantly pregnant, there were soon ten children in the Shoen household.

Suzanne's behavior toward the live-in maids L.S. hired was one of the major causes for Joe's and Mark's objections to their stepmother. When Suzanne was absent from the house, leaving each new maid to become a surrogate mother for the children, the boys basked in the attention. But Suzanne was soon cross with each maid, fighting angrily before firing the maid the boys had come to like. It was as if Suzanne would not allow anyone to mother the children.

The pattern of fighting and passionate reconciliation that had begun during the summer of the courtship was accentuated after the move to California. L.S. spent at least half his days and nights on the road, but when he was home, inevitably he and Suzanne fought, because his young wife was determined to settle issues of dispute immediately. L.S. could be, and often was, cantankerous, headstrong, and opinionated, but he could not understand why reason was insufficient, why there had to be combat. It seemed to him that his new, beautiful wife fed on the shouting and anger, that it was important to her in a way he could not comprehend. These fights were nearly always resolved by furious sex, which L.S. still found overwhelming. Afterward Suzanne would fall into a seemingly contented sleep while he stewed for hours. *There has to be another way to live,* he thought. The next day they would be, as he put it, "all lovey-dovey," until the fighting resumed again.

Lunches, consisting day after day of bologna sandwiches for the children, were a far cry from those Anna Mary had prepared. In more significant ways Suzanne was neglectful as well. One afternoon the children waited at school for their stepmother to pick them up, but she never arrived. When they called home, she was gone, and one of the nuns had to drive them home. When Suzanne told the children later that she simply "forgot" to pick them up, they were was too embarrassed to tell their teachers when asked.

There was, however, a dedicated side to Suzanne's personality. From the time he was a baby, Mark had been small for his age. Since the death of his mother he had become increasingly ill tempered. During his many absences L.S. did not see how bad the situation was becoming, and it was Suzanne who pointed it out to him, in a calm and measured manner. She arranged for an appointment with a psychologist and faithfully took the ten-year-old to his sessions until the worst of his behavior had ebbed.

It was much the same with Joe. When he was in the eighth grade, Suzanne noticed that his feet were not properly developed. She arranged for treatment to correct them with casts, but by then it was apparent his body was also not growing normally. She took him to a doctor who diagnosed a scoliotic condition that, if untreated, would leave his spine permanently bent. From then and nearly through high school Joe was periodically forced to wear a body cast and for a time could move about only in a wheelchair.

Joe and his wheelchair were an unpleasant experience in the house since he delighted in running into the smaller children with it. When Mary Anna was lying on the floor watching television, he sneaked up behind her, then ran the wheel of the heavy chair over her fingers. Joe also organized the younger boys and sent them off to do some mischief with cherry bombs. Neither L.S. nor Suzanne punished Joe for this behavior, and it continued unchanged. As much as she could Mary Anna stayed in her bedroom, away from Joe and her stepmother, and grew into a sensitive, artistically inclined child.

Despite, or perhaps because of, his small stature, Mark prowled the neighborhood and picked fights, fights he often required a bigger friend to finish for him. This was a pattern very similar to the one his uncles James and Hap Carty had followed at the same age.

L.S. was upset with himself for not having seen his sons' physical problems and was grateful to have Suzanne there to take care of them. Both Sam and Mike, he believed with relief, were coping very well with the changes in the family and were less in need of his attention. L.S. still felt sorry for Joe and Mark, and their physical problems only enhanced his need to coddle them. Whereas the two oldest boys were on occasion spanked with a strap, L.S. dealt with Joe and Mark by spending more money on them and by making allowances for their misdeeds. When it came to Joe and Mark, L.S. experienced an enhanced measure of guilt that tainted every decision he made about them.

U-Haul had a substantial operation in Phoenix, Arizona, and L.S. frequently flew there because it was a short hop from Palm Springs. Someone in the company came up with the idea of Trailer Mates, attractive young women who were sent on the road for photo opportunities to promote the company and encourage agents to service the equipment by demonstrating in skimpy, tight-fitting clothes just how easy it was. L.S. assigned himself the task of supervising the comely young women. Each district in the country had at least one, and the Trailer Mate for Arizona was Suzie Whitmore.

L.S. was attracted to the well-dressed Suzie Whitmore and made a point of befriending her and her roommate whenever he was in Phoenix. One night he flew the two of them with him to Las Vegas, where he was scheduled to attend a conference the next day, and they spent the night. On another occasion he followed the pair to Hawaii for a three-day vacation. Whenever he was in Phoenix, he went out of his way to see Whitmore and her roommate.

Much to his displeasure Mike spent his eighth-grade year in Palm Springs while Sam attended a new boarding school in Los Angeles. Until now he had considered Suzanne's performance benign neglect as he observed nothing sinister in her behavior, just a lack of interest in being a mother to her husband's children. His opinion changed very quickly not long after Sam had left for school.

That year Mike was thirteen, and Suzanne was twenty-four

years old. Mike was big for his age, the second-largest student in his school, where he had been elected class president. One night, when his father was away on an extended trip, Suzanne went to Mike, who was already in bed. She told him she was frightened and wanted him to come with her. Mike was confused and uncertain. This did not feel right, but he followed his stepmother to the master bedroom, where she had him slip between the covers. Then she removed all her clothing except for her bra and panties and climbed into bed beside him. She took her stepson into her arms and pressed her large breasts strongly against him. He could feel her naked skin hot against his own.

Mike was very frightened, though of what he was not certain, and tried to will himself to shrink. He became cold all over and lay there terrified as Suzanne pressed herself against him for what seemed painfully long minutes. He lay motionless and for one awful second suddenly realized what was about to happen.

"I've got to go," he stammered, the words hardly coming out of his dry mouth. Slowly, even reluctantly, Suzanne let go of him, and Mike slipped quietly from the bed and went to his own bedroom. He lay there thinking a long time about Suzanne and this episode. He decided she was dangerous. After that he did everything he could to avoid her and told no one what had happened.

Mike joined Sam at Loyola High School in Los Angeles the following year and was glad to go. They worked as busboys to help with expenses, and so tight was the money their father allotted them that Sam had to drop off the junior varsity football team because he could not afford to buy cleats.

Even after the Shoens had moved from Oregon, the Cartys stayed close to their deceased daughter's children. Bill Carty had been an athlete in school, and Mike threw himself into track and field with a vengeance. He wrote his grandfather about his training, and Carty wrote back advice on how to win. Mike mailed clippings of his races and, when he began to place, sent the ribbons to his grandparents.

During Mike's junior year Bill Carty died, but L.S. decided against telling either Sam or Mike until after Easter, saying that he had wanted to spare them the grief, though how this would be achieved by telling them later rather than earlier, he did not explain.

Mike asked his father if he could spend the summer on the farm because he wanted to be of help to his grandmother, but L.S. said no. The Carty farm, he explained, was something the family was moving away from, not clinging to. Instead Mike and Sam spent that summer with L.S.'s good friend and senior employee Tom Safford, who took them on an extended motor trip across Canada, working at various U-Haul agencies, repairing trailers. Mike did not enjoy the summer at all and was angered when Safford drove past the Carty farm and refused to let the boys visit their grandmother.

This was a typical summer for the oldest boys, whom L.S. wanted to teach the value of money. They had spent the first summer of L.S. and Suzanne's marriage digging ditches for the sewage system at the Gearhart beach house, then in painting it. Both boys at different times were assigned to other U-Haul employees L.S. trusted and worked on the most menial tasks in the company.

It was not uncommon for L.S. to use the same techniques with his children as he did with his employees. His dressing down an unfortunate employee was an embarrassing sight for other workers because L.S. rarely stopped before he had humiliated and humbled the man, making him feel like an imbecile. L.S. was not reluctant to address his own boys in such a manner in the presence of strangers.

Five years after moving the family to Palm Springs, L.S. decided he had made a mistake and must move to a metropolitan area to which the company could also be relocated. Perhaps with Suzie Whitmore in mind L.S. decided to relocate to Phoenix.

In January 1964 L.S. flew to Arizona and quickly bought a furnished Frank Lloyd Wright-designed house on Tatum Boulevard beside the exclusive Paradise Valley Country Club, paying $410,000. He placed the title in the name of his ten children and Suzanne, then flew to Palm Springs, where he informed Suzanne for the first time that he had bought a house and they were moving to Phoenix.

On the trip to Phoenix L.S. spoke enthusiastically of the house, which was nearly five thousand square feet in size and sat on nine acres of desert. Constructed in 1954, it had seven bedrooms and five baths. But when they arrived, Suzanne voiced her immediate displeasure. She wanted something easier to live in. Even worse, deed restrictions prohibited moving the furniture or for that matter changing the color of the fabric or the house. It was to remain exactly as Wright had designed it, and that suited L.S. very well.

He had acquired the house on a Thursday, and by Sunday he and fourteen-year-old Mark were loading furniture into the Tatum House, as it came to be called by the family. So quickly had the move occurred neither Sam nor Mike knew where the family was for a week, just one more indication of the chaotic life the Shoens were leading.

Visitors to the Tatum House experienced mixed feelings toward it. Some considered it a museum and could not imagine any normal family living in it with all its rough edges and picture-perfect symmetry. Others were enthralled by its beauty and envied the Shoens.

It developed that Suzanne only hated *living* in the Tatum House. It was distinctive in its architecture, a unique, eye-catching structure that was ideal for entertaining. After she had turned the children loose cleaning the place, spent hours coiffing her hair and donning her makeup before joining guests at parties and heard them lavish praise on the house, she loved it and was eloquent about its many virtues. The next day she was back to complaining about it.

Joe and Mark attended nearby Brophy College Preparatory boarding school those first two years. They were home three nights a week, and one of the children commented that a three-ring circus could not have compared with life in the Tatum House when they were there. A distracted and despairing Suzanne demanded that L.S. at least lay down some rules, to which he replied, "I don't think prisons have any rules today," so why should a household? By Suzanne's admission the household was in chaos.

After graduating from Loyola High School in Los Angeles both Sam and Mike attended Holy Cross College in Worcester, Massachusetts. In L.S.'s opinion, the two oldest boys were still least in need of his help. "They could," he often said, "take care of themselves." While they had worked, and worked hard, both in school and during summers, the same could not be said of Joe and Mark, who were indulged. Given jobs over the summer, Joe insisted on supervising crews rather than do work himself, and Mark simply refused to work altogether.

In L.S.'s mind, both Joe and Mark with buck teeth were less physically attractive than their older brothers; "homely" was how he described them. As a teenager Joe remained quiet and in the shadows. He appeared almost pathologically afraid of girls his own age and did not date. Whether that was the consequence of his periodic episodes in a body cast, his natural repressed sexuality, or his relationship with Suzanne wasn't apparent. He constantly sought favor with his father, to whom he was devoted. L.S. continued to be grateful to have the steady Joe home to look out for the younger children while he was on the road.

Brophy Prep discontinued boarding students, and Joe and Mark began living at home every night. Mark was the most overtly unhappy of the four oldest boys. Throughout school he had required tutors to maintain acceptable grades and more than once came home from Brophy disgusted with his performance, slamming his books on the table, insisting that he was going to drop out. He remained easily agitated and combative, and his anger was most manifest in his constant defiance of Suzanne.

However, there was little doubt who the real instigator was behind the trouble with the stepmother. As with the cherry bombs in Palms Springs, always "behind the curtain" was Joe. Outwardly he manifested no emotion toward Suzanne, but in quiet he worked insidiously against her. Joe and Mark commonly called Suzanne "the bitch" behind her back, and Mark often mimicked Joe in agitating others to defy her.

When Mary Anna was fourteen, Suzanne slapped her face. Mark insisted in private that Mary Anna should have struck her back. "Why take it?" he demanded. Mark once persuaded Mary Anna to call Suzanne a "whore" to her face, and afterward Mary Anna felt used and ashamed, while Mark was thoroughly pleased with himself.

Mary Anna's role at home had not improved with the years, and her comparison with Cinderella was as true at fourteen as it had been at ten. L.S. noticed that whenever he and Suzanne fought most violently, Suzanne demanded excessive housework from Mary Anna. Mary Anna, for her part, was concerned with harmony in the house and looked up to her four oldest brothers. It was seven years to the next girl in the family, Sophia, and Mary Anna was more like a mother to her younger sisters than a big sister, a role of which L.S. approved.

Suzanne complained frequently to him about his unwillingness to support her in disciplining Joe and Mark, finally telling him that if he would not back her, she would no longer be held responsible for their upbringing. She was going to care for herself and her own children and no more. Instead of rising to her support or seeking some other compromise, L.S. wrote, "This struck me as a possible solution. It seems futile to try to mother the older six and I explained this to them. No strain from their view."

When Joe turned sixteen, he asked L.S. to buy him an Austin-Healey sports car that was very much in need of work. L.S. decided to buy the car for both Joe and Mark. The Austin-Healey was only the first of many cars for these boys.

In 1955, during his extended road trip with Anna Mary after completing law school, L.S. had met Harry DeShong, Sr., and his wife, Eileen, in Phoenix. L.S., who was impressed by the industrious, constantly smiling man, hired him to help run a repair shop for the company in Portland. Eileen joined U-Haul as a secretary in 1958. In 1964 DeShong, was relocated to Phoenix and made marketing president for the district, but primarily he was responsible for operating the repair facility for U-Haul there.

When Joe and Mark went to work on their Austin-Healey, it was to DeShong's repair shop they took it, as he was always quick to do a favor for any member of the Shoen family. Working for him at the shop were his son, Harry DeShong, Jr., and Darrell Hamby.

Even in those days Harry DeShong, Jr., possessed an ingratiating manner that exceeded his father's with an unvarying smile fixed on his face. He behaved as if something great were about to happen to him at any moment. And though DeShong was quick to work on the Austin-Healey, it was clear he would rather have owned it.

Hamby was the skilled worker, and it was for his help Joe and Mark actually went. He was a man who seemed to want bigger things but never got them. He was good with engines and skilled at painting cars.

When Mark was old enough to drive, he immediately began wrecking cars. L.S. urged caution on him, then repaired or replaced each vehicle. Mark also started racing cars on the local dirt tracks with an inevitable outcome. He drove flat out, forced others to yield, and, when finally they did not, crashed. No one recalls Mark's finishing those early races, let alone winning any.

This was only one way in which L.S. treated Joe and Mark differently from the oldest sons. Joe, though still in high school, talked his father into buying him a hydroplane that he regularly took to the lake and that DeShong enjoyed borrowing. Joe and Mark loved motorcycles and were soon collecting them. Anything they wanted, they got.

In July 1967 L.S. bought twin towers in central Phoenix to establish a national headquarters for U-Haul. Known as U-Haul Towers, they marked a significant step up for the company, and over that summer, using U-Haul trailers and trucks, L.S. transferred the company's administrative functions from Portland to Phoenix. He established an office to help his employees find housing and covered the expenses of their moves. Some employees who were unwilling to relocate were let go, but most who did not want to move were given jobs in the portions of U-Haul that remained in Portland.

When Sam and Mike returned home from Holy Cross for holidays, the tension between Suzanne and L.S. was palpable. In private their father complained frequently to them of his marriage, and it was apparent that Joe and Mark were in a virtual state of rebellion against their stepmother.

Suzanne, who resented L.S.'s devotion to U-Haul, was viewed by some employees as openly hostile toward the company, though in light of her husband's behavior, this was, to some degree, justified. L.S. was gone at least half of the time and, when he was home, worked out of the house. He had a WATS line installed and lived on the telephone. The talk was U-Haul, U-Haul, U-Haul.

The support he had taken for granted from Anna Mary simply did not exist. To L.S. it seemed that Suzanne, with her constant complaints, wanted to destroy him.

Not every aspect of life in Paradise Valley was unpleasant for Suzanne, however. She was gone from the house most of the time, attending the luncheons and meetings of the wives of the movers and shakers in the community. Already U-Haul was one of the state's largest private employers, and she was readily welcomed. It was a role she relished, and her reputation in social circles was impeccable.

When L.S. was on the road, he rarely called home because of the tirades Suzanne delivered about the misconduct of his boys. Usually he caught Joe on the telephone since Suzanne was absent so often and heard his side first. But it was an unending list of more of the same, and early on he decided it was better not to call at all. L.S., in fact, took to dodging his wife when he was away. If she wanted him, and she often did, she started calling U-Haul offices all over the country, demanding to know if some employee had seen her husband recently. Employees covered for L.S., and if she suspected that was the case, she became even angrier.

But not all of L.S.'s road trips were entirely unwelcome. More than once, as he prepared to leave, Suzanne told him not to come back for at least a month. She needed the break.

In addition to her involvement in social circles, Suzanne became active in the Pentecostal renewal charismatic movement of the Catholic Church and hosted gatherings of twenty or so well-dressed people at the Tatum House during the day. Neighbors were already unhappy with the Shoens because of the fast cars that raced up and down Tatum Boulevard and the oversize bright orange U-Haul trailer mailbox L.S. had erected out front. Word quickly spread of Suzanne's strange behavior.

One day Mary Anna came home from school with a neighborhood friend and found Suzanne and her charismatic group gathered in a circle, holding hands, staring intensely into the void, and speaking in "tongues of fire," as Suzanne called it. Mary Anna's girl friend was shocked while Mary Anna just rolled her eyes and took her friend to her room.

Besides speaking in tongues, members of the group laid on hands to cure disease and to drive out spirits. Suzanne searched for opportunities to lay hands on one of the children as a means of solving a problem. Whenever she attempted this, Mike firmly refused since he could think of nothing worse than to have Suzanne corner him, then lay her hands on him. When she was in this mood, he avoided her completely.

Mark talked to Mike, and the two agreed that God was not on Suzanne's side, even though she and her friends insisted he was. Mark had located a record called "Power over the Devil," a fiery sermon by a fundamentalist preacher. He played it over and over until both he and Mike knew sections of it, applying it to Suzanne especially when she was stalking the hallways of the vast Tatum House, searching for someone on whom she could lay hands. "Power over the Devil" was their code for fending her off, for standing up to her, and whenever she was nearby, but out of earshot, they broke into sections of the sermon, followed by hysterical laughter.

But Joe showed no interest in the humor; in fact, he rarely demonstrated a sense of humor at all, especially as concerned Suzanne. His relationship with her was so twisted emotionally it appeared incomprehensible to L.S. and some of his siblings.

As a solution more than once Joe suggested that the boys should kill their stepmother.* "Let's take her to the lake," one brother recalls Joe insisting, "and push her overboard." Sam was amused by Joe's constant talk of doing away with Suzanne and considered it a joke, just so much tough talk, his sober version of "Power over the Devil."

Joe's memories of his mother had faded to the point where he scarcely remembered her. His father, Hap Carty, and others spoke lavishly of Anna Mary, and when Joe talked about her, he spoke with the rapt breath reserved for the Virgin Mary. There was much the same in his manner when he talked about his father to others or shared the dreams he had at night in which he was head of U-Haul. There was the disturbing look of the zealot in his eye.

By his late teens Joe's desire to destroy L.S.'s relationship with

---

*Many years later, when confronted with accounts he had planned to kill his stepmother, Joe denied that this incident and others took place.

Suzanne was becoming obsessive, and his hatred of Suzanne appeared pervasive. If Suzanne had ever taken Joe into her bed, as she had Mike, he never spoke of it, though apparent by this time was his unrequited hatred for "the bitch."

Toward the end of high school, when Mike and Sam were home from college, Joe pulled them and Mark into his bedroom and shut the door. In Joe's eyes, Suzanne had committed an unpardonable sin. "We have to do something," he said feverishly.

Mark agreed. "There's a problem. Our father can't deal with her."

"He's suffering," Joe said emphatically, "and something has to be done." He went on to say that he had been keeping "book" on Suzanne's misdeeds, and it was time to do something about them. Then he squinted his eyes and said, "We have to kill her."

Joe repeated Suzanne's perceived misconduct and was working himself and Mark up emotionally. How should we do it? he asked rhetorically, then led a discussion of options. A knife was suggested. Then maybe poison. Perhaps a gun would be better.

Until now this had seemed like a bad joke to Sam, just so much more of Joe's big talk. His usual threats against Suzanne sounded a lot like the times he had argued that someone at school should be beaten up. But this day the mood was clearly different.

With the talk of weapons and of specific ways to kill his stepmother Mike became frightened. Joe and Mark had said things like this to him before, but he had never heard it with this intensity or singularity of purpose. As Joe and Mark debated the proper instrument to use for Suzanne's destruction, Mike had no doubt they were intending to do it. Mike was feeling very much as he had when he had been in Suzanne's bed, and again he pulled into himself, willing himself to become smaller, unable even to protest. *I don't want to kill anyone,* he thought.

But Joe and Mark continued planning and talking. Finally the emotion passed, and once again it turned into just so much big talk from Joe. Mike left the room then, but for years he had nightmares that he had actually gone ahead and murdered someone, so close had this been, so clearly had that been Joe's wish.

* * *

This wasn't the end of attacks on Suzanne. In September 1968, when Mark was seventeen, L.S. had just arrived at the Tatum House. He was upstairs in the bedroom and heard a commotion below. When L.S. ran into the kitchen, he spotted Mark landing lefts and rights to Suzanne's body. She had grabbed a butcher knife and was waving it in the air, screaming at the top of her lungs, as Mark continued to punch her. L.S. broke the pair up, but Mark had hit Suzanne so hard she insisted the police be summoned. When they arrived, she gave them a full report and demanded that Mark be permanently barred from entering the Tatum House.

Behind U-Haul Towers were modest brick houses, and L.S. had made a point of buying them as each fell on the market. A few were cleared for employee parking; another was used as a day-care center; some were maintained as living quarters. L.S. moved Mark out of the Tatum House into one of these houses, which was also convenient to Brophy College Prep, opened a checking account for him, then hired a recent Miss Arizona who was Catholic to stay with him and do the housework. One of the secretaries working at U-Haul was assigned the job of seeing to Mark's overall needs.

All this should have been a clear message to L.S. that his marriage was dysfunctional. In light of Mark's behavior, L.S. was unreasonably blaming Suzanne for the problems at home. He should have been able to see the adverse effect this was having on his children, but if he did, he did not act to end it.

"My God. What next?" L.S. wrote. "I am sick to death with Suzanne's neurotic behavior. She insists that people be forced to comply with her plans...." There was no doubt whom L.S. blamed for the fight. "...Suzanne [was] acting like a mad woman," he wrote, "called the sheriff and want[ed] to bring an assault charge vs. Mark. It should have been vice versa....I can't blame Mark for his hitting Suzanne."

CHAPTER SIX

PRIMA DONNAS

For the children in general life was typically, if affluently, American. Mary Anna attended Xavier High School, the exclusive Catholic all-girls school beside Brophy College Prep. Most of the other children were at Brophy or the ultra-exclusive Paradise Valley Country Day School.

The family had grown so large it now spanned more than a single generation, the youngest children having been born when the oldest were young adults. Surprisingly the family did not divide by natural mother. If L.S. had been unsuccessful in persuading Anna Mary's six children that Suzanne was their new mother, he had succeeded in melding the children from two mothers into a single family. Suzanne had played an important role in accomplishing that by treating all the children, Anna Mary's and her own, in the same manner. Mary Anna's initial dislike of her stepmother had been tempered considerably over the years and the same thing occurred to the oldest children as they reached young adulthood. Only Joe retained his anger, which became even more vitriolic, and Mark, at Joe's instigation, continued to spar with his stepmother.

While L.S. confessed in private that family "holidays drive me out of my tree," they were the only times the whole family gathered and for that reason were especially cherished by the youngest. There was a genuine effort to keep family differences outside the Tatum House, and Christmas in particular was a warm and lavish affair. Not for many years had L.S. bought used bikes for any of his children. Christmas in Arizona was a celebration of conspicuous, amazing consumption.

The children could be generous with one another and often were. Once Joe bought cowboy hats for the family members and had them pose for a family picture in front of the sheriff's office at a local amusement park, L.S. with a cigar. Another time, without telling anyone, Joe arranged and paid for a week's rafting trip down the Colorado River for Sam, Mike, Mark, Paul, and Jimmie. Still again, he financed a train trip for the older children through Mexico.

The oldest boys were like uncles to the youngest children and in some cases, especially Joe, were nearly fatherlike figures. It had been Mark who delivered her first lecture on sex to Mary Anna. Sex for a woman, he told her sternly, was a carrot you hold in front of the man to get what you want.

Sam and Mike were not judgmental in their dealings with the younger children, and their arrival for vacations or holidays was greeted with enthusiasm by them. Mike was a bit of a poet, mild-mannered and sensitive. When Mary Anna came home one evening at about the time Mark was instructing her on the nature of sex, she found Mike quietly crying alone for no reason he would articulate. She had taken him into her arms, and they had held each other for a very long time. Ever since Mary Anna had felt a special affinity for him.

Sam was a family favorite. He was gregarious and warm by nature, with an open, sweet disposition and the hearty Shoen laugh. He was extremely intelligent and possessed a slightly professorial air in formal settings. Almost he alone of the children had a clear memory of the early days of struggle in building U-Haul and appreciated just how far the Shoen family had come. He understood that his father had made this privileged life possible for all of them.

L.S. was constantly looking for opportunities to expand U-Haul operations into related areas. Adding one-way rental trucks to trailers in the late 1950s was inevitable. Trailer hitches were a specialty item no national business was serving, and men who needed to haul trailers in their work were soon coming to U-Haul for help. The company had become expert at installing temporary hitches on all kinds of vehicles, and it was a logical extension of the business first to sell, then permanently to mount a hitch on someone's truck. Out of this came Hitch World, one of several U-Haul subsidiaries that sold rather than rented moving related equipment.

One of U-Haul's vice-presidents in Florida suggested to L.S. that U-Haul consider renting boats. L.S. knew nothing about boating, so he decided to learn by buying a Chinese junk located in Texas. The thirty-five-ton junk had been constructed for a New York businessman, and though it was intended for sailing, it also had formidable diesel capacity. Over seventy feet long, painted jet black, it was an attractive craft with ample cabin space. L.S. intended to have the older children join him for a trip up the coast of the Gulf of Mexico, then cross the Gulf to Florida. This was to be a father's trip with the older children, a real adventure. One of the senior U-Haul managers with sailing experience would accompany them. L.S. thought he'd know enough about boating by the time he reached Florida to start asking intelligent questions.

Joe was attending Holy Cross at the time. A Buddhist statue of luck for ships called a hotai went with the boat, and the twenty-year-old agreed to drive through New York City, pick it up from the owner, then transport it to Texas, where he would join his father and brothers for the trip.

On June 6, 1969, Joe called Sam, who was in medical school at the University of Arizona in Tucson, and said he had been arrested for driving a hundred miles an hour in a fifty-five-mile-an-hour zone in New York State. He asked his older brother for a hundred dollars' bail money because he did not want their father to know what had happened. Sam didn't have that much cash, but he passed the hat among his fellow students, then wired it to Joe.

Accompanied by a college friend, Joe resumed his trip and later that night drove into the small town of Rye, New York, at a speed in excess of a hundred miles an hour. A local police car was parked at the edge of the road when Joe struck it full force. Two police officers were seriously injured, as were Joe and his friend. All were hospitalized. Joe had suffered a concussion and received multiple face lacerations and contusions. So serious was the wreck that Joe's companion was unconscious for three days, and first reports were that Joe might not survive the night. Joe recovered, but the family learned that when he was released, he was to be charged with reckless driving, a criminal offense, and that police guards were posted outside his hospital room.

Rather than go to Rye, L.S. flew on to Houston, where he met Tom Safford, his close friend and senior U-Haul official, and his sons Mark now nineteen; Paul, age thirteen; and Jimmie, ten. Sam's summer vacation had just begun and he was intending to join the family on the junk.

Working closely with his father by long distance, Sam carefully orchestrated Joe's extrication from trouble; he retained a local Rye attorney with the right political connections and saw to it the officers were compensated for damages. It wasn't easy or cheap, but within days the criminal charges had been dropped. Once again there were no consequences for bad behavior.

For eleven days Joe lay in the hospital while L.S. supervised the fitting and repair of the junk in Texas. When Joe arrived on June 27, L.S. was shocked by his son's physical appearance. He was not just covered with cuts and abrasions, but his head was mis-shapen as well. L.S. had not thought his son that badly injured despite what the doctor first told him. Joe was furious with his father for not coming to see him and behaved as if he were more than a little hurt. But if he knew of L.S.'s and especially Sam's efforts to keep him out of jail, and he surely must have, he made no mention of it and offered no thanks. Such effort on his behalf was what he had come to expect as his due.

L.S. ran the boat as captain and delegated tasks to the children, but the original plan for the voyage quickly proved an illusion. After a month's worth of repairs on the junk, it was at last pro-nounced seaworthy, and they hoisted the sail. But soon the main-mast snapped. When the trip resumed, L.S. headed for New Orleans by running on the diesel engine and stuck to the channels and locks of the safer inland waterway.

Sam arrived just as the junk was about to leave Texas and was greeted at the airport by the quick-tempered Mark, who headed at once for the family plane with a suitcase in hand. "There's the

car keys," he said, pitching them to his brother. "I'm going home."
Sam asked him what the trouble was, and Mark let loose with an
unending list of abuses to which he had been subjected this past
month. Mark said he had been delegated all the dirty jobs on the
junk and was having a miserable time. Sam persuaded him to stay,
however.

Joe had assumed control of the wheel once he arrived and had
been doing a studious, if inept, job of it. When Sam arrived, L.S.
told him to try his hand, and he quickly established himself as an
able yachtsman. Joe joined Mark in the menial tasks and did not
take well what he perceived as his reduced status. Sam had assumed
his place and on top of that was receiving his father's lavish praise.
Joe was openly bitter and antagonistic toward his older brother
and conspicuously defiant toward his father. He constantly sniped
at Sam and displayed a pronounced temper that startled L.S.

The older Shoen boys all possessed the slimness of youth and
were vigorously fit though they were already losing their hair. In
apparent compensation Mark had grown a scraggly beard that
enraged his father every time he looked at it. Joe had a beard as
well, and the older boys sported overgrown sideburns.

L.S. loved an adventure, but this expedition with the junk was
proving too much with one failure after another. The boat was
exhausting to operate and tested everyone's patience. At one time
or another it seemed every part of the boat broke.

But not everything about the trip was unpleasant, and during
the periods without breakdowns it was enjoyable. Mark was
hoisted to the top of the mast with a grin on his face, and more
than once the family used a chase boat to film the junk roaring
across open water with the throttle wide open. Overall there were
more smiles than frowns until they reached New Orleans.

They were in one of the many locks waiting for the water to
rise when Joe glanced up and spotted a smiling Suzanne, waving
at them from the bridge. "There's the bitch!" Joe shouted savagely.

Mark looked up. "How did she find us?"

The trip might not have been perfect, but until now it had been
their trip, their time with their father.

L.S., who had been lonely without a woman was not unhappy
to see his young wife. By this time he was fifty-three, and she was

a stunning thirty-four. Their marriage was less than perfect, but he was emotionally bonded to Suzanne and enjoyed their robust sex life.

Any attempt to cross the gulf by diesel proved a fiasco when they ran out of fuel during a violent storm and were towed to shore by the Coast Guard. When L.S. considered how much money he had spent on repairs during the past eight weeks, it was obvious to him that U-Haul could never rent boats and make a profit. From what he could see, the only money to be made from boats was in owning repair docks.

Not long after this trip there occurred a strange incident that at first did not appear to touch on the Shoens directly. Tom Safford's daughter was arrested and charged with attempting to hire someone to murder her boyfriend's wife. That seemed to L.S. an especially ugly way to solve a problem, but he lent Safford ten thousand dollars to hire a lawyer for her defense, and she was eventually acquitted.

By now the personalities of the four oldest sons were set. They were distinctively identifiable as Shoens, yet diverse in their own ways. Each bore aspects of his father's personality; all held good and bad traits. All these were aspects of the father, and taken together, the four oldest sons very likely constituted L.S.'s total personality. But it was as if nature, or fate, had cleaved the four into two sets, and each set bore more distinctly certain facets of their father's personality.

Sam and Mike were warmer and generous in nature, more tolerant and forgiving than Joe and Mark, who were secretive, darker and moody, conspiratorial in their behavior, self-absorbed and narcissistic. It had always been the two oldest boys and the two next younger in the pairings, but now that distinction held a real difference.

This same year L.S. was once again reorganizing his nationwide network of thirty-five corporations by placing them under the control of a new holding company to be called American Family Corporation, or Amerco. He had always favored a large number of corporations, both to minimize liability for U-Haul and to provide titles to pass around rather than large paychecks. U-Haul had more presidents and vice-presidents than the average bank. Lending institutions had been reluctant to lend money, and forming a single holding company with all the assets in one pot would ease that problem.

During 1969 L.S. was busy transferring stock of the new company to his children, now grown to eleven with the addition of Katrina three years earlier, and was attempting to equalize ownership as much as he could. The reality was that the six oldest children held larger percentages because they had inherited a portion of their mother's stock upon her death.

Suzanne attributed less than noble motives to L.S. for these stock gifts. She told friends that her husband was giving away the company to keep her from getting any of it should they ever divorce. In private she scoffed at his plans and told him, "The boys will just take the company from you when they grow up." But it had no effect.

By this time L.S. had transferred all but a small percentage of his company from his hands. Nearly all the stock was held by the children, though he still voted the minors' stock as their guardian. He could have created more stock and, by issuing it to the younger children, made them all equal owners, but he rejected that as fundamentally unfair. The real effect of such a maneuver would have been to dilute the stock of the oldest children, which they had received in large part from Anna Mary, and that simply would not have been right.

L.S. could also have issued additional shares of common stock to himself or placed them in a trust for the children, which he could have voted even when they had reached majority age. But he had always seen U-Haul as the ultimate property of his children, his legacy to them, and he could see no option other than the one he had chosen, giving the company to them.

Katrina's birth had served only as the latest example of the difficulty he faced. The ten existing children and Suzanne each held joint ownership of the rapidly appreciating Tatum House. L.S. created a separate estate for Katrina in an attempt to equalize the wealth, but he could not know how much one eleventh of the Tatum House would eventually be worth.

The problem of equitably dividing the money was not theoretical though those lacking such assets might wonder why he was concerned. At its peak the oldest children would be worth an estimated $160 million each while even L.S.'s paltry 2 percent was worth nearly $30 million. Some of the younger children held stock valued at $40 million, but as adults they complained bitterly of the disparity with the older offspring.

Ownership in U-Haul, however, was like holding Park Place in Monopoly because the stock was not publicly traded. L.S. paid no dividends since he reasoned that U-Haul's income was taxed when it was received; if he paid his children dividends, the money would be taxed a second time, and that struck his business sense as just so much foolishness.

Generally either he or the company provided his children with every financial need. With their stock in U-Haul each child was worth tens of millions of dollars, money he or she would see if the company ever went public or U-Haul agreed to purchase portions of it, both possibilities L.S. anticipated eventually.

But he also wanted all his children to hold wealth in their own right. He had not forgotten the grinding poverty of his youth, and although U-Haul appeared to have acquired a life of its own after these years of hard work, anything was possible in the business world. By the mid-1950s each child had an estate established upon birth to which L.S. gave valuables or cash on a regular basis. Since the minor children had no need of the money and U-Haul could always use an extra source of cash, the estates were highly leveraged by U-Haul. The primary growth of the estates took place through fleet ownership, an opportunity no longer commonly available. Once U-Haul was well established, L.S. had stopped making opportunities for fleet investment available except to select employees and family.

The children's estates were carefully monitored so that at age twenty-one each Shoen child held cash in the amount of approximately one million dollars. Because of economics, the money might still be leveraged, and not all of it be available, but by their mid-twenties the debts were clear. Because of the manner in which the estates were funded and the varying interest rates that existed during their formative years, the value of each estate when the child reached twenty-one could vary by as much as two hundred thousand dollars. Some of the children were grateful for the estate; most took it for granted; a few were angry that others' estates had higher values than theirs and complained about it.*

There was another reason for the convoluted finances, however, that L.S. never discussed. In large part he kept his children cash-poor so they had to come to him for help as young adults. In this way he exercised a heavy-handed control once they were grown. Perhaps he was consciously aware of it, perhaps not, but it was just one manifestation of his controlling personality, a tendency that had been exacerbated over the years as U-Haul had grown and prospered at his direction. In every way he could muster, he sought to manage the family the same way he ran the company, and in many regards the two were one and the same.

The Shoen children benefited greatly from their birthright. They

---

*An examination of just one estate is demonstrative of all of them. Sophia was born in 1960. By 1983 her estate held the following:

Cash	$13,382.00
Money market savings	2,571.00
Credit union	2,100.00
Merrill Lynch Ready Asset Trust	38,946.00
Smith Barney Nat'l Liquid Reserves	11,385.00
U.S. Treasury bills due Jan. 1984	100,000.00
Amerco (U-Haul) note due Jan. 1984	100,000.00

TOTAL CASH AND CASH EQUIVALENTS	$268,384.00	
Tax-exempt bonds	362,000.00	
Gold bullion (325 oz @ $375/oz)	121,875.00	
TOTAL LIQUID ASSETS		$752,259.00
Tatum House (1/11th interest)		120,000.00
IRA cash reserves		4,000.00
Amerco (U-Haul) profit-sharing plan		1,500.00
U-Haul fleet income (@ 1983 earnings)		101,433.00
		$979,192.00

In addition, her yearly income from wages paid by U-Haul, interest (more than half of which was tax-exempt), director's fees and rents, less tax, was:
1981—$99,990.00 1982—$132,238.00 1983—$112,389.00
Sophia's one-eleventh interest in the Tatum House became approximately $400,000 in cash. After deducting capital gains tax, she was left with $320,000, or $200,000 more than listed for her share above. Sophia was one of the children who objected to how L.S. had managed their estates, though some years later she acknowledged the Shoens were "luckier than ninety-nine percent of the people in the world."

held company credit cards, flew in company planes to private functions, and drove company-provided automobiles. When they were adults, their life and medical insurances were paid for by the company, company houses were available at no cost, and they drew salaries, whether or not they actually performed work for U-Haul.

L.S. was slow to inform his children, especially the two oldest boys, of their estates. Mike first discovered he had an estate when he mentioned in passing to L.S.'s secretary that he lacked the money for a car and didn't know what to do since he needed one. The secretary quietly handed him his estate accounting, and only then did Mike learn he was a millionaire in his own right. It took some convincing by the secretary but finally Mike cautiously withdrew fifty-one hundred dollars and bought a Volkswagen Beetle that he drove for twenty years.

L.S. also fretted about U-Haul's future. It was his oft-stated dream to see his children, and by that he meant his four oldest sons primarily, take over the company from him in some capacity. Not all the oldest boys were showing an interest in that, but L.S. still held out hope they would see matters his way. He was well aware of the history of the second generation's assuming control of a family company and then falling into a destructive feud. He repeated the quote "Shirt sleeves to shirt sleeves in three generations" so often to Joe that the young man complained it was a disparaging comment directed personally at him.

L.S. needed to look no farther than Suzanne's family for an example of what he did not want to happen to U-Haul. He repeated the story often to his children as a lesson from which they should learn. The Gilbaughs had done very well with the Portland Casket Company, but when Suzanne's grandfather, the founder, died, her grandmother had retained control of the company. Her four children constituted senior management, but under her direction. Suzanne's father was president of the company. He had a flair for marketing, but his mother was a bean counter who saw no wisdom, only needless expense, in expansion. The company stopped growing, and in time the four children fell out among themselves and lost the company.

L.S. knew it was arrogance on his part, but it was hubris he could not resist, and he believed with all his heart and logic that it would be different with his children. He was a man who wanted everything, and he blinded himself to the reality that it was not possible.

Though Mike initially attended Holy Cross, just as Sam had, he disliked what he viewed as the Jesuit college's hypocrisy and received his father's permission to transfer to Arizona State University just outside Phoenix to complete his undergraduate work. Mike loved his father profoundly and was always the dutiful son, but obedience had taken a terrible personal toll on him. Day in and day out Mike was told in personal ways what to do and how to live, and he did it. When he finished his undergraduate work, L.S. directed him to attend ASU's law school. Mike reluctantly agreed but found other ways to rebel.

That first year in law school and through the summer he began racing motorcycles in his spare time. More than once he stood at the starting line with the other racers and, scanning the cheering crowd, was struck by the oddity of his situation. He was, he thought, very likely the only college graduate in the place, and certainly the only millionaire. As he raced, he improved his performances by taking reckless risks and slowly began to win, but after a time he saw he could never beat the best, not in motorcycles.

He switched to racing cars but had a similar experience, though with cars he could push harder and cut his edge with the best drivers even farther. At one track he did very well because of a peculiarly dangerous curve. The raceway rose so fast at one point that a sharp turn was invisible to the drivers and cars slowed down to make it safely. Mike used this point to pass cars, steamrollering blindly into the turn. The risks were enormous, but he no longer cared.

He went through the motions at law school but felt gutted. As he walked the hallways, Mike thought, *I am dead,* so acute was his sense of having no control over his life, and he wondered if people could see it just by looking at him.

At this time the Carty farm was sold, and its loss was another cause for Mike's heartache. He knew that Anna Mary had made his father pledge never to sell off the family farm, and he could see his father's ambivalence over the transaction, but as he had told his son, the farm was something from which the Shoens were moving, not clinging to.

James Carty had waited years for this opportunity, and with the death of his mother the farm had passed to the Carty children. James, who had held local political office was able to have the farm made eligible for federal acquisition as a wildlife refuge. Once the farm was bought by the government, the old house and barn, which Mike had so loved, were dismantled. The farm Bill Carty had tended with devotion was allowed to go to weed and was soon overgrown. Very shortly it was as if it had never existed. James Carty achieved his dream: The family farm had been destroyed.

In time Mike recognized the lunacy of what he was doing on the racetracks and came to realize that this building of his courage had occurred because he lacked the courage to stand up to his father. He decided when he graduated from law school he would make a life for himself away from U-Haul and free of his father's control.

During his years as the trailer man, L.S. had frequently moved heavy equipment and, in 1969, injured his back seriously. In his house he installed a whirlpool and an elaborate traction device. Suzanne ordered a pyramid constructed over the bed and told L.S. its focused power would heal his back. Occasionally L.S. was laid up in bed for weeks at a time, and more than once he tolerated her gaggle of charismatic pseudo-Christians, as he called them in private, and had them lay hands on him.

To cope with the pain, he was taking a wide range of pills, including Valium and Quaalude. The same year he tried lithium, a drug most often associated with the control of manic depression, but was very unhappy with it, blaming the drug for disrupting his thinking and causing him to be irritable. After less than two weeks he discontinued its use, but his chronic back trouble persisted.

In corporate circles U-Haul was known for its unorthodox management style and tough-talking staff. By 1970 L.S. had become concerned about what he regarded as some senior officers' lack of consideration in spending money. Too many of them were recarpeting adequately carpeted offices, holding needless, and expensive, conferences, and purchasing cars when replacements were not necessary. He called a special meeting on the eleventh floor of U-Haul Towers to bring an end to the practices and planned a demonstration to make his point. He ordered the doors locked and guards posted to see to it no one left until he was finished.

"We don't want to join the businesses that are in trouble," he told the men. "We can sweat [hard times] through and make a dollar at the same time. But we'll have to try to serve our customers, not try to serve ourselves."

Earlier L.S. had received a thousand dollars in cash in repayment of a personal loan, and it was this thick wad of money that had first given him this idea. He pulled out the money, everything from one-hundred-dollar bills to one-dollar bills, and held it conspicuously in front of him.

"I know that many of us in this room have thrown away a goodly amount of money already this morning. And I'm included in that group." He asked for suggestions on what this amount of money could buy and made a few of his own. He then invited the men out onto the balcony and explained that the way money in the company was being spent was no different from tossing it out onto the street.

He extended the bills toward the startled group and suggested throwing them away. No one took him up on the offer. He tried again, but still, there were no takers. Finally he called over a secretary and ordered her to do as he said. She gingerly took a handful of one-hundred-dollar bills and, at a nod of approval from L.S., pitched them off the balcony. With that L.S. flung the rest of the money into the air, out over Central Avenue, during rush-hour traffic.

L.S. had thought the money would just drift down around the towers, but instead it fluttered out, landing on the cars and in the street. He was startled by the ensuing traffic jam, as drivers climbed out of cars and scrambled for the money. Horns were honking and people shouting as they rushed to grab a bill before they all were gone. L.S., amazed by the reaction, watched a single bill float like a paper plane and land in the lap of a woman sitting on a bench.

By the time police arrived all the money was gone. An officer went upstairs and told L.S. that because there was no evidence, he could not cite him for littering but asked him please not to toss any more money into the street.

The story quickly made the rounds of the company. L.S. had an audiotape of the meeting distributed nationwide to his offices, and it became a staple in the stories of the eccentric founder of U-Haul. "We work for a man," employees told newcomers, "who throws money into the street just to make a point!" With each retelling the amount he had tossed away grew larger.

U-Haul also had rough edges in senior management because of L.S.'s propensity for promoting service station operators who had served as rental agents into positions of authority in the company. He believed men accustomed to running their own shops on a small scale made the best senior managers in his companies. Because these men were generally unschooled, U-Haul paid them less than comparable managers in similar companies. The men were fiercely loyal to U-Haul and L.S. personally, in part because they had risen farther here than they could reasonably expect and in part because they had nowhere else to go. They also felt great loyalty to L.S. because he was one of them, a workingman who had made good. Here was a man who was not averse to getting grease on his hands and talked a language they used and understood.

In the often ruthless business world L.S.'s commitment to loyalty was not a casual matter and caused more than one rental agent or employee to tough out a difficult work situation. For example, L.S. had brought into the company the young man who had mowed his lawn in Portland in the late 1940s and placed him into increasingly responsible positions until he became president of a state U-Haul corporation. When he was summarily fired by someone immediately subordinate to L.S., his longtime friend and rental agent Jack Adair gave L.S. a call to inform him of the injustice. L.S. looked into the firing and called Adair back. He agreed that it shouldn't have happened but said he could not overrule his man, for whom he must show support. "But you tell him not to worry. I'll take care of him," he told Adair. He was true to his word. The discharged employee kept his company-leased car and was carried on full salary for one year until L.S. found another, better job for him in the company. Such stories were quick to make the rounds and played no small part in building fierce personal loyalty to U-Haul's founder.

In 1968 L.S. bought Legend City, a western-style theme park in Phoenix, as a means to acquire real estate for the company and to give his oldest sons management experience. The Tatum House wasn't a very pleasant place in those days, and in part Legend City gave L.S. a playground where he could be with his children.

Purchasing the park had primarily been the brainchild of twenty-year-old Joe and his friend Darrell Hamby. L.S. heard rumors that Joe, Mark, and Hamby were beating up customers and throwing them off the premises. He found the stories incredible, especially when he considered how small both Mark and Hamby were. Even when Joe and Mark personally related a few of the incidents to him, L.S. refused to believe they were true.

One summer Mike ran the sky ride at Legend City and, as he worked with and around his younger brothers, developed a new perspective toward them. Both Joe and Mark bragged of beating up customers, and Mike was told there was a peephole in the women's rest room but declined his opportunity to use it. Then Joe pointed out one of the young cancan dancers Legend City employed and told him she was his if he wanted her. Mike could see the girl was uncomfortable in Joe's presence and realized just how far some people could be pushed and made to do things for him because his last name was Shoen. Again he declined.

Sam had a similar experience when he was home on vacation from med school. Joe, he noticed, ran Legend City as if it were his own private reserve and treated its employees as if they were serfs. One night Joe brought a lovely blond cancan dancer up to him and said, "Here she is, Sam. She's yours." Sam found the situation peculiar and declined to take the girl out.

Throughout high school Joe had been in and out of body casts and had waged his running war with Suzanne. He acted every bit like a young man in mortal fear of normal contact with women his own age, and here he was offering Sam a young woman as a gift. It was especially odd because from what Sam knew, Joe didn't date and from all appearances was frightened of women.

Accusations of thuggery were not limited to Joe's and Mark's conduct at Legend City. That summer Mary Anna was eighteen years old and preparing to go off to college in New York City. Her boyfriend was a much older musician, a man L.S., Joe, and Mark disapproved of very much. L.S. had tried repeatedly to reason with his daughter, but she continued her affair. The night before she was to leave for college Joe told her he wanted to meet her after work at Legend City, where she supervised one of the children's rides. She thought he, Mark, and Darrell Hamby were behaving oddly when she spotted them whispering suspiciously together, so she just left work and dropped by her boyfriend's place to say good-bye. While she was there, Joe, Mark, and Hamby jumped out of cars and confronted her boyfriend and his roommates. The boyfriend was trying to be reasonable and avoid a fight, but it was clear the others intended to beat him up. Mary Anna was crying and begged them to stop, but Mark and Hamby wouldn't listen. They demanded she leave, and finally she did.

When L.S. learned what was going on, he drove as quickly as he could to the place. When he arrived, he found Joe, Mark, and Hamby had smashed bottles of beer on the cement and were brandishing the jagged edges in front of them. L.S. could see that Mary Anna's boyfriend and companions were not interested in a fight, but his sons were spitting on them, screaming obscenities, and demanding they leave town. His sons, even with the beer bottles gripped in their hands, struck him as being in over their heads, and L.S. moved between the groups to restore order. It wasn't easy, but finally his sons and Hamby drove off.

Mary Anna learned later that her boyfriend was harassed, investigated, and finally driven from Phoenix. She heard from him when she was at college and, expecting him to be angry with her, was surprised by his voicing sympathy for her situation, telling her that he had had no idea what she had to tolerate at home.

Mark's involvement in fights was not always so fortunate for him. He had taken to riding an expensive motorcycle and hanging out in biker bars. After smarting off to bikers one night with a finger gesture, he was taken outside and beaten senseless. Another time he picked a fight with a biker who worked him over and broke his nose.

There was a bizarre incident that also occurred that summer. To add to the color, Legend City had several buffalo. Joe, Mark, and Hamby decided to hunt one of them with a bow and arrow and thought it would add to the spectacle if they killed it in view of a trainful of parents and children. The animal fell to its knees, then to its side and lay there, puffing air, while the little children in the train screamed in horror. The wound was not fatal, and the young men had made no provision for killing the animal if an arrow failed. They ran about the park, trying to find a gun, as the train circled the bleeding animal repeatedly. Finally they obtained a .22 caliber handgun and dispatched the creature with a sloppy series of shots that brought fresh waves of screaming. Joe and Mark thought it had been great fun and laughed repeatedly about it, and when Legend City employees complained, they were fired on the spot.

As a result of this and other episodes, L.S. paid closer attention to Joe and Hamby and wrote, "Neither can accept any controls. . . . [Hamby] is acting like a spoiled [child], and Joe is aiding. . . . [T]ried to make clear to them both the policy restrictions on operation of Legend City and they both took off like a shot when they thought they had disposed of me."

Joe lacked the patience of maturity and in the minds of more than one of his siblings had become a classic Shoen brat. L.S. could not see such self-centered, insensitive behavior in any of his children and rushed to their defense no matter what they did, but the selfish conduct was obvious to others.

If L.S. learned anything about Joe from his conduct in management at Legend City, it was not the lesson others thought was evident. Instead, L.S. chastised himself for putting too much pressure on Joe and for failing to give him enough leadership.

L.S. had developed islands of tranquillity away from Suzanne where he would hole up for days or weeks at a time to plan and work. One was the company's Manhattan apartment. Another was the home of Suzie Whitmore and her roommate, who were now living in Cleveland. L.S. made a point every few months to fly to Cleveland for a few days, and at some point he began a sexual affair with Whitmore.

Generally the relationship between L.S. and his wife was miserable. To those who knew the family or worked with L.S., Suzanne appeared genuinely befuddled by her older husband and lacked his mental acumen. One senior member of U-Haul who socialized with the Shoens watched Suzanne visibly cringe at her husband's disgusting eating habits. Not only did he wolf down food when he was on the road and eager to make time, but he shoveled it in as fast as he could at social dinners as well, and he rarely chose silence as he chewed the food. He discussed business at any time and on any occasion.

The couple bickered relentlessly, and their arguments were a staple in their public relationship. L.S. would remove employees from office responsibilities to the Tatum House for sudden staff meetings with no consideration for what Suzanne had planned for the day and often without informing her. Her anger with her husband appeared entirely appropriate, and there was considerable sympathy in the company for her predicament, even though its employees commonly understood she had no love for U-Haul.

As early as 1968 Suzanne threatened divorce, and she frequently accused L.S. of infidelity, which he doggedly denied. Their feuds could last for days and were conducted in the manner of a public spectacle. They made up, then fought, then made up a half dozen times in a single day.

L.S. was constantly surprised by how much Suzanne stayed away from home. She often disappeared without explanation to give him the impression she was being unfaithful and became angry when he did not appear upset at the thought.

Perhaps L.S. summed up his feelings toward Suzanne best in 1969, eleven years after their wedding, when he wrote in private, "Fed up to the gills with Suz. and her shitty behavior. Doesn't give one damn about anyone in the family. Kids run wild while she consorts with pseudo-Christians. . . . "

The most serious crisis of their marriage to date occurred over the Fourth of July in 1970. For days the couple had engaged in a relentless running fight while Suzanne claimed that she had just learned the man she had stopped seeing in Portland to marry L.S. was now a successful lawyer in Los Angeles and was obtaining a divorce. She was leaving L.S., she said, and going to join his earlier rival. L.S. told her he did not want her to go, but if she insisted, she was free to—but he would be keeping the children.

Once when she booked a flight to Los Angeles, after L.S. spent most of a morning talking her out of the trip, he called the house and learned she was on her way to the airport. He had her paged there and tried again to talk her out of the trip. Such ongoing arguments were routine.

On July 3, 1970, Suzanne disappeared. L.S. was frantic and searched everywhere. When she called, she refused to say where she was. He heard nothing for the next two days. In fact, she had not gone to Los Angeles to see her former boyfriend but was staying locally with sympathetic friends.

Whatever the reason for Joe's deep-seated hatred for Suzanne, he at last decided to act on it. That weekend he obtained a gun and went to the Tatum House, where he found the darkest spot in the master bedroom and sat in an agitated state, determined to kill Suzanne when she walked through the door. He waited all night, steeled in his courage to act. She was spared only because she did not come home.* His brothers were surprised to learn just how close Joe had come to killing their stepmother, to committing murder.

When Mike heard that his younger brother had actually sat in the dark with a loaded gun waiting to kill Suzanne, he was fascinated by the mental image this invoked. His tough-talking brother had finally decided to do something. He asked Joe what this had been all about, why now? "She was out fucking some Holy Ghost asshole," Joe told him, naming the senior member of U-Haul he believed was her lover.

Later one of those present when Joe had talked of killing Suzanne wrote of feeling regret for not following through with

---

*Some years later Edward J. "Joe" Shoen publicly denied this incident ever occurred.

the plan. "I don't know how many times that creed [of getting along with Suzanne for their father's sake] stopped us kids from beating her senseless," he wrote his father. " ... [N]one of us ever got down to killing her, unfortunately for some mysterious reason. Although every one of us has had the means and the motivation. It would have been a true case of mercy killing." She should have been murdered, Joe once suggested, to cleanse her of her multitude of "sins."

When L.S. was laid up with back trouble, Joe wielded a disproportionate degree of influence not only over Legend City but in U-Haul operations as well. He was, after all, a Shoen, and employees generally were unwilling to disobey him. At the Tatum House Joe would jump L.S. in his sickbed, much as Suzanne was inclined to do, and insist on some course of action, then not let up until his father agreed.

Because of his Legend City experiences, Joe appeared to have gained confidence from his ability to manipulate his father. Even though he was still in college, Joe was engaged in an unrelenting program to press L.S. on how he should run U-Haul. The tactics he engaged in were very much the ones he had learned in combat with Suzanne. He simply wore L.S. down until finally it was just easier to give in to his aggressive son.

Joe was by now the epitome of the "Shoen brat," having expanded its definition by his conduct toward U-Haul employees. He spoke disdainfully of employees, whom he referred to as "slaves" or as "pigs feeding at the trough." He generally treated those with whom he came in contact with arrogant contempt, an attitude and behavior he tried to conceal from his father. More than once Joe, accompanied by Mark, had stormed into U-Haul Towers and fired employees at whom he had taken offense. Joe worked himself into a rage, ranted about the alleged abuses of the employee, then dragged Mark after him to go kick the employee out. Sometimes the employee acquired L.S.'s ear and recovered his job; often he did not. An employee instructed by Joe to remove someone from the payroll obeyed the order unless a superior could be persuaded to override the order. That often did not happen because no one wanted to cross Joe, and in such ways the young man exercised control in the family company in which he held no official position.

L.S. allowed no one to criticize Joe and Mark, and rather than confront his unruly offspring, he covered for them, made excuses, or ignored their conduct. It was in this way, and through his indulgent behavior toward Joe and Mark, that L.S. was primarily responsible for the creation of the Shoen brats.

By the end of 1970 L.S. was questioning whether or not he needed psychiatric help. In his journal he wrote, "I am beat at this year's end. One of the most harassing of my lifetime. I would hate to have to relive it. It has got to get better in 1971 or I may collapse."

Shortly before graduating from law school in 1971, Mike married, a marriage his father bitterly opposed. L.S. had routinely objected to the young women his oldest sons dated, saying they were not good enough. "You shouldn't get married until you are thirty," he told them. Women, he warned, were "just after your money." Then he launched into a list of his problems with Suzanne and told them that was the way marriage ended up.

More than once Mike turned to his wife, Christa, and said, "We've got to get out of here," knowing that if he did not make an existence for them elsewhere, he would be sucked into a life of obedience to his father and the family.

When he graduated from law school, Mike and his young wife loaded a U-Haul truck and drove to Vancouver, Washington, just across the river from the old Carty farm. Mike took a job as a deputy county attorney, working with five other lawyers and learning an old style of lawyering. Sitting around in the office, the old-timers spun tales of the practice of law in rural Washington, and Mike was thoroughly approving of his new life. Here people were polite and considerate. There was no constant struggle for control and for power. He and his wife were content, and Mike could not imagine any circumstance that would drive him to work for his father.

* * *

In July 1971 L.S.'s back problems were reaching a critical stage. Sam located a highly recommended orthopedic surgeon, then carefully drove L.S. 120 miles south to Tucson. The doctor performed a myelogram of L.S.'s spinal column and during the procedure excessively punctured the sac. The doctor was unaware of what he had done but gave routine orders for L.S. to take it easy for the several days he was to be in the hospital. Impatient, L.S. soon grew bored and called Joe, whom he instructed to drive him to Phoenix.

When his son arrived, L.S. explained how carefully he must drive. Joe had brought a station wagon as told, so L.S. could stretch out on a mattress in back, but rather than take the freeway north, Joe suddenly exited onto an old two-lane highway. The road undulated across desert, was poorly maintained, and passed through a succession of small towns, requiring frequent stops and starts. But even this might have been acceptable had he driven with compassion. It seemed to L.S. that Joe drove like a maniac, disregarding his pain-racked father's entreaties to stop what he was doing and return to the freeway.

Joe had picked this trip to explore locations where they might place road signs advertising Legend City. He was wrapped up in this project, whether real or imagined, and single-mindedly occupied himself with it, ignoring his father. In the rear of the station wagon L.S. was rocked from side to side, then slammed into the mattress as Joe raced into dips, took curves at a high rate of speed, and swayed around the many corners.

Joe was typically oblivious of the temperature, and though it was blisteringly hot, he would not turn the air conditioner to high as L.S. asked repeatedly. In the rear of the station wagon, far from the vents, L.S. sweated and grunted from the heat and strain.

It took nearly five hours to reach the Tatum House, and by then L.S. was gaunt and pale. His head ached with an exquisite, excruciating pain, and there was a ringing in his ears that lasted for several years. The violent ride had caused the punctured membrane in his lower spine to leak spinal fluid, and suffering miserably, L.S. was bedridden for ten days.

L.S. believed Joe would understand his wrongdoing, that he had not only caused his father great pain but placed him in danger as well, but that was not the case. When Joe said nothing of his conduct, L.S. finally told him how badly he had behaved and how much discomfort he had caused his father. L.S.'s arrogant son became immediately angry, then denied the incident had ever happened. Joe shouted at the top of his voice that he had always treated L.S. in the best possible way, then abruptly stomped off. It was a side to his son L.S. had never witnessed before, something nearly alien to the reclusive and silent teenager he remembered.

Not longer after this, L.S. had surgery that permanently ended his back trouble, and in late 1972 he sold the money-losing Legend City.

The oldest boys were young adults now and generally ending their educations. It was the four oldest boys who primarily mattered as far as U-Haul was concerned. Though he loved his daughters dearly, L.S. never considered, seriously or otherwise, handing his mantle to any other but one of his oldest sons.

Of the four—Sam, Mike, Joe, and Mark—only Joe regarded control of U-Haul as his birthright. From all appearances, that had been his perception from the time he was a child. Considering the career choices of his older brothers, the right to assume control of the company was falling to him. Joe had every reason to consider himself the heir apparent despite his frequent conflicts with his father, and it may have been what he concluded to be that inevitability which fed his misconduct toward his father. He did not need to be more considerate or cautious; L.S. had no one else.

It was a family joke that Joe actually dreamed at night that he was running the company. His brother and sisters did not consider the implication but were amused further at Christmas or on a birthday when Joe handed out a gift to one of his siblings who held stock in U-Haul and, half jokingly but with a piercing glint in his eyes, said, "This means you have to vote for me." But if Joe believed that control of the family billions should pass to him by right of birth, L.S. had come to view this son as nearly the least desirable of his alternatives.

Still Joe was acquiring a background to prepare him for a career in business. He had graduated from Holy Cross, then attended Harvard Business School and obtained his M.B.A. in 1973. That June he went to work for the company as a full-time employee. Mark had never demonstrated an aptitude for work and remained thoroughly under Joe's thumb.

Sam was set to be a doctor and had voiced no desire to work for U-Haul or to succeed his father as CEO. As it developed, however, he was much less happy in his residency at Cornell in New York than he had expected. So when his father called in July 1973 and asked for his help, Sam was interested. After three years in medical school in Tucson and two years in residency in New York City he was ready to come home. That month he joined U-Haul as assistant to his father.

Finally L.S. began calling Mike repeatedly in tears. Mike's determination to stay out of U-Haul had been reinforced when Joe shipped him volumes of U-Haul documents, including a 1962 lecture L.S. had widely disseminated at the time and hounded him to memorize the material. The 1962 lecture had become like a Bible to Joe, who insisted that any problem in life could be solved by consulting it. Mike found Joe's obsession with U-Haul unsettling.

L.S. told Mike that U-Haul's legal department was a mess. The company had just suffered a five-million-dollar punitive judgment in a case and was in danger of having to stop renting its largest and most profitable trailers. The company, the family, stood to lose everything if something wasn't done to reduce corporate exposure in wrecks involving U-Haul trailers. Though Mike had told his wife over and over, and believed what he said, that he would never work for his father, the plea for family loyalty was more than he could resist, as L.S. well knew. Mike was, after all, a Shoen, and one of L.S.'s dutiful sons.

The final straw came on a plane trip with his father when L.S. repeated again the problems he was facing in litigation. When his father broke down and sobbed, Mike knew he had no choice. So in October 1973 Mike went to work in U-Haul Towers as head of the legal department.

L. S. Shoen had worked to create a company that he would hand as a legacy to his children like a feudal lord. He had wanted his oldest sons to join the company and intended them to take control after him. That three of the four clearly wished for lives elsewhere and had evidenced no desire to work for him was of no concern. L.S. was determined to have his way whatever the cost.

L.S. knew what was in store for him because he summoned his longtime trusted employee Dick Rink into his office and fired him. "My kids are coming on board," he explained. "We've got enough prima donnas and don't need another."

Despite all the warning signs, despite the imperative of logic, L.S. had his wish: His four oldest boys now were part of U-Haul. In the coming years he paid the price for what he came to view as his own arrogance. In time others paid much higher prices.

CHAPTER SEVEN

PRINCES OF THE KINGDOM

In addition to his own desires, economic circumstances worked to push L.S. to pressure his sons into the company. Richard Nixon imposed wage and price controls, and they were having a disastrous impact on U-Haul, playing havoc with the company's careful balancing act of seasonal and zonal adjustments in prices. L.S. was having a fit persuading government regulators that he wasn't increasing prices whenever he made a change. In addition, the 1973 gasoline shortage was extremely detrimental to business. There were by this time fourteen thousand rental agents nationwide. Independent service station operators, the key to U-Haul's success, were rapidly going out of business, and potential customers were delaying plans to move because they could not be certain gasoline would be available on the highway. From L.S.'s perspective, U-Haul was threatened, and it was only proper that his sons do their part to safeguard the family company.

L.S. had pressured Mike in particular so aggressively because U-Haul could not withstand many more losses like the one it had just suffered. Mike's perception that a genuine crisis existed caused him to join the company, that and his father's assurance that he would be left alone to run the legal department.

There was a certain genius in what L.S. had accomplished since 1945. He had managed to make what should have been the boring business of trailer rentals exciting. And if he had failed to create a family environment in his home, he had succeeded in creating one in his company. A typical U-Haul employee in U-Haul Towers was a divorced mother looking for security and an opportunity for advancement. L.S. believed in few frills in the office since they usually cost money, and there was no dress code as the employees did not deal with the public. Each group performed a unique function for the company, and teams were more often than not very closely knit. Potluck suppers were common, and employees worked on a first-name basis.

Within the towers L.S. was nearly a mythic figure. He was absent most of the time, and when he did visit, the only contact with his employees was to share the elevator as he rode to the eleventh floor. One employee viewing the founder of their company in the coffee shop for the first time could not believe it. L.S. was wearing filthy tennis shoes, a pair of baggy khaki pants, an ill-fitting checkered flannel shirt with the price tag still on it, and glasses held together with a piece of tape. Unaware he was the founder, another first saw him in the elevator. When she exited the elevator, she complained about the strange man who had stood in the corner wearing a sweat-stained jump suit and dirty tennis shoes. Informed that was L. S. Shoen, she was absolutely stunned; he did not look anything like her idea of a Fortune 500 CEO.

On the road L.S. was a cheapskate. He once asked his pilot if he would sleep on a cot at one of his rental agencies rather than in a hotel. One employee returning from a six-week plane trip with L.S. complained to his co-workers that he had eaten McDonald's hamburgers three times a day, every day he had been gone.

L.S. had watched the success of McDonald's with envy and preached to his staff that U-Haul must achieve the same level of quality control and uniformity. He mandated that every employee traveling for the company eat *every* meal at McDonald's, and when he took employees to McDonald's on the road, he pointed out the cleanliness and standard appearance of the operation throughout the brief meal.

To some extent L.S. was aware of the dichotomy between his family and U-Haul. He privately voiced his frustration at his inability to "manage" his family when he could so effectively manage his company. He appeared to perceive no difference in the skills or techniques the two endeavors required and was genuinely mystified that the same approach was not successful with both. In his mind the financial wealth of his children and "their spiritual welfare" both were tied to U-Haul. The company was everything for the Shoens.

In his personal life L.S. was returning to prayer and for a portion of each day read Kahlil Gibran and other philosophers in an attempt to bring himself internal peace. He routinely lectured his children on the virtues of Catholicism, as if it were a magic potion that would bring order to his home.

The oldest sons were now fit young men. Mike was the tallest at six feet. He still had most of his dark hair and wore an old-fashioned mustache that connected with burly sideburns which he shaved when he joined the company. Sam and Joe were about the same height at five feet ten inches, but Sam had an elegant gracefulness about him while Joe was increasingly stocky. Sam wore dark-framed glasses and pork chop sideburns while Joe had a pencil-thin mustache unconnected to a Lincolnesque cropped beard. Their hairlines were in significant retreat. Mark was the smallest, perhaps two inches shorter than Joe, and mimicked his brother with a short beard.

Mike was quick to realize that L.S. had not overstated the legal threat to the company. Other court cases with similar liability potentials were pending trial. Mike began by reading the transcript of the latest trial and obtained transcripts of other U-Haul lawsuits to determine where, in a courtroom, the company was vulnerable.

Whereas other attorneys would have focused on the legal aspects of defending U-Haul, Mike took an entirely different approach probably because he had been raised in the family business and had worked summers in nearly every aspect of it and because he was interested in motorcycles and race cars. He began by checking with the U-Haul technical center in nearby Tempe to assure himself that company trailers and hitches were as safe as possible. He reviewed the loading decals on the trailers and had them redesigned and repositioned so renters knew how to load the trailers safely. He ordered new brochures to be produced with a fresh emphasis on safety. His lawyers told him not to acknowledge in the brochures that a U-Haul trailer could *ever* be loaded unsafely since opposing lawyers would use it against them. Mike explained the choices to his father. L.S. told him to go ahead with the new brochures because they would save lives and reduce accidents, and U-Haul would be involved in fewer lawsuits as a result.

Once the changes were in place, Mike drafted a jury trial strategy designed to counter the claims made against the trailers. No one could say in the future that U-Haul didn't care about safety or that its customers had not been cautioned about unsafe trailer-vehicle combinations and loading practices. Key long-term employees were reeducated on safety and jury presentation and from then on were called as expert witnesses.

L.S. was confident enough after that to self-insure the company. So effective was all this that during the mid to late 1970s, when other rental companies saw their insurance rates soar, U-Haul's fell. It came as a surprise to Mike that working for U-Haul could be so satisfying.

Those who worked with him thought highly of Mike's keen legal mind and his willingness to present options to his father that allowed him to make the final decision. Mike was self-effacing and gentle, almost the antithesis of L.S.

Sam, known to employees as Doc Sam to distinguish him from L.S., who until this time had been called Sam, was finding he also enjoyed working for the company. Like Mike, he had not been formally trained in business and knew about U-Haul primarily from his summer work. L.S. took Sam on the road to teach him how U-Haul was run. Senior employees warmed to the soft-spoken eldest son. What they found most remarkable was that this Shoen, born they believed with a silver spoon in his mouth, dealt genuinely with employees without a trace of condescension.

Joe had stormed into U-Haul from Harvard Business School with apparent high expectations. From the time he was a teenager he had compared himself with his father and disparaged anyone else's attempt to draw parallels between L.S. and any of his other sons. Now that Joe was in U-Haul management, it was evident that he was in open competition with his father. When L.S. suggested he join him on the road to learn firsthand how the company operated, Joe told him he wasn't interested. He intended to remain ensconced in an office on the eleventh floor of U-Haul Towers, where he could keep his finger on the company pulse. L.S. explained that U-Haul was not that kind of operation; the real company was in the field. The towers were just the thousand or so employees who dealt with administration, bookkeeping, personnel, and similar matters. But Joe was adamant and remained in Phoenix.

L.S. had little success the summer of 1973 involving the volatile Mark in U-Haul management and was content that his fourth-oldest son would be attending law school at nearby Arizona State University. Though Mark had no significant duties at U-Haul, L.S. maintained the fiction that he was a working part of management, and all four sons attended senior staff meetings initially. Joe and Mark were not reluctant to voice their displeasure with longtime and trusted employees, preferring confrontation and hostility to reasoned discussion. They screamed obscenities at staff and ridiculed explanations. Some present were stunned when L.S.'s response was tempered. The equally volatile, headstrong, quick-tempered L.S., founder of this institution, was being cowed by his twenty-four-old son, Joe.

But L.S. held the real power as board chairman, president of U-Haul International, and CEO for Amerco. Joe's and Mark's tirades were tolerated because they meant nothing, and after the boys stormed out of meetings in anger, L.S. would make a passing apology on their behalf and get down to business. Mike, however, was so affected by his younger brothers' conduct that he told his father he would not attend future meetings.

Joe frequently voiced confidence in his own academic training in business and was condescending to both Sam and Mike. When one senior employee attempted to explain something routine about the company that Joe clearly did not understand, the young Shoen cut him off rudely by saying, "I have a degree in everything."

Sam was uncertain of his ability since his formal training was in medicine, and despite Joe's unseemly conduct in senior staff meetings, Sam sought him out for counsel. At first Joe was quick to oblige, and some of what he said made sense. Joe and Sam were living together in a house on Roanoke Street beside U-Haul Towers, and in late 1973 and early 1974 they walked home together after work while Joe lectured Sam on U-Haul operations.

By this time it was apparent that L.S. was extremely pleased with the job Mike was performing with the legal department, and Sam also enjoyed his father's favor. If Joe had sought to assert himself over his brothers and assume a place second only to L.S., he had failed. So he began a new tack at this time that at first startled Sam.

"The company's going bankrupt!" Joe shouted as they walked down the quiet residential street at twilight. Again and again Joe related a horror story that he believed demonstrated his point. While expenditures at U-Haul were a constant, income was cyclical so that there were occasional periods when the business was less prosperous. Joe used these examples to prove his point. When Sam spoke to L.S. about what Joe was saying, his father laughed it off. It was true this was the most difficult period U-Haul had ever faced since the early years, but the company was very resilient and not in trouble.

But Joe was adamant. With his Harvard M.B.A. and certain manner, he constantly parroted his theme: "The company's going bankrupt." Sam began to question his father's casual certainty. Finally he went to the company's chief financial officer, a senior employee in whom he had confidence, and quizzed the man, citing Joe's examples. The officer carefully reviewed U-Haul's financial position for Sam and told him to disregard Joe's hyperbole. The company had never been in better shape despite the temporary downturn in income. For most of its history it had been a cash cow, and it remained one. L.S. had never carried significant debt, and the company could withstand a great deal more than it was facing now. Joe, Sam was told, just liked to talk that way.

When Sam shared his findings, Joe dismissed them without discussion. Joe knew best. "The company's going bankrupt!" he shouted again. This seemed odd to Sam, and away from his brother's domineering pressure he considered Joe's behavior. He concluded that Joe was *really* saying, "I can run the company better." All this bankruptcy talk was simply intended to discredit their father.

Having observed Joe's conduct firsthand for months, Sam believed him incapable of running U-Haul—period. Only Joe seemed unable to see that.

Within months Sam had grown confident enough of his own knowledge and ability to stop asking Joe's opinion. Sam had seen enough of his brother's behavior and general ineptness in business to respect him no longer. Joe refused to let up at home, and finally Sam moved into his own house to escape his younger brother.

Since joining U-Haul, Joe had accomplished nothing of significance. He had no distinct management style and in the office generally conducted himself as he and Mark did in the senior staff meetings. When he wasn't using intimidation to get his way, Joe was trying to manipulate employees. When he selected someone to work under him, he usually chose a malleable personality to whom he gave bonuses and perks. From his perspective the only competent U-Haul employees were his gaggle of yes-men.

His conduct was very offensive to Mike. Both Joe and Mark used code words rather than names when talking about family members. "The bitch" was Suzanne. New terms now were added. At first Joe sarcastically referred to Sam as "the good doctor," but as his older brother's star rose with his father, Sam became "shit for brains" or "that asshole brother" and finally "the douche bag." Joe and Mark would swagger into the usually quiet legal department and loudly begin their Mutt and Jeff routine of attacks and obscenities.

Mike tolerated their conduct for a short time, then finally told Joe, "Don't come around if you're going to talk like that." He wanted no part of it. A filthy mouth, Mike believed, was simply an indication of deep-seated problems, as well as personally offensive.

Having watched Joe's conduct for some months, Mike concluded that Joe was "crazy," and he believed everyone in the family could see it as clearly as he did.

Shortly before his first-year final exams Mark dropped out of law school in disgust, much to his father's disappointment. Of the four oldest boys, L.S. was primarily concerned for Mark and gave him a job at the tech center in Tempe, where he repaired trucks but his work habits there were irregular, and L.S. later could not recall Mark's making it steadily to his job for more than two weeks at a stretch.

Mark may have had no interest in running U-Haul, but L.S. was determined to mold him for the role. L.S. had fantasies of a rotating CEO in which he passed the reins to each of his oldest sons in turn. The company would benefit from the strength of each while he would be the guiding hand to prevent serious missteps. Under this scheme each of his oldest boys must be made ready for the responsibility.

When L.S. brought Sam and Mike on board, he was unconcerned about their abilities. He was spending a great deal of time with Joe and was attempting the same approach with Mark, but it was like trying to hit a moving target. Mark wasn't around enough for L.S. to take control of him, and clearly resented any direction from his father.

L.S. continued trying to find an area in which Joe could make a contribution. He made him responsible for fleet management purchases and sales, a relatively simple and straightforward operation, but within weeks L.S. had decided this was a mistake and removed him. Late in 1973 L.S. turned U-Haul's self-storage endeavor over to Joe, who had been arguing for months that this was the company's only salvation.

L.S. had understood for years that self-storage was a logical move for U-Haul and agreed in principle. At both ends of a move customers often had need of storage facilities, and where better than the place they rented trucks or trailers? The problem was that U-Haul owned few suitable sites since U-Haul operations were located at service stations. He assigned to Joe the task of developing a plan and making the first inquiries.

"I have not provided the necessary leadership [to Joe]," L.S. had written, and this time he intended to do it. It proved a disaster. Within days L.S. sat Joe down to remind him of the program's objectives and of what constituted acceptable company policy. L.S. left this meeting confused about his son's apparent inability to grasp what L.S. considered simple concepts, especially as he was so proud of his Harvard M.B.A.

The last straw came quickly. Under the plan Joe was advancing,

U-Haul operations were not even to be located at the newly acquired sites. This was to be a separate operation with no visible tie, and no logical connection, to U-Haul—one, presumably, that would be under Joe's sole control. Incredibly Joe did not want to encourage U-Haul's clients to use the service, the very reason L.S. was willing to make this move. He wanted to spend money advertising for new customers.

Challenged on his scheme, Joe chose to offer none but his view that this was how U-Haul self-storage should work. L.S. was shocked by what he perceived to be Joe's ineptitude and unwillingness to see reason and within eleven days, shortly before Christmas, turned the self-storage program over to Sam. Once again, just as with piloting the Chinese junk four years before, Joe had failed, and the job was given to "the good doctor."

Joe's attempts to run his father's businesses, as he had the year before with Legend City, met with no success. What he apparently failed to grasp was that Legend City was never anything but a sideline to his father, an operation whose success or failure meant nothing to U-Haul. It was a business about which L.S. knew little, and he had been willing to allow Joe's asserted competence to prevail.

But U-Haul was L.S.'s baby. He knew it from the ground up, so when Joe brandished his M.B.A. and argued his own position, L.S. knew his son was talking garbage. In this one area of his life L.S.'s vision was crystal clear. He knew good business decisions, he knew how to watch the bottom line, and as far as L.S. was concerned, Joe didn't know what he was talking about. So if Joe had thought he would run over his father at U-Haul and L.S. had believed he would guide his son, both were disappointed.

Joe's tactics against his father *were* effective in distressing L.S. even if they failed to advance his own position. As early as the previous August L.S. observed in his writings, "Joe up tight." In November 1973 he added, "Joe and I have a tough time getting along on some issues and get one another in rough shape."

Finally L.S. came to see Joe's behavior for what it was. "Feel great this morning," he wrote, "but not long before beat down mainly by Joe who I must conclude uses this as a tactic."

The disapproval was coming from both sides of L.S.'s personal life. The truth was he often didn't stay at the Tatum House, partly because Joe was giving him such a hard time for remaining with Suzanne and partly because he wasn't always welcome there. The nights when he was in town, he often slept at the house on Roanoke, where Joe kept up his harangues.

L.S. was finding solace in his personal life where it was available, and more and more that was with Suzie Whitmore in Cleveland. Then, at a time when his relationship with Suzanne was at a new low, Whitmore became pregnant.

L.S. was not prepared to divorce Suzanne and marry Whitmore, yet the thought of his child's being born illegitimate was abhorrent. Whitmore changed her last name to Shoen, and L.S. made financial arrangements for her. He bought her a house as well, and when a son, Scott, was born in 1974, he established a trust fund for him, as he had for all his children. He attempted to do all this in secret and believed he had succeeded, but so many eyes saw the necessary documents that soon Suzanne was demanding to know about his "bastard." L.S. looked his angry wife in the eye and lied.

Without realizing it, L.S. was attempting to establish a feudal kingdom in U-Haul, a company in which the male descendants of the founder assumed positions of power by right of birth, not because of demonstrated competence. In considering Joe's behavior, L.S. felt his difficulties lay in his need for direction. " . . . Joe just expects too much of himself," L.S. wrote, ignoring the fact that Joe may have been unqualified by temperament or ability to work in U-Haul management.

For many years Joe had worshiped his father, and he alone of his brothers had plotted a career in U-Haul. Joe had spoken of L.S. with the enthusiasm of a "zealot," as one family member noted. Even Joe's feverish efforts to destroy his father's marriage were done in the name of love.

Now to achieve the goal of taking over U-Haul, Joe was locked in combat with the father he admired, and as his inability to bend L.S. to his will became more apparent, he was compelled to fight him. Little wonder that Joe was "up tight" so often.

Joe had no social life to speak of. He did not date significantly and lived beside U-Haul not because it was available and rent-free, as in Sam's case, but because he believed he must be available at all hours. U-Haul was his life. What free time he gave himself he spent working on a car in a shop beside the towers. He went so far as to pay ten thousand dollars for a 1967 Mark IV Ford, one of only six ever constructed, that had crashed at Le Mans. He placed the car parts in the house he used on Roanoke and lived for years amid all the machinery.

Joe had allies within the company, for not everyone who worked there supported or admired L.S. James Carty, whom L.S. had fired in the 1950s, approached Mike and asked for a job. James had been a prosecutor and private attorney, so Mike felt no hesitation in hiring his uncle. Hap Carty, locked in his own continuing struggle with L.S., opposed almost every extension of the company into a new area. James and Hap were Joe and Mark's regular companions, and from them Joe heard a new version of the founding of U-Haul.

It had been their sister, Anna Mary, who devised the idea of one-way trailer rentals. Anna Mary, not L.S., had thought up the name U-Haul. Anna Mary had not only discovered the fleet financing scheme that established the company, but while her husband was on the road, she had recruited those first crucial investors. Sure, L.S. did work out of town, but Anna Mary had really run the company. It had been Anna Mary, after all, who had been A. M. Carty and solved the problems for the rental agents, not L.S.

U-Haul was the product of Anna Mary's mind and energy. She had been the force that made it possible; she had been the true founder. L.S. had usurped that role and was now trying to bury her memory. L.S. was nowhere near the businessman he said he was. Anyone could make a success of a business given the start Anna Mary had delivered.

And darkly, with his knowing manner, James suggested that L.S. was responsible for Anna Mary's death. Remember the bruises? The absence of an autopsy? Look how quickly his father had dated after Anna Mary's death. Was that the conduct of a grieving husband? Think about it, James suggested. Just think about it.

* * *

For some time L.S. had been developing a profit-sharing arrangement for employees. When Joe heard of it, he complained vehemently that employees were paid a salary and were undeserving of any further compensation. Nevertheless, in February 1974, over Joe's objections, L.S. adopted the profit-sharing plan.

Almost at once Joe began pressuring L.S. in another direction. Though L.S. had given nearly all the stock in the company to his children in the early days, from time to time thereafter he presented a few shares to long-term, loyal employees, about three hundred or so. These shares held a special place beyond their worth because so few existed outside the Shoen family. Retired U-Haul employees with a handful of shares were known to travel hundreds of miles to participate in the informal annual shareholders' meeting. It was an opportunity to follow the progress of the company to which they had given such loyalty and many years. The fact that they sat there among the Shoens, the royalty of the U-Haul kingdom, was a sign of their privilege.

The existence of these shares rankled Joe, and he harped at his father that all outsiders should be eliminated. U-Haul was a family company, and ownership should be reserved for Shoens alone. He suggested that with the outsiders gone, the family could make money by concocting inside deals, for there would be no one to object. L.S. was appalled at the thought, but again and again Joe lectured his father on the subject, arguing that something must be done about these outside shares. Finally he came up with a hundred to one reverse split of stock.

Normally, as the value of shares increased, companies split them into smaller pieces to hold down the price per share. Joe proposed doing the opposite, taking one hundred shares and turning them into one. Nevada corporate law said a company did not have to tolerate shareholders' holding less than one full share. The reverse split would place many of the non-Shoen shareholders into that category, and U-Haul could force them to sell to the family.

L.S. was dismayed by such a scheme and repeatedly told Joe he would not hear of it, but Joe pressed the point.

Despite Joe's relentless attacks on Sam and Mike and his constant harping on his father, L.S. gave no thought to removing him from the company, refusing to believe he would not eventually work out. Indeed, in 1974 Joe was responsible for accounting and finance, though he was not in charge of the U-Haul Towers operation.

What Joe was unable or unwilling to accept was that his father was simply seeking competence in his sons. All Joe was expected to do was perform well the tasks he was given. Neither Sam nor Mike wanted to follow in L.S.'s footsteps. If Sam's star was rising, working as he was so closely with his father, it was because he was willing to learn. The same was true of Mike.

Neither Joe nor Mark had ever competed in sports and learned the lessons of discipline, cooperation, and controlled competition that came from them. For that matter they had never had a life outside the U-Haul fold beyond college and did not know the real world. They were simply what their father had created: ill-tempered, petulant, overgrown children accustomed to getting their way by badgering or throwing temper tantrums. L.S. could not face that he was beginning to reap the harvest for the seeds of disaster he had sown with his sons.

The spring of 1974 L.S. quietly gave fifty thousand dollars to Marylhurst College in continuing fulfillment of his pledge to his first wife's memory. Far from allowing Anna Mary to disappear, he believed himself obligated to perpetuate her name.

Despite Mark's lack of involvement with the company, he was promoted that year to assistant to the president of U-Haul, L. S. Shoen. Mark claimed it made no difference to him. "It was all the same to me," he said, describing his duties. "... About all I did was carry his briefcase around for him." That, and not showing up for work, appeared to be his primary skills in business.

L.S. was quietly thrilled by the natural ability Sam was demonstrating in contrast with Joe's failings and Mark's lack of caring. L.S. and Sam traveled with increasing frequency and Joe expressed his desire to have them on the road and out of the towers, which he was now attempting to run as his private fiefdom in his father's absence. However, he was unable to make significant changes in the company since he lacked the authority, and senior staff deferred his demands until they spoke with L.S., who was quick to countermand Joe's orders.

In the field Sam strengthened L.S.'s position. He was by nature reserved, a quieter man with a more even disposition than his father. Like all the older Shoen sons, he had an aggressive personality, but it was tempered with maturity and a natural affection for people. As a result, his presence worked to defuse his father's quick temper.

The pair often disagreed, but if Sam was unsuccessful in persuading his father to his way of thinking, there was no dispute. U-Haul was his father's company, and he alone of the boys never forgot it.

In large measure this was because he remembered tires stacked in his living room and secondhand Christmas gifts. He had witnessed the struggle U-Haul's growth had required. For Mike, just sixteen months younger, these memories were less pronounced and those events left less of an impact on him.

In the U-Haul Towers' hierarchy Joe was superior to Mike, though L.S. thought Joe understood he was to assert no real control over Mike. Still, using his areas of finance and personnel, Joe constantly tried to bully his brother, and Mike resented it. Joe also routinely denigrated the job L.S. and Sam were doing, pressing endlessly his claim that the company was going broke.

As it became increasingly clear that Joe would not achieve his coveted position, his claim that U-Haul was going bankrupt became more shrill. He badgered Mike with the story time and again until finally Mike, like Sam before him, checked for himself. The company, he learned, was in fine shape even with the wage-price freeze and gas shortage. "That's just Joe," Mike decided.

So effectively did Joe assert his case, however, that even L.S., who should have known better, sat down with the company's financial officer to be certain he wasn't overlooking anything.

Whenever L.S. and Sam returned from the road "like conquering heroes," as L.S. viewed it, Joe greeted the pair with a scowl and an abrupt "Hi! When are you leaving again? You've got a lot of work to do." Then for good measure: "The company's going bankrupt, you know!"

Sam smiled and shrugged off his brother's rude conduct. That was Joe. But at once L.S.'s glow dissipated, and within minutes Joe was in his office with a long string of abuse that only increased his unhappiness. Any discussion between Joe and L.S. escalated at once into an unpleasant emotional confrontation.

L.S. remained mystified by Joe's behavior and said repeatedly that he could not understand what was bothering him. In September 1974 L.S. entered in his private journal: "[R]eceived telephone call from Sammy saying that Joe was real upset last night and in tears. Tried to reach Joe by telephone and then had Sammy go to his home [to talk to him].... [Joe] showed up for 1 P.M. meeting...but left in less than an hour. I terminated the meeting at 3 P.M. and Sammy and I went over to Joe's. He came in about 4 P.M. and I talked with him for 4 hours.... [C]oncerned about Joe and his happiness."

Since the founding of U-Haul L.S. had been occupied with creating wealth. U-Haul was a money-maker, but except for its fleet of trucks and trailers and bits of property here and there, it had no real assets. L.S. was haunted by the thought that it could come crashing down. The company required real estate, tangible assets, and it needed to expand into new areas.

In 1970 L.S. had paid $3.5 million to purchase A to Z Rental, which rented general merchandise. It was an area into which he believed U-Haul should be moving, and he had looked to buy a company that already had a knowledgeable staff. But A to Z Rental proved a disaster for U-Haul because the franchisees were so angry with the previous company management they would not cooperate. In late 1974 it folded. L.S. did not consider it a failure since a number of very talented people from A to Z Rental were now a part of U-Haul; among them was a young woman named Norma Colwell, whom he assigned to work closely with his children. But to the staff in general the experiment demonstrated that U-Haul should stick to trucks and trailers.

With the quickening collapse of the traditional service stations due to the gasoline shortage L.S. was losing not only valuable rental agents but excellent locations for the placement of his long-anticipated U-Haul centers as well. Of the fourteen thousand locations U-Haul had at its peak, some six thousand had gone out of business by the mid-1970s. Since the 1960s L.S. had considered the possibility of creating centers to make available the entire selection of U-Haul trucks and trailers rather than the usual half dozen items. Most corner service stations were too small for what he had in mind, but not all were, and in other cases adjacent property was available for expansion.

L.S. had attempted the idea of a supermarket for moving equipment in Texas without success. In Phoenix in the mid-1960s a U-Haul rental agent named Ned Saban came up with the same concept and approached L.S. with it. Since L.S. had already failed with it, he disparaged the concept as unworkable. Saban persisted and convinced L.S. to provide him the necessary equipment once he had a suitably sized location.

Saban was every bit as tough-minded an entrepreneur as L.S. though on a less grand scale. As soon as he opened that first center in 1964, Saban went to work providing trailer hitches for vehicles that U-Haul wasn't servicing. L.S. was skeptical, but whenever he saw potential, he hung around and picked up any ideas he could. Saban and his men developed a clever hitch that fitted beneath contemporary bumpers with no damage. L.S. was impressed, and not long thereafter U-Haul was installing a similar device.

Shortly after the Saban center opened, L.S. arrived and was greeted by painted lines leading to expanded services. He was very impressed, and when he returned to the towers, he directed that Saban's rental figures be given directly to him each week. He watched closely as Saban expanded the center repeatedly. By 1974 L.S. knew the center concept would work—Saban had demonstrated it—and now seemed the time for U-Haul to make the move.

Perhaps L.S.'s greatest strength, ironically an attribute that proved his undoing, was his ability to see ten years into the future. He had known in 1964, when Ned Saban made his center a success, that was the direction he would take the company, but it was ten years before the opportunity presented itself. He kept the scheme in his mind, spending countless hours analyzing how it would work. His intention was to plunge U-Haul into real estate acquisition, an area in which it had very little experience and one involving enormous risks. He alone knew it would take a decade to complete what he had in mind. It was breathtaking in its scope for a company that specialized in renting trucks and trailers. Not only would U-Haul acquire one of the single largest holdings of metropolitan real estate in America, but before it was finished in the mid-1980s, the traditional rental agent would be finished. In addition, U-Haul would acquire tens of thousands of employees and sell a wide range of moving-related items as well as self-storage.

This all sounded reckless and speculative when he spoke of it to his staff. But during the summer of 1974 L.S. and Sam scouted countless locations and bought land that appeared right for their purpose. By the end of the year U-Haul had a hundred locations for its new centers.

Since just before the death of his first wife L.S. flew company planes, and his daring in the sky was the source of many stories about him in the towers. One night he was en route to Las Vegas from Phoenix with Ned Saban's son, Dennis. About halfway there L.S. told Dennis to retrieve maps from behind him, then locked the stick with his knees as he fumbled the maps open, turning them first one way, then the other. Finally he pitched them behind him, nonchalantly commenting, "These are the wrong ones." L.S. squinted into the dark, left, then right. "Look for landmarks," he told the stunned Dennis.

Asked once what he thought of his father, Jimmie Shoen replied, "What do you expect me to think of a man who has walked away from six plane crashes?"

Since managing a beauty shop for her older brother, life had not gone well for Patty Lee Shoen. She never married, and L.S. paid for her psychiatric counseling during the years she operated a charm school for girls in Portland and sold her own line of cosmetics. Finally, L.S. gave her a job in U-Haul Towers, established a trust fund from which she received the income to supplement her salary, and provided her with one of the houses on Roanoke in which to live rent-free. She remained a peculiar person, painting all her rooms black and refusing to keep a knife in the house. She was highly opinionated and frequently identified herself as the black sheep of the Shoen family. Despite her outspokenness, Patty

Lee blended in at U-Haul Towers, where it was not commonly known she was the founder's sister. On the occasions when she spoke of L.S., she often said that he had saved her life.

In early 1975 L.S. developed ulcer problems he attributed largely to the continuous abuse he was receiving from Joe. By this time he was taking sleeping pills and an assortment of other drugs to get through each day.

It was apparent that his oldest sons could not meld into the stellar management team he wanted. Through Arizona State University he obtained a referral to Dr. Barbara Levy, a local psychologist. After meeting with her, he told the oldest sons they all were to attend weekly counseling sessions in an attempt to resolve their constant conflicts.

L.S. worried about Joe's behavior and the chronic depression from which he appeared to suffer. Afraid that Joe would commit suicide, he discussed the subject at some length with Sam and Dr. Levy. He was reassured to learn that a personality such as Joe was unlikely to kill himself.

Mark refused to attend most sessions, and in fact, Mike, who had survived at U-Haul by avoiding contact with his father, was not having a pleasant time of it. On August 11, 1975, Mark exploded during one gathering. Rising, he simply blew up and shouted that he would no longer "eat shit." Mike became agitated by all the shouting and at last gave vent to his long-standing anger toward his father with a recital of the abuse to which he had been subjected over the years, most recently from Joe.

L.S. left the session deeply troubled. A blowup from Mark was to be expected—he had always been volatile—but Mike! Mike was a bedrock on whom L.S. had come to rely. Until that day L.S. had no idea of the pent-up emotions Mike held, nor did he understand the implications of his heavy-handed influence in Mike's life over the years.

"I have never done anything except with love and intent to help [Mike]," he wrote. "I am deeply hurt."

By the early 1970s U-Haul had reached the size where it was an attractive acquisition for a larger corporation, but since it was privately held, it could not be purchased without the participation of the family shareholders. In 1973 Westinghouse explored buying the company, and in 1975 Consolidated Foods pursued a vigorous campaign to court L.S. At the same time another group representing Arab money expressed interest. Finally Gil Deakon and Associates began negotiations.

Selling the company and dividing the money according to ownership would make everyone rich; each Shoen would have his or her wealth free of the others and of U-Haul. There were signs even L.S. could see that this might be best for everyone. Mark often complained that people said he was a millionaire but that he didn't have enough money to buy a car. The statement was a substantial exaggeration, but it did accurately state what some of the children may have felt: They were not in reality nearly as wealthy as they appeared on paper.

L.S. asked Sam quietly to poll the children about the possibility of selling because it was apparent someone was going to make an offer. If they wanted to sell, L.S. would go along.

With the possibility that all of them might come into sudden fortunes, L.S. asked Capital Formation Counselors, a company that specialized in family trusts, to study each child's portfolio and potential. Meetings with individual family members began in January 1975 and continued through the year.

In the meantime, Joe had continued to argue in favor of his hundred to one split. L.S. considered it treachery to those longtime employees whose dedication and talent had made U-Haul what it was. But a key aspect of appeasing Joe meant that occasionally he must win. Finally, exhausted from Joe's relentless haranguing, L.S. allowed the reverse split, though at once he felt manipulated and believed, correctly, that he had betrayed old confidants and close friends. Even when a delegation of L.S.'s closest employees met with him to protest this maneuver, he remained firm. In May 1975, at his direction, the board voted the reverse split. Perhaps with an eye to the possibility that Consolidated Foods or someone else would soon buy all of them out or perhaps simply to assuage his guilt, L.S. ordered the minority stockholders affected to be paid one and a half times the stock's worth.

When Joe saw that even this change did not force out all the minority shareholders, he told L.S. that they had to find other means to get rid of them and demanded the legal department prepare a stratagem. There was no place for non-Shoen ownership of U-Haul.

In late August Sam returned with the results of his informal poll. The answer was no, they did not want to sell. L.S. was surprised, then considered the response of his children and wrote that night, "I personally don't want to sell because this is my life and perhaps this is the reason the others don't want to sell."

In October Gil Deakon and Associates offered the family $140 million. On the basis of the input L.S. had received from Sam he declined the offer.

Joe's abuse of L.S. continued despite the counseling sessions. Whenever he could, he also criticized Sam to their father in an attempt to undercut him, but L.S. refused to see these efforts for what they were.

Though Mark had stopped attending the Levy counseling sessions following his outburst, L.S. was still determined to persuade him to participate in U-Haul management. With Sam on the road handling the East Coast the office next to L.S. on the eleventh floor of the towers was vacant. Time and again L.S. entreated Mark to move in and make his place in the company. But Mark had no interest. He was carried on full salary and had all the customary perks but remained absent from the company for the most part, working on something called the U-Haul Racing Team to pass his time, an endeavor in which L.S. subsidized Mark's desire to blow up engines on racetracks.

The quick-tempered, slightly diminutive Mark was actually a family favorite despite his habitual allegiance to Joe. He was like an overgrown kid who just wanted to have a good time. There were significant differences between Joe and Mark. As quickly as Mark's temper flashed, just as quickly he was caring and sympathetic, attributes not seen in Joe. There was another, more profound, difference as well. "Joe's eyes are hollow," one of his siblings once said; "Mark's eyes have pain."

* * *

Capital Formation Counselors met with the adult Shoen children for three days in early December 1975 with the results of their research and a proposed course of action. Its gist was that each child would place his or her shares into trusts that would be managed by trustees who would vote the stock in such a way as to maximize the company's profits and, as a result, maximize each person's wealth. All the children had participated in the process, and all of them, it had seemed, supported the professional handling of their wealth and its potential. They would be rid of the responsibility and be assured it was being managed by expert hands. L.S. had anticipated no difficulty having the arrangement adopted, though it would take the unanimous approval of his sons and daughters.

Joe, it turned out, would have nothing to do with it, and Mark followed his lead. Joe's objections did not stand up to reason, and others of the children were irritated because he was vetoing something they considered an excellent idea for them. L.S. pressed Joe repeatedly on his objections, and finally Joe settled on one argument he repeated obstinately. "They're just in it for the money," he said. "They don't really care about us."

Engaging in business to make money did not strike L.S. as something evil; that was what he had done all his adult life. But Joe and Mark stonewalled the proposal and would not be moved, so it fell through. Joe told Sam and others they could go ahead on their own, and most did, but without everyone's participation certain key aspects were missing.

Joe's anger continued after he had sabotaged Capital's plan, and L.S. was again concerned for his state of mind. Counseling, L.S. concluded, is "a waste of time[,] for Joe is so angry he cannot be rational. He is unpredictable...."

Toward the end of the month Consolidated Foods made its offer—$160 million for the company—and again L.S. turned it down.

For many years L.S. had hidden the family movies he had taken of the boys and Anna Mary since Suzanne disapproved of any reminder that L.S. had been married previously and because he could not bear to see them. At Christmas 1975 he dug out the films and played them for his oldest children.

They had not known that such film existed. For Joe and Mark, Anna Mary was a distant figure about whom they had no real memory. Joe idolized his mother and could not see her as a real woman. Now, up there on the screen, Anna Mary was laughing as she held each child. There they were running to their mother, and there she was bending down, holding them, wiping their noses—a real person who loved them, a woman in absolute contrast with the one who had ultimately reared them. The film had a profound impact on all of Anna Mary's children, but none so much as Joe.

That same Christmas Day Joe was vigorously chopping firewood at the Tatum House when he wrenched his back. So seriously was it hurt that he was virtually incapacitated, though no actual injury beyond a sprain was found. Joe was in such agony he had to be assisted to the bathroom. He was given pain pills and placed in the master bedroom, where Suzanne was to nurse him.

Suzanne's caring for Joe was a practical solution L.S. believed Joe would tolerate since this was one area in which she had been an asset over the years. But Joe would not be alone in the Tatum House, in his father's bed, with Suzanne seeing to him. Within two days he had bolted from the Tatum House in excruciating pain and to everyone's amazement moved into the apartment of a young woman he was dating, Heidi Hatsell.

L.S. was shocked. He knew Joe despised Suzanne and believed that accounted for his sudden departure, but he had not imagined Joe would go to his girl friend. As he had with all the women his sons dated, L.S. disapproved of this one. He feared that Heidi's nursing Joe would create a degree of intimacy that would form "a permanent commitment under circumstances in which [Joe] would not be choosing."

Mike had been the first to marry, followed by Mark in June 1974, just after graduating from Arizona State University. Joe, who had never dated seriously before, started seeing Heidi after meeting her at the wedding of Harry DeShong, Jr. Heidi and DeShong's wife, Patti, had been roommates at Northern Arizona University in Flagstaff.

Heidi had been told about Sam, the attractive, very wealthy heir apparent to control of U-Haul, and attended the wedding with an eye to meeting him. But Sam showed little interest in her, and since Mike and Mark were already married, Heidi appeared to direct her attention to Joe.

Joe, it seemed to many who knew him well, had always been terrified of women and had dated very little even though he was in his twenties. There were, one said, only two kinds of women who did not frighten him: nuns and grandmothers. Very soon Heidi started looking and acting like both. She wore "old lady" shoes and, when questioned about them, claimed she had an orthopedic problem—like Joe's. She wore granny dresses, though they were years out of style, and pulled her hair, which she sprinkled with a light powder, back into a tight bun. She wore no makeup, and when she was with Joe, she presented a pale presence, an unassuming sponge who hung on his every word. Her efforts had succeeded enough for Joe to date her, but no one in the family anticipated the relationship going anywhere.

The differences between the two were vast. Heidi, who maintained formality in her life and kept her apartment like a showroom, had a taste for the material things of life. Joe reveled in wearing baggy pants and scuffed shoes and drove an old Chevrolet he littered with fast-food wrappers. Regardless, Heidi's eyes were set firmly on the wealthy young man. So when Joe moved into Heidi's apartment and she began seeing to his every need, it appeared that at last fate had presented her with a perfect opportunity. Without outward justification, to L.S. it looked as if a gold digger were about to land one of his sons.

Joe and his attitude toward women had always puzzled L.S. One night, when he was having dinner with Joe in Flagstaff at a time when he was living apart from Suzanne, a beautiful young woman who knew Joe came over to say hello. It was obvious to L.S. that she was interested in his son, but despite L.S.'s efforts to persuade his son to have her join them, an invitation she clearly wanted, Joe had declined.

On another occasion a woman Joe had known at Harvard flew to Phoenix to see him. L.S. was thrilled when he saw the beautiful woman at a dinner with Joe. *Now there*, he thought, *is a woman*

Joe should marry. When she was in the rest room, L.S. suggested as much and in a mocking manner said if Joe weren't going after her, he'd better look out because his father just might. When the young woman rejoined them, Joe rose awkwardly and pushed her around to his father, as if he were offering her to him. L.S. was shocked, but Joe persisted. "Take her. She's yours," he said, then promptly spun on his heel and left the woman with his father. It made no sense to L.S. and looked very much as if Joe had just pimped for him. L.S. was mystified by the event.

For a time Sam had dated an Asian woman about whom Joe and Mark made constant racial slurs, but eventually the relationship ended on its own. Sam was thirty years old now and regularly chided Mike's wife, Christa, for not introducing him to her women friends because he was ready to settle down. Christa, a German national, had a Norwegian friend who worked at Copenhagen, a retail furniture store in Phoenix. That Valentine's Day 1975 Christa handed Sam her friend's business card, wrapped with a ribbon. Here was someone Sam should meet. She was very special.

Her name was Eva Erickson.

CHAPTER EIGHT

LOTS OF MONEY, LOTS OF WIVES, AND LOTS OF CHILDREN

E va Erickson had been born Eva Berg in Larvik, Norway, a picturesque town of fifteen thousand located eighty miles southwest of Oslo. The town's main industry was a large pulp mill where Eva's father worked as a foreman. She had a younger brother and had been raised in a happy home, oriented in typical Norwegian fashion toward the outdoors.

Eva grew into an attractive, lithe woman, candid and polite. When she was nineteen, she moved to Oslo to work and in 1966 was sunning in the park beside the king's palace in a bikini, drinking milk when an American tourist ten years her senior smiled and said in English, "That milk's going to make you fat." To his surprise Eva smiled and replied in perfect English that she wasn't concerned about that.

The young man who had been taken with Eva was a shy, bookish American from Chicago, Don Erickson. He had been posted with the Army in Europe for a year and a half and the previous April had taken a ship back to Germany, where he and a friend bought a Volkswagen and set about exploring Europe on a budget. They had visited nearly all of the capitals and had driven as far as Greece by the end of summer, occasionally staying at hostels but more frequently camping out. He and his companion were headed to Munich for the Oktoberfest when Erickson spotted Eva.

He learned over dinner that night that Eva worked for an insurance company and also as a reservations clerk at the Continental

Hotel. In addition to English and Norwegian, she spoke German, Swedish, and French. Erickson watched as she precisely and fastidiously cleaned her plate, and by the end of dinner he was in love with her.

Eva Berg was a bit over average height, and upon critical scrutiny she bordered between pretty and beautiful. She possessed a radiant smile, a quick, fertile mind, and a manner of calm acceptance and gentle sweetness that made her a desirable woman.

Erickson spent every moment he could with Eva over the next two days before he left for Munich, and he could not put her from his mind. After just two days in Germany he left his friend, returned to Oslo, and traveled with Eva to Larvik to meet her family. But within days it was time for another farewell, this one tearful. The couple exchanged letters as Erickson finished his trip.

His last week that October was to be spent in Paris, but he suggested he return to Oslo instead and spend it with Eva. She refused, saying she did not want another sad farewell, but Erickson flew back anyway. Within days he had convinced her to join him on his ship for New York City, which was leaving in only six days, and they spent most of this time arranging a passport and visa. There was other red tape and guarantees for Eva's support that Erickson's parents were required to make, but that Saturday they set sail. They were young and in love, and it was very exciting.

In New York City Erickson's parents met the couple and drove them to Chicago. Erickson worked as an auditor for Del Webb Corporation and after a week the couple took the train to Phoenix, Arizona, where Eva lived a short time with Erickson's sister. On New Year's Eve, 1966, they were married.

Three months later the Ericksons decided to return to Europe, and in 1970 Eva gave birth to a daughter the couple named Aase. In Heidelberg Eva acquired a saluki, then began breeding and showing the dogs. With Aase, just five months old, two saluki puppies, and two grown dogs, the family returned to Phoenix.

After a time Erickson was offered another European job as controller for Sheraton, this time in Copenhagen. The experience didn't work out and in August 1972 they returned again to Phoenix, where Erickson found work with a title company. Eva devoted herself to Aase, to hiking, and to breeding and showing her dogs, and she finally learned to drive.

Don Erickson was a soft-spoken man who held his emotions in close check. For some time it had been apparent that his wife regarded him as she would an uncle or even a father. The love he felt for her, the passion in their marriage were not mutual, but he did not speak of that. He watched his wife slowly drift away from him until in January 1974 she asked for a divorce. Until then he had not believed the distance was so great between them and now for the first time spoke about restoring their relationship. When it became apparent that Eva was not interested in a reconciliation, he became angry, but it changed nothing. Her mind was made up. They agreed that Aase would live with him, and in July the divorce was final.

Eva found a job at the Copenhagen furniture store, where she met Christa, Mike's wife, and, through her, Sam. When they met, Eva evidenced little interest in him and it took a lot of persuading before Eva agreed to go out. They attended Phoenix's prestigious Heart Ball, held that year at the ultraexclusive Arizona Biltmore, where she drew L.S.'s approving eye.

The summer of 1975 Sam was accepted at Harvard Business School and made plans to attend in the fall. Eva was reluctant to become so involved with him, but she finally agreed to join him in Cambridge.

While L.S. was unhappy in his relationship with Suzanne, he was also mystified about Joe's motive for ending it. When he tried to talk to Joe, to explain that he wanted Suzanne for his wife, that he needed her, that divorce was a terrible thing, especially for the youngest girls, Joe would not hear of it. Suzanne, he argued, had tricked his father into marriage and was ruining his life.

For a time again L.S. turned to religion in his unhappiness, and he frequently pondered the unending complexity of his personal life. If he realized that his own excessively controlling personality and behavior had led him to this unhappy state, he did not write or speak of it.

Beginning in 1973, L.S. had silenced Suzanne's constant talk of divorce by calling her bluff. He would divorce her. She warmed to him for a day or two after he made such a claim but soon resumed her threats of leaving. "Blowups" with her were a regular occurrence. Increasingly L.S. was spending his nights at the house on Roanoke and, after Joe moved, was joined by the ever-faithful Tom Safford. The two spent hours in relative silence, playing endless games of checkers.

Joe often stated his preference that his father stay on the road, and L.S. found himself traveling almost constantly in 1975. When he was in Phoenix, there were fights at home with Suzanne and at the towers with Joe. During all the feuding it was not unusual for L.S. when awakened from sleep for the next installment simply to drive to the house on Roanoke to finish the night.

In April 1976 Joe and Mark attended the opening address of the Amerco district vice-presidents' (ADVPs) meeting. Their arrogant, condescending manner and extreme intolerance toward these hardworking men who were the cornerstones of U-Haul embarrassed and puzzled L.S., who was in the habit of apologizing for their behavior. In the presence of others Joe and Mark loudly discussed whom they intended to fire someday. Mark would raise his voice, spout off a name, then crow, "I'm going to X him out."

"... I realized how tough [life] was for everyone," L.S. wrote, "by the time I was fifteen years old." *Why*, he thought, *couldn't these two sons see that?*

What he would not accept was that his sons had had different upbringings from his. As a teenager he had labored as a migrant worker in the orchards, living a hand-to-mouth existence. In their teens his sons had attended a private prep school and lived in a mansion. L.S. had spent a lifetime building a company; his boys had merely inherited it.

L.S. was subjected not only to Joe's ceaseless attacks against Suzanne, but those of others as well. In June Paul wrote to his father:

> I have been uptight for a while because I have not been able to communicate with you about a particular subject. . . . If you have

not guessed by now, it is Suzanne. . . . [S]he contacted [my girl friend's] parent's and informed them of the following:

My past life.

My present sex life (a total & unequivocal fabrication of fiction).

That Mark, [our girl friends,] and I hold a "sex circus" on company trips. . . .

It isn't enough that she isn't my mother. It isn't enough that I have moved out of her house three years ago. It isn't enough that I never tell her anything personal. It isn't enough that I live 2,500 miles away 7 months of the year. It isn't enough that I avoid her whenever possible. What do I have to do to get out of her reach? Move to New York City? Buy a fast airplane? Get married?!?!?!? Stop associating with you??? . . . I'm sure you are tired of me belaboring the obvious, now that I am reduced to ranting and raving. I am sorry about that. I do not know about you, but goddamnit I want things to improve. I have hope & a future. I have not given up. I will not go down on this stinking junk. Things only get worse as time passes. I will not be a part of it. If she is part of the hand you dealt me, I fold. Take it back. I will go somewhere else.

Your goddamned, fornicating Phillistene [*sic*], mother-less, bastard child, son of a bitch, Paul Francis

In August 1976 L.S. moved to the house on Roanoke for two continuous months. When he was permitted back into the Tatum House, Suzanne preferred to be absent, and the children, who were older now, were often out. "This is a lonely place at times," he wrote that fall.

In November 1976 Paul delivered another letter that troubled L.S. very much:

Growing up in Suzanne's household, there was almost never any outward acknowledgement of any kind that us six kids actually at one time had a mother. It was pretty obvious that we sure had none now. That absence of acknowledgement may be never made itself felt on you so much. You had spent 10 + years of your life living and sleeping with Anna Mary. You did not need to be reminded of who she was & what she meant to you. You could never forget. The rest of us never knew her as you [did], and had so much less to remember her by.

Christmas 1975 was a surprise to *one and all* of my siblings when we saw Anna Mary recorded on film. None of us had any knowledge, even knew such a record existed. Is not that a little strange? . . .

I do not feel I know a damn thing about Anna Mary, even though I have studied pictures, the letter you wrote to us, and listened attentively every time she was spoke of, none too often. She was as real to me as the Virgin Mary—not too real. . . . I understand that Suzanne would not allow it, because she would give you an endless raft of grief, which she did anyway. Everyone [sic] of us kids would eat shit from her till we were blue in the face because we thought she would lay off persecuting you. It never did a bit of good as it turns out. It probably just fueled her fire. I don't know how many times that creed stopped us kids from beating her senseless. We all figured if we were going to start in on her we had better finish her off for good, else she would just give you more shit. And none of us ever got down to killing her, unfortunately for some mysterious reason. Although every one of us has had the means and the motivation. It would have been a true case of mercy killing.

I want you to know that I will assist you in any way I can to effect a thorough elimination of Suzanne from our lives. . . .

L.S. began thinking that it might not be so bad to give both Joe and Suzanne what they wanted. At the least, this skewed line of reasoning went, it would bring him peace. And there was another argument in favor of at last taking some action. He could tell that his dysfunctional marriage was having a negative influence on the children. On a trip with Paul, his teenage son had confessed that he was having nightmares about Suzanne.

That winter Suzanne spoke incessantly of divorce. In December L.S. wrote, "Sue on the warpath again . . . " But Suzanne was not going to let this be her husband's decision. On Christmas Day 1976 L.S. awakened early and fixed pancakes for the youngest children. Sam and Eva dropped by later, as did Mark and his wife. But soon Suzanne showed up with a group of her friends L.S. disliked, and by 8:30 P.M. he had gone to bed. An hour later his wife stormed into the bedroom, snapped on the lights, and read a letter prepared by her attorneys. She had instructed them to file for divorce. With Whitmore and L.S.'s child in the background there was no longer any question of who would retain custody of the youngest girls.

L.S. moved into the house on Roanoke, and on January 6, 1977, L.S. conducted a lengthy meeting at the towers. At its finish a process server handed him his divorce papers. "She is stupid and scared..." he wrote that night. "I am sick."

In May the divorce was final. "Don't feel good or bad," L.S. said in reaction. He ate a large dinner, had two drinks, and afterward smoked "a big black cigar" in a mock ceremony. Then, for the first time, he wrote in his journal, "...I truly love Suzanne."

U-Haul's parent company, Amerco, was incorporated in Nevada, and L.S. lived and worked out of an apartment there that summer. He had given the end of his marriage a great deal of thought and now developed an unusual approach. Suzanne had complained for years that while L.S. was rich and her children were wealthy as well, she had no money of her own. The divorce settlement had ended her objection.

L.S. convinced himself that now he was free to remarry Suzanne and be rid of the major problem he had faced. Joe would see he really loved Suzanne, and since his former wife had her own money now, that was one less objection he would have to face from her.

In consequence of this logic, L.S. pursued Suzanne to Portland and proposed remarriage. She became furious with him and left at once for Phoenix. L.S. followed her there with no success. However, when he threatened to marry Suzie Whitmore, Suzanne was taken aback and allowed L.S. to move into the house she had bought at McCormick Ranch in North Scottsdale. Though Suzanne was only a one-eleventh owner of the Tatum House, L.S. had agreed that she could continue to live there and he would pay her expenses. Instead she had moved into the kind of house she had always wanted, a house in which he felt like a stranger. But once there he persisted with his hard sell, and within days Suzanne ordered him out.

The illegitimacy of his son by Whitmore had troubled L.S. ever since his birth, and L.S. flew to Cleveland and proposed marriage. Whitmore would join him in Nevada, and they would marry and file for divorce the same day. Whitmore agreed to go through the legal process to legitimize their son, and on September 16, 1977, the couple were married. L.S. was privately terrified she would suddenly change her mind, refuse to divorce him, and shake him down for money, but she quietly signed the papers and returned to Cleveland as agreed.

For the rest of that year L.S. begged Suzanne to remarry him, and finally, it seemed, he was making some progress. They would move to Las Vegas, away from the mess in Phoenix, he proposed. Their life would be better than before. All she had to do was give him another chance. On December 29 Dennis Saban held a wedding reception L.S. and Suzanne attended, but the couple "had a big fight on the way home," L.S. wrote, "and she hates me with a passion. Anyway I am to pack tomorrow morning and leave. Slept on the floor and Suzanne slept like a baby and so it goes, no different than twenty years ago."

But the next morning Suzanne agreed to fly with L.S. to Las Vegas, where they were to celebrate the new year together. But the trip north proved unpleasant and ultimately futile. Suzanne told a friend that she "never knew how happy she was away from him" before making this trip. On New Year's Eve day Suzanne went house shopping with L.S. "One moment she was saying nice things about me and the next I was a S.O.B.," he wrote. "On January 1, she had me drive her to the airport for the last time. All is over."

The turmoil in his private life was matched by the trauma at work with Joe. On April 1, 1977, Joe and Heidi were married, just as L.S. feared. Joe's efforts did not go entirely unrewarded. He still insisted that L.S. remain on the road, and with Sam at Harvard during the school year Joe had the run of the towers. He had persuaded L.S. to relinquish the title of president of U-Haul International, the corporation responsible for the business activities at the towers, and to appease him, L.S. had appointed Joe to the position, which he held at his marriage.

If Heidi had contemplated moving into a house suitable for the president of U-Haul International, she was quickly disappointed. Shortly after the wedding she bought an elaborate silver service setting and gave the distinct impression that she believed she had arrived and wanted to show it. Joe insisted that he must be at or by U-Haul twenty-four hours a day, and he moved his bride into a small house on Roanoke just down the street from the towers. Heidi rankled at the situation and told others she wanted a house more suitable for her station, but there she remained for some time.

L.S. clashed with Joe almost daily. Mark was busying himself with the U-Haul Racing Team, working on cars in one of two buildings Joe had specially built behind U-Haul Towers, regularly blowing up engines, wrecking cars, and losing races by competing in events that were beyond his skills.

Joe and Mark brought a sinister approach to U-Haul operations. At a meeting about a lawsuit Mark proposed, "Here's the way to solve this. Get two whores and put them in the guy's motel room. Catch them in bed with the guy, take a picture and then break both his legs." One of the men present considered the last superfluous. Either get the photograph or break his legs, not both.

Such comments were not limited to Mark. When the company had difficulties with anyone his uncle James Carty was often heard to say, "Give me ten thousand dollars, and I know a guy who can take care of him." Mark was soon parroting the same speech. "Give me ten thousand dollars," he said at business meetings, "and we'll end it for this guy."

When Suzanne told L.S. in Las Vegas that she hated him and would not remarry him, L.S. was plunged into depression. He was adrift and had no idea what to do with his personal life. L.S. had at one point been very attracted to Suzie Whitmore and found solace at her house. Now he wanted to know the son she had borne him. Within weeks of Suzanne's decision not to remarry him, L.S. flew to Ohio and told Whitmore they should marry again, and this time for real. They would be a family. Whitmore's roommate, and longtime companion, was strongly opposed, but L.S. pressed Whitmore, who finally agreed. They were immediately remarried and moved into the Tatum House with their son.

It was a disaster. Whitmore found L.S. impossible to live with, and he was in no emotional state to take on a new commitment, not with his unresolved feelings for Suzanne. Whitmore missed her roommate terribly, and one day, only weeks after their marriage, when L.S. returned from work, she and his son were gone. For a second time they were divorced.

His teenage daughter, Cecilia, lived with him for a month to ease the emotional strain. He could not sleep or rest and thought for all real purposes that he was dead. To remove himself from day-to-day affairs at U-Haul and Joe's constant haranguing, L.S. decided to return to Las Vegas and use the company residence there. He was alone, very much missed his youngest daughters, who were eleven, fourteen, fifteen, and seventeen, and was extremely despondent.

Sam, who had been monitoring his father's condition closely, became deeply concerned about what he perceived to be a "progressive deterioration over a 1–2 year period." He had attempted to locate a suitable psychiatrist in the Phoenix area, but L.S. had been unhappy with all of his suggestions. Sam had even flown to Connecticut to examine a highly recommended psychiatric facility, but L.S. had refused to go to it.

On a trip L.S. took to Phoenix in July 1978 Sam assumed control of his father and simply drove him to Los Angeles, where he checked his father into a private hospital in Long Beach operated by Dr. Ferris Pitts.

L.S. considered the place a dreary "loony bin" and told Pitts there was nothing to be done for him. "We'll see about that," Pitts said. A moment later he gave L.S. a cup of antidepressant and a sedative drink that he said would make him feel better. Then he put his new patient to bed, and the exhausted L.S. slept for three days. When L.S. woke up and ate, he felt as if the worst were behind him. Each day thereafter he was feeling better, and the hospital, he realized, was actually a pleasant facility. By week's end L.S. had rented a car and was driving about Los Angeles, and within two weeks he returned to Las Vegas.

Earlier on vacation in Las Vegas, L.S. had met Janet Hammer, an attractive nurse whose twin sister had worked for U-Haul. He had seen the pair casually a few times and now began to date Jan Hammer seriously. Feeling reborn and in need of a fresh start, he was soon pressing her to marry him. In the fall of 1978, just a few months after his second divorce from Whitmore, they were married. He bought a house for them in an exclusive district of Las Vegas which she redecorated. But L.S. found it impossible to live with Jan Hammer's teenage daughter from a previous marriage, and in a few months he was again getting divorced.

L.S. was now sixty-two years old. He had been married five times to four different women and had fathered twelve children. A colleague of many years once said of him, "He wanted lots of money, lots of wives, and lots of children. He was a man who wanted everything and got it." With the end of his last fiasco Hammer moved to Denver, and L.S. returned to Phoenix to put in order the one portion of his life over which he truly exercised control—U-Haul.

During the period of L.S.'s marriages, remarriages, divorces, and depression, Joe had seized all the power he could, and it was primarily the consequences of that power grab that caused L.S. to turn his full attention to the company.

Matters at the towers, he knew, were not going well for the company under Joe's management. Mike had been badgered repeatedly by Joe, and it seemed to L.S. that Joe's purpose was to run his brother off. This mustn't happen. Mike had done everything L.S. had asked of him since coming on board, and even if he was still angry with his father and avoided him, Mike was doing a good job.

By 1978 L.S. had at last persuaded Mark to join management at U-Haul, but Mark extracted a price for this concession. He would assume control of field operations for the western United States, U-Haul's most profitable area, but L.S. could not tell him what to do.

In December 1978 L.S. summoned his oldest sons and once again told them of the pain it caused him that they could not work together in peace, in "love and respect," as he so often put it. He drew up a document and had each of them sign it, as he himself did. They agreed to be committed to running U-Haul, to communicate with one another, to "cut one another plenty of slack," and to strive to be personally happy and cheerful.

The written agreement of cooperation made no difference, and that spring L.S. met privately with Heidi to discuss Joe's unhappiness. "I do not understand why [it has to be]," L.S. told her fervently.

Upon his return to the company from Harvard, where he had graduated thirty-third out of a class of eight hundred, Sam and Eva moved into one of the houses on Roanoke. A few days later Joe went down the street and dropped in on Eva during the day. "Hi," he said, "I'm your landlord, and I just stopped by to see how you are." While it was true that Sam was paying no rent, any more than Joe and Heidi were, Joe was not Eva's landlord. Eva told Sam about what had occurred and how ridiculous it had been. They concluded that Joe had delusions of authority that did not exist.

Theirs was at least one prospective marriage of which L.S. wholeheartedly approved. On New Year's Eve 1978 Sam and Eva were married, and Sam said he had never been happier in his life. "She is my life," he told friends.

Perhaps the most conspicuous symbol of the conflicts existing in U-Haul management was U-Haul Towers itself. L.S. had never spent money on accoutrements. Desks inside the towers did not match, and serviceable furniture remained in use long after its best years. The exterior of the building had become so run-down that employees began calling it the Teheran Hilton. L.S. decided to paint the towers, but his sons could not agree on a color. His solution was to have various panels on the north side painted the different colors they wanted, to see which looked best. But no one could agree even then, so that side remained a checkerboard of different colors for more than a year until L.S. made his own decision.

Although U-Haul International was primarily the administrative arm of the Amerco companies L.S. supervised directly, it was still an important part of the operation. Joe's management style was to intimidate employees and to implement decisions by "pushing buttons," as he often said. If you wanted something done, you should just push a button at your desk and it would take place.

Sam was continually amazed at Joe's idea of control. Traveling with his father and working in the field nationwide had taught Sam that the real company was out there, not in Phoenix. At the towers were now about fifteen hundred employees while in the field were more than twelve thousand. Field operations were run by L.S. and the Amerco district vice-presidents, who reported to him. The nature of self-moving meant it was a business that required constant fine tuning because no single answer to problems worked indefinitely. What worked in one place might not work elsewhere, and what was successful one year might not be the next. It was the competence of the ADVPs who ran the day-to-day affairs of the company—and reported directly to L.S.—not Joe and his imaginary magic buttons, that made U-Haul a success.

It was apparent to Sam that paper work was burying field operations, which still used a variation of the initial hand-sorting system L.S. had devised with Anna Mary in Portland in the early 1950s. Computers were an obvious solution, and Sam went to Joe with the request that his operation, which was the clearing-house for all the paper work, devise an automated system. Joe shook his head, then said smugly, "We just don't have the ability to do that sort of thing in [the towers]. Why don't you do it in the field?"

That was an absurd suggestion, and L.S., who soon learned of it, saw it as such. He believed Mark was making a mess of West Coast operations, Joe had guided U-Haul Towers administration into a quagmire, and only Sam seemed to grasp what had to be done.

Joe and Mark attended an ADVP meeting in New York City at about this time. In the back of a company bus, wearing leather bomber jackets and drinking liquor from a bottle, the pair held court, loudly insulting longtime employees whom they held in contempt and berating the jobs Sam and L.S. were doing for the company. For some time now Joe and Mark had openly expressed their disdain toward many of those in senior management, especially those most loyal to their father, men such as John Fowler and Jack Adair, and had bragged that these were men they intended to "X out."

The board meeting in June 1979 typified how such meetings had deteriorated since Joe had joined the company. Whenever business was being discussed, Joe contemptuously closed his eyes as if he were asleep. Then he launched into one of his tirades. The meeting became a "donnybrook," as L.S. described it, with Joe threatening repeatedly to walk out when L.S. refused to back him just as he had at least twenty times before. Mark shouted constantly, and L.S. was unable to figure out just what it was these sons wanted. "I can't understand these people," he wrote, "and their petty arguments."

For Mike that June's board meeting had been enough. Ever since he had won an impressive court victory he had been treated like a superstar by his father. Whenever possible Joe held Mike up to ridicule and vociferously attacked his every suggestion. As a consequence, Mike abruptly resigned during the June meeting. L.S. was devastated. When he asked Mike to explain himself, Mike vented again the long string of abuses to which he believed he had been subjected. L.S. found them virtually incomprehensible, though all of Mike's complaints could be summarized by his simply saying L.S. insisted on trying to run Mike's life and Joe had made his existence at U-Haul unbearable. L.S. retained Mike on the payroll while he tried to persuade him to return.

L.S. went to Sam and said he wanted to reshuffle the Shoen deck. What Joe needed was field experience, to see what it was like out there in the real world, in the "knuckle-busting" business of U-Haul. Sam would assume Joe's duties and run U-Haul International.

Sam wanted nothing to do with the change since he knew what a mess Joe had made of administration. The idea of sitting day after day in that office cleaning up after Joe, convincing employees they no longer had to work in terror, sorting out mind-numbing administrative procedures sounded like a prison sentence. When

L.S. proposed the change, Sam begged his father not to ask this of him, but L.S. could see no alternative. With Mike gone Sam was his only choice. With that Joe was informed that he was no longer president of U-Haul International, that Sam would take his place. Mark would assume Sam's role heading East Coast operations, and Joe would now work in the field in charge of the West Coast, under L.S.'s personal control.

For an entrepreneur who had granted titles rather than paychecks to his managers all his career, it is surprising that L.S. failed to appreciate the stock Joe placed in his position. Indeed, Joe related that he perceived his removal as president of U-Haul International as a demotion. More significant than this, once again Sam was taking his place.

Early that September, knowing he would no longer report to Joe, Mike returned to the legal department.

At first Joe refused his new assignment, and L.S. had to urge him to take it repeatedly. Finally Joe said that the only way he would accept transfer to the field was if L.S. bought him a private plane and provided him with a pilot to chauffeur him about his new territory. Eager to appease Joe, L.S. hurriedly approved the three hundred thousand dollars for the purchase of the plane and hired a pilot.

In Mark's case the concessions were even more severe. In the foulest of language Mark told his father he was not to set foot into his territory, nor was he ever to tell Mark what to do. In addition, L.S. was refused permission to distribute the essential "Agency Bulletin," the unifying instrument of the U-Haul empire. To the amazement of those present, L.S. agreed to Mark's demands, so eager was he to have his oldest sons all working for U-Haul.

Despite these and other concessions, the new arrangement of job assignments proved short-lived, and operations disintegrated quickly. L.S. came to the decision that he needed a new family psychologist and, acting on a referral, acquired the services of Dr. Jerry Day to replace Levy. His oldest sons, he said, were to attend the sessions. It was past time they started getting along. It was clear to him by now that Joe and Mark were the problem, and counseling, to be successful, had to focus on them.

As L.S. moved to reassert direct control over U-Haul that summer and fall of 1979, the power Joe had exercised slipped away from him. In August during a meeting, Joe abruptly resigned from the board, hoping apparently his father would lure him back with more concessions in still another demonstration of appeasement. The immediate effect of Joe's resignation, however, was to improve the tone and competency of the board meetings in the absence of his bellicose behavior and crude manipulations.

Dr. Day attended meetings at U-Haul to observe the oldest sons and their father. He also met with them in long sessions that were not pleasant. "Meeting with Mark and Sam and Joe and Jimmy [sic] and me with Dr. Day," L.S. noted. "Meeting went all day and it was one hell of a mess and B.S. and tiring and exhausting." By October 1979 Mark, expressing frustration with his duties, quit the company rather than be responsible for the East Coast.

Day told the rest of the family that he would not need to see them for now, that he would be working only with Joe, but when Joe learned that Day was focusing just on him, he refused to attend any further sessions.

Joe was at first unwilling to go at all into the field with L.S., then reluctantly on October 9 joined his father to call on rental agents and centers in the Phoenix area. Going into the field like this was a slap in Joe's face. They left the towers at midmorning with Joe driving while L.S. was, once again, explaining how Joe should deal with employees: He must treat them with respect; he must listen; he could not treat them as if they were his personal servants. Joe had heard it all before many times. Just two miles from U-Haul Towers he slammed on the brakes of the car and screamed, "I can't take it! All right? I'm through!" and struck the steering wheel so violently he bent it. He drove recklessly back to the towers and left U-Haul.

Joe's version of his resignation was, predictably, quite different. "I left U-Haul because too many cooks spoil the broth," he said dispassionately. "I just wasn't fitting in."

L.S. had asked Day to prepare a written report to assist him in evaluating his sons, and on November 5, 1979, Day delivered the report along with a special oral briefing for L.S. The report was unsparing in its language:

> The Shoen family, over the past two years, have experienced great stress; as a result of personal conflicts between the working members of the family. The conflict seemed to result from a splitting of the group into two competing camps. Camp number one constituted: L.S., Dr. Sam, Mike and Jimmy [*sic*] and camp number two was Joe and Mark. Joe and Mark expressed very strong feelings of hurt and anger with L.S., Dr. Sam, Mike and Jimmy. The anger and resentment between these two groups became so great that any meeting, in which all were present, resulted in a disruptive shouting match; cooperative behavior was almost nil.

Day then told L.S. what he already knew: that while others had helped, Joe and Mark had "cooperated poorly and did not make the necessary adjustments that would lead to a better working relationship. If anything the family relationships deteriorated further as the deep anger and hurt were brought into sharper focus" during the evaluation period, during which both Mark and Joe left the company. "Joe and Mark experienced a severe trauma when their Mother died when they were six and five years old. After a reasonable amount of time a stepmother came into their lives. In addition to the trauma of losing their Mother, Mark struggled with some severe learning problems as a result of a minimal brain damage problem. Their relationship with their stepmother was terrible."

According to Day, in the situation the sons had faced, children often "develop strong, pervasive feelings of inferiority." They "reasoned that something must be wrong with them. They were not worth loving." As a result, the boys had compensated by setting goals for themselves so high they could not succeed; "therefore they always have an excuse for failing. They honestly feel that they try hard but 'others' won't let them succeed. However, in reality their position is either so extreme or so unrealistically high that they cannot expect to succeed or to get others to support their extreme position." This allows them to blame others, and "their life script" requires someone much like their stepmother to act as a rejecter.

> A second neurotic trend that developed out of their early home experience with their stepmother was the development of a power struggling personality. They felt unloved and abused. Therefore, they fostered the belief that power, and power alone is important. Early on they pitted their power against that of their stepmother and concluded that when they got big they would be able to be powerful like Suzanne. They resisted, as best they could as children, and generally fought her at every turn.... This struggle went on for years.
>
> As a result... they matured into adults who are quite comfortable with power and are willing to fight for it. Their desire for absolute power is insatiable. The more they have the more they want.... [Their] reward is not in winning but in getting significant powerful people to struggle. Winning is secondary and in fact uncomfortable. Because they basically feel inferior, winning a power struggle is undesirable because they would then have to be responsible for success. There would be no one to blame for failure, if they did have "all power." The reward is in the struggle, they may not win but you will know they are around.
>
> ...L.S. is usually the focus of the power plays, however, anyone who stands in their way will experience the struggle.... They skillfully structure a working situation that puts them in direct opposition to another family member. The struggle is then on and when they lose they feel that the failure to make progress is someone elses [sic] fault.... Another way to look at the struggle is thusly: "If you really love me you will do as I say," "Since you oppose me then you don't love me, therefore I am justified in hating you."...
>
> Remember, they had years of training for this personality development with their stepmother. They simply have projected their experiences and feelings from their stepmother to others in power.

Inviting him into the family to help was an important step, Day said, and he suggested that even Joe and Mark "must, at a deeper level, also want to see a better family relationship." The psychologist advised that they must first break up the power struggle.

"L.S., Dr. Sam, Mike and Jimmy must withdraw from the field of struggle.... It is impractical to expect the struggle to lessen as long as there is a close working relationship between Joe and Mark and the rest of the group."

He now suggested that Joe's and Mark's resignations had been a positive occurrence. But he reminded L.S., "Keep in mind that the life goal of Joe and Mark is to match their power against the authority of others. When they successfully get someone to struggle, then their mistaken life goal is rewarded and strengthened; ie to engage in power struggles. It does absolutely no good to resist for awhile and then compromise. For then [*sic*] winning is not as important as the struggle...."

Day recommended that L.S. give Joe and Mark at least two years away from the company. Joe had expressed a desire to become a lawyer, and the psychologist thought that he "is quite talented intellectually and his combative personality could be turned into an asset in the legal department." But Joe must settle his differences first and, ideally, work for an independent law firm for at least two years. Mark, Day believed, should develop his own independent business away from U-Haul: "The best teacher for both will be society or the realities of the business community. They will learn best from the natural or logical consequences of their behavior to befall Mark and Joe. They should not be protected from financial pain or boredom or unfulfillment or vocational limbo...."

Attached to the report was a special message for L.S. "You have been targeted," Day wrote, "by Joe and Mark, as the culprit in their life drama. Although your marriage to Susanne [*sic*] and frequent absences from home had something to do with the development of the present difficulties the main problem is that you have the ultimate power...."

Day suggested that L.S. stop overexplaining himself in meetings and become less excitable. "It is my belief that you often reinforce their outburst by (a) first resisting, (b) then later giving into [*sic*] their position. They have generally concluded that the only way to get you to attend to them is to shout, scream and generally play uproar...."

After reading the two reports, L.S. spoke to Day at some

length to elicit his thoughts beyond what was contained in writing, and the psychologist made a number of practical suggestions. At one point he said, "Recognize that they may be lost to U-Haul. Realize that we all did the best we could and this is it."

Day had devoted most of his report to understanding Joe and Mark, just as L.S. had desired. His comments to L.S. to temper his conduct were nearly an aside, and in taking this approach, Day overlooked the central aspect of this struggle. Although it was true that Joe and Mark had shown behavior that led to the conclusion that they were power-hungry and that the reasons for this very likely were those Day outlined, the fact was that without L.S.'s central role these conclusions would have made no difference. Mark didn't want to be in U-Haul; his father had dragged him into the company against his will. And while Joe wanted to run U-Haul, L.S. was the one who controlled the situation. He was free to remove Joe from any of the positions he held at any time.

The fact was that L.S. wanted his sons in the company so badly he was prepared to overlook almost any behavior. L.S.'s controlling personality and ego were driving this conflict and placed Joe and Mark in positions in which they could struggle with him. Day was looking to L.S., the very man who created the conflict, to implement his commonsense solutions. L.S. was incapable of taking instruction from Day because he was so blinded he could not see what was really taking place, and he was unable to face his complicity with honesty. The problem was Joe and Mark, he decided. When they changed their ways, everything would be better.

Day's role was now largely ended. L.S. weighed the contents of the reports, then tossed them aside. Despite the language that graphically depicted the men his two boys had become, L.S. doggedly pursued them to rejoin the company. He continued their salaries rather than let them suffer economically for having resigned. He compromised with Joe and agreed to let Heidi take Joe's place on the board, ensuring that Joe would have input and that his director's fee would remain in his household.

But Joe would not hear of coming back. L.S. had made his

choice; he wanted Sam over him. Joe had done everything he could all his life to prepare himself for taking control of U-Haul. L.S. had rejected his plans and now told him Dr. Day said he was crazy. Joe was finished with it.

In December L.S. tried again, this time suggesting that Joe and Mark could assume control of U-Haul's Canadian operation and would be left alone. The answer was no. Joe and Mark were out of it.

CHAPTER NINE

THE MANAGEMENT OF GREED

J ames Ryder, the founder of Ryder System, a competing company in one-way rental trucks, lost control of his company and in 1978 founded Jartran. During 1980 Jartran exploded on the one-way truck and trailer rental industry and immediately positioned itself head to head against U-Haul with more than twenty thousand trailers and four thousand trucks.

Until now U-Haul had never experienced a significant national competitor, and never before had competition aggressively pursued its market. Jartran placed its rental agencies at some of the sites L.S. had closed during his expansion into the centers and hired a number of former U-Haul employees. Jartran selected U-Haul's price to rent a truck or trailer from one city to another, then displayed a rate that it claimed was less.

L.S. had determined many years before that the way to make a profit from trailer and truck rentals was to own the equipment. Rental income became a profit only when the equipment acquisition had been paid off. From L.S.'s point of view, James Ryder had made a crucial, and fatal, error from day one: He was buying nothing. All his trucks and trailers were leased. By the time the lease payment was deducted from the rental income, the rental agent paid, and the overhead covered, there was not enough money left for a profit. There might be if Jartran was free to set a profitable rate, but it was forced to compete with U-Haul, whose almost wholly owned fleet established the base price.

But Jartran was depressing the rate for one-way rentals, in many cases to a point below cost, and U-Haul was losing tens of millions in net profits each year it operated. As a consequence, the speed with which U-Haul could add centers was reduced, and the company was forced to assume a greater debt load than L.S. had anticipated and it had ever before experienced.

For L.S. the lesson was obvious. While he did not believe Jartran could survive while leasing its equipment, U-Haul was susceptible to a well-financed rival company with other sources of income. L.S. was more persuaded than ever that U-Haul must diversify and now moved it toward general equipment rentals, the creation of a moving van line, and motor home rentals. They all cost money with no guarantee of success.

The threat of failure did not deter L.S. In fact, most of the new areas into which he had directed U-Haul had not met with success. In 1959 U-Haul had added small camping trailers to its line, but they failed to catch on and were discontinued. A to Z Rental had failed as well. Convinced they would be a hit with weekend hunters and fishermen, Hap Carty had seen to the construction of rugged camper trucks. The hunters loaded the campers with buddies and abused them, even building fires inside during cold weather. U-Haul had created a Rentmobile, a truck for moving to which was added an Extracar, a Ford Pinto, but this also proved a bust. In the late 1960s U-Haul had acquired rental vans, for which L.S. believed there was a ready market. Instead by the 1970s U-Haul was forced to convert them to stake bed trucks for light commercial hauling. Car rentals had appeared a natural move for U-Haul but were also a failure. In Arizona Hap insisted on painting the cars U-Haul's distinctive orange, and renters avoided the garish automobiles in droves.

But for all the failures there were some successes, and one success that produced income for years more than compensated for a host of failures. Hitch World was a steady money-maker, and the insurance companies U-Haul acquired to self-insure were also profitable. Expansion of U-Haul into trucks in the late 1950s had been a notable success as well.

Failure was a part of any successful enterprise. As L.S. pushed U-Haul into diversification, he was not concerned with experiencing failures.

Joe, now age thirty, and Mark, twenty-nine, had resigned or threatened resignation so many times previously it was only in retrospect that this latest departure was seen as such, though their exit from the company and the board did not mean their absence from U-Haul Towers. And despite Day's report, L.S. was not willing to let his boys loose into the real world. He continued their annual salaries in excess of eighty thousand dollars, allowed them to retain their company credit cards, gave them access to U-Haul planes for personal use and private cars. Mark continued his use of the adjacent building for his U-Haul Racing Team, along with the service of two full-time U-Haul employees.

Darrell Hamby suggested to Mark a way to make easy money, and the pair constructed a giant fish tank on a truck that they enthusiastically stocked with exotic fish. Soon they acquired a bear that they took with them to fairs. They charged a fee to see the fish and bear, but Mark soon tired of the enterprise.

Joe was determined to start a business of his own and was away from the house for weeks at a time as he searched for something. He left home at 5:00 A.M. when he was in town and returned after midnight. This went on for months until he finally settled on two endeavors. In 1980 he started Space Age Paint, which he located in Mesa, outside Phoenix. The following year both he and Mark began Form Builders, Inc., a printing operation whose offices were housed with the paint store.

Heidi was surprised once these were going concerns to learn that her husband was buying his female employees gifts, including items of clothing and money for vehicles. When she confronted Joe, he told her this was necessary to secure "the loyalty of certain Space Age women employees...."

Joe dismissed any thought of independence from U-Haul in beginning these businesses. He often told Heidi and others, that he had "orange paint" for blood, suggesting he had spent his childhood painting U-Haul trailers and trucks. Paint was a major acquisition for U-Haul and was potentially a great expense. L.S.

had invested substantial effort in locating a supplier who could provide a paint that held its color and stayed fresh on the equipment for a decade. Painting any more often than that was lost money, so when Joe approached his father to start buying paint from his new company, L.S. refused. He was not prepared to take a risk in this area, which was too important to U-Haul. In addition, U-Haul bought its paint from a producer, and Joe would simply be a middleman who acquired the paint from someone else. Joe was furious at the refusal and raised the subject repeatedly to his father, who continued to say no.

Joe had better luck with Form Builders when he argued that the least his own father could do was to buy printing material from his son's company. He assured L.S. the quality would be the same and the pricing competitive. U-Haul produced most of its material in-house but contracted out for many of its needs.

L.S. agreed but was appalled at the inferior product Form Builders produced from its operation located next door in a U-Haul building. Nevertheless, worn down again by Joe, he ordered the material shipped. And though Joe had promised the prices would be competitive, he badgered the procurement staff out of L.S.'s earshot to pay whatever he billed. Very quickly all semblance of outside competition disappeared, and 99 percent of FBI's business was with U-Haul. L.S. cautioned Joe and Mark repeatedly that this arrangement was wrong, that it was not arm's length, and that it would not last indefinitely.

The use of the acronym "FBI" for Form Builders, Inc. was part of a pattern for Joe and Mark. The truck Mark had used to tow his race car had a personalized license plate that read "SPY 001." FBI seemed an appropriate match; indeed, the name, Form Builders, Inc. may well have been selected to allow it.

And so L.S.'s largess was the key to Joe and Mark's success outside the company. Whereas Space Age Paint was a money loser for Joe for several years, Form Builders, with its main-line feed from U-Haul's coffer, was an immediate, and conspicuous, success.

At this time L.S. took the next logical step for an entrepreneur: He wrote a book. *You and Me* was written as another in-house project. Part family and business photo album and U-Haul manual, it bore a photograph of L.S. in a white dinner jacket on its cover and had 122 pages of photographs, 35 of them of L.S., in its 322 pages. It was dedicated to "all the people who have lived and are now living on Planet Earth."

The book freely intermixed photographs and stories of both the Shoen family and U-Haul and demonstrated once and for all just how much the two were one and the same for L.S.

Now that L.S. was single and had been married twice to Suzie Whitmore he was prepared to acknowledge their six-year-old son publicly. Knowledge of the child was not common in U-Haul Towers. At one of the occasional U-Haul functions attended by employees L.S. proudly lined up each of his children, calling them from the audience and announcing their latest achievements and degrees with tremendous pride. As always he began with the oldest, kept them standing up front as he worked his way down to number eleven. Then, to the startled gathering and the discomfort of several of his grown children, he pulled his twelfth child from the crowd, introduced the boy with pride and forced Whitmore to stand and be acknowledged as the mother.

Longtime employees to the rear of the room looked at the six-year-old, made quick mental calculations, and realized he had been born well before L.S.'s notorious divorce from Suzanne. They glanced at one another knowingly with suppressed smiles on their lips.

L.S. was sixty-two years old now and for the first time had successfully resisted plunging headlong into another marriage. His attraction for young, beautiful women, however, was unchanged, and he was inviting Ned Saban's twenty-five-year-old daughter, Marcie, to accompany him when he socialized with her parents. Marcie's brother, Dennis, was a longtime friend of Mark's, and the two of them were entering a business arrangement that Mark claimed would earn him one million dollars a year.

Marcie Saban was a remarkable woman by any standard. Independent, self-confident, and bright, she often worked with her father. She was a beautiful woman, a debutante whose picture frequently appeared in local magazines.

L.S. was strongly attracted to her, but she held their association at a distance. L.S. had the Sabans, and Marcie, join him in flights across the country, and he even persuaded her to accompany him without her parents on a European trip sponsored by one of U-Haul's vendors. When they returned, L.S. continued to see Marcie from time to time, not nearly as often as he would have liked.

She was by no means the only woman he was dating. L.S. had attended an *est* seminar in Phoenix in the fall of 1979 and met another lovely young woman to whom he was very attracted. Carol Copeland was thirty-two years old and had renewed her interest in *est* following her divorce the previous February.

At the *est* seminar participants turned their chairs around to face the individuals behind them and then engaged in a series of exchanges before breaking into groups of six for discussion. The man seated behind Carol was L.S. Following the seminar partners were asked to remain in contact with each other to monitor progress, and from that point L.S. started dating Carol. Though L.S. was still seeing Marcie, it was Carol who became his constant companion, and for the first time since college L.S. maintained a relationship with a woman without rushing thoughtlessly into marriage.

L.S. was still deeply concerned about the inability of his children to work as a unit inside U-Haul. He asked Paul, then age twenty-four, to attend one *est* seminar with him and in June 1980 Sam, Mike, Joe, and Mark went with their father to Cleveland, Ohio, and attended a seminar held by the Center for Family Businesses.

Mark and Dennis Saban had been close friends since early in high school, and Mark had been the best man at Dennis's wedding.

In the autumn of 1979, just after Mark left U-Haul, the couples traveled to Europe. Throughout the trip Mark complained about having had to change territories with Sam, which had led to his resignation. He told Dennis repeatedly that he had to accomplish something on his own.

When they were in Europe, Dennis bought a Porsche he planned to take with him back to Arizona and sell for a ten-thousand-dollar profit. Mercedes and Porsche had stopped exporting to the

United States some of their sportiest models because of fleet mileage difficulties, and there existed a booming "gray" market that Dennis had exploited for several months. Besides the ready profit from the sale of the car, the exchange rate between the German mark and U.S. dollar was highly favorable. He told Mark he had been importing about two cars a month, which he and Marcie drove until they were sold.

Mark told Dennis, "I'd like to get involved in this." Dennis explained that he could handle only two, perhaps three cars at one time. The beauty of the deal was the lack of overhead, but with more cars than that there would be expenses.

Mark asked, "How many do you think you can sell?"

"Probably six a month," Dennis said. In light of the way he operated, he doubted there was any more of a market in Phoenix than that.

In Europe Mark became increasingly enthusiastic about what he considered the prospects for this enterprise. It would be his chance for a big score. All his life he had heard how tough it was for people to scratch out livings. This looked easy enough to him.

Mark had as little success with his renowned temper in Europe as in a restaurant in Phoenix. At a service station near the Swiss border the attendant spilled a small amount of gasoline on the car they were using, and Mark went ballistic. He ended up punching the man and was arrested. Both wives were crying, and Dennis paid three hundred dollars to get Mark out of it.

This was not the first time Dennis had watched Mark's temper at work. Years earlier Mark had told him how enraged he was at a man whom he had spotted with a U-Haul hitch permanently mounted on his pickup. Since these hitches were not for sale, that meant it had been stolen. Mark had argued with the man about it, telling him just who he was, but the man had refused to return the hitch.

Dennis and Mark were out in Mary Anna's Mustang when Mark insisted that Dennis drive and take him to the man's business, which was closed that time of night. When they got there, Mark reached under the seat, extracted a .357 magnum handgun, and aimed it at the plate glass window. BOOM! BOOM! BOOM! Three times he shot into the window. The startled Dennis sped off, and as a result of these two incidents, no one needed to tell Dennis Saban about Mark's temper.

During the summer of 1980 Dennis imported his usual number of cars with Mark bankrolling the operation. The pair split the profits, and Mark was bragging to his family about the big money he would make from his activity with Dennis Saban.

In September the two flew to Frankfurt to set up the direct purchase of cars. But they ran into difficulties in Germany. Car dealers told them to go back to America and buy their cars there as that was the way it was supposed to work. Dennis located a German middleman who would buy them cars for a fee of a thousand dollars each. Dennis had to return to Phoenix, so Mark remained behind to negotiate the details.

When Mark returned, he told Dennis enthusiastically they were to import a hundred cars, thirty-five in December, thirty-five in January, and the rest in February. Mark had given their new middleman, who they had just met, a check for $100,000 and now told Dennis they had to wire him another $150,000.

Dennis couldn't believe what he was hearing. One of the reasons he had restricted himself to two or three cars was that each one had to have a catalytic converter installed and reinforced beams placed into the doors. That took time. There was absolutely no way they could process thirty-five cars a month, not unless they opened their own shop and did the conversions themselves. Mark's thinking was, as Dennis later put it, "a little bit flawed." Well, it was Mark's money, Dennis reasoned, and Mark had committed them. He just didn't understand how this could possibly work out.

The change in assignments at U-Haul in 1979 followed by Joe's and Mark's abrupt departure had not entirely surprised Sam. Throughout the period he had been responsible for the East Coast both Joe and Mark had complained repeatedly to their father about Sam's lack of performance. L.S. had argued with the pair, pushing aside the figures they thrust into his face, that the East Coast was the most difficult part of the U-Haul operation.

Joe and Mark had always behaved as if they knew best, but from what Sam had seen they actually understood very little about U-Haul. Sam had listened to Mark's braggadocio in describing his business venture with Dennis Saban, and he simply didn't believe the figures Mark was claiming.

These were difficult times for U-Haul, but Sam had great faith in his father's business judgment. After all, L.S. had built this company from nothing, and despite occasional missteps, U-Haul had grown repeatedly. By 1980 U-Haul's annual sales were approximately two hundred million dollars a year.

But more significant was the fact that Sam simply did not have the difficulty dealing with L.S. that Joe and Mark experienced. L.S. was willing to listen to his input though he often played devil's advocate. In the field Sam watched his father run ideas by staff members at all levels, asking what they thought. L.S. was open to feedback and, even after he had launched a new program, was willing to make corrections—or in some cases make one of his fabled 180-degree turns. It might not look pretty to outsiders, and longtime employees found it disconcerting, but overall his father's management style was very effective.

As exhilarating as Sam found running U-Haul, especially in the absence of Joe and Mark, the real joy in his life came from his relationship with Eva and the family they had begun. Eva gave birth to a daughter in 1980, a child they named Bente, which was Norwegian for "blessing." And in 1982 the couple had a son named Esben, Norwegian for "strength of a bear and protected by God."

Eva was a considerable athlete who jogged regularly and took her dogs out with her as well as to shows. She was an expert cross-country skier, and at least twice a year they took skiing trips. She was a strong, graceful, and very attractive woman and "was intimidating to a lot of men" as a consequence. In town they went to dinner with friends and even with Joe and Mark and their wives.

The truth was, however, that Eva did not like Joe and Mark, whom she called "gangsters" or "the goons." As a European she tended initially to be more formal and reserved in her personal relations, and their behavior offended her. Though she was friendly with all of her husband's family and socialized with the sons' wives, she did not involve herself in family affairs or allow herself to be drawn into close friendships. There was an air of aristocracy about her, the sense that she had married the heir to the U-Haul empire.

Her behavior toward L.S. was perhaps the most startling initially. L.S. was a very wealthy, powerful, and domineering man who usually insisted on having his way, in business and his private life. The reality was that in much of his life those around him fawned on him or fussed over him. Eva would have none of that. When L.S. attempted talking business over dinner, she told him firmly this was a family affair and business was out of place.

At first L.S. was shocked by his assertive daughter-in-law and uncertain what to make of it. Eva could see the reaction her forthrightness had and asked Sam privately if she should continue. Sam assured her that his father preferred straight talk and that he, Sam, loved her for daring to engage in it. He was right. L.S. soon came to appreciate Eva's direct manner and had to concede she had a point. He did mix business and family too often.

Eva's disregard for Joe was keenly returned. Behind her back, but in her presence, Joe called the elegant and graceful Eva "horsy," "the moose," that "telephone pole," or, with a snicker, "the big Swede." Joe was not alone. Paul appeared to hold a similar hostile attitude toward his brother's wife. Sam commented once that there was something he needed to do, and Paul responded with a sneer, "You have your tall blond Norwegian to do that for you."

Heidi's reaction to Eva was no less pronounced but even more perplexing. Heidi threw a party for the couples and their children. Eva was in attendance with Esben, who was still an infant. In the kitchen Heidi extended a plate of food to Eva, as if it were an offering, and after Eva made her selection, Heidi retreated, bowing and scraping, over and over until she was across the room.

At first it had looked like a joke of some type, as if Heidi were trying to mock her dignified sister-in-law with the lilting European accent, but it was soon obvious that Heidi was serious. In some bizarre way Heidi believed this was the appropriate way to treat Eva and was determined to show her respect. It was shocking to at least one person in the room—and sad.

The closeness of Sam and Eva, and the love between them, were so apparent people commented on it routinely. Eva possessed a spontaneous, deft sense of humor that filled the outgoing Sam with roaring laughter. Whenever he was in her presence, she was the focus of his attention, and when she spoke, he clung to every word.

By comparison, Joe and Heidi were not doing well. While Heidi spoke with pride of her husband—he had after all gone on to obtain his law degree—and insisted at family gatherings that Joe was every bit the businessman his father was, the tension between the couple was clear to see. To some of those who knew both couples it was obvious that Heidi was jealous of Eva, especially of her relationship with Sam.

Their house was divided into Joe's "space" and Heidi's "space." Heidi's area was immaculate, so formal and stiff that any thought of spontaneity was crushed. Joe's area was as it had been when he was a bachelor, with biker paraphernalia scattered everywhere, leather and chains, gross drawings of scraggly men and buxom women on chopped motorcycles, and a T-shirt with a German Iron Cross, skull and crossbones, and the words "Love is hate, Hate is love."

Joe placated Heidi by buying her what she wanted from time to time. One day when L.S. was visiting, Heidi gave him a tour of the small house, pointing out each of the acquisitions she believed were intended to keep her satisfied by saying, "There's a bribe from Joe," then pointing to another with the same words.

Heidi had married the president of U-Haul International, and it was clear to those around her that she very much wanted to be "Mrs. President." Joe's removal from that position and his subsequent resignation were surely as difficult for her as they were for her husband.

After years of badgering Heidi pressed Joe into moving out of the small place they had lived in since getting married. Sam and Eva had just bought a lovely Paradise Valley house, and the one they had owned was for sale. Joe didn't like it very much, but Heidi insisted he buy it.

Aase Erickson, Don and Eva's daughter, had lived primarily with her father following her parents' divorce when she was four years old. After initially finding Sam standoffish, she soon took a liking to him. She was also drawn to L.S., especially after the first Christmas she met him. She spent a portion of Christmas Day that year with Sam and her mother, who took her to the annual holiday family chaos at the Tatum House. This was in 1975, before L.S.'s divorce from Suzanne and at a time when Sam and Eva were dating. The Shoen children and friends were laughing and carrying on with one another in the immense house.

Because Aase was only five and did not understand that she was the daughter of Sam's girl friend, she had arrived expecting a gift. When L.S. saw the expectation in her eyes, he rushed from the house and bought her a huge teddy bear. It became her favorite gift from her childhood, and she could never look at it without remembering him with affection.

L.S., she could tell, was uncomfortable with children, uncertain how to behave. He was, however, almost giddy with joy at the holiday gathering and scurried around, pinching the cheeks of the younger children, often too hard, and embracing them in his great bear hug.

The last of L.S.'s and Suzanne's children had been born in late 1966, after the family was living in the Tatum House. Suzanne's first child had been a son, Jimmie, born in 1959, only three years after Anna Mary had given birth to her last child, Paul. After Jimmie, Suzanne bore four daughters in a row: Sophia in 1960, Cecilia in 1962, Theresa in 1963, then Katrina three years later. When Katrina was born, Sam and Mike were already in their twenties and Joe and Mark were leaving for college, so she missed their volatile high school years fighting with her mother.

By the time Katrina came along her parents appeared exhausted from their efforts with the other children and their mutual combat. She found herself in a very different world from her siblings', one in which she had few rules, no regular dinner or bedtime. During L.S.'s regular business meetings at the Tatum House the youngest girls were told by the men attending what a wonderful father they had and how very proud of him they must be. Katrina did not disagree. L.S. was gone from the house a great deal, and when he was home, his relationship with Suzanne was combative. But both Suzanne and L.S. made a determined effort to keep their ongoing conflicts away from the youngest girls, who were generally shielded by everyone.

When L.S. was home he cuddled his girls, who could not walk past him without getting a hug. In their presence he was upbeat and optimistic though they could not help noticing how tired he was. For years they worried that he would die at any moment.

The youngest girls had a very different perspective on what the oldest boys called Suzanne's "benign neglect." Suzanne encouraged independence on the part of the children and Katrina viewed it as one of her mother's most positive contributions.

The parents of a girl friend had divorced, and Katrina took comfort from the certainty that this would never happen in her family. But when she was ten years old, the fighting between L.S. and Suzanne could no longer be concealed from the girls. It now took place in the open with shouts from both sides that they were going to get a divorce. The youngest girls huddled together crying, listening to the end of their parents' marriage.

Not long after the divorce Suzanne moved herself and the four girls, now eleven through seventeen years old, to her new house in North Scottsdale's McCormick Ranch. At the Tatum House Suzanne had been required to run the home on a budget, but with her property settlement she was free to spend what she wanted. The girls went shopping with their mother and loaded up the basket with goodies that heretofore had been in short supply at home. In a much smaller house, with just the four girls and her, Suzanne pampered the children and eased the transition for them.

But soon she was dating Donald Anderson, described as a cowboy of sorts, with an interest in Arabian horses, a popular, and expensive, indulgence for the well-to-do in Scottsdale and Paradise Valley. Suzanne moved Anderson into her house, and Katrina, for one, did not enjoy his presence. She disliked the man intensely.

Mary Anna, Anna Mary's only daughter, had graduated from college by the time L.S. and Suzanne finally divorced. L.S. automatically gave his children seats on the board once they were of age if they wanted it, and for a time Mary Anna served there. U-Haul was often the home away from home for the children, and as teenagers they commonly hung out there. Older brothers lived just down the street. There was always a secretary at the towers to type a term paper or a typewriter available to do it yourself. L.S. had encouraged this association by hiring at least two employees at different times to see to the needs of his children in his absence. Children had friendships with long-term U-Haul employees, and when they were between homes as adults, the towers served as their address. Most of them had summer jobs in the company throughout high school, but that constituted the sum of their formal training in the operation of U-Haul. As a consequence, though most of the children were on the board at one time or another, they had little understanding of company operations and generally voted in ignorance of the issues when they were on the board.

Joe continued his maneuverings with his siblings even away from the company. While Mary Anna was in college, she had ridden in a van with others to inspect the tech center. Joe joined them with fudge, which he passed around. But as each sibling reached for a piece, he admonished them, "You have to vote for me if you want one." There were laughter and smiles, but Joe's eyes said he really meant it.

After he and Mark stormed out of U-Haul, they worked on their siblings in other ways. At one meeting at the towers Joe and Mark barged in and began their litany of U-Haul misdeeds caused by L.S. and Sam, bemoaning the sorry condition of the company. Joe nearly shouted, "The company's going bankrupt, you know." Asked what this was all about, why the rude behavior and nasty manner, Joe said abruptly, "I just thought you should know," and left.

Well, that was Joe as some of his siblings saw him, always acting as if he were the prophet: Vague in his accusations, ominous in his predictions, but asserting that he alone knew best and if his brothers and sisters wanted to save the company, they had better start listening to him.

However, Joe was effective in other, more subtle ways in dealing with his siblings and did not always relate to them as domineering or manipulative. He could be extremely persuasive and present himself as being a man of substantial intellect. When he chose, he could be smooth and demonstrate a genuine interest in the welfare and interests of his brothers and sisters.

L.S. felt he had done justice by all his children. Each had an estate, and unless they were incredibly foolish, they all were guaranteed lifetimes of comfort independent of U-Haul. Not all his sons and daughters agreed with him. Joe, for one, had been vitriolic in his condemnation of his father's handling of his estate when he was a minor, and Sophia had expressed her displeasure as well. L.S. hired a full-time financial adviser to manage their holdings for his children after that.

One reason L.S. had given stock to his children was to avoid paying taxes. His own share was now down to 2.26 percent. Sam, Mike, Joe, and Mark each had just under 11 percent. Mary Anna and Paul held 9 percent. Jimmie had ended up with 7 percent, while Sophia and Cecilia each held just over 6 percent. Theresa had 4 percent, and Katrina just 3 percent. As the youngest children came along, L.S. had less and less to distribute.*

For years he voted the shares for his minor children, and the fact that it was they who owned U-Haul was not an apparent reality. But by 1980 only Theresa and Katrina were still minors, and the others were voting their own stock. For several years L.S. automatically asked them for proxies and received a majority of the shares in return. Joe, Mark, and even Mike refused him their proxies and voted their own shares.

What L.S. did not comprehend was that he had become the very type of minority shareholder for whom Joe had always demonstrated such contempt. And once a majority of his children were of age, L.S. was just another U-Haul employee subject to dismissal like any other.

By late 1981 Dennis Saban and Mark were at each other's throats as the cars Mark had ordered in Germany piled up in California. The source Dennis had used to convert them to U.S. requirements was backed up and couldn't get to them. The pair had done nothing about setting up shop to do the work for themselves. Dennis tried to stop the flow of cars and demanded a refund from their new-found German middleman but had no success. At one point, exasperated by the impossible task they faced, Dennis suggested that Mark forfeit his $250,000 deposit, much to Mark's horror.

While the pair was grappling with all this, the value of the dollar

---

*These percentages are correct as of December 1986. Slightly different percentages appear on documents depending on how many shares of stock were in existence at the time.

declined in relation to the German mark. Overnight much of the profit in the cars had been wiped out. Dennis told Mark they absolutely had to have more money, and Mark said he was in such poor financial condition that the only way he could get more was to borrow from one of his siblings.

Dennis had been trading commodities with mixed results and had used Mark's money to try to "hedge" some of their potential losses. For a time he ran an account in Mark's name and enjoyed some success, but overall the pair was losing everything, especially when Mark, on his own, overleveraged and lost.

Dennis suggested that he give Mark as many of the cars to sell as possible and then Dennis would file for bankruptcy. He was gambling, and another business deal had gone sour, so he was technically bankrupt already, or so he argued.

Mark reminded Dennis that their fathers were in business together and that he was in a position to make things very hard for Ned Saban. Whenever they spoke, Mark insisted the meetings take place at Form Builders, where Joe played the heavy while Mark stood by. Joe and Mark both were very angry at Dennis, and he was frightened of them and what they might do to him.

At one of these meetings Dennis told Joe and Mark that he had arranged with a "friendly banker" to overdraw his account by three hundred thousand dollars and had lost the money. He said he was in serious trouble over it and was facing criminal charges.

Joe told him, "You are better off being in trouble with the bank than you are being in trouble with me. You just go get all of the money you can and you get as much as you can back to me—now!"

Dennis had limited resources by this time. He offered to give Mark his house, which Dennis believed held four hundred thousand dollars in equity. Mark declined. Dennis tried again to get money out of his father, telling Ned, "There's not going to be any more U-Haul business," if he didn't help out. Ned agreed to allow his lawyers to meet with Mike, Joe, and Mark, but afterward Ned vetoed the idea of helping further until there was a proper accounting of the money that had changed hands between Mark and his son. This was something Mark refused to provide.

With proceeds from the sale of some cars, Dennis believed Mark was only "at worst a little bit over break-even" in their business deals. Since Dennis was going to eat the losses and faced prison for the bank loan, he thought this was an equitable arrangement.

Mark didn't agree. As he told the story, Dennis Saban had cheated him out of $750,000, and he intended to get it back.

At 8:00 A.M. on Sunday, January 4, 1982, neatly attired in a sports jacket and slacks, as if he were on his way to church, Mark drove to Dennis Saban's house. He stood at the front door with his wife and their young daughter. Joe and Darrell Hamby were also with him, concealed on each side of the doorway.*

When Dennis, dressed in a terry-cloth bathrobe, answered the door, Mark asked politely, "May I come in?" Dennis had taken Joe's statements to him to be threats, but seeing Mark with his wife and daughter put him off his guard, and he opened the door. Joe and Hamby barged in. They demanded to know where Dennis's girl friend and two small children were. Hamby then rushed to her bedroom where she was on the telephone talking to a Realtor when Hamby ordered her to hang up. She refused, and when he stepped forward and took the telephone from her, she bolted from the room.

Mark's wife and daughter stood off to the side but could see what was taking place. "Do you have coffee?" Joe demanded. When Dennis pointed it out, the pair poured it over Dennis's head while they told him they were there to get Mark's money. The men cursed at Dennis, telling him what they intended to do to him. Then they forced him out to the guesthouse by the swimming pool.

Mark produced a legal document and shouted, "You sign this, you son of a bitch!" Dennis sat down and began reading the papers when Mark struck him on the side of his head. Joe slapped him on the other side, then pulled out a handgun. They ordered him straight to the signature page, and as Dennis wrote the first letter of his name, he was certain that these men intended to kill him once the signature was finished.

*Edward J. "Joe" Shoen, Mark Shoen, and Darrell Hamby all deny this event as recounted here.

Dennis's girl friend, who had reached the guesthouse by now, spotted Joe and Mark working her boyfriend over. Joe ordered her back to the main house. Hamby took her to the bedroom, disabled the telephone, then gave her a red pen with which to mark her belongings, telling her they were taking everything else and if she left the bedroom again, he would kill her.

Back in the guesthouse Dennis finished signing his name. Joe still had the gun, and Dennis was convinced the men planned to kill him. Mark told Joe that he had the situation under control, so Joe pocketed his gun and went into the house, where he and Hamby began removing paintings and sculptures from the residence.

When Dennis left the guesthouse, Mark pushed him into the pool. Whenever Dennis tried to swim to the edge, Mark ran over and kicked him back into the water or pushed his head under. Dennis's bathrobe was binding him, and he didn't know what to do. He was convinced Joe was going to come back out and kill him, so he had to get away if he could. He stripped off the robe, beat Mark to the far end of the pool, ran across the lawn, jumped the fence, and pounded on his neighbor's door. Once inside he called the police.

Back at his house Joe, Hamby, Mark, his wife and daughter quickly left, taking a black 911 Porsche Dennis had been driving. Dennis reported to the police when they arrived that the men had stolen $6,000 in cash, a Rolex watch, five paintings, and four sculptures, all valued at $188,000.

Responding to the call was Paradise Valley Police Officer Harry Morrison. Morrison took Dennis's statement and that of his girl friend. Just on its face there appeared to have been a kidnapping when the girl friend was moved and held against her will, robbery, and theft. Morrison obtained a search warrant at nine forty-five the next morning, then, accompanied by other officers, headed for Mark's house near the towers to search for the missing items.

When they arrived, they discovered a newly planted For Sale sign in the yard and a locked house. Two Phoenix police officers were summoned to assist, and Morrison entered the residence, where he discovered most of the furniture and clothing gone, but a number of personal items still there. In talking to the neighbors,

Morrison learned that Mark had loaded a U-Haul truck the day before and been gone by 8:00 P.M. The neighbors expressed surprise at this turn of events as they were unaware Mark and his wife were planning to move.

Marcie Saban was furious when she learned what had happened and called L.S. to tell him she would not be seeing any more of him. "If you knew what your sons did at the house, you'd be ashamed of them," she told him.

L.S. heard none of the details, and it is unlikely he wanted to learn them. He knew that for some time Joe and Mark insisted that Dennis had conned Mark out of much of his estate, and as always L.S. was disposed to believe his children. Whom he actually believed or whether or not his child was right, however, was never really the issue, not this time, not ever. Joe and Mark were in trouble, and as in the past, he gave the orders that they be extricated from the charges they faced.

When Joe and Mark called Sam and tried to persuade him to store the stolen car in one of U-Haul's warehouses in Las Vegas, he refused and withdrew from any effort to save his brothers. But James Carty, who still worked at U-Haul, assured L.S. he could manage this. The man who had often said that for ten thousand dollars he could take care of anyone suggested the family trust him. He would see to it.

A few days after the Dennis Saban incident, accompanied by their lawyers, Joe and Mark presented themselves to police officer Morrison for questioning and related a brand-new story, arguing that they had done nothing wrong. This was very different from what they had told their siblings. With them the pair had bragged about what had taken place and gleefully recounted how they avenged themselves on Dennis Saban. Mark told of pushing Dennis's head under the water and said he had humiliated Dennis.

L.S. instructed his lawyers to keep the pressure on officials—U-Haul was one of Arizona's largest employers—and incredibly no charges were filed. It was Dennis Saban who, charged in an unrelated matter involving his commodities trading, went to prison two years later.

This incident ended L.S.'s friendship not only with Marcie but with Ned Saban as well. Ned came to L.S. and tried to explain that Dennis had not cheated Mark out of $750,000, that there was another side to this story, but L.S. refused to listen, and their personal and business relationship was terminated, though not without a bitter and protracted lawsuit. Ultimately Ned Saban broke free of U-Haul and operated his own rental business in Phoenix.

The story spread like wildfire throughout U-Haul Towers. It was common knowledge that Ned Saban and L.S. were fast friends and longtime business associates and not unknown that L.S. was dating Marcie. The idea that two sons of these men were at each other's throats was titillating. There was little doubt, as the story was told, about who the thugs had been.

Joe was not well regarded by employees because of his intimidating tactics against them when he had been president, and Mark was infamous for his quick temper and violent behavior. The effect of the Saban incident, as it came to be known, was to increase apprehension toward the two sons and affirm what many already believed to be true: Joe and Mark were dangerous.

CHAPTER TEN

MR. MAGOO

In 1982 L.S. and Carol Copeland flew to Japan on a trip sponsored by the U.S. State Department. Along with other entrepreneurs from America, L.S. toured plants, where he was struck by the management style. For years Joe had battered him with his philosophy of push-button management and argued that L.S. was out of touch because he continued to work the field and glean fresh ideas from lower-level employees. In Japan L.S. saw his own approach institutionalized. Line workers were routinely asked for input, and upper management responded. Innovation and progress came from the bottom up, not from the top down, as Joe insisted.

When L.S. returned from the trip, he was reassured that he had always been on the right track in how he managed U-Haul, and he was determined to pursue his ideas even more aggressively.

Following her sophomore year in high school Katrina could no longer tolerate Donald Anderson and moved into the Tatum House with L.S. and Carol. In the vast mansion occupied by only Carol and her daughter, Katrina had her own living space and great personal freedom. She found she enjoyed the experience and was drawn at once to Carol.

Though she was just fifteen years old, Katrina realized that L.S. had an odd taste in his women, and at first it was hard to believe that he had finally ended up with one who had such a sweet disposition. Carol had at last brought peace into L.S.'s personal life. It was plain for everyone to see. With this measure of stability in his private life and his increasing zeal for the management of U-Haul, any thought that L.S. was going to fade away into old age or sink into chronic depression or illness was ended. With his young, beautiful, and supportive fiancée, there was a fresh spring to his step, an eagerness to address new problems, and an enthusiasm for the growth of U-Haul that had been absent for years. He was firmly in control of the company and from all appearances intended to remain so for years to come. This was not welcome news to everyone.

Several months after the Saban incident, during the summer, police officer Morrison received a call and was asked to come to Dennis Saban's house, which was on fire. Although flames were visible when he arrived, the house had not been entirely consumed by the fire. A strong odor of gasoline permeated the structure, and Morrison was told that the fire was a result of arson but that whoever had done it had not been terribly adept. He had doused the house with so much gasoline, it had inhibited the flames.

Looking beyond the fire damage, Morrison was struck by how different Saban's house appeared from when he had been there before. In the dining room were a plant, one old table, and a single picture on the wall. There was no other furniture. Throughout the house most of the original furniture was absent, and beat-up tables and chairs were scattered around.

For some time now Joe and Mark had not been content with, as some said, "beating the rap." The rumor was that they wanted revenge and were engaged in a vendetta to destroy Dennis. Dennis claimed that Mark had hunted him down one night and pursued him across town while Dennis had tried to escape in his Porsche. According to Dennis, Mark had fired at him with a pellet pistol. The exaggerated story making the rounds at U-Haul Towers was that the handgun had been a .357 magnum.

Aspects of the arson pointed suspicions at Dennis, and his situation was not improved when he expressed surprise the house had not gone up entirely in flames and kept revising his loss list. But these reactions had harmless explanations as well, and Dennis steadfastly denied any knowledge of or involvement in the arson.

Asked by Morrison to name suspects, Dennis gave him the names of Joe and Mark Shoen. According to Dennis, when he had moved his girl friend to Baltimore, Maryland, Mark had placed his house under surveillance and had it torched once it was empty.

Others, having watched the feud rage for nearly a year, were prepared to believe Dennis's innocence. Joe and Mark could have burned the house in vengeance. Again word spread through U-Haul Towers, and whenever Joe and Mark were present, employees averted their eyes, stopped speaking, and tended to business.

However, in meetings at U-Haul Joe and Mark claimed that Dennis was responsible for the arson, and to that end James Carty had worked at establishing a close relationship with Morrison. As an ex-prosecutor he talked the talk of a brother law enforcement officer, and Morrison was inclined to trust him. James went to L.S. and said he believed the arsonist could be located if they spread a little "street money" around the city. L.S. gave James two thousand dollars in cash, which James gave to Morrison in an envelope.

Morrison saw nothing wrong in taking the money and within days had located a man named Steve Porter, who confessed to committing the arson for pay. Phoenix's Silent Witness Program declined to compensate Porter, and Morrison claimed he used the payment to keep Porter out of sight until he could testify. To others it looked as if the detective had taken a bribe to pin the arson on Dennis and had pressured someone into doing his bidding.

There was some controversy on exactly whom Porter was going to finger. Morrison believed Porter would testify he had been hired by Dennis, but others thought Porter had said he was hired by a young Shoen from U-Haul who wore a beard, a description that fitted Mark. He was scheduled to appear before a grand jury on a Monday, at which time he was to testify under oath on exactly who had hired him.

That Sunday night Porter went to a seedy bar in central Phoenix near the courthouse. Called Lil's Convention Center, the bar was locally notorious for shootings, stabbings, and the ready availability of prostitutes. During the evening Porter was shot to death in the men's room. No one was charged for the murder, and the criminal investigation into the arson of Dennis Saban's house was dropped. No charges were ever filed.

Joe and Mark were enraged that Dennis was not arrested for Porter's murder or the arson. They repeatedly told their father that they could not accept that Dennis had got away with first arson and now murder. From their perspective it was clear that Dennis had contracted with someone to eliminate Porter.

However, to Dennis Saban it looked as if the contract killer had been hired by Joe and Mark, and it was the two Shoen boys who were getting away with murder as well as arson.

When Morrison's superiors learned he had taken two thousand dollars in cash, they expressed their disapproval by forcing him to resign. When L.S. was informed, he promptly hired Morrison to work in security for U-Haul.

Harry DeShong, Jr., the longtime friend of Joe and Mark and son of one of U-Haul's senior executives, worked for the company after dropping out of college, then entered the Army and was sent to Vietnam. Upon his discharge he paid a call on L.S. in uniform and told his former employer that he had been in the "black berets," that he had seen a great deal of combat and even been wounded. He pulled up his pants leg and displayed where a portion of his calf muscle was missing from the injury.

L.S. had remained close friends with DeShong's parents and could not deny the war hero a job when he asked for one. And because he had known DeShong since he was a teenager, L.S. decided to take him under his wing, to be his mentor in the company. For almost anyone that preferential treatment would have been a guarantee of success.

DeShong worked a short time in the Phoenix area. Then L.S. dispatched him to Logan Frank, an ADVP in Dallas, and told Frank to work with DeShong, that here was a young man with a future in the organization. DeShong was assigned to marketing, but soon Frank was reporting his strange behavior back to L.S.

At a service station that was to become one of U-Haul's centers DeShong had placed redwood pots overflowing with gaudy flowers around the site like a moat. The colors clashed with the facility, and there were so many pots it looked silly. There were other examples of such activity, so L.S. tried DeShong with ADVP Sam Brown.

Brown was another longtime employee L.S. held in very high regard. This was at a time when U-Haul was aggressively going into centers and substantial sums of money were being spent on construction and renovation.

The centers in DeShong's area were losing money. Finally, Brown told L.S. that he no longer wished to be held accountable for DeShong and the money he was costing the company.

L.S.'s opinion of DeShong changed after these experiences. As L.S. put it, the slickly dressed, heavy-lidded man was "full of shit." He was a "braggart" and a "bully" who was incapable of seeing business reality.

At a meeting of ADVPs it was common to discuss difficult employees and try to find a place for them in the company. It was not unusual for two ADVPs to swap each other's problems. L.S. said that DeShong had "lived long enough off his father and mother's reputation." The two ADVPs who had worked with him discussed his problems at length, and no one volunteered to take him on. Finally L.S. looked at John Fowler and said, "You're a tough ass. Find the coldest place you can for him because he loves the warm weather," and then he laughed. Fowler dispatched DeShong to Buffalo, New York.

Fowler had no better luck with DeShong, whose construction projects ran as much as 35 percent over projections. Rather than address the cost overruns DeShong spent his time relating his war stories around the office. Once Fowler commented that it seemed to him that Vietnam veterans were quick to use the war as an excuse for failure. "If we'd done that after World War Two, the whole country would have fallen apart," he said. DeShong replied that that wasn't the case for him. "I was there," he said. "It didn't bother me. You get used to killing."

The last straw came when Fowler inspected a newly built center on which DeShong had installed a mansard roof, one completely contrary to the standard U-Haul design. He appeared genuinely amazed that Fowler was not pleased. After that Fowler clamped down so hard on DeShong that he could not make a decision without Fowler's approval.

L.S. and Carol stayed with DeShong and his wife, Patti, whenever L.S. was in Buffalo on business. L.S. regularly visited with Joe's wife, Heidi, and knew the two women were good friends. L.S. was distressed by what he saw. DeShong's office was elaborately decorated in gaudy colors, and everywhere L.S. looked it seemed to him that DeShong was mismanaging the operation.

DeShong proudly displayed his elaborately appointed basement, complete with a big-screen television, an expensive rarity at the time. That evening DeShong invited L.S. and Carol downstairs to watch a pornographic movie with him and Patti. L.S. declined, then was shocked later when he overheard DeShong aggressively lobbying Carol to join him for the movie. She had no interest, and L.S. was upset with DeShong. His answer should have been good enough.

At this time Sam was still responsible for the East Coast, and he had occasion to stay over at DeShong's as well. On one visit, after Patti had put their children to bed, DeShong blurted to Sam enthusiastically, "There's this video you've got to see!" Sam joined the couple in the basement where DeShong slipped a tape of *Deep Throat* into his VCR. Sam was so surprised he scarcely knew how to react. Finally he started a nonstop conversation and ignored the video until DeShong turned it off.

But DeShong's lack of business acumen and social graces wasn't his only problem. He was a conspicuous braggart around the office and gloried in his stories of Vietnam. He claimed the "black berets" to which he belonged had engaged in search-and-destroy missions. He spoke affectionately of the camaraderie of war and said he often went into battle high on marijuana. When they were stoned one night, he and his men fired tracers into the air to watch them. He had loved the war, or so he said, and one night at a party he leaned over Mary Anna and said drunkenly, "Don't let anybody kid you [about Vietnam], it was a lot of fun."

But most disturbing was his tendency to suggest killing as a means of settling business differences. People couldn't tell if he was joking or serious. When something had to be done about someone, DeShong would say, "If you can't pull the trigger, I know someone who can." More than once he suggested U-Haul should simply kill opponents and described himself and another U-Haul employee, Frank Langford, as combat veterans with "a license to kill."

It seemed to Sam that DeShong was one of those men who had returned in good physical health but was still a casualty of war, diffused, unfocused, irresponsible. His first marriage to a fine woman had ended in divorce, and now he was making a mess of this golden chance L.S. had given him.

But L.S. had had enough and reluctantly fired DeShong. He had hedged for months but decided the man was simply unstable baggage he could no longer tolerate. Heidi was enraged, and Joe expressed his anger with his father as well. With DeShong out of U-Haul Patti was no longer part of the upper management family, and her well-being was in jeopardy since there was little likelihood DeShong could land a job with similar pay. But despite Joe's anger and Heidi's entreaties, DeShong stayed fired.

In the fall of 1982 L.S. and Carol were again out of the country, this time in Europe, and not everyone was appreciative of the job Sam was doing as president of U-Haul International. Of the oldest children Sam was the least likely to cast himself into an adversarial role with his father and as a consequence was accused of being a yes-man. At L.S.'s direction that year Sam was supervising the annual Amerco shareholders' meeting, which for all practical purposes was a gathering of the adult Shoen children who cared to attend or for a voting of their proxies. Joe and Mark, who as always had given their proxies to no one, showed up, expressing their determination to take control.

Joe ranted, as he had for several years, that the company was headed for bankruptcy, that the birthright of the children was threatened by a bumbling and incompetent father who was out of touch with contemporary business practices. According to Joe, U-Haul was tottering on the edge of the abyss and the financial reports for 1982 to date were "frightening." Assets were $1.75

billion, and the posted profit of $30 million was a clear indication that the company was in serious trouble.

On a personal note Joe added that he "had developed the tastes of a wealthy man" over the years, something that came as no surprise to those present, but that he could not afford a house, a car, or private schools for his two children. Space Age Paint, according to Joe, wasn't producing enough money for him to buy a new pair of shoes or an electric typewriter.

What Joe was not mentioning was his sizable estate income or that Form Builders was posting earnings in excess of one million dollars a year with its captive client. L.S. had recently cut Joe's and Mark's salaries to twelve thousand dollars a year when he realized how much Form Builders was billing U-Haul, and that was very likely the reason for this outburst. The two years Joe had drawn full salary were also something he omitted.

Mark now shot to his feet. What he and Joe wanted was a board without their father or Sam. He and Joe would serve on it and set things right. Mark said that if the shareholders reelected the existing board, which included both L.S. and Sam, they all would live to regret it. It was his hope they had better sense than that, but if they went ahead against his warning, "I hope I am still alive to wish all of you and your children ill will."

Finally the pair railed against the two million dollars earmarked for the employees' profit-sharing plan. That money should more properly have gone to pay all of them dividends.

Sam presented the other side for his father and him. Jartran was depressing profits, and debt was climbing as the company continued its expansion into centers. The company was robust and profitable despite that. With his shares and the proxies Sam voted the old board back into place much to Joe's and Mark's anger.

On October 22, 1982, Joe wrote his father:

Dear L.S.

In response to your letter, I am out of U-Haul. If you want to goof off then please do as you want.

You have my never ending respect as my father as a great

organizational talent. In my view you have chosen your subordinates, and you have elected not to choose me....

*The children you have chosen as your subordinates and suc-
cessors in U-Haul have never offered to carry their own weight
let alone help carry part of your burden.*

I am out of U-Haul. I am still your son, you are still my father.
I will do a great deal to help you. U-Haul however can treat me
like a stockholder. That means treat me well, pay me income.
U-Haul is an organization to which I belong only as a shareholder. U-Haul has been playing with me.

Your Son
JOE

I will be a testament to what you have told me many times.
"Shirt sleeves to shirt sleeves in 3 generations." *I am tired of
being called a failure. I have excelled at being your son. I work
hard, I am honest. Tell that to your dope smoking children*
[emphasis in original].

In 1982 Joe located a ranch in Sunflower, a rural area seventy-
five miles northeast of Phoenix called the Circle Bar. Just off a
state highway, it was a remote, private area, and Joe secured the
use of two houses along with more than sixty acres of pasturage
and a shooting range. Mark took over one house, and Joe the
other.

The cattle were tended by vaqueros out of Mexico, rough, unschooled men, reared in a system of patronage and peonage. At
first glance this appeared out of place for Joe, but L.S. had noticed
that his son seemed to prefer primitive people over whom he could
feel superior. On the ranch Joe was *el jefe, el patrón,* absolute
master over these crude, violence-prone men. The Sunflower ranch
was a land to itself and completely secure, a private world with
its own rules. For a time Frank Langford, the veteran DeShong
bragged had a "license to kill," managed the ranch.

There were roundups of the cattle, branding, and butchery, and
on occasion, the vaqueros used a large needle with which they
inoculated the cattle against infection.

Despite Paul's assurances as a teenager to his father, it appeared
his involvement with marijuana had not ended. In November 1982,

twenty-six-year-old Paul was charged in Shasta County, California, with cultivating marijuana. The police had located three fields of mature marijuana plants on a "ranch" of Paul's, complete with a watering system and a greenhouse with seedlings. Paul's associate in the enterprise told Sam that he and Paul were engaged in a commercial scale marijuana operation, that Paul had financed it while others managed the "ranch" and sold the product.

L.S. was relieved some months later when the charges were dropped for lack of evidence.

Mary Anna had served on the U-Haul board from 1975, when she was twenty-two years old, through 1980, when she left because the meetings so often disintegrated into "donnybrooks." Throughout her life she had tried to be the peacemaker with her four older brothers, but she found herself no longer effective in that role. Joe and Mark just did not seem to want to be reasonable. They appeared to be unhappy, insisted on dissecting every issue in a highly combative manner, made outrageous claims about the company, pounded their fists on the conference table to intimidate, and were, in general, thoroughly unpleasant.

Other members of the family coming of age had similar experiences on the board. It was not uncommon for Joe to rave at the top of his voice, then viciously sweep books off the conference table, tossing them all over the room as he stormed out. Theresa, for one, had quit because she could not tolerate the acrimony.

In 1983 L.S. and Carol flew to Las Vegas to be married, then went on to San Francisco for a conference. Shortly after that they traveled to China to attend an international trade meeting of top U.S. business executives. At a massive warehouse in China L.S. was intrigued by statues of dragons, elephants, and lions and for twenty thousand dollars ordered a set to be shipped to U-Haul Towers. The lions were the Chinese symbol of a trading house and signified good luck. He intended to place them beside the entrance to the towers and anticipated that his Asian guests, especially potential financiers, would be subtly impressed with his sensitivity toward China and his commitment to the Orient. Besides, he liked the statues.

*   *   *

By 1984 U-Haul had developed more than one thousand centers and become a major national player in the renting of general merchandise. The number of traditional rental agents was down to five thousand. When L.S. had created the Amerco holding company in 1969, he had given the name very careful consideration because he had come to believe that the name U-Haul was a mistake.

On its face it was a clever moniker that was highly effective in advertising the initial purpose of the company. U-Haul no longer painted its trailers entirely in orange; they were now either silver or white with a distinctive orange band, but the block U-HAUL in black was virtually a household name.

L.S.'s evental plans for the company had become much bigger than simply renting trailers. While Joe appeared obsessed with the idea that U-Haul was trailers, trailers, trailers, L.S. took that as a sign of his limited vision and of how impressionable he had been in his early years. A more fitting name for the company L.S. reasoned would have been U-Move. It encompassed the U-Haul concept but also suggested other ways of moving, such as the van line U-Haul now began, Movers World.

L.S. had been looking far beyond moving and wanted a new, though generic, name that could adapt to cover any direction in which the company moved. Amerco was his choice, and from the time it was organized L.S. ceased using the name U-Haul when he referred to the company. He hoped that as employees grew accustomed to the use of Amerco, it would broaden their vision or at least make them susceptible to new ideas.

Creation of the centers had been a very difficult experience for the company. The old rental agent had a number of advantages, including a service station's extended hours seven days a week. When U-Haul bought a center location, renovated or built a structure, and hired employees, it could not be an eight-to-five operation.

At first L.S. had been unable to persuade staff to buy merchandise to rent out, so he resorted to buying en masse, often when he was in Asia, and just shipping it to ADVPs to whose accounts he would bill the cost. This included VCRs, jet skis, cribs, video cameras, and all manner of tools. In some cases his stratagem worked, but in many situations the expensive items just sat in storage until someone finally put them out for rent. Stories of massive thievery were rampant in the company.

Longtime employees were disquieted by all this, and many viewed it as just more of L.S.'s foolishness. The baby cribs L.S. had shipped proved unsafe, for example, and had to be destroyed. The whole operation looked haphazard, ill conceived, and grandiose. Take the names, for example: Movers World, Hitch World, RecVee World. Employees joked that L.S. thought he was going to take over the world from his eleven-story towers in Phoenix, Arizona.

L.S., on the other hand, did not care about how the program was perceived. Once the bugs were worked out, once U-Haul learned what could, and could not, be profitably rented, the expense would stop, and U-Haul—i.e., Amerco—would be the dominant rental force in the nation. The profits would be immense and more than compensate for the millions the expansion had cost. So when senior ADVPs grumbled to him about the waste, L.S. shook them off. The cost was negligible compared with the opportunity. L.S., nearing the end of his productive years, was a man very much in a hurry, and because he failed to take the time to explain what this was all about, many didn't understand. Joe was no longer alone in his claim that U-Haul was going broke.

In fact, the company debt had grown at a remarkable and disturbing rate. From a maximum of $150 million in the early 1970s, it had ballooned under L.S.'s period of massive expansion and redirection to $560 million by the early summer of 1984. The number of employees had shot up from 12,000 to more than 22,500 the same summer, while the number of centers now stood at 1,200.

L.S. had always addressed the problem of debt with absolute devotion since debt servicing was lost money. U-Haul's cash-rich period was the summer, and it was common for L.S. to position the company's profit-generating operations each spring to maximize income. Then in the fall, when the annual income was essentially known, he cut costs, if necessary, to ensure a profit. Despite the acquisition of thousands of parcels of land, the purchase of tens of millions of dollars of general merchandise, the renovation or construction of hundreds of center buildings, and the diminished income caused by Jartran, U-Haul had posted a profit every year of the expansion that had begun in 1975—this, even though L.S. had concluded that Jartran was costing U-Haul a hundred million dollars in net profit each calendar year since 1980.

The spring of 1984 L.S. cautioned his ADVPs to put on the brakes, but there had been no measurable reaction. He had been concerned with prodding his naturally conservative ADVPs to expand into nontraditional areas. Now that expansion was out of control, in his opinion.

On July 19, 1984, he learned for the first time the new magnitude of the debt and the rate at which it was growing. The next day he telephoned the ADVPs and ordered a stop to all construction and hiring. He dictated a memo to Sam, Mike, and Paul at U-Haul Towers to halt all real estate purchases and cut truck repair costs to a minimum. He made it clear that every nonessential expenditure of funds was to cease.

By July 25 U-Haul's debt had grown to $573 million and was still rising. L.S. ordered that parcels of real estate were to be sold to raise cash. But within weeks the debt topped $600 million. L.S. was finding it very difficult to stop what he had begun.

L.S. ordered the two employees who worked on Mark's race cars transferred to other duties and had the racing team operation disbanded. The company could no longer afford such a luxury no matter how much pleasure it gave Mark. L.S. also hoped that by closing the team, he would reduce Mark's disruptive visits to U-Haul Towers, where he was constantly stirring up trouble. Mark was furious when he learned what his father had done.

Following one more near disaster in the air, L.S. ordered U-Haul's three planes sold as part of the expense cutback and gave up private flying.

In late 1984 L.S.'s Chinese statuary arrived to much local fanfare. It was necessary to block off traffic on busy Central Avenue to lift the massive matching lions into place. Employees streamed out to view another of L.S.'s expensive eccentricities. The statues were written up in the local papers, and the tour bus for the art museum added U-Haul Towers to its route.

By November 1984 L.S. was still not convinced U-Haul's debt, now standing at $621 million, was under control. On November 19 he cut the salaries of all top executives 10 percent and canceled the annual employees' Christmas bonus, then ordered a review of U-Haul's pay structure. He gathered a number of ADVPs and promptly shut down four U-Haul plants, laying off 100 employees just before Christmas. In all he reduced the size of U-Haul from its peak of 22,500 earlier that year to 18,500 in just a few months.

L.S. was fairly niggardly in his salaries, relying on his offer of security and bonuses to retain employees. In the span of a single month he had undercut both. When word of discontent over the cancellation of the anticipated bonus reached him, he was persuaded to reinstate it but almost immediately reversed himself again, at the peak of the Christmas shopping season. That evening, as employees filed out of U-Haul Towers, they quietly taped the notice over his twenty-thousand-dollar statues until the lions were completely covered in a paper cocoon.

Incredibly L.S. was still unhappy that Joe was out of the company. In 1984 they met once again, this time for five hours and Day's report still meant nothing. L.S. offered Joe his old job, president of U-Haul International, if only he would return. Joe refused.

In January 1984 Sam had hired John Peet, a well-recommended local recreational vehicle salesman, to head RecVee World, U-Haul's new motor home rental subsidiary. Throughout 1984 RecVee World expanded rapidly, and more than two hundred centers were adapted to perform maintenance and rentals. Ever since the creation of Form Builders, Sam had been concerned about whether or not U-Haul was in fact receiving fair value for the price of the work it purchased. L.S. had given Sam instructions that Form Builders was to receive all the printing business it was able to handle. More than once Sam attempted to inquire into the profits of Form Builders, but Joe and Mark categorically refused to respond. Twice Sam complained that Form Builders had not delivered material up to specifications, and there had been an argument with Joe and Mark about it, but both times U-Haul ended up accepting the material regardless. When Mark did not approve of the behavior of a U-Haul employee in the purchasing department, which placed orders with Form Builders, he demanded the employee be fired.

Sam simply did not like the client relationship U-Haul had with Form Builders and more than once tried to persuade the U-Haul board to end the incestuous association. Every attempt resulted in hassles, but as long as Joe and Mark enjoyed their father's approval for the arrangement, it continued despite Sam's reservations. The times it appeared Sam might be successful Joe took his young sons over to visit their grandfather while he pointed out that Form Builders was really theirs, not his. The tactic always worked.

Mike's relationship with his father had not improved in the five years since he had joined U-Haul. L.S. met with Mike and his wife more than once to discourse on what he believed it took to be happy in life. Mike took exception to some of what his father said in his book, *You and Me,* and periodically the pair argued when Mike tried to persuade L.S. on a new course of action.

In many regards Mike was the forgotten older brother, a quiet, intellectual with an offbeat wit that took getting used to. It was not uncommon for Mike, in the middle of a business conversation with people he knew, to stand on his head in a corner and continue the discussion as if nothing odd were occurring.

Mike had become a profoundly religious man, though outside organized religion, and had come to view life from that perspective. He was not aware of all of Joe's and Mark's activities, but even at that, his father's approach toward his two younger brothers struck him as dead wrong. *You do not,* he came to realize, *compromise with sin.* By tolerating Joe's and Mark's constant abuses, ignoring their bad behavior, covering for them when they were clearly wrong, L.S. was giving them his implicit approval.

The summer of 1984 Mike was increasingly irritated at being second-guessed by his father. Mike had considered trying to remove L.S. from the board but avoided taking any action. At a meeting in Sam's office in August, Joe and Mark goaded Mike and incited him against his father and Sam. Mike became so agitated that he spit at Sam, then slugged him. The next day Mike apologized. Mike took this as an example of how insidiously manipulative Joe and Mark could be in stirring others into actions they usually rejected.

For some time now Mike had been head not only of the legal department but of the tech center as well. This odd combination had been remarkably successful in reducing U-Haul's liability exposure. L.S. had no complaint about Mike's performance in either area though he was regularly peeved that Mike insisted on voting his shares himself. Hap Carty was now working as the ADVP for Arizona, Utah, and Colorado and refused to travel, preferring to remain in Phoenix. As a consequence L.S. believed his area was not doing as well as it should. L.S. needed a spot for Hap, a place where contact with employees would be minimized. L.S. told Mike that he no longer wanted him to serve as head of both legal and the tech center. He told him to quit the tech center so he could give his job to Hap. Mike refused.

Mike had always prided himself in standing up to his father when he believed L.S. was wrong, and this was such a situation. There was no practical reason for L.S. to insist on this change. L.S. told Mike to choose between the two, and again Mike refused. L.S. told Mike that he should get his M.B.A., that the company would pay for it. After some cajoling Mike agreed but he soon discontinued his studies. In the meantime, L.S. assigned Hap to head the tech center, so Mike quit the company. Or L.S. fired him. It depended on who told the story. In either case Mike was out, though not for long.

Mike returned to U-Haul just after the new year, but only as a staff attorney in the legal department, even though L.S. had decided to overlook his son's "insubordination." Not long after Harry Morrison was hired by U-Haul, Mike fired James Carty because of his continual confrontational manner. James went to L.S., a man whom he constantly criticized, and asked to keep his job. L.S. refused to override Mike but continued James's medical insurance for some time after he left the company and returned to Washington State. Each winter James was a regular visitor at Joe's and Mark's ranch in Sunflower.

* * *

Sam had enthusiastically promoted John Peet within the company and was pleased with U-Haul's rapid expansion into motor home rentals during 1984. Even Joe and Mark had embraced the concept with fervor. To finance many of the first purchases of Winnebagos, fleets were organized and marketed, often to financial institutions now ready to invest in U-Haul, but also to select individuals with the money. Joe and Mark hustled the fleets to their siblings, speaking enthusiastically of this opportunity.

RecVee World was now the leading motor home rental company in America with forty-two hundred units available at eleven hundred centers. Sam was satisfied with its rapid growth, but the expense appeared excessive. As it happened, one of U-Haul's senior employees in Las Vegas had a daughter who worked at a local bank. One day she processed a check for six hundred thousand dollars drawn against a U-Haul subsidiary. She reported this to her father, who called L.S., since it appeared that embezzlement was taking place inside U-Haul. L.S. alerted Sam, who began a quiet investigation.

What he uncovered was that Peet was receiving personal gain at company expense. By the following Monday Sam had frozen all the accounts Peet appeared to be using. He called Peet in for a briefing, then asked him a series of questions suggested by U-Haul's attorneys. Sam then opened the doors to the conference room, fired Peet, and had him served with a subpoena on the spot.

Ultimately, through legal action, U-Haul was able to recover over one million dollars, all but two hundred thousand of the missing money. The criminal case against Peet was eventually dropped.

There was no criticism of the way Sam handled this matter, but his loyalty to Peet, who some believed had taken the company for personal gain, and the fact that Sam had not realized it was occurring caused some to lack confidence in him.

Mark had always bristled at his perceived lack of wealth and, regardless of which side of the Dennis Saban incident one believed, clearly Mark's business dealings there had cost him a great deal of money. Form Builders was receiving more than two million dollars a year from U-Haul, and Mark profited from that.* And while he ran the U-Haul Racing Team, he enjoyed the customary U-Haul perks. Regardless, he was eager to cash in his stock and during 1985 approached Sam, asking that the company buy his shares.

U-Haul had never previously bought such a large block of shares. In fact, the only buyback had been from minority share-holders. Mark pressed Sam to make an offer. After consideration Sam allowed that U-Haul might buy Mark's shares for one-half value, the amount paid to the minority shareholders. Sam went on to say that he did not recommend Mark sell at that price, but it was the best the company could do in the circumstances.

Even at one-half value Mark would have received tens of millions of dollars just for having been born a Shoen. Sam added that he did not know if there were any alternatives, but if Mark wished to investigate, U-Haul would pay the cost.

Mark was furious at the pittance being offered him. And he wasn't going to investigate anything. He said that it was up to Sam to figure this out for him and with that stalked off.

Early in 1985 Joe displayed on his desk at Space Age Paint a copy of a lengthy tract he had written. Hamby noticed on one of his visits that it was entitled "Getting Rid of the Founding Father."

It was not uncommon during this time for Joe to telephone his father and curse him for the death of his mother, Anna Mary. Joe portrayed himself as the only one who had ever suffered in life

---

*Half of Form Builders was held by Mark's minor daughter; the other half was split between Joe's two sons. An example of the income posted to Mark's daughter is as follows. A like sum was divided between Joe's minor sons:

	1983	1984	1985	1986
General rental equip. rents	$ 60,836.00	$ 11,890.00	$ 42,700.00	$ 45,797.00
Building rents	25,000.00	39,000.00	36,000.00	36,000.00
Printing equipment rents	240,000.00	460,000.00	375,348.00	359,436.00
ANNUAL INCOME	$325,836.00	$510,890.00	$454,048.00	$441,233.00
		Sale of Tempe Property	297,542.00	
	1985 ADJUSTED ANNUAL INCOME		$751,590.00	

because he had lost his mother. He attacked L.S. for this, as if he believed that L.S. was responsible for his loss, a position James Carty often held.

To others Joe regularly said, "I suffered big time," then told of the death of his mother. Sometimes when he mentioned an enemy, he suggested the enemy's children should lose their mother as he had as a way of getting even.

Joe's and Mark's campaign to discredit L.S. and Sam was relentless, and increasingly Joe and others were discussing the state of L.S.'s mental health. Twenty-nine-year-old Paul met with Sam to ask what he knew about L.S.'s treatment with Dr. Pitts. Because he was a medical doctor and L.S. had given him liberal access to his physicians, Sam had more information than his brothers, but he was not free to discuss it. Sam asked Paul to keep his speculations to himself because he was concerned how others might use them. He followed up with a letter to Paul.

That April Mark, not Paul, responded in a letter to Sam with copies to his siblings:

DEAR SAM-

Your recent letter to Paul may raise some doubt concerning your reputation as a liar. For this reason let me set the record straight. You are certainly a liar, your words and behavior demonstrate this. You are a willing participant if not the designer of a charade of prejudice and discrimination against members of your own family.... [Y]our specialty has been to create a system in which only you can work with our father.

Mark then accused Sam of providing only certain information about the business to his siblings and "misinformation" regarding their father's "medical diagnosis," and of fostering ill will against those members of the family not employed in the company.

... Sam, when will you apologize to family members [and others] for your continued incompetence, insubordination, deceit and purposeful divisiveness[?]. It has gone beyond an apology—your resignation—is the only acceptable means of saving what little integrity you may still have.... Who are you to "Imagine" what terrible things that "Mark and Joe would do" with information about their fathers [*sic*] illness.... You are an arragoant [*sic*] asshole to think I would use my fathers [*sic*] illness to hurt him....

On April 3 L.S., not Sam, responded:

DEAR MARK:

I am truly sorry and saddened that you feel it necessary to write to Doc Sam as you did a few days ago and then copy your letter to his brothers and sisters. You apparently do not realize that you are using him as a scapegoat for your relationship with me. Sam is not a liar in any sense of the word. He is a competent business leader and manager....

The medical diagnosis of my health [you refer to] does not come from my doctor. [The man you used] is a psychologist, not an M.D. Sam has not discussed anything with my doctor except in my presence and I and he never heard the words that some of my sons now think is my diagnosis from Doc Pitts.

You and others seem to want Doc Sam to quit. Just how do you think we are going to operate this business then? Sam is considered to be my successor by the organizations's personnel, bankers and suppliers. He has worked hard and long to gain the respect and trust of these groups....

You, Joe, Mike, Paul, etc., sure are not out of [U-Haul]. You and Joe own a printing company that does essentially all of its business with U-Haul and these purchases totaled $2,163,526.89 for the Fiscal Year 1985. This is a wired business and plenty profitable. The two of you are using the two buildings next to the Towers and have two mechanics on the U-Haul payroll. This alone is worth more than Doc Sam gets paid for working full time with no side deals....

Mark, you are very precious to me. I love you dearly as I do all my sons and daughters....I apologize for any and every injury that I have done to you or any of your brothers and sisters....

But this was not the end of it. Any thought that Mark's comments were his alone ended shortly thereafter. On April 16 Paul sent Sam a letter accusing him of duplicitous conduct concerning their father's mental health. "It is true that you didn't explicitly admit that you knew the nature of L.S.'s emotional disorder for the last seven years," he wrote, "and yet made the conscious decision to keep this information from all those who ethically have the right and responsibility to know."

Paul informed Sam that he had "been designated as the liason [sic]...in the family" concerning L.S.'s mental health. He informed Sam that he knew that Dr. Pitts had diagnosed L.S. as "manic-depressive, a.k.a. bipolar affective disorder," and he accused him of withholding this information from the children. "[Y]ou denied both the relevance and accuracy of the diagnosis, and relentlessly stonewalled the process of getting to the truth and creating an action plan."

These attempts to characterize their father as mentally ill were in Sam's view simply another power play, and their father's diagnosis, if there ever had been one, was their father's business, not his children's. But Paul had taken considerable exception to Sam's not playing along with this family approach to deciding L.S.'s mental health treatment, which had the potential of becoming an end run in the removal of their father from the company.

"You may disagree with people who characterize you as a liar," Paul wrote, "but you can't disagree that I don't trust you as far as I can throw you."

When L.S. saw the letter, he became furious. He knew that he had never received any such diagnosis, and he believed he knew who was really behind this effort. "Paul. There is so much B.S. in this letter," L.S. scribbled across the face of the letter. "Go take a good hard look at yourself.... Your concern for my health is a sham. Your actions speak clearly. You want me dead. This may be an unconscious desire but the effect on me is the same.... Sure it depresses me, but mostly because you and others make Sam the scapegoat." By characterizing L.S. as mentally ill, then attacking Sam for concealing it and failing to see to his proper treatment, these sons were discrediting both L.S. and Sam at the same time.

L.S. took comfort when Mary Anna told her father that Dr. Pitts thought L.S.'s problem was that he had given ultimate control of the company to his children.

It was clear to L.S. that Paul and others were looking for an "action plan" all right, one that would get rid of him. "Some of my sons," he wrote, "confuse health with wealth."

* * *

At about the same time, reacting to his trip to Japan as well as the behavior of Joe, Mark, and now Paul, L.S. wrote the current members of the board, nearly all of whom were his children: "First, I want, and need, to make clear to you that I have finally realized that you each need and must be free of me, as well as of [U-Haul] and all that this implies. You need to and must make your own personal decisions as to how and where you are going to live your life. You must not be bound to me or [U-Haul].... It is cruel to bind you to me or it...."

He had given the matter a great deal of consideration and had decided he had been in error to stock the board with his generally uninformed offspring. He was surprised he had not thought of the solution previously. The new board, he told his children, would be entirely composed of ADVPs, seasoned professionals who knew the company's needs. No more shouting matches, no more power plays, no more fistfights, no more bogus concerns for his mental health.

In addition to their attacks on L.S. and Sam, Joe and Mark had been raising a commotion over U-Haul's financial performance. Its depressed earnings and excessive debt, they argued, were about to cheat them out of their due. Sam arranged a meeting of all the Shoen children at which top financial people would review each of the company's statements in detail. But at the meeting Mark was unconcerned with hearing what they had to say. Instead he demanded to know what sweetheart deals Sam had cooked up for himself in order to skim money out of U-Haul. When Sam said there were none, that all he earned was his salary and director's fee, Mark told him bluntly that he didn't believe him.

During the fall of 1985, with sufficient proxies from his children, L.S. replaced all his offspring, including Sam, and elected his ADVP board. The new board then held a series of meetings to adopt long-needed policies. L.S. stated that the ten-year period of expansion was at an end. Jartran was at last on the ropes, its expensive financing having finally caught up with it, and U-Haul was to enter a period of "circular flow," as L.S. called it, a time when the problems created by expansion would be remedied and the company would refocus on generating profits. L.S. was now satisfied that he had resolved his long-standing board problems and that U-Haul's debt was under control. The cost had been high in hurt feelings and angry employees, but he had done it.

L.S. bought a vast house on Viking Street in Las Vegas and moved there with Carol to maintain the distance from the towers he required to think and plan. By the summer of 1986 members of the ADVP board understood that Sam was the heir apparent and that L.S. would gradually become more of an adviser and consultant. Others understood that message as well.

Generally the Shoen children had conflicting attitudes toward their father. A number of them had grievances against him, real or imagined; others were merely perplexed. Too often his rambling dissertations came across as moralizing. Until recently his own personal life had been a shambles, and the past ten years had been unsettling. U-Haul was not the company of trailers and trucks in which they had been reared and with which they were comfortable.

Joe and Mark, at the least, had learned a revisionist view of the birth and development of U-Haul that enhanced Anna Mary's role and diminished that of L.S. As a result, they were less beholden to their father. For the others, so much of what L.S. tried didn't work. His legendary 180-degree turns were simply failures, and when a new direction did succeed, it appeared to be more by accident than plan.

L.S. understood how his children felt. Most of them didn't know business and did not grasp what he was doing. Some of his closest executives called L.S. a buccaneer behind his back, with pride, and perhaps that explained him best.

But to too many of his children L.S. was Mr. Magoo, the nearly blind, bungling old man, saved from great failure time and again by fate and luck.

CHAPTER ELEVEN

WITH LOVE
AND RESPECT

The previous decade of expansion through which L.S. had directed U-Haul had taken a toll on the confidence most of his children placed in his business acumen. L.S. used conservative bookkeeping practices and carried a debt load substantially lower than that of comparable public companies. U-Haul's debt at the beginning of 1986 stood at between five hundred and six hundred million dollars, about three times higher than that in the early 1970s, but significantly less than that of other companies with nearly one billion dollars a year in income and a value approaching three billion dollars. Had U-Haul used the common accounting practices of publicly held companies, a direct comparison of worth, income, and debt would have clearly demonstrated its sound financial position. But L.S. was the original do-it-yourselfer and would not consider such a switch.

But Joe and others attacked L.S. for being set in his ways. These were modern times that called for modern management techniques. In addition, L.S. and Sam had placed a great deal of confidence in John Peet, who now was shown to have been a thief. How many other thieves were in the company? Taken together, these attacks on L.S., and to a lesser extent on Sam, were having an adverse effect on the shareholders—L.S.'s sons and daughters.

The same sons and daughters were no longer children. Of the offspring born to Anna Mary and Suzanne, who owned voting shares of stock in U-Haul, the youngest, Katrina, was twenty years old and Sam was forty-one with the others spread between them. They were now adults with their own needs and personal expectations that had been shaped by childhoods of privilege.

Only Sam, Mike, and Joe had ultimately prepared themselves in terms of education and in varying degrees by experience to understand business and the operation of U-Haul. The others were for the most part ill equipped to make business decisions, and at least one knowledgeable observer believed that in their judgments they were driven primarily by their own insecurities and fears about losing their wealth. In many ways their material advantages had made them weak and vulnerable, insecure in their natural abilities and fearful that they could lose what they had.

Their father's perceived missteps had shaken their confidence in him and left them feeling exposed. As L.S. moved aggressively with his all-ADVP board, those on whom he depended to retain control of the company had less faith in him than ever before.

That summer L.S. and Carol decided to live in Phoenix at the Tatum House. L.S. wanted to reconcile with Joe and Mark and was determined to find a way to bring them back into U-Haul management. When the sons invited L.S. and Carol to a weekend visit at their Circle Bar Ranch in Sunflower, L.S. was happy to go, viewing this as an opportunity for rapprochement and relaxation.

L.S. and Carol spent a great deal of time in Sunflower, and Mark made a show of preparing a room for his father's use. He told Carol to decorate it as she wanted. He was, she thought, being very "kind and sweet," and she felt that he must really love his father to make such an effort. Later that day, when she saw Joe's wife, Heidi, Carol said that she believed Mark was genuinely trying to heal matters with his father.

The following weekend Mark displayed his other side when he walked up without provocation and whispered in her ear that she had better watch it or he would get rid of her as he had Suzanne. Carol was dumbfounded but decided this was typical behavior for Mark. He was unpredictable, as if the good were struggling with the bad in him. In one telephone conversation he would be solicitous, very calm; in the next he would be highly agitated.

Generally the stays at the ranch were pleasant with the grazing cattle, small lake near the houses, and horseback riding. While L.S. accepted the pleasantries as a sign that at last Joe and Mark were willing to put aside business differences, others were not so certain. That summer there was an air of courtship in the family.

Mary Anna, now thirty-three, who lived out of state, was getting the same message. For the past two years Heidi had been exceptionally gracious to her. Mary Anna was invited to functions at Heidi's house at which the other daughters-in-law, including Eva, were in attendance. Heidi hosted a gala of old college friends, including Patti DeShong, at the Tatum House and made a point to include Mary Anna. During the summer that L.S. and Carol stayed at the ranch, Heidi and Mary Anna took a train trip to visit Anna Mary's alma mater, Marylhurst College. The purpose very likely was to heighten the legendary role Anna Mary had played in founding U-Haul, a theme Joe used routinely to denigrate L.S.'s part.

During the same time Mike decided to make another attempt at reconciliation with his younger brothers. He shared Mark's love of auto racing, and Mike agreed to go with him on a Baja California road race from Ensenada to La Paz.

The brothers had agreed that each would drive half the race. Mark had burned up most of the clutch when he road-tested the car, and it soon gave out on Mike who was leading the race. Mark told him he had figured Mike was going to crash anyway, so what difference did it make?

On the trip back to Phoenix Mark was elated that Mike had burned it out, that Mike had lost the race. Over and over Mark crowed that it had been Mike's failure. That was when Mike understood what this had always been about. Mark may have feared the possibility of his own failure and with Mike's failure, Mark had, in his own way, achieved a victory. On the way back, at every shift of the gears, Mark told Mike when to shift—not occasionally, not usually, not often, but every single time. When they reached Phoenix, Mike had concluded that Mark was "a controlling monster." The entire trip had been one of relentless conflict and Mike decided once again that he had been correct in his earlier decision not to have anything to do with either Mark or Joe.

But just as L.S., Carol, and Mary Anna were being courted that summer, so, too, was Mike. Joe and Mark approached him and asked for his help. It was time, they said, for L.S. to slow down. In principle Mike agreed with them and to that end was willing to cooperate, though he rejected their suggestions that L.S. suffered from a mental illness. They agreed that L.S. should be more accountable to the shareholders and should refrain from acting on his own, as he often did. By shareholders they meant, of course, his children. Then the pair asked for Mike's proxy, which he refused to give, and he doubted, knowing Joe and Mark as he did, that anyone else in the family would give them his or her proxy either.

L.S.'s younger sister Patty Lee had worked for U-Haul over the years and lived near the towers, rent-free, in a company house. For fifteen years she had been in nearly continual psychiatric counseling, which her brother had paid for. Besides her salary, she drew a modest income from a trust L.S. had established for her, but despite this support, she suffered from insecurity.

She had demonstrated fierce loyalty toward her brother and commented more than once that his children were spoiled and failed to appreciate what he had done and was doing for them. She was aware of the situation at the Tatum House prior to L.S.'s and Suzanne's divorce and in her way had tried to be a mother to the children. Joe and Paul had taken immediately to her in this role.

But Patty Lee was in some ways like a child who needed attention by being bad, and while her behavior was acceptable, if strange, she was conspicuously outspoken. She talked frankly with the Shoen boys and shared her opinions freely.

Her insecurities were fed in more than one area. L.S. had become the Shoen family's huge success, eclipsing even his younger brother, who had gone on to become a doctor. And though he had been generous with her and his siblings, none of them shared in the immense wealth of U-Haul. L.S.'s son Jimmie lived next door to her when he was in his mid-twenties. She said that one day he came over to tell her that his dogs would run through her carefully maintained flower beds at will. However he said it or meant it, this so upset her that she pulled out all the flowers herself rather than watch them be destroyed by her nephew's dogs.

She knew that someday L.S. would die and that control of U-Haul and of the house in which she lived would pass to his children. Because of her experience with Jimmie, she became upset about whether she would be allowed to remain in the house once that happened. She had, after all, nothing of her own, not even the trust, which L.S. had never placed in her name.

From her brother's point of view, he had more than fulfilled his obligation to his sister. So when he was desperately fighting to reduce U-Haul's debt and laying off employees and Patty Lee approached him to open a trust for her that she could use to buy her own house, he refused. He spoke without considering her sense of vulnerability or the trivial amount involved.

A second incident soon occurred. Patty Lee had worked in a dead-end job at U-Haul in relative obscurity for years. The manager of her department was absent temporarily, and Patty Lee was asked to fill in. She was a great success, and at the end of a month she asked her brother to make her the permanent manager. L.S. refused.

Not long after that, when a replacement was needed for the receptionist on the eleventh floor of the towers, Sam asked his aunt to fill in. Though a loner by nature, Patty Lee was customarily jovial and a nonstop talker with a loud voice. L.S. was routinely disturbed by Patty Lee's incessant chatter in her new job and told Sam to replace her. According to Patty Lee, the mild-mannered Sam was unnecessarily harsh. She returned to her former job, and when Sam learned she was telling everyone how awful he had been, he apologized, then apologized again and again. It made no difference. She shunned him.

Patty Lee no longer spoke in support of L.S. or Sam. In fact, she routinely railed against them. While Joe and Mark had condemned the two for years, the other children had not. But here was their aunt, Patty Lee, a Shoen herself, condemning L.S. and denouncing Sam, who ran the company. If she could rail against them, just how loyal did other Shoens have to be?

A few years earlier, when Mary Anna approached her father for assistance in starting her business in San Francisco, he had declined, calling her a dreamer; she had been very disappointed. A month later a contractor called her out of the blue and asked how she wanted her building remodeled. L.S. had instructed U-Haul to buy the structure and was paying for the renovations.

She had been very pleased with the progress of her business, but in December 1983 she received a letter from her father that read:

DEAR MARY ANNA:

I have thought and agonized over [your business] ... for as long as is sensible. ... The problem is that where we come from and where we live on a day-to-day basis is so far from the sophistication of [your business] and your lives in that environment that I cannot find any reality in supporting [it] for myself or for the thousands of people working daily in U-Haul. ... Secondly, I watched my sister, Patty Lee, as a beautiful, talented young woman, squander the best part and most of her life, doing what I viewed and still view as the same thing. ... I must get you out of it. ... [I]t is not too late to make a 180 degree turn. ... I am going to, and I ask and need you to help me close [the business] on January 1, 1984, and close out the corporation and get this off your back and off my back. ...

With much love,
L.S.S.

This had been a bitter disappointment, and ever since, though she had her estate income, she wanted greater access to the cash her shares in U-Haul represented.

In 1986 Mary Anna was in counseling to reconcile herself to her mother's loss. She had never fully grieved, and as part of her therapy was induced to re-create conversations with Anna Mary in a dreamlike state. That summer, after Mary Anna returned from her trip with Heidi to Marylhurst College, Joe began calling regularly, soliciting her vote for the fall shareholders' meeting. He was aware of what L.S. had done with her business and said that an enlightened management would have long since been paying dividends. With her shares she could reasonably expect hundreds of thousands of dollars a year in additional income.

Joe called as often as twice a night and in a quiet, insinuating voice told his younger sister that their father was old and had earned a rest. They all loved him and wanted only what was best, but like many successful entrepreneurs, he would have to be shown the door.

Sensing perhaps her emotional vulnerability, Joe poignantly told Mary Anna a story about how he had witnessed a decrepit L.S. at the tech center, so broken down, so beaten up that others had had to help him into a car. The man simply did not know when to stop, and U-Haul was killing him.

Mary Anna had serious misgivings about Joe but still listened to him. He suggested that in her counseling sessions she take this issue to Anna Mary. Mary Anna should ask her mother what she wanted her daughter to do. Mary Anna agreed.

Twenty-year-old Katrina was a student at Brown University in Providence, Rhode Island, when Joe, who was seventeen years older than she, first approached her about the shareholders' meeting set for that fall. She had always understood her 3 percent of stock was a responsibility, and she knew that eventually she would be called upon to make decisions about how it would be voted. Like all of L.S.'s five daughters, until 1986 she had routinely given her proxy to her father and intended to this year as well.

Katrina did not know either Sam or Joe very well but considered them both to be of equal influence. Sam had been running U-Haul since she was in her early teens, and Joe appeared to be a success with Space Age Paint and Form Builders. In the summer Joe called her regularly and spoke very technically about the company. In time she came to see him as a "wordsmith," someone who used talk to get what he wanted, and later she noticed how he always left himself an out, but that summer he was just her older brother expressing his concern for the company in which they both held shares and for the well-being of their father.

She was aware that there were cunning and scheming people in the world, but she believed that basically all or at least nearly all men were good at heart. Certainly this applied to those in her family.

Joe represented to Katrina that he was being neutral and fair when he told her that U-Haul was badly managed by their father. He reminded her that he held a Harvard M.B.A., had previously served as president of U-Haul International when it did very well, and that he was the respected CEO of a highly successful company in his own right. He suggested that others should be given a chance to run the company, that others, including himself, possessed expertise and had a great deal to offer the family. He gave her figures that appeared to her untrained ear to support his presentation. Several times she attempted calling others in the family but reached no one. All the while Joe continued his gentle touch and portrayal of himself as a calm professional.

That summer no one else was courting her. L.S. had no reason to believe that the usual group of children—that is, all those except Mike, Joe, and Mark—would not give him their proxies, and he had no reason to make special appeals to any of his children. Mike knew what Joe was up to but thought it inappropriate to attempt to influence his siblings. He believed Joe was "crazy" and considered that this was obvious to all the children.

Joe's pressure on others of his siblings continued relentlessly. To Mike he suggested that with L.S. more responsive to the shareholders the company would buy back the Carty farm. To Cecilia, age twenty-four, he misrepresented that U-Haul was forced to finance its debt through the commercial paper market at expensive rates because banks would no longer lend it money. Other siblings were told various stories tailored to suit their desires, and always Joe represented their father as old, possibly mentally ill, and frail and urged the children to act to save L.S. from himself.

As the tide turned against L.S., almost no one fully appreciated what was taking place. L.S. had ensured what was about to occur because he lacked the heart to dilute the shares of his oldest children. If he had issued himself more shares, he could have guaranteed he would always have control or if he had modified the rules, only a supermajority of shareholders could have ousted him. He had further sown the seeds for his own removal by failing to educate properly the owners of U-Haul so that they were prepared to make informed business decisions. He had alienated and angered several key players without considering the potential consequences. He had behaved arbitrarily for years, but especially over the past eleven years, neglecting to take the time to explain to his children why he was doing what he was doing and where he was taking the company. He had overestimated the ability and involvement of his younger children.

In planning the future, he neglected the present. Like a football team looking ahead to the championship, he failed to consider the current game—the shareholders' meeting in the fall at which the board of directors would be elected.

Finally he couldn't comprehend how ruthless Joe had become, indeed had been for years, and what he was capable of. Deep in his heart L.S. knew, beyond any doubt, that whatever the differences, his children would never turn on him.

Joe's wife, Heidi, played an aggressive role in returning her husband to U-Haul management. Her motives could be evaluated only later, and not everyone agreed, but it appeared that she was still angry that L.S. had fired Harry DeShong, Jr. She had included her longtime friend Patti at her Tatum House party, perhaps with an eye to getting Patti's husband reinstated.

In many ways Heidi was regarded as the perfect wife for Joe. At first her mother had refused to let her date Joe because she reportedly said L.S. was a gangster who had people murdered, and Heidi's relationship with her mother was just as combative as Joe's was with his father.

Theirs was not a happy marriage. One uncharitable observer once said that Joe had managed to marry Suzanne by marrying Heidi. Joe, for all his faults, appeared genuinely perplexed over how to make his wife happy. Once after an especially ugly scene with her he had turned to the woman beside him and asked, "Is it like this at your house?"

There are those who believed that Joe acted only because of Heidi's instigation. They say the message he received at home was that if he wished to keep his wife, he must again become president of U-Haul International.

This theory contradicts the reality of Joe's behavior during his adult life. He had been locked in a struggle for control of U-Haul with his father before he ever met Heidi. And even in high school Joe had dreamed that he sat on the eleventh floor, pushing buttons, running U-Haul.

Also, there was considerable evidence that all his life Joe was jealous of Sam. He said that he was resentful that Sam, "the good doctor," had known their mother longest. Joe was envious of Sam's close relationship with their father and his happy marriage to Eva. "The good doctor" had taken his place as president of U-Haul; "the good doctor" came first when Joe wanted to be first.

There are many who believe that Joe held animosity toward "the good doctor." This was Joe's chance to act on it.

L.S. and Sam received long-awaited good news with the announcement that Jartran had folded. Jartran had cost U-Haul an estimated half billion dollars in profit during the years when U-Haul's debt had grown threefold. The feisty competitor had made U-Haul's ten-year expansion more difficult and expensive than necessary, and there was rejoicing in the towers at word that it was at last out of business.

In the fall of 1986 U-Haul was, despite early setbacks, the national leader in general equipment rentals, the number one motor home rental company, and first in self-storage. With Jartran out of the picture U-Haul's profit and loss statements would get healthier very quickly.

On September 3 L.S., now seventy years old, wrote his customary letter to his "sons and daughters" soliciting their proxies for the next shareholders' meeting, scheduled for October 25. "It is my judgement that the organization is under control and it is my intention to keep it in this mode for the foreseeable future. Exploiting present targeted markets will give us enough to do for the next ten to twenty years.... With love and respect, L. S. Shoen." L.S. had been even more pleased with the all-ADVP board than he had expected and planned to continue it the following year.

The members of the board had been just as satisfied with the progress the company was making. For years ADVPs and other senior employees had grumbled about the children's influence in the company. Sam was well regarded and the acknowledged heir apparent, but Joe was seen by many ADVPs as an egotistical jerk.

ADVP John Fowler, for one, had held Joe in low esteem from the late 1970s, when Joe bragged that he knew all about the company. It had been clear to Fowler that Joe wasn't interested in learning the basics of the company; he already believed he had the answers. It was also apparent that Joe wanted to work at U-Haul, but only if he was running it. And that was not a pleasant thought since he had this feeling about Joe that he would step on people.

Within a few days L.S. received unexpected proxies from Paul and, of all people, Mark. He could hardly believe it and told Sam enthusiastically that at last his children were prepared to work together. If Mark was willing to give his proxy to his father, could Joe be far behind?

But Sam cautioned his father not to place much trust in the proxies. Either son could rescind his proxy or show up at the meeting in person and vote the shares as he wished. Sam suspected L.S. was being lulled but wasn't certain for what reason.

Despite Joe's blandishments, Katrina forwarded her proxy to her father, as he had requested, and L.S. remained enthusiastic. With increasing confidence he turned his attention toward the American Entrepreneurial Institute, an enterprise he had dreamed about for years through which he would educate young business-people and share his lifetime of experience.

From October 9 to 12 L.S. conducted a combined board and ADVP meeting that Joe attended. Any thought that Joe was pre-paring to become cooperative was put to rest when he started a fight with the head of marketing over paint purchases from Space Age. Joe became enraged with the man, cursed him savagely, then spit in his face. L.S. did everything he could to calm Joe, but his son was so angry he had to be physically restrained.

By mid-October L.S. had received proxies from Sophia, Cecilia, and Theresa. Along with Mark's and Paul's this gave L.S. 51 percent of the shares, but he had yet to receive Mary Anna's or Jimmie's proxy. Perhaps Sam was right about Mark and L.S.

wanted the others just to be on the safe side. These two proxies were ones he counted on, and he was shocked when he spoke to Jimmie, who said he was giving his proxy to Joe. "This puts the shit in the fan again," L.S. wrote. He then learned that Paul would be attending the shareholders' meeting, meaning L.S. could not count on that proxy.

L.S. calculated the numbers. With his 2 percent, Sam's 11, Sophia's 6, Cecilia's 6, Theresa's 4, and Katrina's 3 he believed he controlled approximately 33 percent of the vote for certain. Even though Mike refused to give him his proxy, he usually voted with his father, and that raised the number to 44 percent. If Sam was right about Mark, and L.S. was beginning to think he was, then L.S. needed Mary Anna's proxy. Her 9 percent would give him a comfortable 53 percent, and along with another percentage point or two from minority shareholders that was enough. Once he had that, the others would come back.

Though Mary Anna later realized that she should have sat down and considered what to do with her vote by applying logic, at the time she took Joe's suggestion and during a guided session engaged her mother in a dialogue about what she should do.

Mary Anna had reservations about Joe, but many of his arguments made sense to her. Her father was seventy years old, and she had seen him age noticeably these past ten years. She could easily believe Joe's story of a decrepit father, tottering toward an early death caused by excessive work. She was also upset with L.S. for withdrawing his support from her business, and the prospect of dividends held a strong appeal for her.

Finally Joe had called Mary Anna repeatedly and told her that he controlled a majority of the shares. "This is going to happen anyway," he told her, suggesting it would be best for her if she were on the winning side. He also argued that it would be a more compassionate gesture for the children to act in unison; then L.S. could see they were together in doing this for his own good.

As his oldest daughter Mary Anna held a special place in her father's heart. Like Sam and Mike, she had weathered the loss of her mother without apparent harm, but unlike them, she had been raised by Suzanne yet still emerged a strong adult in whom L.S. had great confidence. She was bright, loving, and supportive, so when he called three days before the meeting to request her proxy, he was certain he would receive it.

Mary Anna told him about her conversation with her mother. In that dreamlike state Anna Mary had told her only daughter that she wanted L.S. to rest. The time had come. Mary Anna told her father that she was giving her proxy to Joe.

It is unlikely that any defection, except perhaps that of Sam, could have devastated L.S. as did that of Mary Anna. Mary Anna had been his bedrock. When L.S. could not depend on Suzanne, it had been his oldest daughter who mothered his youngest children. He believed that he had always been a good father to her, and her decision was nothing less than a betrayal. In one telephone conversation Mary Anna caused L.S. to consider seriously for the first time that he ought to step aside and stripped from him any thought of fighting.

Though the commitments from some siblings were still in doubt, Joe and Mark, wearing their signature leather bomber jackets, barged into Sam's office at the towers and submitted a list of ten unreasonable and unacceptable demands. After a loud fight Sam threw them out. He called his father and the general counsel in for a strategy session.

It is likely that even without legal action L.S. and Sam could have swayed enough votes their way by engaging in tactics similar to those Joe had used. But L.S. believed that his children should be able to see for themselves what he had done for them and he should not have to do anything more than ask for their support.

The lawyer said there were many ways to fight what was about to happen. Joe and Mark were now in the big leagues. "Turn me loose," he promised, "and I'll bury the sons of bitches."

"No, we're not going to have war in the family," L.S. said, vetoing the idea. He would place the family into a win-win situation. In an attempt to discover common ground L.S. called Joe to learn what he was after. When he finished the conversation, L.S. was convinced that Joe had taken a deep-seated hatred of him and transferred it to Sam. But L.S. was still determined to find a way out of this and told all parties that he would step aside if they agreed to a mediated settlement.

L.S. quickly arranged a telephone conference meeting of the twelve ADVPs. All were adamant that they did not want Joe on the board. In a rambling discourse he shared intimate details of his conflict with Joe, revealing so much that one ADVP was moved to ask if he was certain he wanted to tell them these details. L.S. asked that the shareholders' meeting, scheduled for the next day, be delayed, and they agreed uneasily. Then he asked one of the staff attorneys to work with all sides and find a resolution.

When word spread that the shareholders' meeting had been canceled, that Joe controlled a majority, other children quickly switched sides until only Sam was still firmly in their father's camp.

Mediation continued for ten days in an explosive atmosphere and was largely a farce. While Joe attended sessions, he simply made demands others considered unreasonable and refused to yield. One observer described him and Mark as displaying "controlled fury."

"Our father has been too hard on us," Joe said repeatedly. "He must give the company back to the children," suggesting that they had once had it and somehow L.S. had taken it from them. At the beginning session, in which L.S., Sam, Mike, Joe, Mark, Paul, and Jimmie participated, Sam was subjected to such a torrent of rage and obscene language that he was stunned. He and L.S. had tolerated this behavior from Joe and Mark for so many years they were no longer in a position simply to walk away. The meeting was the turning point in the mediation, a pivotal episode that ended any possibility that L.S. or Sam could emerge from this in a positive position. So hostile, so brutal were the negotiations that the first mediator backed out, claiming he had come to dislike Joe too much to remain impartial.

It was clear that Joe had a purpose behind his behavior. If it drove people away, Joe would have the field to himself.

On October 27 Sam and Eva met with L.S. and the new mediator at the Tatum House. For days Sam had looked as if he were in emotional shock. L.S. suggested he would retire and collect the three-hundred-thousand-dollar consulting salary provided for in the employment contract he had negotiated several years earlier.

L. S. Shoen at Oregon State University in 1937

L.S. supported himself in college by operating barbershops such as this one, pictured in 1940. L.S. stands to the extreme right.

L.S. and Anna Mary shortly after their wedding in 1943

Early U-Haul trailers were quite primitive. This was the company's first furniture van trailer, 1949.

L.S. with one of his boys while they were still living in Portland

Sam, Mike, Joe, and Mark in 1953 in front of their Portland home

U-Haul's "First Family" in Portland, 1954, before Paul was born

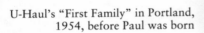

L.S. and his second wife, Suzanne, just after the marriage ceremony in 1959

L.S. and Suzanne in New Orleans in 1964.
L.S. already had a lover.

L.S. and Suzanne at a U-Haul open house at
Tatum House in Paradise Valley in 1968.
The strain in their relationship was already
apparent on Suzanne's face.

Joe bought everyone cowboy hats, then had the
family pose at Legend City in 1969.

With Larviksfjord in the background,
twenty-year-old Eva Berg posed for
her fiancé, Don Erickson, in October
1966, during the week when she
decided to leave Norway with him for
Arizona.

Sophia, Katrina, and Theresa beside
the Frank Lloyd Wright Tatum
House in Paradise Valley, Arizona

L.S., Suzanne, and the eleven Shoen children at the Tatum House in 1971. Not pictured is L.S.'s twelfth child, born the previous year to his girl friend. Mark, Joe, Mike, and Sam (*from left, standing*) comprised U-Haul's senior management when this picture was taken.

Mike and his wife, Christa, share a court victory with U-Haul employees. U-Haul was as much a family to employees as it was the place they worked.

L.S. and Suzie Whitmore at their second marriage. Months earlier they had married to legitimize their son, then divorced. The second marriage lasted three months.

Joe in 1977. Since he was a boy he had dreams of running U-Haul.

Most of the Shoen children with spouses, circa 1977. Joe's wife, Heidi (*holding baby*), is still wearing "old lady" shoes and matching dress.

Eva, with Mike's wife, Christa, and Katrina Shoen, on the outskirts of Phoenix. The boys' wives and the Shoen girls often socialized together.

L.S. hugs Joe the night of the Celebration of Love, even though his son has just ousted U-Haul's founder from power, 1986.

Mike in 1979. Though he worked for his father, he was still very angry with him.

L. S. had his four oldest sons pose with him (*from left: Sam, Mark, Joe, and Mike*) the night Joe successfully engineered his ouster.

Mike displayed for the press the bruises he received from his brothers at the Reno shareholders' meeting. For years before Eva's murder, threats and violence had been tolerated at both board and shareholders' meetings.

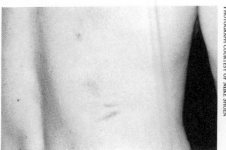

Dr. Sam and Eva in 1986, four years before her murder. Joe called her "horsey."

Sam, Eva, and Bente with Aase and Esben in front, taken in Phoenix; 1988. "Sam is my hero," Eva told friends.

Sam's favorite photograph of Eva, taken on the trail to Hope Lake near Telluride the summer of 1989

Eva walking her dogs on the road outside her log cabin in Telluride that last winter

Eva on a mountain trail near Telluride, spring 1990

Eva and Esben on the coast of Norway, July 1990, just a few days before she was murdered

Telluride officers believe one of Eva Shoen's killers watched the log cabin the night of her murder from where this photograph was taken.

Investigator Kim Pound with the San Miguel County Sheriff's Office pursued Eva Shoen's murderers for over a year before resigning to marry one of L.S.'s former girl friends.

Sheriff Bill Masters at the murder scene, August 1990. In his ten years in office this was his first homicide.

Dr. Samuel Shoen at the reception following his wife's funeral. Had he only agreed to sell his shares in U-Haul to his brother Joe for $16 million, one-tenth their worth, he believed Eva would not have been murdered.

Sam said he was prepared to stick this out for the good of all the family and would serve as CEO even if Joe were on the board. But he would be CEO for only ten years, then quit and someone else could take his place. L.S., relieved to hear this, relayed this news to Joe.

To save face and let his employees know what he intended, L.S. dispatched a cryptic note saying that he had decided to retire. Within the towers word spread that L.S. was being forced out, that it was an ugly scene and L.S. was not retiring, his children were pitching him out.

Two days after Sam's assurance L.S. tried to relax while the mediation proceeded in his absence. "I am exhausted," he wrote. "Carol is happy and I am relieved and joyful but also some sadness. This decision is precipitous and not as orderly as I would have liked but the wise thing under the circumstances as I am able to tell." He told Carol that he was going to keep his "mouth shut" from now on.

Hap Carty, who had spent his business life playing to L.S.'s concept of family loyalty, was busy shifting allegiance behind the scene. At least that is how his behavior was interpreted by some. Initially Hap had expressed shock at the thought of Joe's leading a coalition to oust their father and urged L.S. to fight it. But as its inevitability became apparent, Hap leaned toward Joe and Mark, intent as always to land on his feet.

The shareholders' meeting was now set for November 8, 1986, and L.S. told his children that all he asked was that they "love one another" as a gift to him. Sophia and Mark arranged a buffet at the Scottsdale Hilton, a gala that was given the formal title of "A Celebration of Love." L.S. made it clear that no matter what feelings anyone had, it was his wish everyone attend. As one put it, "We were all to hug each other and act like nothing horrible had happened."

During this time Mike called his father and suggested he look to God in his life. This was not the end of the world, he said, and for a short while L.S. was uplifted. At home Mike spoke with his father-in-law, who asked him rhetorically, "Would you want your son to do this to you?" Mike returned to his father's camp and lobbied his siblings to abandon Joe and elect their father instead.

Mediation was still making no progress as the meeting loomed. Joe adamantly refused to allow Mike to serve on the new board. Sam felt just as strongly then that Joe should not be on the board either. For Joe to continue exercising his proxies, it was understood that Sam must be CEO, otherwise too many who sided with Joe would withdraw their support. His younger sisters had confidence in Sam though his reputation had been sufficiently tarnished by John Peet and the allegations that Sam had not properly seen to the medical treatment of their father that he was unable to knock Joe out of contention for a place on the board.

The night before the meeting L.S. went to the towers at midnight and for the next two hours hammered out a resolution. Sam was finally forced to agree to Joe's inclusion on the board when Mary Anna voiced her support for him. The board would be comprised of Sam, who would be CEO of the company, Joe, who insisted on being chairman of the board, Paul, and Jimmie. These four agreed to represent the interests of their brothers and sisters. To reduce and perhaps eliminate conflicts with Joe, Sam was to report to the full board. Because as a practice, board meetings were held no more than once a month and sometimes even less, this arrangement was considered viable.

The meeting ended around 2:00 A.M. with assurances all around that everyone would strive for the common good. L.S. nevertheless drove to the Tatum House with a sinking heart. For more than a week he had been trying to convince himself that this could work, and at times his natural enthusiasm overcame a sense of foreboding.

Sam was unable to sleep as he did not believe Joe would work cooperatively with him. He called his three brothers and requested a 6:00 A.M. meeting at the towers. The situation was as bad as he feared once they were together. Joe was unrepentant in his father's absence and openly hostile toward Sam. Paul and Jimmie were contrary as well, and at 6:30 A.M., when L.S. passed by the meeting room, he could hear the raised voices. This was what he had feared, and he went in to learn the trouble.

Sam was in tears. "These people don't know the meaning of support," he said. Joe jumped in to say that assuredly he was prepared to support his brother. L.S. stared each of his sons in the eye. "Do you understand what you have to do, Joe?" he asked, and waited for an affirmative answer. "Do you know what you have to do, Paul?" he asked, and then went on to Jimmie. Once he had their direct assurances he suggested they all move on to begin preparations for the shareholders' meeting.

The day before, Joe had been especially solicitous of Mary Anna and had given her Heidi's company-leased car to drive, over his wife's objections. The daughters from out of town were staying at the Tatum House, and there was scarcely unanimity the morning of the vote.

Twenty-four-year-old Cecilia was accepted as the most outwardly loving and affectionate of the children and was a peacemaker by nature, so it came as a surprise when she said in the living room, "I don't want to vote for Joe. He acts like a jerk, and I have no confidence in him."

Someone else said, "We all feel that way."

Now that she had committed herself Mary Anna was the most aggressive and was apparently not interested in any defections. "I know," she said. "I feel that way, too, but he can't be that bad." Then: "He deserves a chance."

But a few minutes later Cecilia was standing in the kitchen when she said again, "I don't want to vote for Joe." It was time to leave for the towers.

Mary Anna with purse in hand snapped, "Well, you're voting for him. Let's go."

L.S. had asked a priest to attend the shareholders' meeting, believing he would lend a measure of civility to the occasion. One of the chief financial officers delivered a speech supporting L.S., then gave his appraisal of the status of the company. "[N]et earnings for the first six months are up $24.6 million compared to $9.3 million last year.... [There was a] $93.6 million decrease in debt after acquiring $90.5 million in capital assets. This positive cash flow of $180 million in an 18-month period is very close to an all-time high.... [O]ur '87 forecast estimated net earnings after tax: $25.5."

Of the children, only Cecilia rose to speak about her father and to thank him for all that he had done for them. She said he deserved credit for what he had accomplished in building U-Haul and they all should acknowledge that.

L.S. had written an article to be published later entitled "A Gift to You Children" and passed it out. Then he rose and delivered a rambling speech in which he unconvincingly said retirement had been his idea and he was confident of the company's future with the new board. He looked tired and haggard.

"I feel very comfortable and joyful personally that this has occurred," he said. "It's a significant accomplishment. . . . I want you to know that I trust my sons and daughters . . . absolutely." Addressing those senior staffers who were present, he said, "Key people are in place to make the transition smooth. I want them to know . . . how important they are at this time to help my sons and daughters."

Then he turned to his family. " . . . What are the problems we have? The first one is that the Shoens need to be able to love and trust one another. . . . The problems with the business are the Shoen stockholders need to claim their birthright and elect a board of directors. You see, they got all the votes. . . . I'm a minority stockholder too. . . . " In the recent expansion of U-Haul, he said, "[t]here were many victims, casualties. I was one of the casualties. Some of you people may not know that, but Joe knows it. My son Joe knows it. . . . "

L.S. discussed the history of U-Haul at some length; at times he was almost incoherent. Stress was written all over him. Finally, with more hope than expectation, he said, "I will go out of this world with what I came in with, and what I leave behind is going to be defined as love."

It was not a long meeting and largely a formality. At last the shares were voted, and the new board was installed. For the first time since 1945 L.S. was not in control, indeed had no place in the management, of U-Haul.

Back at the Tatum House L.S. found little rest and at 6:00 P.M. went to the Scottsdale Hilton to the Shoen gathering. Katrina was in Italy and Heidi who had had minor surgery that day, was not in attendance either. But there, glitteringly attired, buzzing from group to group like a queen bee, was Suzanne, apparently there to enjoy these hours of her former husband's demise. If anyone present that night really understood what U-Haul had meant to L.S. and what this day had taken out of him, it was Suzanne.

Joe looked stunned as if he could scarcely believe that he had pulled it off. He was uncommunicative and drifted at the edges of the affair. Suzanne, spotting him, positively glowed with approval and approached him repeatedly. Whatever unhappiness Suzanne had ever felt toward Joe was no longer apparent.

To the absolute amazement of almost everyone, Joe responded to "the bitch." He was polite, even friendly to her. Here was the woman he had despised all his life with her. He had once told a brother that if Suzanne ever set foot in Joe's house, he would burn it to the ground.

Then it became clear to many present what was taking place. Suzanne could be expected to exercise a measure of control over her five children, all of whom had voted to oust L.S. Joe, it seemed, needed "the bitch" as an ally to help keep those votes on his side. The gala had now acquired the aspect of a Fellini film.

Sam had grave misgivings and attended, accompanied by Eva, only to honor his father. Mike had been assured by Joe all along that the changes he had in mind were intended only to make L.S. more accountable to the shareholders, and he had been shocked to witness his father's ouster. He had voted with the majority only at his father's request and was sick at heart.

Despite his outward joviality, L.S. understood that this day was one of closure for him. What he had dreamed of accomplishing forty-one years before as he lay in bed at the naval hospital in Corona, California, had largely been achieved and in many ways exceeded. He would be seventy-one years old in just three months, and this might be the last time so many people who had played a role in building U-Haul would be together.

He bounded from group to group, putting on a happy face, and increasingly he spoke of the old days, of the beginning. At one point he placed an arm around Suzanne, the other around Hap, and told his children that the company wasn't made up just of Shoens, that the bloodlines of the company came from the Cartys and the Gilbaughs and they should always remember that.

By 9:30 P.M. L.S.'s adrenaline was spent, and he left with Carol for the Tatum House. He was exhausted and slept soundly for the first time in ten days. In a strange and unexpected way he had what he always said he wanted. The new board was comprised of four of his sons. His children had taken over.

There had been a brief ceremony at the gala. His sons and daughters had ordered a large sheet cake which L.S. sliced. Written atop it were the words "For Dad. A Celebration of Love and Respect."

CHAPTER TWELVE

TAKING OVER
THE TOY BOX

For weeks word of the turmoil among the Shoens had spread throughout the towers. When the vote was in, employees shared their apprehension and anger. Telephones rang as the word spread: "Did you hear? L.S. is out and Joe is in." One longtime employee thought savagely, *You little brats. How could you do that to your father?*

An uneasy calm spread over the company. Many workers had not been there when Joe was last involved in management, but rumors said he was a terrible boss. There was considerable apprehension because only "Doc Sam" was remaining on the board and more than one employee was not certain he would have enough power to save them. Then, ominously, once the change had taken place, all communication from the eleventh floor ceased.

The first meeting of the new board was an immediate abrogation of the agreement creating it. The first order of business was to elect Joe its chairman, and this occurred unanimously. Sam suggested that as CEO he should hold the formal position of president of Amerco, the corporate holding company. Joe objected, arguing that Sam required no position.

Sam pressed the point. CEOs always held a formal position in the company; that was the basis from which they operated. Joe was adamant. He claimed to see no reason for that matter why Sam should even be CEO. After all, it wasn't a real position. Joe

213

said he would not be party to "giving any executive that kind of malignant power."

After hours of haggling the board finally elected Sam president without any mention of CEO. Sam decided to ignore it; all this fighting over a title was pointless. There was a company to run.

The next morning Heidi arrived at the towers before the first U-Haul employees. Like a queen greeting her subjects, she stood at the door smiling as workers filed past, nodding and bidding them good morning. The former "Mrs. President" was now "Mrs. Chairman of the Board."

In the meantime, L.S. had called the twelve ADVPs to urge them to support the new board and falsely to reassure them that this had been his idea. For the most part these men were not fooled. They knew that L.S. had been booted out, and more than one was concerned for his own future. Joe and Mark had made it plain enough over the years that there were ADVPs loyal to their father whom they planned to "X out" once they held the power.

After talking to his senior managers, L.S. called his four youngest daughters to reassure them, most of all to let them know that he loved them.

Approximately one week after the gala, Joe called his father in Las Vegas and angrily accused L.S. of stealing his money by taking it out of U-Haul. The very distinct message L.S. was receiving was that he was to give no meaningful input to the board even though his employment contract called for him to serve as a consultant. Joe made it very clear that L.S. was to consider himself excluded from U-Haul.

Sam went about U-Haul's affairs, refusing to be stayed by the board's failure to act on company issues. Joe soon called his father and complained that Sam was not behaving like a member of the board because he was acting independently. Joe had presented his older brother with a series of reports he had prepared on what was wrong with the company and demanded that Sam as president correct these mistakes. These objections were nothing new and, in Sam's view, required no action. Joe responded by announcing weekly board meetings.

These meetings were marathons lasting twelve hours and consisted almost entirely of abuse directed at Sam. Joe demanded an immediate reorganization of the reporting responsibilities of key executives and an inquiry into selling the U-Haul Canadian subsidiary. He also wanted Movers World closed at once, RecVee World dissolved, and the general rental program ended. In short, the expansion of the company into diverse areas was to be abandoned.

Sam countered that this was turning the clock back. As things stood, half of U-Haul's income was about to come from the diversification that had just been completed. Nearly all the expenditures were finished, and with interest rates falling the debt created by the expansion would be renegotiated to less backbreaking levels. To make his point, he reminded his brothers that earnings were up three and a half times.

Joe would hear none of this. U-Haul was to be once again trucks and trailers, and that was all there was to it.

The diatribes against Sam were endless, and at the conclusion of the meetings Joe would lay out a week's worth of work for Sam for which he would lambaste him at the next meeting. It took Sam one day to prepare for each board meeting, one to endure it, a third to recover. There was little time left for managing U-Haul. During the first eleven weeks after the takeover Joe held seven board meetings, skipping two weeks for Thanksgiving and Christmas.

The struggle was taking a personal toll on Sam, who was developing chronic back trouble that often sent him to bed. At home he despaired of the situation and called Joe and Mark a couple of "yahoos." But the tactics were having an effect because he was finding it harder and harder to cope with Joe.

Katrina was uncomfortable with what was taking place in U-Haul. At Christmas she went to Phoenix to visit her mother and stayed at the Tatum House. She heard that Joe was demanding weekly meetings of the board intended to harass Sam and not to accomplish anything constructive. But when she asked Joe about his conduct, he countered, "You'd do it, too. They've been running the company without anyone asking them anything for years. Of course, they're upset about it." He repeated his assurances to her that he was concerned for the company and for the well-being of the family. He just needed time.

Katrina's concern was heightened when she noticed that Ryder System was advertising heavily on television and U-Haul was not responding, letting Ryder take the initiative in gaining market share.

Because she made it a point not to discuss business at family functions, as did L.S., Sam, and Mike, she did not ask them about what was taking place. Joe had no such reluctance and lobbied her fiercely that Christmas season.

L.S. did not understand the magnitude of what was taking place inside U-Haul, for Joe's behavior, sometimes joined and often abetted by Paul and Jimmie, appeared to have one objective: to run Sam out of management.

Jimmie was having personal problems. That month a female employee of U-Haul filed a complaint against him and the company alleging that in January 1985 he had first hired her to be his office manager and later consultant in Eureka, California, where he was working. While employed by Jimmie, she alleged they entered into a sexual relationship, which in February 1986 she had terminated. Thereafter, she alleged, he "began a systematic campaign of sexual harassment, intimidation, and violence" against her "which included, among other things, non-consensual touching, verbal propositions, and discriminatory job assignments." She stated that he had made it known to her that "he would cease such harassment if she consented to sexual relations with him, which she refused to do." The conduct continued, she said, until April of that year, when he had changed her shift back and forth to force her resignation. When she "attempted to leave the premises she was physically restrained by" Jimmie. That had resulted in "the constructive termination" of her employment.

Jimmie denied the allegations in his formal answer to the court, and the case was subsequently quietly settled out of court.

Word of the allegations did not come as a surprise to some U-Haul employees. The disdain Joe felt toward female employees had been apparent for a long time. Joe had told one senior employee years before that he did not want to see "any pussies pushing pencils behind the counter."

The day after Christmas L.S. wrote Sam a brief letter with suggestions since it appeared to him this new board was ineffectual. As a clear sign of how little he knew, he first suggested Sam give a budget to the board for its approval. Then he told Sam that he had to stay in regular contact with the ADVPs, something he thought Sam was neglecting. And then: "You are not reporting to Joe Shoen. You report to the . . . board as a group. You must make this distinction."

From Sam's position this advice was largely irrelevant. Neither Paul nor Jimmie was showing any grasp of business; they were utterly ill equipped for the roles into which they had been placed. "Dumb" was the word Sam used.

Over the holidays Joe engaged Mike in an unpleasant conversation that demonstrated forcefully how Joe was reversing Suzanne's and L.S.'s roles. Joe explained in a very hostile way that their father was responsible for the mess the Shoen family had become. Since Joe was ten years old, the blame had been laid at the feet of "the bitch." Now in the space of a few weeks the fault was entirely that of L.S., a man who, according to Joe, was no longer a victim of Suzanne, as Joe had been, but was the real cause of Joe's personal unhappiness and everything else that was wrong with the family. Joe made this explanation as if it had come to him as a sudden discovery.

For some time U-Haul had been contemplating acquiring a Nissan automobile dealership, and at a board meeting Sam ran the final proposal by the board for approval. This was routine and represented U-Haul's interest in expanding into related areas. Joe was furious and denounced the deal. One of the reasons Sam had been willing to tolerate Joe on the board was that the chairman did not vote except to break a tie. With such a small board Sam would need only Paul or Jimmie to join him, and this time one did. The proposal passed two to one.

Sam took the documents to the legal department to have them executed, but a few days later one of his executives said, "I thought this passed a board of directors meeting."

"It did," Sam replied.

"The legal department says it did not."

Sam was then told by one of the attorneys, "We have two sets of minutes." Paul had been responsible for recording the vote, and Sam went to him. Paul said that after the meeting Joe had told him that he had changed his mind and the vote was a tie, two to two. Sam explained that Joe had not voted at all, that the chair voted only to break a tie, not to create one. Besides, the chair couldn't vote once the meeting was adjourned. Paul said he had prepared a second set of minutes and submitted those as well to the legal department.

While Sam was president of Amerco with overall authority, Paul was president of U-Haul International, the job Sam and Joe had previously held. Routine matters such as this were within his province, and if he couldn't get straight something this simple, Sam knew he was in "deep trouble." Rather than stay available to settle the issue Paul left at once for a two-week motorcycle vacation down the Baja peninsula.

The hassles and confrontations with Joe were relentless and occasionally trivial. Sam ordered a bulletin posted and, when he returned from a business trip, learned Joe had taken it down. Sam ordered it put back up. Joe began calling Sam, screaming obscenities into the telephone, until Sam simply hung up on him. Joe then called Sam's home.

Sam was talking to Mary Anna, and others about what was taking place, but he believed they weren't listening. They seemed to think Sam would find some way to make this work. Before L.S.'s ouster Sam would have turned to his father, who would have ended this foolishness in a heartbeat, but L.S. no longer had the power. Neither did Sam. The only ones who could end this were the shareholders, and they weren't paying attention.

Ever since L.S. had persuaded Sam to join the company rather than complete his residency, Sam had tolerated Joe and Mark for the good of the family. He knew his younger siblings depended on him. But he alone had voted against this change. Immediately before the election, when he attempted to tell his brothers and sisters that he required their support, they had instead listened to Joe.

Sam had agreed to this charade with Joe, expecting things to be as bad as they turned out, for love of his siblings. Yet after the change, when he had gone to them, only Mike was on his side. The others were traveling the world, spending time with their families, or pursuing hobbies—having lives of their own, without the burden of running U-Haul.

On January 6, 1987, not quite three months after the election of the new board, Joe brought a motion before it to approve job assignments of employees through three levels of management. It was absurd and utterly impractical. It was also a slap in Sam's face since assignment of personnel at those levels lay with him or his management team. Sam demanded to know why Joe wanted the board, which should be concerned with company policy and direction, to be concerned with such administrative matters.

"I just think we ought to do this" was the only reply Joe would give.

"This is very foolish," Sam said to Paul and Jimmie. "If this motion passes, you're going to need a new president."

Joe shouted at him, "You can't threaten us!"

"It's not a threat," Sam replied, "but it is what I'll do."

The motion then passed. Sam quietly left the room and cleared out his office, then drove home to tell Eva. He left with no regret. He had given this his best, and most of his siblings had turned their backs on him. He felt as if the weight of the world had been lifted from him. He would soon be forty-two years old and finally his life was his own.

At home Sam called L.S. in Las Vegas and gave him the news.

Before L.S. had a chance to respond, Joe was on the telephone, shouting at his father. He renewed his accusation that L.S. had been looting the company for years. L.S. urged a return to mediation, but as the intensity in Joe's attack increased, L.S. returned the harsh words. He told Joe that this was going too far, that things could get out of hand. People could get shot over things like this with emotions running so high, with so much at stake. They had to settle their differences. Finally he shouted that Joe was nothing more than a "con man" and said he would not rest until he was out of the company.

The next day L.S. caught a plane for Phoenix, planning to meet with his sons and get matters back on track and it was up to him to engineer it. At the towers the paranoia and apprehension were palpable. At first Joe refused to see him. The way L.S. heard it, after their telephone conversation Joe had run about the towers, repeating and embellishing what he had said, twisting his words to make them come out that L.S. had threatened to shoot him.

When they finally met, Joe was cool toward his father, and completely unrepentant. Nothing that had taken place was his fault. Hadn't Joe been trying for years to point out Sam's shortcomings? L.S. argued the need to make changes, but Joe stonewalled him.

Mark learned of the shooting comment and immediately called his father, screaming into the telephone, "If you kill Joe, I'll get you!"

L.S. explained to Mark, as he had to Joe, that he had not threatened to shoot anyone, least of all his two sons, whom he loved very much. "Mark, take it easy. There is no way I'll kill Joe." It was Joe who had talked about shooting. The point L.S. had been trying to make was that emotions were so intense that if things continued like this, someone could get shot. Mark was hearing none of it.

In the meanwhile, Joe was still running about the towers, fanning the flames, telling people that he was afraid of his father, who was planning to kill him.

There was apprehension among longtime employees and senior managers when the change in power became apparent, especially among those who had close dealings with Joe and Mark in past years. One such employee turned to his co-worker and said, "Well, we're goners. Markie's taken over the toy box and he's going to twist all our heads off."

It was apparent that L.S. would find no support for his proposed change in directors with the current board. On January 23 he wrote the first of what became many letters "To: Sons and Daughters of L. S. Shoen."

"I feel compelled to write to all of you about the composition of the . . . Board of Directors that we elected last fall. I know that all of you did what you thought you had to do under the circumstances. . . . " He said he did not blame them, and since then he had stayed "out of the way and prayed." But the new board was not working. "I believe that it is cruel to hold the present Board responsible for the appropriate management of this organization. . . . I am asking you to quietly re-establish the [ADVP] Board of Directors. I am not asking to be any part of this. I will, and am trying, to find a new career. I will stay out of your way."

He proposed Sam as CEO, and any member of the family who wanted could "have meaningful work" within the company. He concluded, "Making the 180 degree turn has saved my life and fortune many times. We can all truly say that what happened last summer and fall was right and good and necessary. But continuing on this course is another matter entirely. . . . With Love and Respect, L.S."

There was no response to his letter, so two weeks later he wrote again, this time volunteering to serve as CEO until the board was restructured. He enclosed recent articles about the Schlitz Brewing Company and the Bass brothers, of Texas, who had similar family disputes.

Still, there was no response. The company was rudderless. Who knew what Joe was up to as chairman, and his children were not acting. One week later L.S. wrote his sons and daughters again. "Last fall I asked that you love one another. If that would have occurred, perhaps the Shoens could have had a second generation manage [U-Haul]. I prayed and was able to create joy in my life. My life is now Shit! . . . "

He chastised his children for not having read the Schlitz material, a family story he thought very much paralleled theirs. Schlitz, once the leading brewer in the United States, was now virtually extinct. The same fate awaited U-Haul if this continued. They must get professionals running the company. " . . . I pray that you will come to this realization soon. With Love, L. S. Shoen."

The Shoens' squabble was by now national news. Jan Parr wrote an article for *Forbes* magazine entitled "King Lear," comparing L.S.'s treatment at the hands of his children to that of Shakespeare's tragic figure.

Joe was quoted as saying, "[My father] had to retire and be run off simultaneously." Then he added, "There has been no bloodletting."

Parr was not convinced. "It is clear that this drama is far from finished."

L.S.'s frustration was only growing. Now that the company he had built from one trailer needed to make the most important about-face of its existence, L.S. was discovering he did not have the power to accomplish it.

That rested with shareholders who refused to act and a four-man board run by its chairman, the very man L.S. wanted out. L.S. had stumbled on Dr. Day's long-forgotten report from seven years earlier and read it with new insight. He then wrote his son with copies to all the other children.

"Joe, this letter is not an attack on you...," L.S. began his letter in late February 1987. "...[Y]our behavior is destructive, not constructive. Your problem is fear. This was probably engendered by the loss of your mother when you were still a child. This fear has made and makes you very insecure. Your security became 'U-Haul.' Your fear manifests itself in anger and attacks upon whomever [sic] you believe is threatening 'U-Haul.'"

For fifteen pages L.S. offered his version of Joe's life history. "...Mark shares many of your behavior patterns. You learned to do this as children.... This aggression is probably in your genes as well as your experience after your mother's death.... You and Mark talk and behave as if this organization was your personal kingdom and that you can do with its people and property as you damn well please.... You even try to make me and others think that my (L.S.S.) mind is incapable of functioning properly. That I should not work. You have secretly told outright lies about me...."

L.S. asked for Joe's resignation from the board. He reminded Joe that he had promised to support Sam; instead he had worked against him. "You did this in a devious and manipulative way.... [N]o large and complex organization...can long endure under the environment that you create. Your lust for power and greed blind you.... As I told you, I will not, and cannot, rest until you are out of power in this organization. . . . Deceit is a part of your everyday life. You are a 'con' man. . . . I am ashamed as to the part I played at the shareholders' meeting last year. . . . I feel like my nose is a foot long. . . . "

He called Joe's attention to the *Forbes* article, then attached an addendum for his other children in which he suggested a special shareholders' meeting. If he could not get the two-thirds vote required to change the board, then with 51 percent they could "add enough new members to change the balance of power. . . . " He proposed placing a majority of the shares in a ten-year voting trust that would be managed by professionals.

He concluded, "It is . . . difficult for me to believe that you can trust Joe as opposed to me. . . . Think carefully. There has been and will be no peace otherwise. Not for me nor for you. You can take that to the bank. . . . "

They were to be the truest words L.S. ever penned.

Joe's subsequent behavior indicated that he clearly sensed that he needed to solidify his power. Enough shareholders had requested a special meeting that one was scheduled for May 1987. Joe, Mark, Paul, and Sophia met secretly with representatives of T. Boone Pickens, a junk bond takeover specialist. Then Joe and Paul quietly met with First Boston, an investment banking company, to explore a plan to buy out shareholders. Joe's overture to Drexel Burnham Lambert was rebuffed since one of its senior men was a personal friend of Sam's. None of these activities was presented formally to the board.

In the absence of a CEO, Joe as chairman was behaving very much as one. Joe's unwillingness to hire a CEO had only one message. "To me," Sam later wrote, "the real reason was simple. After my departure, Joe had assumed the power and had no intention of relinquishing it."

Though he was no longer president, Sam resumed attending board meetings, which had now been reduced to once a month. With Sam present someone would have an idea of what Joe was up to. Each time Sam urged a search for a replacement CEO Joe scoffed at the idea. "We'll just hire another manic depressive"; "We need to reorganize before we hire a CEO"; or "We don't need a leader for this company." What Joe's behavior said was he was in power and no one else was going to challenge it. Then Joe would smile and say, "Heads will roll. Faces will change."

They already were. ADVP John Dodds was dispatched to Ohio to call on longtime ADVP John Fowler. He told Fowler that there was "an awful fight going on in Phoenix." Fowler, who owned a few shares of U-Haul, had heard that Dodds was soliciting shares from others on behalf of Joe. "I hope by now you're smart enough to know who runs the show and which side your bread is buttered on," he told Fowler. Then Dodds asked how Fowler planned to vote his shares at the special shareholders' meeting.

"Were you told to ask me this?" Fowler inquired.

"You don't have to worry," Dodds responded evasively. Others might be fired, but Fowler was safe.

Fowler saw no point in not answering him. "Everyone knows my opinion." He was a longtime L.S. man who didn't care for Joe and would vote accordingly.

A few days later Dodds called and asked if Fowler was going to quit. Fowler said he had no intention of quitting. Dodds asked if he was going to retire. Again Fowler said he didn't plan on that, at least not now. "In that case you're fired," Dodds said over the telephone. Fowler wanted to know just who had ordered this. "It comes from Joe Shoen. He runs the place," Dodds said as he hung up.

Ten years before, Jack Adair, who now operated a U-Haul rental center in Roseburg, Oregon, had been honored by the company for being its longest rental agent, since 1947. With the changes in Phoenix the word going out from Joe was "Daddy Warbucks is dead; the gravy train is over." Adair had no illusions about his future under this management and started wearing a cap to work that read, "Daddy Warbucks is alive and well."

The same month Fowler was fired the state president drove up to see Adair. "Do you want to resign?" he asked without preamble.

"You've got to be kidding," Adair said. "I know more about this end of the business than anyone in the company."

"I agree, but I have to let you go."

"This has got to be a joke. I'm going to call Sam," which was the name he still used for L.S.

"It won't do you any good," the state president said. "He's out." So was Adair.

These men weren't the only ones to be fired for no stated reason. Heads were rolling left and right, just as Joe had promised. There were also additions to the U-Haul team. Harry DeShong, Jr., was back with his slick clothes, ingratiating grin, and insinuating manner. Heidi had taken care of her friend Patti.

Mike had been having no more success influencing his siblings than his father, but the firings enraged him. He wrote Joe, Paul, and Jimmie with a copy to the rest of his brothers and sisters:

> Last November after Mark had finished shouting obscenities at my wife and while still cursing me for supporting Sam, he voiced his main complaint, that I "had my own agenda." Apparently, I didn't have Mark's agenda, or Joe's.
>
> For years, Joe has dumped a cesspool of degrading language ... on Sam: "the douchebag," "shit for brains" and "that asshole brother of ours." All we had to do was get rid of Sam.
>
> The same attitude extended to John Fowler. I can remember many examples of Joe's hateful, spiteful language toward John, vowing to "X him out."
>
> I trusted Joe not to continue this mind-set and voted for him on the board. The result was 7 board meetings in 11 weeks, after each of which Sam went home physically sick and was unable to work the following day.
>
> Sam finally broke down to where today, he is literally having trouble forming words when speaking about the business.
>
> ... This company was built on serving others, honesty and integrity. The opposite will kill it and kill you. . . .

A few weeks later, in March, increasingly concerned about the growing hostility in the family and unable to work for Joe, Mike moved his family back to Vancouver, Washington. He wrote his siblings: "When we removed L.S. from the board last fall, I never seriously imagined that Joe would end up as the designated leader of this organization. . . . " He urged his brothers and sisters to listen to their father.

At this time Mark called Mike's wife, Christa, at their home and in the most vile and hate-filled language cursed her and said he would do everything in his power to destroy the estate plan

Mike had created for their children and then would take care of Mike as well. Cecilia was visiting the family and watched as Christa started crying. By the time Christa hung up they both were in tears over what Mark had said.

Also in March L.S. wrote Sophia to wish her well on her twenty-seventh birthday:

> ... It is your lot in life that I made you rich and powerful.... It is my lot in life that God is leaving me here on earth to see what would have happened after my death to my sons and daughters relative to the organization. It is clear to me that God wants me to fix that which I did wrong.... I have been given a chance to correct my past mistakes (sins) and there is no way out of this for me except death or the resolution of this behavior.... I understand well your comment "that the ancient Greeks would have killed me. That such is what *King Lear* is about." I also understand very well what your brother Jim was saying when he explained to me that "the ancient Chinese took away all the possessions of their ex-leaders." I am indeed fortunate to be living in the U.S.A. and a couple of thousand years later....

On April 14 Joe called his father in Las Vegas. They spoke for a time with increasing aggression. Then Joe asked, "Now can I tell you a story?"*

"Go ahead."

"Same year. Suzanne goes off.... You take some sort of a pill that puts you to sleep to the point where you can't talk. OK. I come home at midnight. You are full of some medication. I don't know what it is. I call Sam, I interrupt him. I get Sam in Tucson. He says get you up, walk you around and do my best and maybe you will live. Then he tells me to get a gun and find a place and lay for Suzanne and, when she comes through the door, to blow her in half—not to blow her in half—to kill her. What I did was I got you up and walked you around."

"When was this?"

"It was right before your operation. It was one thing that pre-

---

*When Edward J. "Joe" Shoen was subsequently questioned about statements reported to have been made during this conversation, he denied the conversation had taken place.

cipitated you going down for surgery. It was when Suzanne [was gone] a day or two over there. She told you she was going to get fucked by some guy, is what she told me. You then took a gob of prescription or something or another. And I called Sam because I got home from Legend City that night."

"Well, that may have happened, but I didn't, I—"

"No, no, let me finish the story because it did happen, you see. Sam told me to get a gun and to kill her. He did not tell me to take you down to a hospital and get your stomach pumped. Now that I am an adult I know that is what you do with drug overdoses. That's my brother in med school. What he suggested was not that I get your stomach pumped, but that I kill Suzanne. So I sat there all night long with a gun. I found the darkest spot up in that bedroom where there was no light coming in. I unlocked the door, and I patiently waited. Unfortunately she did not come through the door."

"Well, thank God."

"Isn't that a bitch?"

"And to think that you would do that," L.S. said solemnly.

"I was asked to.... By my older brother, the doctor. He didn't suggest that you pump your stomach. He suggested that I shoot your wife."

"Well ... "

"I'm not real bright frankly."

"I ... was not overdosed on drugs.... "

"Oh, yes, you were! And you can ask Sam. He remembers that part. He has a hard time with the part where he told me to kill Suzanne. But he will remember the part about you being overdosed on drugs."

"Joe, listen—"

"I, I—"

"I know the time this was going on ... and I did not overdose on drugs."

"No, you did not. You lived."

"I did not [get] anywhere near it [overdosing]. Yes, Suzanne may have told me what you said she told me."

"She did go over [there].... "

"All right, whatever it was."

"You were frantic. Out of your mind. Frantic."

"Well, Suzanne used to torture me."

"Of course she did. I was around when she tortured you. And we are not mad at her for it. But she did. And it is also true that Sam, who was in his middle twenties, instructed me, who was under twenty, to get a gun and wait for her."

"I . . ."

"And the truth is that I did that."

" . . . That may be the way you remember it, Joe."

"That is the fact."

"Well, here's one. . . . I don't know. . . . "

"That's the facts."

" . . . [L]et's agree that Sam said that. . . . Now come back to the situation just a month or two ago. I called you, and I talked to you about saying we have got to do something now to correct this thing, Joe. . . . And I said you know people can get shot over things like this. We can get so angry that is a possibility."

"Yup."

"Now you interpreted that to be that I was going to come down and kill you."

"Yup. That's how I interpreted it."

"Joe, that was so far from a threat to you. I was not thinking in any way of doing that. That is not my behavior. And you told that to other people."

"Then I misinterpreted that totally."

"Now I just wonder about what you misinterpreted about what Sam said."

"Nothing! Nothing! Not a thing. Nothing! Nothing! Not one thing did I misinterpret."

"One of these days, Joe—"

"I will admit. I will admit and I will admit, but Sam never did a mother-fucking thing wrong in his life!"

"Wait a minute. If you could only get it, Joe . . . that your attitude is that you don't do anything wrong."

"No."

"You don't remember."

"I misinterpreted."

"Didn't you understand that I had that punctured spinal column and that I could lose that fluid?"

"Sure I did."

"And I tried to tell you.... "

"Sure you did."

"And I tried to tell you, 'Don't do this.' "

"Sure you did."

"Then you drove like a madman. Then the next ten days I was in bed."

"No. I remember that the third day out of that you were up and directing how to wash the windows. And you felt so good that you never felt that good in your life."

"You can go through my diary . . . and show that."

"Would you?"

"Sure. I'll go through my diary."

"Great. Go through the part about [Suzanne], back up about a month to see if you find anything about taking sleeping pills—Suzanne being over at [someone's house]. That's one of the reasons I have a problem with [that man] since then. It ain't something he did to me; it is something he did to you."

"I know one thing," L.S. said, "[he] certainly did not have intercourse with Suzanne."

When the call was complete, L.S. stopped to consider what Joe had said. First, Joe had been twenty-one when the events occurred, not under twenty, as he claimed. L.S. checked his diary and learned that Sam had not even been in Tucson when these incidents occurred, so Joe could not possibly have talked to him there. The entire overdose story was also untrue. L.S. knew that during that period he was occasionally heavily sedated, but he had never overdosed, and Joe had never walked him around a room and saved his life. Everyone knew how Joe had felt toward Suzanne, and the gun story was also common knowledge. Joe had never before claimed Sam put him up to it. This was bizarre and, to L.S., one more example of Joe's manufacturing reality to suit himself. He had once told his father that he could program his mind in such a way that he could pass any lie detector test. L.S. sensed this might be just how Joe went about it.

One thing was clear: Dr. Day's report had been extremely accurate. L.S. wrote, "Joe cannot work for me or for Sam." L.S. was seeing more clearly now that this was a power struggle and that in the end he or Joe was going to run U-Haul. There was no middle ground.

With his children still dragging their heels L.S. wrote, almost in desperation, "I beg you to study the material in this notebook. A house divided against itself cannot stand...." Included with the letter for all of Joe's brothers and sisters to read was Dr. Day's report as well as tapes of conversations L.S. had recorded of Joe and him.

In apparent retaliation for Sam's attending board meetings, Joe issued a notice in mid-April announcing *daily* board meetings from April 20 through May 3. Sam canceled several business trips, then reported each day for the meetings, only to be told, one at a time, that each had been canceled.

Sam missed his work and did not seem to know what to do with himself. He had no real hobbies, having always preferred to work. One of his great pleasures was in doing a job well. Eva suggested he try landscaping, but he threw himself into the yard project with such determination he was exhausted by evening. Finally he took a job with a medical consulting firm.

Mary Anna's support for Joe first wavered when she heard Sam had walked out, then collapsed with the firings of all the men she had known for most of her life, men she knew were good, loyal employees and the backbone of U-Haul. She called Joe and said, "What the hell is going on?" Joe was upset she had called and treated her question like an attack. He behaved as if she ought to feel sorry for him and offered no explanation that made sense to her. When she tried to get him to understand that he was making significant decisions for her and the rest of the family and accepting no input from them, he made it clear he intended to continue as he was. Mary Anna became angry and shouted sarcastically into the telephone, "Whatever you think is best for me you just do that!," then hung up.

L.S. believed he could secure enough proxies to place himself, Sam, Mike, and a senior financial officer on the board. Even with

Joe's disruptive tactics there would be a solid majority to allow Sam to run the company as CEO until the next regular shareholders' meeting.

But Joe threatened a lawsuit if anyone assigned proxies to vote. No member of the Shoen family had ever before used such tactics on others in the family. As a result, his brothers and sisters were so intimidated they decided to show up and vote individually.

There was by now a great deal of confusion over what was taking place in the family company. Mike and Mary Anna had been quick to jump ship, but the other children were less informed and were uncertain. Chaos such as this was not something they had come to expect in U-Haul, and Joe was aggressively pitching his version of events.

After all, he said, the company was going bankrupt. Sam had put his tail between his legs and run, and only selfless Joe was staying the course, to save the company for everyone. Sam was a quitter, and quitters had no place on the board. Katrina, for one, had originally given her father her proxy, but when everyone except Sam was voting to oust L.S., she had given it to Joe. Now she, and others, felt that he deserved his chance.

Until May 1987 U-Haul shareholders' meetings had been casual affairs. It was not unusual for them to take place around a conference table in the towers. L.S. would arrive with a pocketful of proxies, Joe and Mark might storm in to bitch, but the outcome was never in doubt. They were short, informal matters, basically a gathering of those of the Shoen clan who chose to show up along with a handful of minority shareholders.

On May 3 Joe called to order the special shareholders' meeting in a vast shed at the tech center. Hundreds of chairs had been lined in neat rows for the approximately twenty-five people in attendance. A huge buffet, more food than everyone present could possibly eat, sat warming in the room. Placed in the aisle was a microphone, and no one could speak from the floor except from the microphone. Joe and his crew were up front, decked out in Brooks Brothers suits, the first suits some present had ever seen them in. Spotlights were in place and created an artificial separation between management and shareholders that had never before existed in U-Haul.

The sight was nearly obscene in its formality. Here were Joe and Mark, overgrown boys with a love for motorcycles who often arrived at meetings in Levi's and bomber jackets, dressed up like real businessmen. It looked as if Joe were trying to conduct himself like the chairman of some board he had once seen in a movie. This certainly was not U-Haul.

Across the front of the stage were charts and graphs with enlarged photographs of U-Haul's new trucks, projects Sam had been working on for years, displayed now as if they were entirely Joe's doing.

For several years and especially these past months Joe and his followers had been presenting an image of L.S. as a doddering old man suffering from a mental illness or the infirmities of advanced age. Unfortunately this day L.S. played into the role. His leg was acting up with a thrombosis, and he was required to keep it straight and elevated. Joe had arranged a special stuffed chair for him off to the side with a separate microphone. L.S. was displayed like a curiosity or as if, in the words of one in the room, "They were setting him up for execution."

For most of the day Joe put on what was generally referred to as a dog and pony show, complete with gratuitous speeches by the sycophants with whom he surrounded himself. The speeches were predictable, as they lavished praise first on the L.S. of days past, then on U-Haul, and finally on Joe, savior of the company. When someone attempted to move the meeting to its real reason, control of the company, Joe was quick to hide behind *Robert's Rules of Order,* a book in which he had shown no interest until now.

Joe had refused entry to anyone but shareholders. Outside fired ADVPs and longtime employees with horror stories were not able to have their say to the controlling shareholders. Heidi owned no shares, nor did Mark's wife, but Joe made an exception for them since their role was to court the youngest sisters. Sophia, who sat beside Mary Anna, was obviously bored by the entire affair. She kept asking if Mary Anna liked her new hosiery.

As the mind-numbing meeting dragged on, Joe strutted back and forth across the stage with a forced smile on his face, waving a ruler like a riding crop. The spoiling food drew a swarm of flies, and every now and then Joe would swat one with a crack of his ruler.

The meeting disintegrated, and for once L.S. was unable to assert himself, bound as he was to the chair and lacking proxies to exercise real power. There were those present certain that L.S.'s slate of new board members had passed when it was voted on, but Joe claimed it hadn't, and afterward when participants requested copies of the tapes of the meeting, they were told the recordings had been lost.

There was another vote which Joe did recognize. His siblings said they wanted a bigger board, as if the size of the board were the only issue, and they said they wanted experts, so his slate included three outside directors no one knew, Joe's own new men to pad the board. There was also Hap Carty, another of Joe's directors; clearly Hap had decided where his bread was buttered.

At the request of some of the children, one of U-Haul's financial officers outlined options for the shareholders to obtain liquidity—that is, to get money for their shares. Without being asked, he suggested an employee stock ownership plan (ESOP) or master limited partnership. Sam was enraged when he heard this. An ESOP would have the opposite effect: It would entrench Joe and freeze out the other shareholders. While it was true that it would create a pool into which shareholders could sell, the pool would be voted by a trustee appointed by the board. Once the ESOP had enough shares to guarantee management a majority, it could stop buying stock. Also, the company could simply create shares and place them into the ESOP for the same effect.

When Sam spoke, Joe launched into an attack, accusing him of having enriched himself by unspecified actions when he had been president, the same sort of accusation he had made against his father. Sam sputtered and denied any wrongdoing, but the accusation was planted, and without details he could not prove it false.

When the meeting ended, Mary Anna confronted Katrina in the parking lot to demand an explanation for her voting, but it was soon plain that Katrina had simply not understood her significance. As Mary Anna tried to explain the opportunity that had just slipped from their grasp, Katrina broke into tears. The sight brought Mary Anna up cold. Katrina was only twenty-one years old. Joe had fooled Mary Anna as well. How could she expect any more of her younger sister than what had just happened?

L.S. was enraged at the outcome. Joe had successfully turned the special meeting into a three-ring circus. He wrote, "... [Hap] Carty threw in with Joe and company and the destruction of [U-Haul] and the Shoen family began in earnest. Hap Carty's dreams were fulfilled."

Within weeks Joe summarily closed Movers World just as its peak earning season began, not bothering to sell the enterprise where it would have fetched money but simply trashing the company and discharging 1,000 employees in the process. Soon U-Haul was down to 12,000 employees from 18,500. Employees in the towers were crammed into floors so other floors could be vacated and air conditioning shut off. In the packed floors the temperature was set at higher levels to save air-conditioning costs. Employees sweated at their desks, except on the eleventh floor, where Joe worked.

The rumor mill had been running wild since L.S.'s abrupt departure from U-Haul. Effective communication from management was at an end, and longtime employees were forced to sift through the contradictory versions of events in an attempt to determine what was taking place in the company. As one employee axed by Joe put it, "You could not walk down the hallway or get into the elevator or go down to the smoke shop without the rumors being a subject of conversation. Over morning coffee, at lunch it was a constant subject of conversation. It was a very tumultuous period in the company."

A despondent L.S. wrote in his journal, "We have only one visible product, the [U-Haul] truck. Everything else has been eliminated or gone down hill.... Ignorance reigns."

Mark at least was taking no chances with the new board members. He wrote them a letter that read in part, "Let it suffice to say that I will closely scrutinize your behavior on the Board of Directors...." One new member of the board commented that he felt "like punching Mark in the nose."

During fiscal 1987 Form Builders received $3.5 million from

U-Haul, and L.S. was not the only one concerned about its manner of doing business. Technically Form Builders was owned by Joe's two sons and Mark's daughter, but since they were minors, Joe and Mark exercised decision-making authority over the company. Though Form Builders had income in excess of $1.5 million a year, it had been sold in 1983 to one of Joe's high school friends for just $32,000. Joe had confided in Mike that this putative sale would allow him to "snooker" the government out of taxes. Despite this ostensible change in ownership, there was little confusion about who really ran the company, and that was Joe and Mark. More than once Joe had boasted that someday his sons would be the wealthiest men in the United States.

In 1987 the Internal Revenue Service brought a case against Form Builders and Joe and Mark. Joe's anger with L.S. was rising to a fearsome degree. He hotly accused his father of having turned him in to the IRS, something L.S. vehemently denied.

In early June 1987 Mark accused Sam of furnishing information to the IRS and threatened in turn to "expose problems" he claimed existed in Sam's family estate plan. He ordered Sam "to make it right" with the IRS or Mark would retaliate even if "innocent" brothers and sisters were harmed as a consequence.

Any IRS examination of other siblings turned out to be routine, but the IRS investigation and lawsuit against Form Builders resulted in formal action and had a profound impact on Joe. Just months earlier he had reportedly engaged in a shouting match with a female IRS agent, calling her vulgar names at the top of his voice, conduct that certainly had not helped his position.

For some time he had confided in Heidi that he feared he would be sent to jail. When Heidi first heard this, she thought he was joking, but as he kept insisting, she believed him. When Heidi asked why he said that it was better if she didn't know; that way if she were ever asked, she could truthfully deny any knowledge.

Heidi had persisted, and according to her Joe confided that Form Builders hadn't been sold in 1983 on the date represented, that the sale had been backdated and that the true reason for the sale was that he and Mark had too close a relationship with the children who were supposed to be its owners. Heidi claimed that almost as an afterthought Joe added that he had also been taking cash from the register, but everyone did that because taxes were so exorbitant.

For several years, according to Heidi, Joe had continued to tell Heidi about his fear that he would go to jail, and when the IRS brought its suit against him and Mark, it appeared his prediction was coming true.

Board meetings were now back to the standard once a month, but even that seemed too often for Joe. Sam attended regularly and wrote his siblings just what Joe was doing. The effect was to frustrate a number of initiatives Joe appeared eager to begin. Sam was as much as ever an unwanted thorn in his side. In June Sam went to the office only to discover Joe had ordered his name removed from the door. At the same time Joe insisted he exercised no executive control, and Sam took to calling him the "phantom CEO." During one board meeting, when Paul apparently became confused about what he was to do, Joe grabbed him by the arm and pulled him into the hallway to "explain" what Paul was to agree to, then went back into the conference room. It was a complete charade.

Mary Anna was as disgusted as Sam by the turn of events, and the two of them considered their options. Since refusing to go along with Joe any further, Mary Anna had felt ennobled and was proud of herself for standing up to him, but there was still a great deal of money at stake. She and Sam were interested in taking what wealth they could out of U-Haul and getting on with their lives. It was not possible for them to act alone; they required the active participation of shareholders possessing a majority of stock.

Sam explored the possibilities, and there seemed to be only two solutions: Either acquire enough money, about seven hundred million dollars, to buy a majority of shares and gain control of U-Haul, or have a majority of the shareholders sell in a block to outsiders, who then would have control.

Though Joe was participating in similar inquiries, directed in part to finding a way to rid himself of Sam's ownership and, to a lesser extent, Mary Anna's, he portrayed Sam's efforts as an attempt to destroy U-Haul. But Joe was having less and less influence over his siblings, and within months of the May 1987 special shareholders' meeting the balance of power was down to Katrina's 3 percent. If she jumped sides, Sam would have enough shares to replace the existing board and perhaps sell control to outsiders.

Katrina wrote her father a letter expressing in part the emotional pain this conflict was causing her. On June 30 her father replied and told her that he was "embarrassed" to have tried to pressure her during the special shareholders' meeting. "I simply can not wash my hands of this matter of how the shareholders vote. I can not simply do nothing," he wrote. " . . . I did not create this turmoil. It tears me apart. . . . Anything I say or do seems shitty to me. . . . 'Old Dad,' Leonard Samuel Shoen."

Katrina was not aware that her vote was crucial. In fact, Joe represented to her that she was part of an overwhelming majority of shareholders who supported his "reforms" in U-Haul. When she asked him why Sam had left management, Joe told her, "He couldn't stand it. I'm taking care of the company now." Joe courted her extravagantly while Sam and Mike held back, unwilling to press her by explaining their side in detail, waiting for her to see the reality of what was taking place.

That summer Joe worked with Paul in filing with the Arizona Board of Medical Examiners a formal complaint against Sam, who was licensed to practice medicine in the state. Paul alleged that his brother was addicted to drugs, was psychopathic, abused alcohol, and prevented L.S. from obtaining proper medical treatment. The doctor assigned to the complaint spoke with Sam and told him that he had never seen people who wanted to get someone as badly as these two. "I shouldn't tell you this, but you have got trouble I wouldn't wish on my worst enemy."

Sam explained that the accusations were unfounded and based on a family feud for control of its company. "Moreover, it is very sad for me to read these allegations, not so much because of their untruthfulness, but because they indicate the breadth and depth of the schism in my family." L.S. wrote the Board of Medical Examiners and attributed the same motives as did Sam, then enclosed Dr. Day's report for good measure.

It took some time before the complaint was rejected by the medical board and was just one more sign of the means to which

Joe and those supporting him were prepared to go to destroy individuals.

Under pressure Joe had agreed to learn the desires of the shareholders and was informed that there was general agreement to explore options for liquidity. Sam attempted repeatedly to persuade the board to hire an investment banker to perform an analysis, but Joe stonewalled his efforts, saying incongruously that to give the shareholders that kind of knowledge would be "like me walking around the campus of Arizona State University and being tempted by beautiful coeds."

When Sam pressed Joe on the issue, Joe criticized Sam for "wanting to sell the company." When even Paul and Jimmie suggested they might support the preparation of an analysis, Joe said, "I don't understand the board's direction." Pushed further, he attacked such an effort as "a waste of money," then finally dismissed it with the comment "Investment bankers are not objective." But because Paul and Jimmie were not prepared to abandon the effort, Joe finally resorted to walking out of any meeting if the subject was raised.

For L.S. this was nothing but heartache. When Joe closed Movers World just as it was poised to turn hefty profits, he had in effect "dug up the orchard" as well as laid off a thousand employees without ceremony. Longtime faithful employees wrote and called L.S., and the effect was to increase his anger and certainty that Joe must be stopped.

On July 7, 1987, Joe called his father and renewed his accusation that L.S. had turned him in to the IRS. He claimed further that L.S. had broken into his office. "It was a mistake, you got it?" Joe said threateningly.

"Well, Joe..." L.S. began, but before he could finish, Joe shouted into the telephone.

"You fucked yourself! You just did it, asshole. You just admitted it!"

"Admitted what?" L.S. asked.

"That you hired people on me, and I knew you had been. You dirty cocksucker!"

"Yes, I have."

"You fucked yourself," Joe said savagely. "Fuck yourself. You got it straight? Can I help you with it? You fuck yourself. I ain't your kid. You fuck yourself. You hire people on me. You fuck yourself." He hung up.

On July 14 Sam was at the towers, stuffing envelopes, when Joe and Mark entered the office and closed the door behind them. They launched into a verbal attack against Sam that grew in hostility. Finally Sam asked Mark if what he wanted was a fight, to which Mark replied, "OK." Sam stood up and said, "Then let's get it on."

Very quickly after the fistfight started, Sam had the upper hand. Then Joe jumped Sam from behind, wrestled him to the floor, and held him down as Mark kicked him in the head. John Dodds heard the commotion and broke it up. Employees watched a disheveled Sam with a bloody, torn shirt leave the building.

Joe's and Mark's version was, of course, different from Sam's, and they were very concerned about how the assault would be interpreted. As part of damage control Mark wrote his brother:

DEAR SAM--

Your letter to Joe describing our little disagreement tuesday [*sic*] 14 July is certainly amusing. In fact had I not been in the room at the time I might even believe you. I am sure your letter is intended for general distribution prior to the shareholders [*sic*] meeting. For this reason I will attempt to jog *your* memory so that at least you know you are lying.

You Sam, are a premeditating, sucker punching, ball busting, eye gouging asshole. You do tell a good story and no doubt are proud of it.

Let me be real clear, the next time you sucker punch me at least do the job right, hit me with the first punch or don't start the fight.... Anyway Sam, like I say you spun a pretty good yarn--every *liar* does.

With all my love and respect,
MARK

P.S. Be sure to circulate this letter with the others.

Each time Sam was in the towers after that, Mark asked him if he wanted to fight again.

Joe wrote Sam a memo instructing:

Do not deal directly with anyone [other than me or the board] unless specifically authorized.... The use of company people... as either conduits of your communication to me or as fall guys for your displeasure with me [is] to be discontinued.... Make all further communications regarding fraud...by me or other parties...in writing.... [O]therwise keep your slurs on me personal, and make them personally, not in the guise of concerns about [U-Haul].... I obviously have difficulty interacting with you on a daily basis.... Your hatred of me is as likely to fade as grow. The damage to the company and to individual people I will no longer tolerate. Deal by the book around the company or don't be around the company.

Sam replied, "I am simply no longer going to be a verbal punching bag for you or Mark. Specifically your 'bully boy' tactics won't work any more. You are the one desiring conflict, not me...."

At a board meeting Paul suggested a six-point plan in which point number five was "to get rid of dissident shareholders." That same July Joe ordered cancellation of the Shoen family estate life insurance polices maintained by the company, netting U-Haul $4.6 million. This act effectively wiped out the estate plans his brothers and sisters had in place since insurance would not be available to pay estate taxes for their children when one of them died. Joe's and Mark's children were covered by the estate plan they had established at Form Builders and were unaffected. The adult Shoen children were still technically employed by U-Haul and received the standard employee package of life and health insurance for themselves and their offspring.

Sam suggested that Form Builders be independently audited since U-Haul was virtually its only customer. He had pressed for such an audit many times in the past without success, and Joe had always refused. This time Joe went "nuts" and told the board that any audit of Form Builders would be done by auditors in U-Haul's control. When the audit was concluded, Sam requested a copy but was refused. He asked Joe if it was true that Joe's sons held an interest in Form Builders, information until then not commonly available, and Joe replied inscrutably, "Since they are my children, they are related to me," and refused to say more.

L.S. wrote Joe on August 1, 1987, to respond to his son's oft-repeated allegations against him:

> I am saddened by your accusations relative to me turning you in to the IRS. You cursed them and told them what you thought of them last November. . . . Yes, I am and have been concerned by what I believe was and still is a "rip-off" of U-Haul International by Form Builders and I have hired a firm to try and get me data on what is truly happening. . . . Your cursing me as the S.O.B. that turned you in to the IRS sounds like you have something to hide. What do you have to hide from the IRS? . . . You have taken over [U-Haul] from me. This was my meaningful work and its welfare was and is critical to my health and happiness. You have turned my creation upside down and set it back 10 years. . . . You are my son and you are dear to me. As King David said of Absalom, his son: "I may be your enemy, but you are not mine." . . .
>
> With Much Love,
> your dad, L.S.

Joe felt compelled to respond to only one portion of the letter, and he interpreted his father's words to mean something L.S. never intended. Joe called Mary Anna, who was staying at the Tatum House, and in a highly agitated state told her, "I don't have a father. He's hired someone to break into my house."

Mary Anna knew that this was not true, that their father had hired someone to conduct research, not to commit an illegal break-in. "Joe, it sounds like you have a real problem with your father. Maybe you should call him." In his tirade he was attacking not only their father but also Sam as if somehow he were ultimately responsible for what was taking place. Joe continued in this vein, refusing to listen to her assurances, and then out of the blue told her that no one had the right to learn about his sex life.

Mary Anna was dumbfounded. This was the first anyone had said anything about this, and she tried repeatedly to explain that was not what their father was doing, but Joe spoke as if his mind were made up.

As he rambled on and on, seeking her support, trying with every word to cast himself as a victim, it was apparent that he was agitated over the IRS investigation and lawsuit. "I'm going to keep a gun to protect myself," he said hysterically, and he would carry it on him at all times. If anyone tried to break into his house to harm his wife or children, he would shoot that person.

Listening to Joe in this state gave Mary Anna heart palpitations. So that there later was no confusion about what exactly he said she scribbled notes as he spoke. Mary Anna knew of Joe's increasing hatred for Sam, and because she knew Joe as she did, she believed this reference to a gun was intended for Sam. With Joe you always had to read between the lines, and this led her to a frightening thought. Joe kept repeating that he was going to be carrying a gun from now on, and he sounded very unstable to her. The whole conversation was very frightening.

When he hung up, Mary Anna immediately called Sam and said, "I just got this scary phone call from Joe." She repeated what Joe had said, that he had sounded on the edge, very unstable, and told Sam that Joe must be feeling threatened. It was as if he had a vendetta against Sam, and she was very concerned for Sam's safety since she knew he went to the towers for a portion of nearly every day. "It sounds to me," she said, "like he is flipping out." She told her brother, "Stay away from Joe."

Sam called Eva at their Paradise Valley house and told her to get the children into the house and to call 911 if Joe showed up. Then, uncertain if Joe was going berserk and meant violence against him or his family, he drove home. Eva dismissed Joe's words as the ravings of an idiot and was much less concerned for her safety and that of their family than Sam was. But to spare her needless worry, Sam intentionally had not told her everything he knew about his brother.

Not long after Mary Anna spoke to Sam, Joe was on the telephone again. "Forget everything I said," he said, then explained in a highly unconvincing way that he had meant none of what he had told her. He wasn't going to carry a gun, and by the way, let's get together as a family while you are in town. Mary Anna did not believe his denials, and no, she wouldn't be visiting with him as a family, not until these problems were ended once and for all.

Ever since his ouster and, in fact, for several years prior to that L.S. had been trying to understand Joe's and Mark's actions. From his perspective every logical approach had met with failure. Now his company was in the grip of a man who was behaving as if he intended to ruin it.

After months of study and analysis L.S. reached a conclusion. The primary culprit here was genes. For decades L.S. had had a preoccupation with the role genetics played in human behavior. The Carty side of his children's line had seemed to him to be volatile and violent. It was as if Joe and Mark were really Cartys at heart.

Searching further for reasons, he was reminded of Mark's encephalitis as a child and came to believe it had caused Mark's violent temper for all these years. And when he looked back on it, Joe's car wreck and his subsequent concussion could well have caused *his* change in personality. L.S. read about brain trauma, and increasingly this combination of bad genes and trauma explained what he was witnessing.

Rejected in this analysis was any consideration that L.S.'s own behavior had played a role in the kind of men his sons had become. By blaming their genes, L.S. blamed no one, not even Joe and Mark, who only needed to understand that they were being victimized by bad genes and seek psychological help.

Genes, L.S. was convinced, had created a predisposition that had been actualized by events. L.S. reread Dr. Day's long-ignored report with wisdom gained from hindsight. He could see now that he had neglected to implement Day's most basic suggestions and that Joe's present behavior had been anticipated and interpreted by Day. Dr. Day had written of Joe: "If you really love me you will do as I say.... Since you oppose me then you don't love me, therefore I am justified in hating you." This certainly made sense now. Sam was attending board meetings and routinely opposed Joe's every move, and Joe seemed to hate Sam more with each passing month.

"Their desire for absolute power is insatiable," Day had written about Joe and Mark, shortly after they had left U-Haul. That was obvious enough to L.S. now. In fact, the entire report appeared prophetic, and L.S. cursed himself for his stupidity and arrogance in having disregarded it.

At the time the report was given to L.S., Day had provided him with special verbal instructions. L.S.'s notes were attached to the original report. A portion of them disturbed him very much in light of current events as he understood them. Twice now Joe had made reference to shooting or to a gun: once when he had acted as if he really believed L.S. was going to shoot him; the second time when he said he was going to start carrying a gun.

L.S. had observed Joe in action for years and believed that when Joe accused someone of doing something, it was because Joe was threatening to do it or thinking of it. Joe had accused Sam of enriching himself with sweetheart deals when L.S. believed it had been Joe who was doing that, as in the case of Form Builders. He said Sam hated him when it was Joe who hated Sam. He had accused Sam of tax irregularities in his family estate, and L.S. believed if there were any irregularities, they would be discovered in Joe's estate finances. And Joe falsely claimed the outside group intended to dismantle—destroy—U-Haul when it was he who was dismantling it and who, in L.S.'s opinion, would destroy the company if he remained in charge.

All this talk of guns and shooting taken in that context was very disturbing. There had been a troubling moment of sobering insight during L.S.'s private meeting with Dr. Day. The psychologist was advising L.S. on what he should, and should not, do about Joe and Mark. Day had told L.S. to understand that he could not satiate Joe's and Mark's "hunger for power."

"They are like a wounded animal in the corner," who tended not to care when they were engaged in a struggle, and they "can easily turn to revenge."

Then, this as a word of caution: "When they are very seriously defeated, they will get a gun."

CHAPTER THIRTEEN

RAPE AND SEDUCTION

"**D**ear Son's [*sic*] & Daughters of L. S. Shoen. In a very short time there will be another shareholders' meeting," L.S. wrote on September 8, 1987. Just the month before Duff & Phelps had lowered U-Haul's credit rating for senior debt and commercial paper, and L.S. was deeply concerned about the future of his company. "How you accept the responsibility for your ownership in [U-Haul] and how you vote your shares will dramatically effect your life...."

He enclosed a transcript of the previous year's meeting and urged his children to read it, hoping they would see how differently matters had turned out from what had been promised. He took upon himself most of the blame for what was occurring. "Separation blocks love. If we can come together...and obey God's commandment to love one another we can expect much good...."

A few days later he wrote a less charitable letter:

> We were both raped and seduced at the May 4th Special Shareholders' Meeting....I am sickened and disgusted with this behavior on the part of these two sons relative to me and to their brothers and sisters....I will never be able to stand by and rest while [Joe and Mark] use the organization as their playground....They must come to realize they will destroy them[selves]...and will destroy many other people....I am

pleading for your help. Believe me there are thousands of others praying for this miracle.

With love and respect,
Old Dad, Sam, L.S., Leonard.

The shareholders' meeting took place on September 27, 1987. Gaudy drawings were displayed conspicuously. Each picture was based on a theme associated with a state and was splashed on the side of a U-Haul truck, distracting from the carefully composed advertising package. It was clear that Joe was placing his stamp on the company's trucks and trailers. He passed out T-shirts with the same design.

Challenged on his use of these pictures, Joe said that U-Haul was showing respect for the states, and of course, anyone against the change was being disrespectful to the states. L.S. looked at the pictures and what they were doing to his trucks and muttered, "Circus wagons."

When Sam was allowed to speak, he explained how ESOPs were used by management for entrenchment, not as a benefit for shareholders. After that most of the Shoens verbalized their objections to the adoption of any ESOP, and Joe assured his brothers and sisters that the establishment of a company ESOP was only in the planning stages.

Then the shareholders were exposed to the chairman of the board's version of communication. Joe stood before them and delivered a rambling, disorganized, mind-numbing oration, directed at defending his behavior.

"You hear that?" he asked when one of his board members agreed with something he said toward the end of the speech. "Now, I didn't force that out of his mouth, and I don't have his wife in a fucking motel room gagged and bound, OK?, and I don't got [sic] power over that man, and if you think I do, you should go tell him that because what you're doing is downgrading him, not upgrading me. And you oughta all be proud of the way you're downgrading the people running the company.

"The final [point] is on market share. OK, no one asked. One thing that Mark didn't bring up that nobody asked about. Now

Sam has a way that he can explain market share, but, and that is some mathematics, and I only went to Harvard Business School, so I don't get [it].

"Market share is essentially one half of what it was in 1973. One half. I was able through my misinformation campaign, in which I do engage in a little bit of it, to get a magazine—namely, *Newsweek*—to print that we had sixty-five percent market share. I lied. I lied. I must confess. You see our market share at that time was thirty-eight percent. OK, not half. Thirty-eight percent. Now you see I lied to that man, but I figured, basically, fuck him. He was from Miami, Florida, and I lied to him. The truth is, and don't yell . . . , and then I got, my lie got repeated in *Truck Insider Newsletter*. OK? U-Haul giant falls from seventy-five percent of the market to sixty-five, so I got my lie repeated. OK? And I am capable of lying, but I won't lie to you. It's at—it's hovering between thirty-nine and forty percent, and [we are] working full fucking [time] trying to increase that and [don't] know if [we] can do it. . . ."

Someone attempted to get the floor several times. "I'd be scared for you," Joe snarled, "and I'll go through [it] again. I still got the mike, and I'm a jerk, I'm a jerk, and I still have the mike." Joe continued for some time, then near the end of his soliloquy said, in defending Form Builders' highly profitable relationship with U-Haul, " . . . I say, you wanna know about FBI, you talk to Ed Henderson, you talk to Tim Carty. OK? I got their wives held in a motel, too. OK? So you got to get them tomorrow before I let the women out. . . ."

The directors' election was conducted in a manner never before seen at U-Haul. Joe's nominating petition was read aloud until someone rose to speak against it. At that point Joe, as chairman, cut off *all* discussion of *any* nomination. Then the rest of his nominating petition was read, and only at that time did the shareholders learn that if the resolution passed, no other names could be placed in nomination nor could there be any discussion of the proposed directors. In short, Joe was ordering a straight up-and-down vote of his selection with no discussion from anyone.

Joe had begged Katrina to give him just one more year to show what he could do, and at the meeting L.S. was pressing Katrina hard to reject Joe's slate. Confused, uncertain, and wanting to trust Joe, she had agreed to vote in his favor, and not aware that her shares were the crucial handful that allowed him to cling to power, she did.

The shareholders passed two resolutions they believed would limit Joe's ability to adopt an ESOP and to prohibit the issuance of any U-Haul treasury stock, but Joe claimed one resolution had not passed and indicated he intended to ignore the other. When Sam attempted to obtain a tape recording of the meeting, his request was denied, and later he was told the tape had disappeared.

The hands-off approach to Katrina most of the family had observed prior to this meeting now ended, and family members from all sides began writing and calling to win her support.

At the first board meeting following the shareholders' Joe was elected president of Amerco as well as CEO. He did not speak to his docile board of the "malignant power" inherent in those positions. Had L.S. remained in control he had planned to start converting the aging U-Haul truck fleet into a modern one. His technique would have been to retain the old trucks for local rentals since a breakdown for a customer moving across town was something to which the company could easily respond. The new trucks would handle one-way rentals because there comfort and dependability were more important. Trucks would be purchased incrementally so that the warranties did not expire simultaneously, resulting in U-Haul's being faced with the same problem of worn-out vehicles in three of four years.

Instead Joe ordered thousands of new trucks and replaced the fleet as fast as he could. And to demonstrate that he understood modern financing, whereas his father had not, the thousands of new trucks were leased, not bought. In 1986, the last full year during which L.S. had control of the company, U-Haul had spent two and a half million dollars in new truck purchases. In 1988, the first year Joe had complete control, U-Haul spent thirty million, not to buy trucks but to lease them. While the company's book debt stood at just over five hundred million dollars, a debt load

Joe had once condemned as excessive, the lease payments were carried as an off-book debt.

Joe now had his chance to show rank-and-file employees just what he thought of them in a company memorandum: "The... Board of Directors has decided... we will not declare a discretionary Christmas bonus for 1987. This decision will, of course, be unwelcome news to our thousands of System members who had perhaps anticipated this discretionary bonus. Unfortunately, the $1,600,000 cost of this bonus is an expense to which I will not commit this company as we proceed in our determination to get back to basics and rebuild our fleet to insure our continued leadership in our industry. Joe Shoen, President...."

An anonymous letter was distributed in U-Haul Towers in response:

To: Joe Shoen....

Unfortunately, your name is on the bottom of [the memorandum canceling our bonus], the Shoen name, the name of *our employer* with not so much as one word of thanks, a few words of empathy, or sorrow for U-Haul employees. THAT MR. SHOEN, IS VERY SIMPLE TO DO AND WILL NOT COST YOU ANY MONEY!! ... Mr. Shoen, I ... can remember what your father used to say many times, "our most important asset is our employees"!!! ... Your father is one hell of a person and I will always think of him as "Mr. U-Haul." I am sorry to say that I along with many other people feel that you are nothing like your father.... Good Luck to you Mr. Shoen. I am sending a copy of this letter to your Dad, Mr. U-Haul.

Joe for years had described U-Haul employees as "pigs feeding from the trough" and now demonstrated his feelings directly. His claim that U-Haul could not afford Christmas bonuses was shown to be disingenuous a few weeks later, when he declared U-Haul's first-ever dividend, at a cost of $1.5 million.

But if he meant the dividend to placate his brothers and sisters, he was disappointed; they were still angry at the cancellation of their family insurance policies.

In December Mike met with Joe and Mark in Phoenix. He told

them at one point that their behavior had to end because "this type of conduct is going to destroy what we've got in this organization." As Mike later put it, "Joe looked at me and basically said, ... 'I will kill you.' "

The next day, when Mike was at a Scottsdale hotel, Joe and Mark ran up to him, and Joe began shouting, "You hate my children! You hate my wife!" over and over. He was soon joined by Mark. The pair were very physically intimidating, puffing themselves up in anger. Joe and Mark were nearly pressed up against him. They were red in the face, with saliva spitting out of their mouths, and behaving as if they were going to attack Mike, they shouted repeatedly in unison, "You hate my children! You hate my wife!" So threatened did Mike feel that he surreptitiously peered over the nearby balcony and tried to spot a place to land in the event they pitched him over the side.

Shortly after the first of the year Katrina wrote her family:

> I am writing you to verify my incompetence, ignorance and inability to deal with the current and recurrent problems which have infested our family and the U-Haul company. . . .
>
> I want you to know that I am doing more than just reading the letters you have sent me. I am trying to understand them. . . . You see, I am perhaps the most isolated Shoen family member. I am also the youngest. Neither have I had the extent of life experience, nor have I had the extent of sibling interaction that you all have had. . . .
>
> Specifically referring to my siblings, I have listened to and read diametrically opposed views on the same issue and I have seen the truth in both views. I have believed what has been presented to me as fact only to later be told that the same information is actually false (in most cases I have not been able to decipher the real truth). I have supped with an alleged devil and dined with a maniac and all the while I have loved these same people. . . .
>
> . . . I do not really think that right and wrong is the issue any more. In fact, what I do know is that in the past there have been nasty exchanges initiated by both "Shoen camps." . . . I so desperately want the family to get along. . . .
>
> My experience has been that the proposal for a forum for

discussion leads to a brick wall in every case....I have been told that there is not time for such efforts...or that they really do not want to be in the same room under such stressful conditions for such a long time. What I understand is essentially that people want to be cured of an illness without going through any kind of treatment—that they really do not want to commit themselves to dealing with the problem!!!!!...

I do not need to be convinced any further that there is a severe problem. I got that a long time ago. Now I am just floundering in a sea of futility where drowning seems to be the most painless way out. I would really like to see something positive happen to bring this family together voluntarily....Do I hear any suggestions?

Sincerely,
KATRINA

At Katrina's request Mike persuaded a majority of his siblings to schedule another special shareholders' meeting, which was set for January 9, 1988. At the same time Joe authorized an advisory committee to which most of his brothers and sisters were appointed. Incredibly, and as a sign of the degree of cooperation Suzanne and Joe were now exhibiting, Joe appointed his former stepmother to the committee though she owned not one share of U-Haul stock.

L.S., who feared that an acrimonious meeting like the one held just nine months earlier would cause more family conflict, asked his children not to attend. Sam warned his father this was very foolish. If those prepared to vote against Joe boycotted the meeting, he could do whatever he wanted. L.S. disagreed, so as a consequence, when the special shareholders' meeting did take place, Joe controlled an absolute majority of the votes present and wasted no time passing a series of resolutions.

The gathered shareholders approved the ESOP Joe had just finished telling his family was nowhere near completion, authorizing twenty-five hundred shares at sixteen hundred dollars a share. Joe also increased the number of shareholders it would take to call a special shareholders' meeting in the future, effectively ensuring this would be the last.

Of the two measures, it was the ESOP that was more sobering.

If Joe implemented its provisions in the way embattled management in other corporations had, he would become very difficult indeed to remove from power, and he would have the vast resources of the company his father had built with which to fight.

Sam was also upset over the value placed on these new shares since it set the price U-Haul said its stock was worth. Any attempt to sell to outsiders would be governed in large part by that floor, and Sam considered sixteen hundred dollars to be about 15 percent of what the stock was really worth. He believed that he "was in jeopardy of losing 85% of the real value of my stock through [this maneuver] of Joe's." Even worse, he seemed to be the only one of the group that was becoming to be called the outsiders who was concerned about it. "...I was on my own," he later recalled.

The same day as the special shareholders' meeting Harry DeShong, Jr., was arrested in Scottsdale, just outside Phoenix, for possession of cocaine. He was charged with possession of a narcotic drug, a class four felony.

Also in January, L.S. roughed out a letter only portions of which he included in communications with his children though its theme was one he used repeatedly. His draft said: "If we were all on the [U-Haul] board we could learn and know what is truly happening and eliminate the discord.... We who oppose this do so in the name of unity and because of fear. We fear the responsibility that knowing would make clear. However the exact opposite would occur. We would know the truth & the truth would make us free."

In February Sam and Mary Anna met with representatives of Bear Stearns, an investment banking firm in a position to advise and assist them in converting their U-Haul stock into cash. Bear Stearns's assessment was that if 10 or 20 percent of the shareholders wanted out, they would take a substantial beating in the price for the stock. Sam and Mary Anna decided to wait until summer before making a final decision.

On April 16, 1988, the new Advisory Committee met for the first time, and any thought that this would be an independent body free to reach its own conclusions and to request action from the board was quickly ended by Joe's antics. Though he did not serve on the committee, he insisted on attending and construed himself to be in charge. He stood in front of the gathering with a pointer that he jabbed at an endless stream of charts and graphs. It was, as one participant said afterward, another dog and pony show.

To assuage their fears, Joe assured his brothers and sisters that there were absolutely no plans to implement the ESOP adopted in January, declaring without reservation, "The ESOP is dead." And under no circumstances would U-Haul issue any type of voting stock that would dilute the voting rights of his family. "Management will do nothing," he said, "that ten, twenty, or thirty percent of the shareholders oppose."

Some present were not prepared to take his assurances on so important an issue and asked probing questions of the handful of senior employees Joe had brought along. Paul shouted that they were harassing the men, and Joe sent the employees away.

Joe told the gathering that the company was running well and that morale, despite the cancellation of the Christmas bonus, was at an all-time high. A few minutes later, apparently unaware of what Joe had just said, Mark acknowledged that morale was at a record low. But Mark and Joe agreed on one thing: their contempt for Sam.

Not long after this meeting Sam and Mike held a private conversation. They agreed that if Joe ever believed he was about to be ousted from power, they felt he was capable of taking violent action against either of them, though more likely Sam would be his target. The men agreed that if one of them were killed, the other would assume responsibility for his children. From time to time in the coming months, as the anger and hostility increased, they would ask each other if it was time to worry, then agree it was not.

For some time Sam and Eva had complained of the summer heat in Phoenix, a phenomenon known as desert fatigue. They had skied in many locations over the years and decided to look for a residence away from Phoenix that offered skiing in the winter and a vigorous outdoor life in the summer. They selected Telluride,

Colorado, and bought a spacious, comfortable log cabin in an exclusive estate just outside the small town. They began making regular trips up to escape, frankly, not just that summer's heat but the family feud as well. The fact that Joe had told Mary Anna he planned to start carrying a gun still weighed heavily on Sam's mind.

A disturbing incident at about this time also motivated Sam to move. It was Eva and Sam's practice in their Paradise Valley home not to pull the drapes at night since the house was set off on a secluded lot. One evening Sam was napping upstairs when a stranger simply walked into the house. "Do what I tell you," he said, "and no one will get hurt."

Eva responded coolly by calling out for her husband, "Sam, there's someone here! Get the gun!"

In fact, they had no gun, but hearing his wife, Sam knew there was trouble, and he bolted from the bedroom in his skivvies, without glasses, which meant he was virtually blind, and charged, stumbling down the stairs, shouting, "I'm coming! I've got the gun! I'll shoot the son of a bitch!"

The stranger was so frightened he bolted out of the house straight through the front window, but the episode caused Sam concern about the safety of big-city life. The pristine beauty and quiet congeniality of Telluride were a strong magnet and among the reasons he and Eva selected it as their retreat.

Not long after the intruder incident Eva participated in self-defense training sponsored by the Young Presidents' Organization in which Sam was a prominent member. Joe had never been invited to join, and that was another sticking point between the brothers. The course was taught on the West Coast by the San Diego Police Department, and when Eva returned, she was filled with enthusiasm. She made a point to tell her women in-laws what she had learned and urged them to be trained as well.

The course was oriented toward what to do if attacked in your own home. The instructor taught that the best defense was to be aggressive, and, if at all possible, not to let the assailant have privacy. Eva had been taught to run screaming if she could, even if that meant abandoning children in the house, because the intruder would flee. If escape was not possible, she was to struggle.

Whatever the man had come for he was going to take, and bargaining or begging would accomplish nothing.

Joe was spending an inordinate amount of time and effort in courting Katrina. She was in her last semester at Brown University and received regular calls from him. That spring he arrived unannounced at her doorstep late one night. He told her he had been working all day and was exhausted, but speaking with her was too important to be put off. He had Katrina and her fiancé join him for coffee, and at the intense meeting he outlined plans for U-Haul on napkins. He was presenting an image of the harried, concerned business executive and was so successful at it she was genuinely appreciative that he had fitted her into his busy schedule.

In May Joe arrived to attend her graduation, dragging along Heidi and his sons. L.S. phoned to tell Katrina that he and others of the outside group would not be coming because he was certain there would be a scene and he did not want to spoil this special occasion. Katrina was crushed though she understood her father was speaking the truth. If someone had asked her what she wanted, Joe would have stayed home and her father would have been there in his place.

Shortly after her graduation Joe presented Katrina with a U-Haul–leased Corvette to drive and informed her that the company would be picking up her costs to study that summer in Aspen, Colorado. When Katrina complained about the car and said that she did not feel comfortable taking so much directly from the company, Joe assured her that these were normal perks for a Shoen adult with 3 percent of the shares. Owners in similar billion-dollar enterprises received considerably more, so she was to take it as her due.

L.S. was increasingly distressed at Sam's apparent decision to sell his stock and seek a life free of U-Haul. L.S.'s solution was a return to the all-Shoen board. He was not even opposed to Joe's remaining as president and CEO because then his behavior would be scrutinized by his brothers and sisters who would discover the truth for themselves. Even now, as the acrimony rose, L.S. was trying to force his children into the company and to deflect any attempt on their part to be free of it.

"I know how frustrated you must feel," he wrote Sam, "after honestly caring for your brothers and sisters and for me from the time you were 12 years old and especially these past 14 years. . . . [But] we should persist in a quest for unity while enjoying life. . . . I am very saddened to see you work towards separation even from Joe. . . . I am for making your siblings accept the responsibility their ownership in [U-Haul] has placed on them. . . . "

In late June Sam prepared an "AMERCO Action Plan" to assist the outside group in countering Joe and his tactics. He believed educating Katrina, Sophia, Paul, and Jimmie, who still supported Joe, must be one of the outsiders' primary objectives, so he suggested that L.S. and he help inform them about the "excessive profits" and the "conflict of interest" represented by Form Builders. He advised providing them with a list of more than sixteen highly respected senior U-Haul employees Joe had summarily fired or forced out of the company. They were also to be made aware of Joe's tactics.

A. Projection (it's you not me who is psycho).
B. Intimidation (shouting or loudly talking the words he wants others to believe).
C. Arouse fear (we are bankrupt or we were conned).
D. Lying (makes no real effort to speak the truth).
E. Uses others to promote his scheme (Paul as to ESOP . . .).

He argued that the outside group should tell the others how Joe was caring for select individuals by "employing Sophia's boyfriend" and "entertaining or otherwise supporting Suzanne and Patty Lee." Finally Sam urged the outsiders to devise an alternative in the event they could not elect a board. And if at all possible, members of the inside group were to be encouraged to work in U-Haul for Joe; that experience by itself he believed would drive them into the arms of the outsiders.

If tower employees still carried any doubts about how profoundly management had changed, those doubts ended in July 1988, when U-Haul's marketing department employees were administered lie detector tests after Ryder System had begun using a slogan very similar to one then under consideration by U-Haul. At the same time reports from the towers said that certain telephone lines there now had recording devices. Company attorneys were reportedly so upset a number were seeking new jobs elsewhere.

On July 8 L.S. wrote Paul, Mary Anna, Sophia, Cecilia, Theresa, and Katrina about the pending Advisory Committee meeting:

> ....Try to remember that I did not create this situation.... *We are in a lot more trouble than I imagined would happen even in my most pessimistic moments* [all emphases in original].
>
> ...I made a most serious mistake when I gifted some 94 percent of the voting stock of [U-Haul] to my daughters and sons. I, they and thousands of others are paying dearly for *my foolishness*.... Bear this in mind. *My ignorance has resulted in much evil*.... [H]ow any of us can stand by while the Shoen family and [U-Haul are] destroyed is difficult for me to understand....
>
> Voting [U-Haul] stock once per year in ignorance is irresponsible.... *It is unnecessary, stupid and cruel. We will all pay and pay for this carelessness*. It gives credence to the line in the book, The Great Gatsby, to the effect that "*the rich are different in that they are careless.*"...
>
> The Advisory Board of Directors is a farce.... I am interested in learning how some of my sons and daughters rationalize taking my work and my life from me.... *I personally have been treated cruelly. So have thousands of others. This was stupid and unnecessary.... I have been compelled to watch my life's work be invalidated and destroyed.... This is preposterous. This borders on insanity*. Ignorance rules and it is manifested by prejudice, fear and confusion.... Harry DeShong Jr. is [now a] boss. This is ridiculous. Harry's only qualification for this job is that his wife is Heidi's best friend....
>
> Christ said, "You will know the truth and the truth will make you free." ... *I am not going to go away or get lost*. Maybe you too think that I am an old man and should lay [*sic*] down, conveniently die or while away my life. You need to know that this is a dream that some of your brothers have been harboring for years.... Nothing that you or others have done or will do

can change the fact that I love you, your mother, your sisters and your brothers. I believe that this love is reciprocal and that it exists among and between my daughters and sons and your mother. This is another reality that some members of our family would like to deny. . . .

The next day he wrote eight of his children: "Some of my daughters or sons have been behaving as fools, some as knaves. If the shoe fits wear it. You can change shoes.

"Do not expect me to speak and act as if darkness were light. . . . [Y]ou cannot get me to exhonorate [*sic*] you from your stupidity and cruelity [*sic*]. Ignorance is no longer an acceptable excuse. . . ."

Shortly before the second meeting of the Advisory Committee, scheduled for mid-July 1988, Joe contacted Sam to discuss buying his shares in the company. Sam was the recognized leader of the outside group, and if he no longer owned shares, it was unlikely he would continue in his efforts to oppose Joe's control. Joe suggested U-Haul would pay not full value, not even half, which Sam had suggested to Mark at a time when the company was strapped for cash, but rather ten cents on the dollar, or sixteen million dollars.

Though this was more money than he would ever use in his life, Sam considered the offer outrageous. He might have accepted a 30 or 40 percent markdown, but 90 percent was too unbelievable to contemplate. Sam refused, and again he and Mary Anna contacted Bear Stearns to see if there was any way they could disengage from "this whole mess" and take no more than a "moderately severe financial beating." They were tempted to hire Bear Stearns but decided to see what the second Advisory Committee meeting brought.

If Joe were primarily concerned with winning—that is, with keeping his power—he would have made a more reasonable offer to Sam or, if he were not interested in enriching his oldest brother, to Mary Anna. He had the ability to pay a figure much closer to the actual value of the stock, and once he acquired a block of their size, his worries over retaining U-Haul's helm would have been at an end. But Dr. Day had placed his finger on the pulse of Joe's personality when he wrote, "Because [Joe and Mark] basically feel inferior, winning a power struggle is undesirable because they would then have to be responsible for success. There would be no one to blame for failure, if they did have 'all power.' The reward is in the struggle. . . . " If Joe bought Sam out, he would lose one of his two primary adversaries, and when things went wrong, Joe would have no one to blame.

Katrina had been perplexed for months and was looking for answers at the second Advisory Committee meeting. She was beginning to think that her brothers and sisters not on the board were being deceived by participating in an Advisory Committee that held no power.

Just a week or two before this she and her fiancé had stopped seeing each other briefly. They were now reconciled, and he told her a surprising story about what had happened during their separation. Joe and Mark had jointly called him and said they appreciated how he had helped keep Katrina in their camp. They wanted to know if there was anything they could do to get the two of them together again so he could renew his influence on Katrina on their behalf. Mark said they would be pleased to hire him to work for U-Haul, and the company was prepared to fly him anywhere to reunite the couple. They wanted him to keep Katrina in line.

When the fiancé was not responsive, Mark cautioned that if he told anyone about this call, he would personally "bust his balls." The calls continued until her fiancé began hanging up on the pair. Then, just before the Advisory Committee meeting, he had received a call from Harry DeShong, Jr.

"How much do you want to work here?" DeShong asked gratuitously.

Katrina's fiancé was intrigued and flippantly decided to test him. "One hundred thousand dollars," he said.

"Consider it done," DeShong replied.

"I'm just kidding," her fiancé hastily said. He was not going to work for U-Haul.

DeShong persisted, but Katrina's fiancé would not change his mind. DeShong reminded him that he'd better not tell anyone about this or he would "bust his balls," the very words Mark had used.

Her fiancé considered this a grotesque manipulation of a personal relationship and afterward told Katrina that he believed it would be wrong for her to continue siding with men like this. With this information and recommendation in mind she flew to the Advisory Committee meeting.

The committee met on July 16 in a conference room at a local resort, the Plaza Hotel. Joe arrived prepared to chair the meeting, but this time those on the committee from the outside group were not going to let him turn this into a dog and pony show. Joe was aggressive about participating, so they voted to exclude him from the room while they prepared an agenda. Joe was furious and outside in the hall paced back and forth "like a trapped animal," according to one participant. Over and over he expressed his disbelief that those not supporting him were finally organizing themselves.

L.S. believed those present would feel freer to act if they did not think they were taking a position against their father. "I give you my permission to sell the company," he told them, though in his heart he hoped they would find some other way out.

Sam and Mary Anna made their position very clear. They were planning to sell. If more shareholders joined them, they would receive a better price. So it was either stay with Joe and all that was coming to mean or go with them and at least listen to what Bear Stearns had to offer.

Ever since Sam had resigned as president eighteen months before, a number of his siblings had made known their displeasure with him for having walked out, leaving them at Joe's mercy. That came up again now. Sam repeated his reasons for what he had done, pointing out he alone of them had opposed Joe when their father was ousted and that all of them but Mike and Mary Anna had ignored his pleas for help in the weeks prior to his resignation. He said that surely by now they could see why he had been forced to act as he had and could perceive the wisdom of joining together to sell their shares. After a discussion of Joe's behavior, participants began nodding. Yes, they were prepared at the least to listen to Bear Stearns.

During a recess Joe and Mark confronted Mike at the rear of the meeting room and shouted that he was the real problem, that he wanted to be president of the company and move it to Portland. "You're the cause of all the trouble in the family!" Joe screamed.

L.S. approached and told his sons, "This is wrong."

Mike said, "They have to do this to someone. Let them do it to me."

Joe was permitted into the meeting following the recess but not to make a presentation. Rather, his brothers and sisters wanted him there to answer questions about what he was doing with the family company. Just the month before, he had been quoted in a news article saying, "The organization is not the same organization as it was one year ago." Joe dodged pointed questions about U-Haul finances and said that he was not prepared to disturb the chief financial officer's Saturday to have him attend. When the committee insisted, the CFO was summoned, but each time the committee put a question to him, Joe shook or nodded his head before the CFO gave a cryptic response. Even that wasn't acceptable because more than once after an answer Joe whispered fiercely into the man's ear and the officer changed his response.

The committee told Joe to leave the room so they could speak directly without his interference. Joe said he would not stand for that. He had to be present for any questioning about finances. Rather than let the matter disintegrate into a brawl, Sam suggested ending the meeting and gathered those of the outside group to decide where they should meet later. As they tried to talk in private, Joe barged into the room and was asked to leave. He exited the room, then charged right back in, accompanied by Mark or Paul or both. This went on for several minutes until most of those who wanted to talk moved out of the conference room to get away from Joe.

Once they were gone, Joe headed straight for Sam's place at the table as Katrina watched and began going through his brother's notes. Sam entered the conference room and saw what Joe was doing. "Give me back my goddamn notes!" he shouted, running over.

Joe was enraged. "You're going to sell the company!" he cried out. He refused to surrender the notes, and Sam grabbed for them, but Joe held the papers away as the two men grappled with each other. Chairs crashed to the floor, tables slid, and pitchers of water tumbled over. People were screaming and shouting for everyone to stop—"Just give him the notes, Joe!"—but Joe was having none of it. He was very rotund by this time in his life, and as Sam reached for his papers, Joe started "belly-bumping" him in one of his favorite techniques of physical intimidation. He was screaming at Sam as he pushed him across the room with his gut, his face right against Sam's, contorted in rage, spittle flying from his mouth as he shouted obscenities.

Mike rushed over, followed by Paul. Sam was backing away from Joe, who was pressing down hard on him. "Let's get out of here," Mike called out to Sam as he moved to place a table between himself and Joe.

"No," Sam answered, "I'm going to get my papers."

Joe and Paul each held one of Sam's arms and were spinning him around toward a wall as if to slam him against it. Mike grabbed Paul and wrapped his arms around his younger brother and said, "That is not the way to love your brother." Then Mike began kissing him on the face playfully, telling him over and over that he loved him.

"Get away from me, you fag!" Paul shouted.

Sophia missed the scene because she was in the hallway, as she later said, "having my own nervous breakdown." Cecilia was also outside when the fight broke out and went into the conference room. For months she had been attempting to placate Joe and had grown increasingly frustrated that nothing she did "could make him happy." He always seemed to be "very angry." Watching Joe belly-bump Sam across the room, she stared closely at him and realized that not only were Joe's eyes showing anger, but "they were evil-looking" as well.

Katrina was taking the whole scene in as if it were a revelation.

When she watched Mike with Paul, she laughed out loud, but what she saw in Joe's eyes chilled her. In her short life she had never before witnessed such hate. It was a "profound moment of truth" for her, and she realized that Joe was "a complete liar" in her view. He wasn't taking care of the company for the good of the family, and he wasn't the competent, detached businessman he presented himself to be. She had come looking for the truth, and here it was, in the form of a sweating, corpulent, hate-filled brother who had mouthed lies into her ear in the name of brotherly love.

There was an instant when Joe caught her look. He reacted so instantaneously that it was as if he had read her mind: He had gone too far. As suddenly as it started, the melee stopped, and Sam had his notes. When Sam asked Katrina if she was willing to drop by his house the next day to discuss options with others, she readily agreed. She had her answer and had made her decision.

Joe wasn't finished. As Mike was leaving the conference room, Joe came up to him aggressively and shouted, "You hate me, and you hate my kids!" He chanted this over and over into Mike's face, working himself up into a rage until Mike was able to get away.

Since that earlier incident when Joe and Mark had shouted a nearly identical message in unison at him, Mike had given this behavior considerable thought. On the surface it was their usual bullyboy tactics, but now it had an extra edge that Mike found unsettling. Joe, Mike had observed, had a "projection thing," meaning that Joe would do "something that's improper, then he looks around the room and looks over at somebody that has nothing to do with it and says, 'You did it.' . . . " So when Joe shouted at Mike that Mike hated Joe's wife and Joe's children, it meant that Joe was actually the one who hated Mike's wife and Mike's children.

On Sunday the meeting at Sam's was a reasoned discussion of the dilemma they were facing. Sam told the outside group, "Now we're in trouble," since Joe obviously knew that Katrina was switching sides. He said that the one hundred million in preferred stock Joe was considering issuing could potentially dilute all their wealth, and they could not procrastinate in making a decision about how to respond.

Mike, Mary Anna, Cecilia, Katrina, and Theresa listened soberly. Though L.S. was coming to see that this approach might be the only one that would work for everyone, he still believed the family just ought to sit down and work this out. He had not built U-Haul only to see it sold to strangers.

The message Sam and Mary Anna had taken from their meetings with Bear Stearns, which Sam was repeating, was that they could not sell their shares without adequate information, and it was surely apparent to everyone that with Joe in charge they would not be able to acquire that information. One obvious solution was to regain control of the board. With that they could sell out, and if Joe wanted to keep running U-Haul, he was welcome to it.

The outsiders' decision was that no one in the family, not even Joe, should be financially hurt by their actions. They were, after all, family. Sam cautioned again that delay could jeopardize them all, but L.S. and others did not want to press and thought that those who were less certain should take a few days to think about this. During this time Sam was to arrange an appointment with Bear Stearns in New York City. Before leaving, they signed an informal agreement to work together "to maximize the liquidity and value of the common stock of [U-Haul]."

Calls were made that week to Sophia, Paul, Jimmie, and others to ask that they come along and explore options, so the pending meeting was not a secret. L.S. wrote to Mark, Paul, and Jimmie: *"[P]lease construe this letter as a plea as well as an invitation for you to write, telephone or meet with me at any time so that we might open up communications designed to achieve harmony and love in our lives and the lives of your brothers and sisters* [emphasis in original]. I need something magnificent, something perhaps miraculous. Miracles do happen....I need for us all to love one another as well as our fellow man. I believe in miracles...."

*   *   *

When Joe called Katrina in Colorado that week, there was no doubt in her mind that he knew he had crossed a line the previous Saturday. He was his old self, spieling a line of "Joe-speak," attempting to seduce her into signing a voting trust that would let him vote her proxy. Katrina knew that he had convinced Paul and Sophia into similar agreements and was working on Jimmie, so she had consulted previously with her attorney, who told her she absolutely should not sign the agreement. Joe assured her that he would release her from it any time she wanted, but her lawyer had already cautioned her not to accept such a verbal assurance. Once she signed the trust, the promise would be meaningless.

Joe pressed Katrina very hard, but she used her lawyer as an excuse and refused to give Joe what he wanted.

By this time Katrina was angry with her father and others in the outside group for not pressuring her as Joe had these past months. How could they expect her to make decisions on her own like a fifty-year-old businessman? This simply wasn't fair.

On Sunday, July 24, the group arrived in New York from various destinations. The day before, Paul had called Katrina and threatened unspecified retaliation if the outsiders took any action. Cecelia was joining the group, and on Saturday Joe called her house to talk. Her husband told him that Cecelia was in New York City with others consulting on what to do with their shares.

That Monday, July 25, 1988, the outsiders held a long meeting with Bear Stearns and learned how it could assist them in selling their shares. Bear Stearns suggested three approaches: It could help create a public market for their shares, reconstitute U-Haul's debt and pay a large dividend; it could sell some of the company's significant assets to accomplish the same purpose; or it could sell the company to a third party. But its central message was that these shareholders must have control of the board to accomplish any of these objectives.

It was difficult for Bear Stearns to tell those present how much money they could expect to make since the necessary information was not available, but if it took a conservative figure of the company's worth, one billion dollars, that would mean each percentage point of U-Haul stock was worth ten million dollars. Bear Stearns agreed it would pay fifty-five hundred dollars per share.

Mike cautioned his brothers and sisters that Joe was the kind of person who would stop at nothing to consolidate his control over U-Haul. He emphasized that in his opinion, it was not possible to overestimate the measures he might take. Still, some of the younger girls voiced their concern about angering Joe. They loved him and did not want to do anything that would be unfair, but they also said they hoped this would "resolve the rift in the family."

There was a consensus on that point, but beyond the need to gain control there was no unanimity on how to proceed thereafter. Some voiced the desire that when Bear Stearns finished its financial analysis, the family would sit down and work out a consensus on how to proceed.

More than one person present expressed sorrow that it had come down to this and wished there were another alternative. One of the Bear Stearns representatives later recalled the obvious "emotional pain" this decision was causing. But in the end the outside group agreed to pay the company a quarter of a million dollars as a retainer, and Bear Stearns said it was prepared to purchase another half million dollars in stock from those present to capitalize their effort.

Under Nevada corporate law a majority of shareholders could add to a board at any time without prior notice to the other shareholders. While still in New York, L.S., Sam, Mike, Mary Anna, Cecilia, Theresa, and Katrina signed a consent agreement intended to add enough members to the board for them to take control. This group controlled 49.66 percent of U-Haul's stock while those with Joe had 45.8 percent. The remaining shares were held by various individuals in small amounts while a Portland bank had 2 percent of the stock in a trust L.S. controlled. L.S. called the bankers, who said they could not approve anything over the telephone, so L.S. and Mike flew to Portland that day. On Wednesday, July 27, the bank signed the consent agreement to effect the election of ten new directors to the board. The next day, Thursday, July 28, the group informed U-Haul in Phoenix that a new board was in place, that Joe was no longer in control of the company.

At long last a majority of the Shoen family had seen Joe for what he was and acted accordingly. It was unfortunate that the result meant most of them would be selling large parts, if not all, of their stock and that control of U-Haul would pass out of the family, but that was the decision Joe had forced on them. They could now get on with their lives.

CHAPTER FOURTEEN

BUTTON, BUTTON, WHO'S GOT THE BUTTON?

What L.S. and the children allied with him failed to understand were the means that Joe was prepared to use to keep control. Mike had been correct in his admonishment. Whereas L.S. for all his faults had kept his children informed of what he was doing and had religiously avoided diluting the stock they held, Joe worked in secret and held no such commitment to his family.

On the previous Friday, July 22, 1988, Joe had frantically called a special meeting of the board to take place on Sunday as the outside group was arriving in New York. Gathering those he wanted on such short notice was not an easy task. Jimmie was flown to Phoenix from a remote location in Oregon, and John Dodds was on an island in the upper Midwest and was brought out by floatplane at U-Haul expense. From Friday through Sunday U-Haul Towers was busy with activity as teams of lawyers prepared various documents.

On that Friday Mark and Paul drove to Sophia's apartment and told her that if the inside group didn't act immediately, they would be out by Tuesday at the latest. It was important that they be the "first to the punch." They told her this was a "hostile takeover," and it was essential that current management act at once.

Sophia had known that something was up for at least the past week. Joe had pointedly asked her to persuade Theresa to come over to his side. If Sophia succeeded, Theresa's shares would replace those he had lost with Katrina's defection. But Sophia had declined to say anything to her sister because she knew that Theresa objected to family members' pressuring her, and Sophia did not want to lose her friendship.

From Sophia's point of view, there was little difference between her father and Joe, and this maneuvering was just more of "the same old shit." Once asked if Joe had destroyed documents, she replied, "I don't know if there have been any documents destroyed or not, but like father, like son. I wouldn't put it past either of them very much." She held business in contempt, judging it to be "the dirtiest work around because it's the easiest way to make a fucking buck."

For some time Sophia had been tired of what she viewed to be her father's pontificating. She had had "enough of him acting like he has the ultimate truth for us all." She "honor[ed] and respect[ed] him and support[ed] him . . . but my truth is a brand-new thing."

More than once Sophia had said that no matter what happened, the Shoen children "were luckier than ninety-nine percent of the people in the world. . . . What am I going to do with all that money? I'm not interested in selling. I don't want ten million dollars. I'm having a tough time dealing with the million dollars I have. I have a financial adviser, a lawyer, and I'm still afraid it's going to disintegrate."

Mark and Paul told her they were concerned that the outside group would create an all-Shoen board, then proceed to sell the company. Sophia was not pleased by either prospect. She viewed it as a "flipflop" from where the company was now positioned, and she shared Mark's and Joe's concern that the possibility of its taking place "was so close." In her experience "the family [didn't] function as a board." This would "be a catastrophe, incite conflict, and anger and grief for everyone. . . . "

She had seen people in their quest for power behave in ways of which she did not approve, and in the end that was what this fight was really all about: power, created by U-Haul's vast fortune. Sophia examined the shareholders' agreement Mark and Paul had for her, then signed it. Watching the subsequent events at U-Haul Towers that weekend, she commented wryly, "They were busy boys."

For the amount of lead time Joe had been given, the measures he took late on Sunday were surprisingly sloppy. Harry DeShong, Jr., later took credit, claiming he had convinced Joe of the course of action while the two stood in Joe's kitchen. The board, and by that presumably Joe, selected five key employees. These included John Dodds, DeShong, two company financial officers, and an attorney who had been employed by U-Haul for not even one month. The board hastily created 8,099 shares of common stock, which these men dubbed the Golden Five were allowed to buy. As Joe said, he was "changing the math." Once the shares were purchased, they were placed in a voting trust exercised by the board. The board set the value of the stock at $2,715 a share. Each of the five men was to receive just over sixteen hundred shares, which would cost more than $4 million.

The problem with the scheme was in the financing. None of the men could afford to buy the stock. Dodds's annual salary, while substantial at $100,000, did not allow him to make the purchase. Joe agreed to accept promissory notes for the money, but the men insisted the notes be nonrecourse, meaning they could not be pursued in court for failing to make payment once they had surrendered their shares to U-Haul. To avoid having the transaction appear an utter sham, the board insisted the men pay at least $100 a share as down payments, but even this was still more than $160,000 each. The men didn't have it, so Joe personally lent them the money. So hasty was the transaction that he set no interest rate for this loan of more than $800,000, and, as he later said, "no loan documents [were] executed...." Once the certificates were issued, they were tucked away into a fireproof filing cabinet on the eleventh floor.

Joe and the others involved insisted this was a bona fide transaction intended to hold key employees in their jobs with "golden handcuffs." But yearly interest alone on each note was later set at more than four hundred thousand dollars, an amount none of the men was capable of paying. Dodds didn't bother to keep his paper work. Once back in his office, he tossed his copies into a trash basket.

The irony in all this was in the source of the eight hundred thousand dollars. For years L.S. had tolerated Joe's and Mark's pipeline into the U-Haul coffers with Form Builders. The men had taken millions out of the company, while employees had claimed the prices they received were inflated. The pair claimed the profits were in trust to their children, but Joe had no trouble accessing the money even with these flimsy loan arrangements, and it was from Form Builders that he took the money he lent. Had L.S. not allowed Joe and Mark to enrich themselves through Form Builders, it is not likely either would have possessed enough personal wealth to make this transaction possible.

If this transaction was valid, when the outside group sat down on Monday, July 25, Joe had indeed "changed the math," and his inside group now controlled 50.01 percent of U-Haul's stock. L.S., Sam, Mike, very likely all the outside group were shocked when they learned that their shareholders' consent was rejected on Thursday as invalid. Less than a majority of shareholders had signed it.

Most of those in the outside group had never considered the possibility that Joe was prepared to diminish the value of stock held by the family to entrench himself in power. Sam had feared something like this, and Mike was not surprised either, but despite their warnings, the outside group had behaved naïvely.

Joe conducted himself as if this were business as usual. On Friday, the day after the consent was refused, he called his father seeking sympathy by complaining the IRS was going to send him to jail and that the government was demanding $1.7 million in settlement for the Form Builders' suit.

The same evening Mark called Cecilia and claimed he was upset that he and Sophia had not been included on the board the outside group had attempted to seat. Cecilia told her brother she was simply sick of all the fighting.

Almost at the same time Paul called Mary Anna to discuss developments. "What are you going to do now?" he demanded. He told her that all families behaved like this and reminded her that U-Haul had the resources and the money to fight the outside group.

He asked her repeatedly what she thought the company was worth, and finally she told him, "Three billion dollars."

Paul apparently misunderstood her, for he replied, "For your stock?"

"No, dummy. For the company."

Shortly after Mark's call to Cecilia, Sophia was on the telephone to her in an attempt to justify her actions. Sophia said that if the outside group had succeeded, the stock she and the others in the inside group held would have been worth a lot less.

There was a heightened sense of concern for security at the towers. A special memo was issued to the guards on July 25 instructing that greater care be taken with the sign-in sheets. "We have noticed that many sheets have been missing, possibly taken by employees," the memo said, and this was to be stopped. A security guard responded in writing: "The *only sheets* that were missing were removed by Joe Shoen *last Sun* [July 24]. He told [security] that he didn't want people seeing the names of those that attended the special meeting on 11 fl Sun evening."

Apparently as a joke intended to tweak the noses of the increasingly paranoid management, a U-Haul employee entered L.S.'s and Sam's names on the log all visitors were now required to sign upon entering U-Haul Towers. When Mark learned his father and brother were believed to be in the building, he ordered an immediate search, and when Harry DeShong, Jr., was informed, he raced his car back to the towers, talking on his car telephone. When they realized it was a joke, every attempt was made to learn who had pulled it off but with no success.

On July 29, 1988, the U-Haul board adopted "golden parachutes" for certain senior employees, including the board members, which provided lucrative termination terms in case they were removed.

On July 31 Mark issued orders that read, "Do not allow into the bldg. or open any doors for the following members of the Shoen family: Sam, Mike, L.S." A handwritten addition to the memo read: "Also Joe Shoen instructed ... that no one including Guard was to enter 11th fl. this weekend."

Employees who asked to remain anonymous called L.S. on August 1 and reported that between midnight and 4:00 A.M. earlier that day, Joe and others had secretly loaded a U-Haul truck with papers from the towers.* Mike received a telephone call that contrary to the story Joe and the others were spreading, the paper work for the 8,099-stock issuance had not been completed until the early hours of Monday, July 25, and had been backdated to Sunday, but he was unable to gather any proof to support the claim.

Events now took off at a furious pace. On August 2, 1988, Sam and the outside group filed suit against U-Haul, challenging the validity of the 8,099-share transaction. They were granted a temporary restraining order to prevent management from voting the shares.

On August 22 Katrina contacted Norma Colwell, one of the U-Haul secretaries who had seen to the well-being of the Shoen children for years, and reserved the use of the Tatum House and of her old Mustang while she was in Phoenix. Colwell wrote a short memo to Paul but received her response from Joe. She scribbled his instructions across the bottom of her copy of the note: "Joe Shoen Called @ 10:15 AM & advised that Katrina is involved in a law suit against the Company & is not stay @ Tatum. I am not to take calls from L.S., Sam, Mike, CeCe, Theresa or Katrina. They are to be referred to Joe Shoen on the 11th floor."

When Katrina went to the Tatum House, she found she was locked out. She called Colwell, who apologized for the inconvenience, but there was nothing she could do as she was no longer authorized to make such arrangements. Colwell said that as she understood it, Katrina could no longer stay at the Tatum House. Katrina was very upset.

Some weeks later, when Suzanne asked to use the Tatum House for out-of-town guests, Joe responded by writing, "OK by me."

Mike was not concerned that the outside group would win eventually and told a friend he considered the case a "slam dunk," but he was concerned about Joe's reaction when the outsiders won and Joe lost control of U-Haul. He confided to the same friend

---

*Those alleged to have participated, including Edward J. "Joe" Shoen, later denied under oath that this event had taken place.

that "Joe could not accept defeat and would feel driven into violence."

As a precaution the outside group checked on the status of their personal corporations. Historically these were managed by a financial officer who was employed by U-Haul but was responsible to each of the Shoen children. Sam was shocked to learn that though this officer had sent each person in the outside group his or her corporate annual report for signature, he had then *not* forwarded the documents to the Arizona Corporation Commission. In consequence, the corporate charters had been revoked.

Sam confronted the accountant and demanded an explanation. "Joe told me to do it" was his lame excuse, though later he testified under oath he could not recall who had told him to hold the documents. The outside group members were able to restore their corporations, but had the revocation not been discovered, they would have incurred a tremendous tax liability.

Joe was not finished. On September 6 he wrote a note to one of his secretaries: "What company cards exist I want them all cancelled gas, Amex etc. for Sam, Mike, MA, Theresa, Katrina, CC. Joe."

Also in September, L.S. became depressed when he learned that Standard & Poor's had reduced U-Haul's credit rating to an all-time low of BBB+.

Since the granting of the temporary restraining order the outside group had spent more than one million dollars in attorney fees. From L.S.'s perspective, this was just so much money squandered. The resources built up over a lifetime were being wasted on this struggle for control of the company. Since January he had tried to get along without the medication he had taken for years to stave off depression, but now the nemesis was returning. That fall he spoke to Joe by telephone and told his son that he was sick and wanted to find some measure of common ground on which the 8,099 lawsuit could be settled. What he secretly feared was that Joe would find a ruse to cancel his employment contract, which was essentially a retirement income. At least he wanted to be released from this burden of worry in these final years of his life. Joe rebuffed him.

L.S. shared his concern with Sam and others in the outside

group, who assured him they were prepared to shoulder the economic responsibilities and to make the difficult legal decisions that lay ahead.

On September 30, 1988, Harry DeShong, Jr., resolved his pending criminal case by entering into a consent agreement with the court that allowed him to participate in an adult deferred-prosecution program for one year. In exchange for regular appearances before a drug counselor and urinalysis testing, the criminal charges against him were dropped.

On October 13, 1988, attorneys arranged for the major shareholders to participate in a settlement conference. This time Joe remained largely silent while Mark did the talking. He told his brothers and sisters that management was in control of the company now and would "drive it until it crashes." Considering Mark's long history of blown race car engines and collisions, this was taken as an indication of just what the outside group could expect.

But Joe wasn't entirely silent and did propose a settlement. The suit was to be dropped and the outside group to sign a voting trust giving Joe control of their proxies for ten years. At that preposterous suggestion the meeting broke up.

On December 12, 1988, a preliminary injunction hearing began in Phoenix and lasted for most of a week. On the third day L.S. persuaded Joe, Mark, and Paul to join him for lunch across the street from the courthouse, at which time he tried to reason with them. Joe had told his father for some time that if Sam were "out of the picture," all would be well. Today was no different. All Joe and the others wanted to know was how to get Sam out of U-Haul. Joe said over and over that everything would be fine without Sam. The lunch proved pointless.

Back at the courtroom the purpose of the proceeding was to determine if the temporary restraining order should become an injunction to bar the use of the 8,099 shares until the lawsuit over the legality of their issuance went to trial. If the outside group failed to obtain the injunction, Joe would be free to use the majority vote those shares created to adopt all manner of policies and to run the company as he wished.

Prior to the early 1960s corporate law generally held that last-second stock issuances such as the one the U-Haul board had engineered on July 24 for the purpose of entrenching management were illegal. After paying their first attorney's staggering legal bill, the outside group members had retained local Phoenix attorney Marvin Johnson, who agreed to take a portion of his fee on contingency. Johnson had a solid reputation in Phoenix as a litigator, but nearing the end of his career, he was reputed to be cantankerous and unfocused in recent trials, even known to swear at opposing attorneys or threaten witnesses during depositions.* He had no special experience in this type of corporate law and relied on the traditional legal position as it related to last-second stock issuances.

Since the early 1960s a new doctrine in corporate law permitted such measures to prevent hostile takeovers or to protect corporations from harm. Mike had a passing knowledge of the law and was comfortable with his group's position. It was not possible for a majority of *existing* shareholders to conduct a hostile takeover. A majority of shareholders *were* the company, and measures to prevent them from asserting control were clearly illegal.

So Mike was stunned when Johnson didn't make this simple argument. During the four-day hearing Johnson rambled on about Form Builders and how Joe and Mark had enriched themselves for years at U-Haul's expense, "a constructive dividend" he called the profits. If left in place, they would continue to do so. Since Form Builders had nothing to do with the 8,099 stock issuance

---

*Deposition of Edward J. "Joe" Shoen on December 1, 1988:

MARVIN JOHNSON TO OPPOSING COUNSEL: Listen to me, you son of a bitch. Don't you ever say I did anything improper.

Deposition of Michael Shoen on January 19, 1990:

MARVIN JOHNSON TO MIKE SHOEN: He's not interested in hearing your philosophy on matters and it really doesn't—don't do it or I'll crack you over the head.

Deposition of L. S. Shoen on December 17, 1990:

MARVIN JOHNSON TO HIS CLIENT, L. S. SHOEN: What's this you're telling us about personal disorder? What the hell are you talking about? Are you answering his question here?
L. S. SHOEN: Maybe not.
JOHNSON: Figure out how to answer his question before you answer his question.
L. S. SHOEN: What do you want me to do?
JOHNSON: Sit up and talk to him instead of being like your son Joe. Open your eyes.

and L.S. had permitted the arrangement for years when he had been in control, it was difficult to find any relevance in the argument.

Only secondly did Johnson argue that the 8,099 shares were issued to keep Joe in power and that such an issuance was contrary to statute. But there was no such outright prohibition in the law.

U-Haul's lawyer muddied its arguments, but its basic position came through very clearly. U-Haul was one of Arizona's largest private employers. If the outsiders took control, they would move U-Haul out of state and take all the jobs with it.

The argument was preposterous, for there was no plan to move U-Haul, but it was persuasive. The court denied the motion for the restraining order, and the temporary restraining order was lifted. The judge was reported to have told his Rotary group that he had acted to save Arizona jobs.

The outside group was thrown into disarray by this unexpected development. The judge had suggested they have an expedited trial on the merits of the case, but Johnson opposed that. He told the group he would appeal the judge's ruling. That meant Joe had the company for the long months it would take the State Court of Appeals to rule, and if the ruling was adverse, there would be another year or more after that before the matter could get to trial. It meant the family was in for a long legal fight, one in which Joe held the company's resources.

Since August 1988 the Shoen family had engaged in an orgy of litigation. The outside group's 8,099 lawsuit was just the first.*
On August 8, the group sued U-Haul to block an offer that would have allowed the company to buy up shares of private individuals. U-Haul settled the case the following month by agreeing to withdraw the tender.

On November 23, 1988, U-Haul sued Sam and Eva in what

---

*From 1988 until the publication of this work the Shoen family filed more than one dozen lawsuits. Suits were filed, dropped, refiled, and amended in more than one state and federal district, defendants and plaintiffs added and dropped in such a fashion that the courts expressed frustration at trying to keep them straight. In addition, the issues in the lawsuits were often fluid, and rarely was there a final resolution. The primary participants and basic issues are all that are presented here because a complete treatment of the suits would consume several volumes.

was to be called the scheme lawsuit, alleging essentially that by contacting Bear Stearns and speaking to the press Sam had engaged in behavior intended to harm U-Haul. Joe had intended to raise one hundred million dollars by issuing nonvoting stock, and *Business Week* had quoted Sam stating his desire to sell the company. The suit alleged that as a result, the stock offering had to be withdrawn. Later Mary Anna, L.S., Mike, and Mike's wife were added to the suit.

On December 30, 1988, shortly after the request for the restraining injunction was denied, at Johnson's direction, L.S. and Mike sued Joe as conservator of his sons' Form Builders trust, alleging essentially he had breached his fiduciary duty to them by lending more than eight hundred thousand dollars to his business associates. This case was dropped when the judge suggested the issue properly belonged in the 8,099 suit.

And while the outside group spent over one million dollars on lawyers during this short period, U-Haul spent five million dollars for the same approximate time.

Also in December Joe sent Cecilia a short memo with copies to L.S., Suzanne, Theresa, and Katrina. He referred to a conversation they had at the injunction hearing: "[Y]ou appear to believe that I am on a program to take something from you. This simply is not the case. I want you to gain as a shareholder and I want to do the same.... We are all at risk because of our exposure to [companies like Drexel Burnham and people such as Michael Milken, Paul Bilzerian, and Ivan Boesky] over the last 18 months. It is more likely that these people will do us all out of our stock, than any of us will take from the others. Somehow we need to circle our wagons, stop fighting each other and recognize the common foe...."

L.S. responded first: "Joe, you write to Cece and copy to me that we should 'circle our wagons, stop fighting and recognize our 'common foe.' ... Joe, you know damn well by now that none of these people or companies are involved in 'taking ... U-Haul away from us.' What were you doing when you contacted T. Boon [*sic*] Pickens, First Boston and coincidentally Drexel-Burnham [*sic*]? ... What I am compelled to do is defend myself from you. *You are*

the corporate 'raider' that I have to deal with...."
On December 24, 1988, Cecilia responded for herself:

DEAR BROTHER JOE,

I usually try not to get involved with the back and forth letter writing which is so common in our family.... However, your recent letter ... demands a response because it perpetuates the inaccuracies which you persist to perpetuate....

You state in your letter that you are not taking something away from me. However, it is clear that you did act by issuing the 8099 shares to "change the math." This has taken away my ability to vote as powerfully by diluting the relative voting value of my stock and that of the other family members.

... There is absolutely no truth to the rumor you acted upon July 24 that I had been involved with any takeover specialists. I ... would never consider selling my shares to anyone who I felt would act to destroy the company. I am shocked that you as well as Paul, Sophie, and Jim clearly believed that this could have been my intention as of July 24.

Joe, if there is any business man that I need to fear it is becoming increasingly clear that it is *you.* You are the one who has contacted First Boston, T. Boone Pickens, and Drexel Burnham. You are the one who deprived me of my rights as a shareholder. And you are also the one under "massive scrutiny" for your business practices....

... I have no fear that [others] will "do us all out of our stock," and did not "bring these people to U-Haul." However, I did vote you into your position and that has clearly been a grave mistake.

Sincerely,
CECE

As it developed, Joe's accusation that L.S. was providing information to the Internal Revenue Service to be used against him was well founded though L.S. denied he was doing so and in discussions was evasive about any role he might be playing. The IRS trial was set to begin in Phoenix in early February 1989, and three weeks before, L.S. wrote a confidential letter to J. Robert Cuatto, district counsel for Internal Revenue. This communication left no doubt about the role L.S. had been playing in creating income tax trouble for Joe, trouble Joe had frequently said he believed would cause him to be sent to jail.

"...First you need to know why I am providing the IRS information...," L.S. wrote before explaining how Joe and Mark came to possess more than 20 percent of U-Haul's common stock. He acknowledged "yield[ing] to their tactics" in the company over the years.

> ...What they ended up learning was that they could get what they wanted via intimidation and power tactics. Now they are in control of a multi-billion dollar organization...and are using these same tactics to destroy people and property.... *They have fictionalized reality, manipulated the truth and corrupted relationships in the [U-Haul] organization* [emphasis in original]. I have experienced employees lying in depositions. These employees do this because otherwise they will be fired.... Simply stated I am now trying to discipline these sons to alleviate to some extent my failure to do so in the past. Their destructive behavior needs to be stopped for the good of society and for their own good....

He went on to describe as a "sham transaction" the sale of Form Builders to Joe's longtime friend. "I still treat [Joe] and Mark with 'kid gloves.' They could and would cut off my salary as a consultant ...at any time and make me sue them to get it reinstated.... Finally, I think it would be wise for you to treat both my son, Samuel, and myself as hostile witnesses if possible...."

L.S. was called as a government witness at the IRS trial. Asked if he had seen anything wrong in the relationship of U-Haul and Form Builders at the beginning, L.S. testified that he had. "At the time I approved of it and supported it because of a lot of reasons, mainly to keep peace, but also because Mark had been conned out of about $725,000 and Joe was starting a paint store, and I wanted to help them, and I wanted to keep peace with them." Asked why the arrangement had not been kept at arm's length, L.S. replied: "[I]t [was] because these two young men were able to intimidate me and have done it and they're still intimidating me, and, they, of course, are easily able to intimidate the people

. . . doing the purchasing in U-Haul International, and I know that went on." He was asked why he had agreed to testify for the government. "Because I decided about two years ago that I'd better stand up and tell the truth and quit letting these people get away. They now are leading and got control of a large business organization, and they can do lots of damage and have done." After four days the trial was recessed to resume in Washington, D.C., in April.

L.S. tried once again to persuade his children.

CONFIDENTIAL MEMORANDUM
DEAR DAUGHTERS & SONS: Feb. 20, 1989

I am sending this letter to all of my daughters. It is short and it is on point. It puts the monkey on your back as well as mine. My son, Edward Joseph Shoen, "Joe," has taken the [U-Haul] companies back in time to the early nineteen-sixties era. . . .

Joe manipulates the truth, fictionalizes reality and corrupts relationships. To quote a famous U.S. Senator, "like a dead mackerel in the moonlight he shines as he stinks."* . . .

You, who are buying his "con," are the fools in Rudyard Kipling's poem, "If." . . . Because he is my son this truth has been difficult and demoralizing for me to admit. However, I do not want to leave this world with you or he in doubt as to what my son, Edward Joseph Shoen, has done and is doing. What has and is occurring is unnecessary, stupid and cruel. It is also inhuman, illogical and uneconomic. It is not creative. It is destructive.

> With love and respect,
> LEONARD S. SHOEN

The same day Joe mailed his father a letter.

Re: *Breach of Employment Contract*
DEAR MR. SHOEN:

Since at least February, 1987, you have been compensated under Section 3.04, Salary Continuation During Disability, of your employment contract with [U-Haul] (the "Company")

---

*"He shines and stinks like rotten mackerel by moonlight."

dated December 27, 1979, a copy of which is attached hereto as Exhibit "A" (the "Employment Contract").

The Company recently learned that you testified under oath that you do not suffer from a bipolar affective disorder. If you are not disabled, your past failure to act in the best interest of your employer constituted a breach of your Employment Contract and your compensation is therefore being immediately stopped.

If your testimony is controverted by a physicians [*sic*] certificate indicating that you have a medical condition that would excuse your above-mentioned failure, please provide that evidence to the Company for its consideration.

> Very truly yours
> EDWARD J. SHOEN
> President and Chairman

Joe had fired his father. Though L.S. had feared this very action for more than a year, he could hardly believe the manner in which it took place. First, he had no idea that U-Haul claimed to be paying him his consultant's salary on the basis of the disability clause of his contract. Second, "the Company" had not "recently learned" about his testimony concerning his sound mental health. Joe had been sitting in the courtroom when he said it; indeed, Joe had just finished whispering in his lawyer's ear, and at the time L.S. thought the question came from his son. Now L.S. was certain of it.

It was not possible to tell from reading the letter, except perhaps from the coincidence of last names, that this was a son writing to his father. Joe, who owed everything material he had in life to his father, wrote to him as if he were a stranger.

The insidious part of the dismissal was the suggestion that if L.S. was prepared to submit a doctor's statement that he was mentally ill, Joe would have his salary reinstated. There was, of course, no assurance that once that occurred, it would not be stopped again with another promise of resumption when L.S. jumped through another hoop. And Joe would use any admission that L.S. was mentally ill to discredit his father.

L.S. was distraught. He had never set aside a personal fortune though for forty years he had possessed the means to do so.

U-Haul had been his fortune, and his employment contract was his retirement. He became even more annoyed when his sister, Patty Lee, called from Phoenix to persuade him to obtain and submit a doctor's statement. L.S. had no difficulty in figuring out where her loyalties lay. If she had felt exposed when L.S. was in control of U-Haul, how must she feel now that erratic, manipulative Joe held the power?

U-Haul had called a shareholders' meeting for March in Reno, Nevada. The company had no significant corporate presence in Reno, and members of the outside group decided Joe had done it to make matters difficult for them. L.S., who had been aggressively arguing for his all-Shoen board, had the support of the outside group. The plan was to force Joe to vote his 8,099 shares to retain power so that when they won their case, the election would be invalidated.

The meeting was held in two conference rooms at the Sands Hotel in Reno. This was the first time the shareholders had met since the issuance of the disputed 8,099 shares the previous summer. L.S. chafed at his firing by Joe and for the only time since the initial success of U-Haul faced economic privation. He was emotionally distraught and unable to function effectively. His primary concern was to bring the family together, to stop the senseless and destructive fighting. It was a minority position.

Once again the meeting was elaborately staged and formal in presentation. The first room had comfortable dining tables for a meal, and the second was arranged for the meeting in chief. The outside group noticed at once the presence of security guards, which some of them took to be a form of intimidation. The insiders were represented by Joe, Mark, Paul, and Jimmie. All of the Golden Five were present as well. U-Haul had twelve men in attendance, two of whom were lawyers, plus four more attorneys for a total of sixteen. A reporter who had driven up from Las Vegas was refused entry.

Representing the outside group were L.S., Sam, Mike, Mary Anna, and Theresa. They had an attorney present, and one minor shareholder, Bertram Miller, was also in attendance. Miller had worked for U-Haul years before and received nine shares in the company. He had not spoken to L.S. in more than twenty years before that day. Miller said that he "had a feeling these boys in power now [are] skimming the cream off the milk, and I [want] to talk to them about it."

The outside group noticed immediately that the inside group wore brilliant green lapel stickers, or buttons, on their suit jackets. The demarcation between the two sides of the family was now formalized.

Though only twenty-three people were there for the meeting, chairs had been set up for a throng. About ten of the inside group took their places at the front with a conspicuous distance from them to the others. An elaborate brochure, entirely inappropriate for such a closely held nonpublic company, was distributed. The outside group had decided to do its own taping, so both Sam and Mike, carrying tape recorders, took their seats. Mike's recorder had been provided by a newspaper reporter in Phoenix who was planning to run a story on the family and the dispute. Mark seated himself beside Sam and immediately began mouthing obscenities to him about Eva and his children.

Joe took the podium. "Good morning," he began. "I would like to call to order the meeting of the 1988* Annual Deferred Shareholders of [U-Haul], a Nevada corporation. My name is Joe Shoen. I am the president and chairman of [U-Haul]. I will be conducting the meeting today."

Except for some of the newly retained attorneys and the two guards there was not a single person in the room who did not know Joe on a first-name basis. His formal beginning only emphasized the absurdity of the situation. This was not a publicly held corporation with thousands of shareholders in attendance. This was family.

"No recording devices of any kind will be allowed to be used during this meeting. I know there are at least two of them that I have seen in here today. The people that have these devices please turn them off at this time."

"May I ask why [we can't record]?" Sam asked.

"It is the rule of the meeting."

*The 1988 meeting had been delayed until March 1989.

"What do you think is going to be said here that you don't want to have repeated?" L.S. asked.

"It's just the rule of the meeting," Joe repeated. Mark started to speak. "Mark, you are out of order. It's the rule of the meeting. We are going to have rules at this meeting. The rules are going to be the rules, basically."

L.S. spoke again. "Mr. Chairman, may I ask you one question? Is this the rule that 'he who has the gold makes the rules'? Is that the fundamental rule?"

"That's your rule," Mark interjected.

Joe said that he was going to try to keep the meeting "as businesslike as possible." L.S. wanted to know if he planned to run this the same way he had run the late-night meeting in July when he issued 8,099 additional shares "and thereby 'changed the math' "?

"Get the guard! Get the guard!" Mark shouted.

Joe assured everyone that he was not going to railroad the meeting. Mark leaned over to Sam. "Turn the son of a bitch off, asshole," he snarled.

From the podium Joe repeated, "We are not just going to have tape recorders."

"Either play by the rules," Mark said rudely to Sam, "or get the fuck out. You turn it off, the son of a bitch. Take these guys' tape recorders or throw them out of the goddamn meeting!"

Mike explained the difficulty he had experienced attempting to get tapes of earlier meetings. "[T]o protect your reputation and to benefit the corporation, I think it would help if we had a tape recording. I also believe that as an individual I have that right."

Joe said rules were rules.

Miller spoke up: "Why were not the rules and regulations sent out, stating that we would not be able to have a tape recorder? Instead of a situation where everybody's wrong but you."

"I do not have a good answer to that question," Joe replied. "[I]f those rules are out of order, you will have all the remedies that are available to people. I don't know what they all are."

Miller persisted. " . . . I cannot understand how Mark Shoen can act the way he did and you act the way you did. . . . "

"Yeah, you gotta problem, Bert?" Mark said.

"No, sir, I do not have a problem," Miller responded. "But I have a right to speak."

"Now, let's let one person speaks [*sic*] at a time," Joe said.

"Why are you here all of a sudden, Bert?" Mark demanded. "All of a sudden your stock may be worth more than nine hundred a share, huh?"

Joe said that there was to be order. "... If we do not have order, we will either have to ask you to leave the room or cut the meeting off. I do not want to know what you want to do. Honestly I do not have any way to control you."

And now it was clear. Mark had always been Joe's pit bull. There was absolutely no way Mark was behaving like this on his own. Joe was going to pretend to restore order, but Mark was going to receive all the license needed to disrupt the meeting.

"... I want to get the tape recorders out of the room," Joe said. "It will be a nonissue. It is clear Mike's objections are noted on the record."

Mike replied, "When they killed the Jews in Germany, it became a nonissue. I will give up the tape recorder when I am allowed to bring a court reporter in here. I want an adequate time to bring a court reporter in here because I know you have nothing to hide."

"I would like to speak to the issue," Mark said. "Are the Jews in Germany under discussion here?"

"No," Joe said, "they are not under discussion."

Mark persisted. "He has specific knowledge about the Jews in Germany because he is married to a woman whose father was an SS man. Let's talk about the Jews in Germany. Check it out."*

"... What I have to say," Mike resumed, "is that I will give it up when it is taken from me physically. I feel that I have the right."

Joe looked to one of the guards. "He does not want a fistfight. He just wants you to pick it up."

Mike was unperturbed. "If you want to assault me, be my guest."

---

*Mike's father-in-law was a Pole of German descent who was drafted by the Germans during the Second World War and compelled to serve on the Eastern Front. Twice wounded, he was 95 percent disabled after the war and was one of eighteen in his mechanized company of two hundred to survive.

"He does not want to assault you..." Joe said.

For now Mike was left with his recorder. L.S.'s daughters demanded to know why their father had been fired. They asked the board members to confirm that Joe had acted with their knowledge, and the men stammered incoherently.

Joe interrupted. "I am the only one that could verify that. So I can verify that for you."

They asked Joe why this had been necessary. Joe would only reply, "Ordinary course of business is what I am going to say."

The sisters wanted to know if he had ever read the employment contract, which called for arbitration of disputes. "I have read it several times," Joe said. What he refused to do was explain his conduct.

All this while Mark was goading Sam with an endless stream of obscenities and abuse directed personally at him and his family. When L.S. was able to speak, he urged them to resolve their differences. It wasn't right having one side of the family sitting up front, the rest facing them from the general room. Why not just sit down around a table and talk?

"Point of order!" Mark shouted.

"Thank you very much," Joe said to his father. "Your allotted time is up."

"Point of order!" Mark repeated.

"...[W]hen you spoke at any place or time, did I ever cut you off once?" L.S. asked Joe.

"No."

"Mr. Chairman, do you have any money or resources or assets or education that you did not receive as a gift from me or that you did not steal from your brothers and sisters and other people?" L.S. asked.

"OK. That's out of order, too. Thank you," Joe said. "The next person who wants to speak I'm going to ask you to stick to the—"

"I move for the question!" Mark shouted.

"Someone moved for the question," Joe said as if he could not see Mark sitting ten feet from him or recognize his voice. "Now we are going to have a vote."

"I move to table that motion," Sam said.

"That's a nondebatable motion. It's a nondiscussable motion. The question has been called for," Joe said.

L.S. objected on the ground that this was exactly how Joe had presided over the meeting when he ran his 8,099 shares through. He then objected to many members of the current board. "I don't think they are qualified—"

Joe had his own way of dealing with this. "Someone called for the question," he repeated.

Mary Anna said, "I don't think that is fair. I want my five minutes to speak."

"Shut your trashy mouth!" Mark snapped.

"Oh! Jesus," Theresa muttered.

Joe said Mary Anna should have objected sooner. "I am asking Mark to rescind his call for the question to let me have my five minutes," Mary Anna said.

"Well, do you want me to speak to that?" Mark said. "If we have to listen to the type of trash that comes out of this man's [indicating L.S., who still had the microphone] mouth. . . . "

"Out of your mouth," the mild-mannered Theresa said.

"Out of your mouth!" Mark shouted. "I maintain that I have a right to call for the question. We don't have to listen to this. Nobody has to put up with this. You people owe us! We don't owe you!"

Joe asked if Mark would rescind his call for the question.

"Certainly not. I think it is extremely important that these type of people—"

"That's enough," Joe said, interrupting.

" . . . Well, I'll say it anyway," Mary Anna began. "This board did not earn the right to be on the board. They issued themselves the right to be on the board, and they stole . . . the eight thousand ninety-nine shares. They stole it from me and every other shareholder. You did not earn it. You stole it, and that is the way it is. You stole it for the purpose of entrenching yourselves and powering down other people." Throughout these remarks Mark was repeatedly calling for a point of order.

Again Joe suggested someone ask Mark nicely to rescind his motion, so Theresa did.

"Can you be serious, Theresa?" Mark replied.

"Yes, I can be. I'm asking you very kindly."

"We don't have to listen to this trash. This is not acceptable" was his response.

"I'm asking you to give everybody—"

"Absolutely not. Absolutely not."

"So you are saying that the only people who have rights are the people up there?" she said.

Joe answered for Mark, "No."

But Sam disagreed. "You've got it."

Theresa said, "Is that what you are telling me? Are you telling me that shareholders, unless they are on your side, have no rights?"

"I've been on both sides, sweetheart," Mark replied.

"Don't call me sweetheart."

"We have a ballot," Joe interjected. "Call for the question."

Theresa said, "Jesus Christ. He, L.S., handed it to you on a silver platter."

"What do you call this?" L.S. asked. "People should at least have the right to their five minutes."

Joe said, "I'm all for it."

"Rule of order!" Mark shouted.

"The question has been called for," Joe said. "We are going to vote now. Let's not all lose our ability to vote."

"This is unacceptable!" Mark shouted. "This is unacceptable! This gentleman [indicating his father] has gone far over his time limit."

"He is using my five minutes," Theresa said, "because you won't give it to me."

"Tell him to sit down," Mark demanded.

"No, he is using my five minutes."

"They don't want anyone to talk, and that is clear," Sam said.

Joe suggested again that someone ask Mark sweetly and perhaps he would rescind his call for the question.

"Why don't you ask him?" Mary Anna demanded. Joe ignored her.

"You tell me it's appropriate to listen to this?" Mark asked rhetorically.

"I have to listen to you," Theresa pointed out. Mark had yet to stop talking even when others were speaking. "You can listen to me. You have already been bitching and screaming at your father, who handed to you everything you have."

"I'm earning mine, baby," Mark said.

"Calm down," Joe said. "Apparently no one is able to ask Mark in a way that will work."

Mary Anna tried again. "Mr. Chairman, will you ask him?"

"Oh, sure. I'm happy to ask him," Joe replied. "I'm going to speak for a minute, and then I'm going to be out of order, too. Unfortunately I have the microphone."

"That's true," Mary Anna said, "it is unfortunate."

Joe made his desires known. "I think that a call for the question is a legitimate remedy for anyone.... It was properly made. I am unable to get people to stick to five minutes.... I apologize for my inability to do that."

"You have not even tried," Sam retorted.

They now argued over how long L.S. had actually spoken. Then Joe called a recess. He and Mark huddled off to the side. They glanced repeatedly at Mike's recorder, which had been running until now.

When the meeting resumed, Bert Miller was able to speak briefly. He expressed his displeasure with the annual report, then said, "Over the years I figured the people here were capable of running the corporation. Well, after reading [the proxy of U-Haul management], it was at times reading from a political speech—I got half a story.... The biggest lie in the world is from the guy who will tell you half a story. I checked around and found that they had diluted the shares by eight thousand ninety-nine, and the people who owned it were basically on the board of directors. There is something wrong, gentlemen, with the Shoen family. From the standpoint that—"

"Hear, hear," Mark shouted, interrupting. "Ta-da." He clapped his hands.

"—you all did not start this corporation. You inherited it, and I just wonder if you are capable back from 1950 or 1949 to be able to do what Anna Mary Shoen and Sam Shoen could have done..." Miller said.

"Shove that shit up your ass!" Mark snapped.

"That's out of order," Joe said, then: "And, Bert, I think you are out of order, too."

"You talk about my mother one more time, pal, one more, just one more..." Mark snarled as if Miller had insulted rather than complimented Anna Mary.

"No. No. I think she was a fine woman..." Miller started to explain.

"You don't know her from shit. Shove it up your ass," Mark repeated.

Joe said, "Mark, would you let him talk?"

"Out of order!" Mark shouted. "I insist that we adjourn this meeting. I make a motion to do that."

Sam moved to table the motion.

"You can't table that motion to adjourn, asshole," Mark said.

"Can I be recognized?" Sam asked.

Miller said, "You all got problems," then sat down.

"Oh, you figured that out?" Mark crowed. "Hey, you are brilliant."

"...We have a motion to adjourn, and we are looking for a second," Joe said.

Sam asked to be recognized. Jimmie seconded the motion to adjourn. "You are out of order," Joe told Sam, "if you are not on the motion to adjourn, unfortunately."

"The motion was seconded after I asked to be recognized," Sam explained.

Mark leaned toward him. "Don't say shit, asshole."

"This is all unnecessary to do. You guys control it," Sam said.

"I agree entirely," Joe responded.

"This guy is out of order," Mark sneered; "he needs to be ejected. It's over."

"We have one motion in front of us," Joe said.

"Well, then do it!" Mark shouted.

"We have one motion in front of us," Joe repeated, then: "Mark. Mark! You are out of order now, Mark."

Mark was leaning aggressively toward Sam, goading him on. Throughout the meeting he had muttered a steady stream of obscenities at his older brother. "Take a swing," he now said, taunting Sam. By now Sam and others present had concluded that the purpose was to get Sam to do exactly that. Then Joe and Mark planned to have him arrested. "Take your best shot. You've done it before. Hit it! . . . These people have one thing in mind, and it's for litigation. Yeah," Mark said as he slid up against Mike, "got right in here so I can talk to you."

Joe called the motion, but Mark was preoccupied. " . . . Your father-in-law killed little Jews, didn't he?" he said to Mike.

"What's that?"

"Your father-in-law killed Jews, didn't he? He was SS, wasn't he? Your father-in-law was SS. He was a Nazi. He killed Jews," Mark said.

"Mike, the meeting is over," Mary Anna told him.

"Wait a minute," Mike said. "I just want Mark to finish this."

"Your father-in-law is a Jew killer," Mark repeated. "He killed Jews in World War Two."

"What do you mean by that?"

"Can't you hear?" Mark asked.

"But I want to understand it, Mark. Hey, Harry. I want to get this thing finished about what Mark was saying."

"Don't fuck with me, you SOB," Mark said savagely, turning to Sam.

"I'm just trying to finish what you had to tell me, Mark," Mike said again.

"Back off, Mike," Joe warned. "Back off, Mike."

Mark grabbed Mike's arm, then slugged him in the face. There were shouts as Joe ran over from the podium. Mark turned back to Sam and took a swing at him. L.S., who had seen Mark building up to this, escorted one of the women from the room.

Mark was still swinging at Sam, who was defending himself. Mike moved toward the door to get his tape recording of what had taken place to safety and to avoid any further confrontation. Suddenly he was struck violently, and hands were pulling at his recorder, which he clutched fiercely to himself. He curled up into a ball to protect the recorder and fell to the floor while Joe pummeled him with his fists and feet.

All at once the assault stopped. Mike got to his feet and moved toward an open door. Joe ran to the doorway and ordered the guard to leave, implying he would give his brother the assistance he needed. The moment the guard turned away Joe moved his body to block the view, then punched Mike brutally in the stomach. Mike could see the hate in Joe's eyes and moved the recorder, hoping now to block blows with it, but it made no difference as Joe continued striking him. Mark ran up and grabbed Mike who again curled into a fetal position, offering no resistance because he didn't want to fight with his brothers, and fell to the floor. Joe and Mark were beating him with their fists and feet, only this time it was far more severe than before. They kicked him savagely, over and over, screaming obscenities. Mike took the blows in his kidneys, head, and back.

An executive with one of the U-Haul insurance companies ran up to them and shouted, "Stop, Joe! Stop! We've got to save the company! Remember! We've got to save the company!" The beating suddenly stopped, and for a moment Mike did not look up as he did not know what to expect. When he did, he spotted Harry DeShong, Jr., with his arms wrapped around Joe, wrestling him backward away from him.

Mark bent and resumed the attack when a uniformed guard ran to him and wrenched him from on top of Mike. "Not me, asshole!" Mark snarled. "I've got the button!" He jerked the lapel of his jacket and shoved the green button into the guard's face as Mike made his escape.

CHAPTER FIFTEEN

JUST SPECULATE

W hen L.S. returned to the conference rooms, he found them empty. He went upstairs to where the outside group was staying and saw Mike, who was battered and bruised from the assault but under the circumstances in relative control of himself. Mike told those present that he intended to charge Joe and Mark with assault. Sam paced back and forth, saying repeatedly that Joe and Mark were "sick."

A reporter came into the room for statements. L.S. shook his head sadly when he attempted to explain what had taken place and finally said, "I created a monster."

Back in Phoenix at three in the morning, Mike was treated at a hospital for deep bruises on his neck and back. He went to the *Arizona Republic* offices to give his story to the state's largest newspaper and posed for a photograph, which the paper ran, graphically depicting the bruises. Asked for his version of the assault, Joe told the reporter mysteriously, "After the meeting, people acted as human beings."

L.S. wrote to the outside group on March 12, 1989:

I want you to realize how my sons, Edward J. and Mark V. Shoen . . . scheme and work as a team. They program themselves and others to do, or say whatever is needed. They do it using the same basic tactics as Hitler.

They replace killing with "firing." . . . As you know, *they have*

294

*now "fired" me. I do not want this to make you unhappy. I do
want you to realize what we are up against [emphasis in original].
... Edward J.* Shoen is a master at using rape and seduction....
I know because I was one of his lackeys for many years. I did
and said things that I am now embarrassed to tell....

That month Mike was informed that the mortgage held on
his home by U-Haul was in arrears. It was not, but Mike understood the warning and paid off the mortgage to the company.

Employees at U-Haul Towers expressed shock when they
learned that Mike had been beaten, and increasingly the speculation was that U-Haul would fail under Joe and Mark. Top
salaries, once sixty thousand dollars, were now in the hundreds
of thousands of dollars. Upon returning to U-Haul, DeShong's
star rose, and he and his wife, Patti, were "thick as thieves"
with Joe and Heidi. DeShong occupied an office that one employee described as being the size of an "apartment" and that
was usually referred to as the Taj Mahal.

Physical intimidation had also become a common management
practice. One supervisor brought in by the new regime screamed
obscenities during staff meetings and threatened subordinates by
shouting, "Shut up or I'll Velcro you to the wall!" Firing had
become a way of life in the towers and was performed with
relish. By one estimate more than half the employees who had
worked there in 1986 had been terminated. On one occasion
DeShong informed an assistant that he would be firing a number
of employees that day. "We're going to have a good time," he
said with a grin.

On March 21, 1989, L.S. informed Cecilia, Theresa, and Katrina that Joe had terminated their employment with U-Haul.
They had received relatively small salaries of about twelve thousand dollars a year from the company, but what they valued
most was the standard U-Haul employee benefit package of health
and life insurance. L.S. told them, "You will need to sign up
for the continuation of [the] policies. These can be continued
for eighteen months for a monthly fee. We will be out of this
mess by then."

L.S. then updated them on the status of their appeal regarding the adverse 8,099 court ruling. "I did not mince words [when I met with Marvin Johnson] and we got very specific. I am now convinced that we will prevail in this litigation...."

The Shoen feud was now all over the papers in Phoenix. L.S. had shunned publicity his entire life except to advertise U-Haul. Though he had lived beside a country club, he had not belonged to one since moving to Arizona. His children had generally attended the best private schools in the area, but they were schools to which a middle-class family could send a child with some sacrifice. The Shoens were not often pictured on society pages, and very few people in Phoenix had ever heard of them or even knew that U-Haul was headquartered there. All that was ending.

At the end of March 1989 the *New Times,* a local weekly tabloid, ran an eight-page story detailing the history of U-Haul and the family. It was written by Paul Rubin, often regarded as the paper's best reporter. "Joe and Mark embrace belligerence and arrogance," Mary Anna was quoted as saying. "I call it bizarre." Joe refused to be interviewed, but Rubin unearthed a quote from a recent deposition: "The kind of lies that we have seen here, that I cut my thumb off in a paper shredding documents..., that I hustled documents out of the building in the middle of the night, that I carry a gun. These sorts of things have prejudiced me massively in my dealings with the I.R.S. They think I'm this sort of a person, that I engage in this sort of behavior on a systematic basis, and that they have reason to apprehend me as an enemy of society. I don't view myself as an enemy of society."

L.S. was asked to account for what was taking place. "When they're young, you see such promise and you want to do everything for them. Practically all babies are beautiful.... But you notice how they get when they get older. The genes take over. With some of my children, greed took over."

Rubin located Suzanne and wondered why she supported Joe when he acknowledged having plotted to kill her. "We were protected by God," she responded piously. "Joe is very intelligent, bright, well read and very, very capable. I don't think U-Haul could be in better hands." She did not volunteer that months earlier Joe had seen to it that she was provided with a new Cadillac.

Katrina spoke for those in the family trying desperately to remain noncombatants. "I think in my family it has gotten far beyond a fight over money. It's power and greed, stuff I don't understand.... [T]here is so much hurt. It's all overwhelming."

What Katrina did not tell Rubin was how much she struggled with her emotions even though she was now firmly in her father's camp. She was compelled to reexamine her life and the behavior of the family members in it. She had come to see the Corvette Joe had given her to use the summer before as "sinful" and typical of the false values Joe represented. She had also decided that Joe had flown east for her graduation for an ulterior purpose, that his display of brotherly love had been a form of manipulation.

Mary Anna had already reached the same conclusions, but in her case because the memories went back so many years, they meant that Joe had schemed "the destruction of the family" since he had been in high school. She remembered the bits of candy and his "This means you have to vote for me" as he passed them out. The cowboy hats they received from Joe the day they posed as a family at Legend City were just a way to curry favor— just as the train trip to Mexico and the Colorado rafting trip had been. His behavior toward her had been kind or charitable only to an end she now saw had loathsome motives. And even if she was mistaken, how could she know for certain? Like her sister, she did not share her thoughts with reporters because they ate at her soul.

Katrina voiced her concern in the article and spoke effectively for a number of her siblings when she told Rubin that her concern about ulterior motives "goes for either side of my family. You don't know whether they're doing something because they love you and they want you to be happy . . . or because they want your vote and want you to be on their side. You never can be 100 percent sure. Never."

With the increased acrimony and Sam's sense that he might be in danger, he and Eva decided to move permanently to Telluride.

In making this decision, they joined scores of other like-minded affluent couples who sought quieter lives away from cities in the bracing air of the Rocky Mountains. Telluride was a small, rustic former mining town situated in a box canyon, a place where neighbors kept an eye on one another's children, and no one locked doors. It had been settled in 1875 and for its early history been a boomtown. The mining boom collapsed after the turn of the century, and hippies discovered it in the 1960s. The story went that when the last flower child left Haight-Ashbury, he went to Telluride to stay. By the late 1980s families such as Dr. Samuel Shoen and his wife, Eva, were buying expensive log homes. The fear in the town was that Telluride would turn into another Aspen.

With a year-round population of just eighteen hundred there was strong resistance to growth. Some people preferred walking to driving cars, and the permanent residents knew each other by their first names. Another sector, however, wanted economic growth. Little by little what made Telluride so desirable was slowly destroyed, and the festivals once held two or three times a year to stimulate business now frequently swelled the town's population to twenty thousand. The nearly weekly events were essential to keep the shops and bars filled to maintain prosperity and further diluted the qualities that had attracted residents.

The house Sam and Eva selected was scarcely the most luxurious in the region. It was situated in the Ski Ranch estates outside Telluride, where large lots and meandering roads offered privacy. The two-story cabin was spacious, and Eva's dogs had a large yard to exercise in.

Sam put his Paradise Valley house on the market, and a couple who worked for Harry DeShong, Jr., agreed to house-sit until it was sold. Driving or flying to Phoenix when necessary, Sam settled down to a life in the mountains, and he experienced little apprehension in leaving his wife and two children behind. If there was danger, it lay in Phoenix, and each time Sam made the journey there he had to steel himself for the confrontations that were almost certain to follow.

At first Eva enjoyed the change from Phoenix. Privately she confessed that she might have preferred a bit more civilization in her life, but she raised no objection. Eva confided to a close friend that she wished Sam did not have to wage this fight, but she understood that it was necessary. Once, beaming at a party, she had patted Sam on the arm and said proudly, "He is my hero." She was lonely during his absences, but that was something else she kept to herself.

By her own choice Eva had lived a life of comfort but not of affluence during her marriage to Sam. She shopped at sales and more than once told her daughter Aase that money was for essentials, travel, and education; beyond that it was just money and not important.

That first summer Eva rode in the Fourth of July parade dressed in a Norwegian costume. During Christmas she went to the local elementary school to share the stories and customs of Norway with her children's classmates. To help pass the time during Sam's absences, she took a part-time job working with a local veterinarian. The locals hardly knew who the Shoens were or that Sam was engaged in a bitter struggle for control of one of America's best-known corporations.

The Form Builders IRS trial resumed in Washington, D.C., on April 3, 1989. Joe was called to the stand. "... You sat in this courtroom when [your father] testified [previously], didn't you?" the IRS attorney asked.

"I believe I was there, yes," Joe said.

"Based on that testimony, did [U-Haul] terminate your father's employment contract with the company?"

"No."

"So, it is your testimony that your father still is employed by [U-Haul]?"

"No."

"So, has his employment terminated since he was testifying in this courtroom?"

Joe, who had written the letter, answered, "I'm not sure."

Joe's attorney objected that nothing that had occurred in 1989 was relevant to the trial, which was about taxes due several years earlier. The judge allowed the line of questioning to continue.

"Did [U-Haul] terminate your father's employment contract with the company after he testified in this court?"

"I think it's been since then, but I'm not absolutely certain. I can't recall the date."

IRS district counsel Cuatto had Joe identify the letter he had sent his father, over the objection of Joe's attorney, then placed it into the record.

Later Joe was asked by his attorney how he had come to be chairman of the board and president of U-Haul.

"In the fall of 1986, [U-Haul's] financial performance was in a severe decline, nearing a loss situation. I was approached by shareholders, including primarily my brothers and sisters... if I would come back on the board. I was elected to the board.... In about June of 1987 the board of directors elected me president of the corporation."

"Did you seek that job? Did you campaign or run for that position?"

"No, I did not."

"...Why does your testimony differ on so many points with your father?"

"My father's whole mental state has changed in the last 24 months."

"Have you ever punished or attempted to punish an [U-Haul] employee because of testimony unfavorable to your case in front of this court?"

"No, sir, I haven't."

"Does that apply to your father, L. S. Shoen?"

"Yes, it does."

"...Why did you have additional [8,099] shares of stock... purchased by these [five] key employees?"

"It was a board of directors'... decision. I'm one member of the board, six member board. It was voted on."

"Would it be true to state that that was done so that you could insure that you could continue to run [U-Haul]?"

"No," Joe said, "that would not be a fair characterization."

In mid-April the trial ended, and the court took the case under advisement to issue a written decision at a later date. When L.S.

reviewed the transcript of the trial, the portion he found most interesting was that in which Joe testified that there were risks for Form Builders because U-Haul represented nearly all of its business and that business might not have remained with it because of family discontent. L.S. had set Sam up to take control of U-Haul, and Sam's opposition to Form Builders had been well known for years. Only his father's insistence that U-Haul use the printing firm had kept the work coming. It was reasonable to expect that once Sam was in control of U-Haul, Form Builders' free ride with U-Haul would have come to an abrupt end.

During the trial, according to Joe, Heidi took their two sons to California. One evening she called him at his office while he was in the midst of trial preparations. She said that she would not bring the children home unless Joe deeded their Phoenix residence to her. Joe agreed, and that Monday she arrived at his office to have him sign a deed in her name to the residence and to the ranch in Sunflower. She then recorded the instruments.

In April L.S. prepared a twenty-seven-page evaluation of the situation to be mailed to shareholders. He warned that Joe was acting like a corporate raider, and the paper, primarily an attack on Joe's management of the company, defended L.S.'s own behavior. It concluded on a decidedly personal note: "Getting a handle on E. J.[Joe] Shoen, reminds me of the North Dakota farmer's reference to the prospect of 'trying to shove butter up a wildcat's "rectum" with a red hot poker.' I am also reminded of a former U.S. Senator's remark that 'like a dead mackerel in the moonlight he shines as he stinks.' . . . "

L.S. watched Joe's conduct as CEO of U-Haul and was appalled. With the collapse of Jartran, Ryder System had emerged as U-Haul's most major significant competition. By stripping the company of new businesses, Joe had eliminated the diversification L.S. believed essential to U-Haul's long-term well-being. Joe had set U-Haul in a disadvantageous position with Ryder, which had a profitable airline-supply business as a component on which it could draw for profits. U-Haul was essentially back to trucks and trailers, and the sizable real estate assets L.S. had acquired were now being

systematically sold. L.S. had always believed his company was
vulnerable to a well-financed rival, and that was exactly where Joe
had positioned the company.

The incomprehensibility had extended even to the product liability litigation department Mike had created and nurtured in
U-Haul. Early that summer it was dismantled.

There was now an ominous feeling spreading through many of
those who had watched this vicious struggle for control of
U-Haul. None of the outside group lived in Arizona any longer
except for Theresa, who ran a local business. Cecilia had married
Dr. Christopher Hanlon in 1988. During the summer of 1989
it seemed to Cecilia that matters were getting out of control.
When she spoke with her husband, he admitted he had been
having the same thoughts. The litigation was getting "heated,"
and considering the personalities involved, "something could happen," he said. By some estimates more than three billion dollars
was at stake, and "people were going after each other in a
personal way and using everything that they could to make life
miserable for Sam or Michael or Mary Anna," including the full
weight of U-Haul's resources. Chris "figured anybody who is
going to go to all this effort, anything could happen." He told
his wife that his primary concern was for the safety of the outside
group.

Cecilia shared these concerns, and they even discussed calling
in the Federal Bureau of Investigation. They remained uneasy and
fearful. "I just got the feeling," Chris said later, "that this was
taking... an eerie turn."

Cecilia and her husband were not the only family members
concerned for the future. At about the same time Katrina's fiancé
had been staring at a photograph of Sam and Eva for a while
before he looked at Katrina and said, "Someone's going to die in
this picture."

Joe's faith in the Golden Five, as the key employees were commonly
known, appeared ill founded. At least three of the five retained
firms to sell 4,869 shares of the stock issued to them the previous
summer. Interest payments of over $400,000 each were due that

coming July, and if the three could sell the stock for the $10,800 a share they were asking, the men would instantly be worth $10 million.

The outside group was, of course, interested in changing Joe's new math, and on May 27, 1989, L.S. and Sam met with one of the representatives for the three. The representative presented a comprehensive plan to sell the stock that he argued would permit an immediate shareholders' consent agreement placing the outside group in control of U-Haul.

Most of the outsiders gathered to consider the offer at a meeting on June 5. They would have to put up more than fifty million dollars to buy the stock, which would eliminate their personal wealth and place them deeply in debt. In addition, the proposal was not as simple as presented. The Golden Five had signed a voting trust, and Joe could be expected to take the outside group to court if it attempted to implement a new share-holders' consent. In the meantime, the U-Haul board could issue more stock to change the math again. In the end they decided to pass on the offer.

The good news from the attempted sale was in the standing of the men involved. "[V]aluable, long time employees . . . want out," L.S. wrote. "[T]he scheme planed [*sic*] and executed by my son Edward & company is falling apart."

Joe apparently learned what had occurred, and in July, just before the Golden Five notes fell due, U-Haul purchased most of the shares from four of the men and placed them in the board-controlled ESOP. The men each retained 430 shares and were paid $478,803 for them. Dodds, who had not been party to the attempt, kept his stock longer before selling it to the ESOP and earned more money as a result.

Placing most of the disputed 8,099 shares into U-Haul's ESOP was the catastrophe the outside group had feared since the stock had been issued. ESOPs had been created by federal legislation that was intended to prevent any diminishment of the stock held in them. Subsequent court rulings had created an impenetrable wall around ESOPs, holding that it didn't matter where shares came from, for once they were placed in an ESOP, they could not be touched. While the outsiders could win their lawsuit on the ground that the 8,099 shares were issued improperly, the stock in the ESOP could no longer be voided. It would remain there under the board's control. It would be necessary to go one step farther in the lawsuit: They would have to persuade the court to give them control of U-Haul *despite* the existence of the 8,099 shares now in the ESOP.

Mike had reported the assault in Reno, Nevada, to the police. Although the case was considered a misdemeanor, the city prosecutor showed a willingness to take the matter to trial. During an oral proceeding in July one of the defense attorneys denigrated Mike and others in the outside group by saying, "These people are basically the idle rich and have nothing better to do than go around engaging in litigation and fomenting trouble, as in this case."

Twice the case was scheduled for trial, and once the witnesses were gathered the case was continued at the request of Joe and Mark. At one proceeding L.S. told a reporter, "This is not a family feud." The struggle for control of U-Haul was the result of greed. "I've got seven sons and five daughters and there are two bad apples. If they had all been born in a litter, I would have been happier if I had culled those two out."

In the meantime, U-Haul transferred the finance department of the company to Reno and made a show of being a new local employer. The prosecutor received another job shortly after that, and not long after his replacement took over, Mike was informed there would be no trial because the case was being dropped.

In August 1989 Duff & Phelps gave U-Haul a rating of D-8 for senior debt. This meant that U-Haul was virtually unable to borrow money through normal banking channels.

For months now members of the outside group believed U-Haul under Joe's control was abusing the court system to harass them. On Christmas Eve Sam had suspected his deposition was being delayed to force him to spend Christmas in Phoenix away from his family. Mike had been served with a lawsuit on a Friday night while in his pajamas at home. The next day, while he played ball in his front yard with his children, the same process server gave him the pleadings. The lawsuit and pleadings had been filed with the court at the same time and were customarily delivered to the defendant together. Mike asked the process server what this was all about. She apologized but said the plaintiff's lawyer had instructed that the papers be served in this manner.

Such treatment was not restricted to members of the family. Norma Colwell, the longtime U-Haul employee, was served with a subpoena while stopped in traffic seated behind the wheel of her car. A man had seemed to be trying to run her off the road, and she was upset. Then, when she stopped at a red light, he ran up to her car and gleefully slapped the subpoena under her windshield wiper. Colwell, who had believed she might be in danger when he ran up to her, described the experience as "harrowing."

On August 10, 1989, the Superior Court judge assigned the U-Haul scheme suit against Sam and the others issued an order that read: "The Court is shocked that 787 interrogatories, questions, and requests are served [by U-Haul] within seven days after service of process. The Court is further shocked at the number— 787 questions.

"The Court finds this to be unreasonable and oppressive, and is an abuse of the discovery rule...."

The order was copied to the state bar of Arizona.

L.S. had referred to U-Haul as the "birthright" of his children. Increasingly, however, it appeared that the family feud for the company was its true legacy.

Joe and Heidi's marriage had suffered since Joe had taken control of U-Haul, and in August 1989 they separated. Joe began staying at the ranch in Sunflower and was increasingly absent from U-Haul Towers. It was not a pleasant separation.

"His attitude [to me]," Heidi said, "is you get nothing, you are nothing. I will discredit you. I will put you in the streets.... Humiliation is the name of the game here."

Heidi told a friend that when she and Joe traveled to England, they had stood on line and met Princess Diana. While Heidi spoke to her politely, Joe "was just shrinking back." Heidi considered it a "wonderful" experience and believed she had represented her husband well. But instead of being proud, Joe "just gave me crap the whole night," she complained, "and left early in a huff. It's as if he wants to be competitive with me, like he treats me like another man instead of being his counterpart. It's the strangest thing. . . ."

L.S. had long believed that James Carty had influence on Joe. James had been a regular visitor to the Sunflower ranch, and Heidi had noticed that Joe "has the same expression, facial expression. Carries his body in a similar way, and he is prone to get petty, name-calling and that, like Jim is. Very, very childish compared to how smart he is. . . . "

For some time Heidi had been concerned about the man to whom she was married. He stayed up at night watching films of Nazi Germany and of Hitler, seemingly obsessed by them. "He's getting farther and farther away from reality," she confided. "He lives in his own world."

Heidi said she had felt compelled to leave. She told a friend that at times Joe said he believed he was evil.

Joe scheduled the 1989 shareholders' meeting for September 29 to be held in Tonopah, Nevada, population 1,952. Challenged on why he had chosen this location, which was a five-hour drive north of Las Vegas, Joe responded, "Why don't you just speculate?" Tonopah was an obscure desert town so remote that the Air Force had based the ultrasecret Stealth fighter there in the years before it was publicly disclosed.

Only Mary Anna of the outside group was unable to attend. Each shareholder was to receive two five-minute opportunities to ask questions or to make a statement. L.S. wanted to maximize their time by spreading the issues around the group. He knew the delays and repeated meetings were having a wearing effect on his group. "Our plan is to make the trip enjoyable," he wrote. "To have a good time. . . . Carol is to check out the Tonopah area to see if there are any sights or National Parks nearby. . . . "

On September 10, 1989, L.S. again attempted reconciliation with his children: "This is a great tragedy, an unnecessary tragedy.

A tragedy which ultimately may devastate our lives and the lives of our children and grandchildren. . . . Wise people throughout the ages have counseled love. At this time of my life I can come from no other place. I have signed my personal and business letters 'With love and respect' for the past six to eight years. I feel this way towards all humans, towards all life. I feel this way towards each and every one of you. . . . ''

L.S. distributed a list of nine inquiries he wanted made before Sam presented their case. These included an explanation of the sale/leaseback transactions of U-Haul real estate, how the Golden Five were funded by U-Haul, the true profit picture from trucks and trailers, which were now basically all U-Haul had left, the company's cash flow, and an earnings forecast for the next fiscal year.

Around 10:00 A.M. the outside group left Las Vegas in three cars headed for the Tonopah Convention Center and the 5:00 P.M. shareholders' meeting. Some of the shareholders had taken L.S. at his word and were attempting to have fun by wearing T-shirts that proclaimed, "Why Tonopah?—Just speculate."

Mike had no doubts about why Joe had selected Tonopah. It was inconvenient for the outside group and Mike believed Joe flying overhead in the corporate jet enjoyed the sight of the outside group lumbering up in cars.

The meeting was held in what appeared to be a theater. Joe arrived in a limousine to run it, along with Jimmie, a U-Haul attorney, and John Dodds. Their car was parked in the rear near a handy exit that avoided the press. Management took its place on the stage. In the audience were about twenty shareholders, including the outside group, and once again U-Haul had arranged for the presence of a uniformed guard. Mike was accompanied by a court reporter to transcribe the proceeding.

As a result of the brawl in Reno, there was significant media presence. A reporter for *The Wall Street Journal* had flown out; there was another from the *Arizona Republic,* a Nevada television crew, and a camera team from *Hard Copy.* Initially the reporters were refused entry until L.S. distributed proxies to each of them.

Joe began by reading the minutes of the last shareholders' meeting and skipped the traditional presentation of the company's financial condition, other than to make general statements that U-Haul was doing well. Then several shareholders were allowed to speak, but the answers to their questions were platitudes. Sam was permitted to make a short presentation to which Joe took exception though absent were the acrimony and profanities of the last meeting.

Joe announced he had enough votes for the reelection of the board. He then said that proxy votes could be filed only by mail and must be postmarked before midnight. Joe and Jimmie abruptly left the room and went straight to their car and drove off.

The entire meeting had lasted just over an hour. The outsiders were angry and dumbfounded at their failure to influence it but not as angry as they were a few minutes later, when they learned the Tonopah post office had closed at 5:00 P.M. If the outsiders wanted their proxies filed, they had an immediate five-hour drive back to Las Vegas.

On October 3 U-Haul informed Bear Stearns that it was amending the scheme lawsuit and would be naming the financial company in it. Under the terms of its agreement with Bear Stearns the outside group was required to pay the legal expenses of the New York-based firm. The next day Bear Stearns requested payment to the law firm it had retained. L.S., Sam, Mike, and Mary Anna also each had a $150,000 note owing to Bear Stearns.

Oral argument in their appeal of the court's denial of the injunction was still two months away with a written opinion to follow months thereafter. Regardless, L.S. was optimistic that they would prevail and the injunction would be imposed. This would enable the outside group to take immediate control of the company even without a trial. L.S. informed his group he anticipated victory in the spring of 1990. "Remember," L.S. wrote, "it is always darkest before the dawn."

That fall L.S. wrote Theresa, Katrina, Mark, and Sophia as each of their birthdays fell, including the portions of his diary about their births. To Sophia he wrote, "This was a good time in my life. You were a beautiful child.... Even tempered and a real joy to me. I remember saying repeatedly that you had restored my faith in the human race.... For many, many years I kept a photo of you at about age two in my billfold. I would look at it when in a motel and away from home. I still have that photo in the right upper drawer of my desk...." He concluded the letter by asking her not to fly to Las Vegas to visit, as she had planned. "What has occurred in the past sixteen months has caused too much pain for me...."

That fall Sam was asked to speak to the Arizona Harvard Business School Club but declined. The invitation then went to Joe, who elected to speak on the topic "Leadership in a Family-Owned Business."

Dodds wrote L.S. asking if the outside group would abandon its effort to regain control of U-Haul. "The answer is never," L.S. replied. "Not now, not tomorrow, not ten years hence. Hell will freeze over first. I would quote to you a sentence attributed to Churchill, 'In the bowels of Christ, consider that you were not only wrong in what you did, but that your motivation is pure crap....'* Someday you and your associates will be called on to account for your actions. I will be there...."

In mid-December Joe made another offer to resolve the feud. All sides were to drop their litigation, leaving him in control of U-Haul. L.S. and the outside group refused to consider it; L.S. referred to this as the "Have You Had Enough Offer."

L.S. was forced to face the reality of his personal situation. For nearly a year he had received virtually no income, and if he continued as he was, he would become bankrupt. There appeared to be no reasonable prospect that he could soon win his case against U-Haul for canceling his employment contract.† The only tangible asset L.S. possessed was the $1 million Viking house in which he lived, which held a mortgage of about $200,000. The house was beautifully appointed and would fetch top dollar if

---

*Oliver Cromwell: "I beseech you, in the bowels of Christ, think it possible you may be mistaken."

†Indeed, L.S. lost the case eventually when a Nevada court ruled the agreement was an illegal lifetime employment contract.

sold furnished. L.S. put the house up for sale, then located a middle-class house that he bought fully furnished for $120,000. When the Viking house sold, for less than he hoped, he took the remaining investment money and sank it into a Resolution Trust Corporation auction of apartments in Las Vegas and houses in Colorado that were rented out. L.S., founder of the multi-billion-dollar U-Haul corporation, was now a landlord to support himself.

Converting a porch on his new house into an office, L.S. transferred his files there. Lawsuits and his efforts to regain U-Haul filled virtually every waking hour.

On February 15, 1990, the federal tax court issued its decision in *Form Builders*. The opinion said, "[W]e find that no partnership existed between petitioner [Form Builders] and the Shoen children" and that they had never "truly intended to have a partnership." The court held that the payments to the children exceeding one million dollars during 1984 that were in dispute "were intended as rent and compensation for services" and were not "ordinary and necessary business expenses." As income the money was subject to taxation.

The court further found that the sale of Form Builders to Joe's friend altered nothing in the operation of the company and that "[h]is purchase did not change the closer-than-arm's-length nature of the transactions."

The court held Form Builders—i.e., Joe and Mark—liable for more than eight hundred thousand dollars.

In April the Arizona Court of Appeals finally heard oral argument on the appeal of the injunction. A decision was expected in late summer. L.S. wrote letters of encouragement to his group suggesting they would certainly win. With increasing frequency the inside group made overtures to individuals of the outside group to drop the litigation. They were clearly shaken at the prospect of losing.

For some time now, working in U-Haul Towers had been described as living in a police state, and allegations of sexual harassment were relatively common. One female employee of many years was approached by a male supervisor with the words "I like a full-figured woman." The same man routinely showed up for work in a T-shirt that said: "Oral Sex. It's dirty, dark work but somebody's got to do it."

Younger, attractive women were receiving quick promotions, and at least one freely acknowledged she was sleeping her way up the corporate ladder. Mark, Jimmie, and DeShong were widely accepted as bringing girl friends on board.* There was also a circulated unofficial hit list that proved surprisingly accurate, and employees named on it lived in dread of the moment when they would be escorted out the door.

Despite her long and intimate association with the children, Norma Colwell's employment at U-Haul had not gone smoothly since L.S.'s departure. Both Joe and Mark had worked for her when they were teenagers, and later she had managed Legend City for one year. The end for her came in early 1990, when "one of [Mark's] girls that worked in the marketing department...wanted to start a Jazzercise class [on the premises]...." In a memo Colwell turned down the request because there was no available space. She sent a copy of the memo to Mark. Shortly thereafter, when she saw him on a routine, unrelated matter, "he became very irate because the girl had told him, and he told me that I was to get the Jazzercise space and he didn't care if they jumped from one side of a carpet to the other;...he screamed that out in front of half the staff, and I...set up Jazzercise."

Not long after, in late April, Norma Colwell's job was eliminated, and she was fired. The effect on her was so devastating she remained in bed for three days afterward. When she called John Dodds to ask if she could find another job in the company, he told her that Mark had given orders that anyone in U-Haul who tried to hire her would receive the same treatment as she.

An unknown employee wrote about Colwell, and the testimon-

---

*Mark Shoen, James "Jimmie" Shoen, and Harry DeShong, Jr., refused to be interviewed, and it should be taken they deny such conduct.

ial was distributed surreptitiously among what was once called the U-Haul Family. It spoke for the thousands who had been summarily fired:

THIS IS DEDICATED TO THOSE PEOPLE IN UHI WHO HAVE NO POWER AND, WHO QUIETLY GO ABOUT EACH DAY DOING THEIR JOBS WHILE THE POLITICIANS SCHEME AND PLOT. AND, THIS IS DEDICATED TO SOMEONE WHO UNDERSTOOD THE DIFFERENCE AND REFUSED TO COMPROMISE HER PRINCIPLES...TO OUR FRIEND NORMA COLWELL

On April 24, 1990 a light went out in the Towers. A light that has burned brightly for the past twenty-two years has been extinguished by the hateful and destructive power politics of the Shoen Family holy war.

And why, you may ask?...Norma Colwell refused to join the maggots in the political dung-heap, and, while she was busy doing her job...these malicious little cretins were busy crawling in and out of the excrement spreading their hate and venom. Whispering in corners, whispering in hallways, whispering behind closed doors, and then one day Norma's name was on the "hit list" and now she is gone!

...I overheard one of our illustrious potentates, who, while carrying on a conversation with some of his cronies, said, with obvious relish, "Well we finally got rid of that bitch Norma Colwell!" Then they all had a big laugh out of how they "had boxed her into a corner and pulled the rug out from under her!" ...I don't believe, until then, I fully realized how cold, calculated and callous top management has become.

...I've done a great deal of soul searching in the last few weeks. I find it increasingly difficult to give my all to a company where the people who control my destiny are out of touch with reality. All it takes is a little whisper in the right ear and you become a suspect and then one day you're on the "hit list" and the following day you're history. Qualities like years of service, loyalty, competence, honesty, integrity mean nothing when our UHI politicians get the scent. They're after blood and guts and anyone is fair game. Their answer is to replace the competent with the incompetent, exchange excellence for mediocrity and when they finally get their clones together all shaking their empty little heads "yes" in unison, the syndrome is complete.

...When the news of Norma's termination spread throughout the towers and the field, it was as if there had been a death in the family.... [T]here was shock, disbelief and anger that the Shoens had actually terminated the most respected executive in the System. It was as if the soul had been torn from the company....

You have been a great success Norma Colwell and you will not be forgotten by your many friends at UHI. GOD BLESS YOU ALWAYS....

Katrina had scheduled her wedding for May 1990 in the red rock country in Sedona, Arizona, and was determined there would be no repeat of last year's debacle when Joe had come to her graduation and her father, to avoid a confrontation, had not. She was forced to ask Joe and those with the inside group not to attend her wedding so her father would be there to give her away. It was just one more sign of the destructive effect the struggle for control of U-Haul was having on the family. She accepted the necessity of what she had to do but it made her very unhappy.

On June 18 Joe sent his father a handwritten letter:

DEAR L.S.

...I too am for stopping the insanity. The waste of attorney's fees needs to be stopped. The waste of people lives needs to be stopped.

I will not re-run my litany of the injuries done me, my family and U-Haul by your group. I expect that all parties feel confident of the righteousness of their position.

Money can heal a lot of wounds. Call off your group. [U-Haul] can then cease spending money to defend itself. This savings will run into the millions.

Dividing money up is not that difficult.... Identify the wounds in your group, and lets [sic] format a plan to heal them in a manner fair to all shareholders.

What has your group got to lose? I can not imagine that you label the present and immediate past and future as being a success. A change in your course could lead to an improved situation for all.

Sincerely,
JOE SHOEN

Joe also attached a letter telling L.S. that Tom Safford had suffered a stroke and "Aunt Patty would appear to me to be dying of cancer.... A call or visit to both of them would be in order I should think...."

L.S. replied on June 29. "...I am aware of the illnesses of Tom and Patty Lee. I have known and loved them a life time. I am doing what I can." He denounced Joe again for issuing the 8,099 shares of stock and for spending "in excess of Ten Million Dollars ...to defend your personal acts of July 24, 1988.... You can heal the wounds by returning the 8,099 shares to [U-Haul's] treasury...."

The same day that letter was dated, a Sunday, L.S. went to visit Patty Lee in the hospital in Phoenix where she was dying of lung cancer. He spent the day with her, and to his surprise Paul showed up and asked to speak to his father. They went into the doctors' lounge, where L.S. uncharacteristically listened as Paul rambled on for some time. L.S. did not trust Paul and was not certain what this visit was about.

Paul had always seemed to be more concerned about his good name than most in the inside group. He said he was concerned that anything he told his father could be used against him in a lawsuit. And if Joe and Mark were to learn that he had talked to their father, they would "bust his balls." L.S. promised to keep the meeting private.

Paul said that business was not going well for U-Haul, that the company had had to manipulate the books to report a modest twenty-million-dollar profit during the past fiscal year. He and others in the inside group were also concerned about what the outside group would do at the fall shareholders' meeting.

For the first time L.S. learned that Joe was no longer involved in the day-to-day operation of U-Haul, that he was distracted by his failing marriage and was under tremendous stress. Mark was running the business, and Paul said that his father could easily imagine what it was like working for Mark.

When L.S. suggested that Joe must be unhappy because he required absolute control, Paul disagreed and suggested that Joe was a good person gone bad.

Paul confided that he and Sophia did not intend to renew the voting trust agreement with Joe and Mark when it expired in January, and Joe and Mark knew it. The brothers had subjected

Paul and Sophia to "a kangaroo court" after learning of it, but the pair had held their ground. Sophia had told Paul that she was no longer certain the trust was even valid.

Paul said he had been resisting Joe at board meetings by abstaining from voting. He was certain Joe and Mark were going to do something before the shareholders' meeting to make their votes unnecessary; they had been talking about staggering board terms so only a portion of them could be replaced in any year. From what Paul could see, Joe and Mark had serious problems other than those with U-Haul, though he wouldn't say what.

Paul asked for L.S.'s help in learning if he and Sophia could get out of the trust right away; he said that he was willing to pay the costs so the two of them could elect a board in the fall. L.S. asked if Jimmie would be willing to cross over, and Paul said to forget him. He was in too deeply with Joe and Mark.

Paul cautioned his father not to talk to him on his home telephone because it was tapped. Paul had a lot more to say, but L.S. was still uncertain how much he could rely on any of this, so he cut him off by suggesting they should not risk being seen together. Paul left, and for the rest of the day L.S. pondered his son's credibility.

That night, when L.S. was back in Las Vegas, Mark and Joe spoke to him by telephone, sounding suspicious and paranoid, very concerned about losing control of the company. They suggested in a rambling, confrontational way that they would like to end the fight. Mark was highly volatile and demanded, "Do you want to have my head on a platter?" L.S. assured him that was not the case at all. It seemed to L.S. that there had surely been a great deal of truth in what Paul had said earlier that day. Joe sounded agitated. But when L.S. suggested some reasonable settlement, Joe became adamant. L.S. argued again that they settle the feud and elect an all-Shoen board. Joe's voice changed profoundly, and he said they would never, ever settle the cases.

After the call L.S. wrote Mark and told him that he had always been special to him. "You were born smaller than the rest. Maybe that is why. But you were perfectly proportioned, and your facial features were beautiful." Then he turned to the business at hand. "I can understand how you feel about what would happen to you and others should you not prevail in the litigation as to the 8,099 shares.... Your natural instincts are so aggressive and you [sic] life experience seems to affirm that if you lose you get badly beat up...."

He compared their situation with that of Germany and Japan following the Second World War. The Axis had "lost," but the loss had resulted in an immediate improvement in the lives of their citizens. "Losing is not really hurtful. Normal people reject revenge as a solution even as to brutal murderers.... Life is a win-win or it is not life. Winning and losing only happens [sic] in games and sports. But even as to sports the winners and losers are really buddies when it is all over. God must love you a lot. Pray for me...."

The news from U-Haul was not good and was reported as such in the media. Earnings for the company had fallen by nearly one half during the previous fiscal year, and though the company attempted to dismiss this as a minor incident, in fact, it was a dramatic fall. Revenues for the company were no greater than the last year L.S. had run the company even though they were inflated by the sales of used U-Haul trucks and trailers. Joe had abandoned his father's nearly sacred policy of dismantling trailers and now routinely sold them whole. Former U-Haul trailers were a common sight on highways, and it was impossible any longer to tell a stolen trailer from a sold one.

U-Haul acknowledged that it was compelled to borrow money to finance new trucks and to pay for leasing, thus compounding the debt. Costs for the seven pending lawsuits were now estimated at eleven million dollars, and an analyst with Duff & Phelps reported that the suits were "a distraction to management."

By the summer of 1990 Sam and Eva were well settled into lives of quiet domesticity in Telluride. In Phoenix Sam was subjected to constant abuse, but here in the Colorado mountains they had found a sanctuary. Eva's parents were aging, and Sam agreed to an extended vacation in Norway. Before leaving, he redrew his will. His shares in U-Haul were held in a trust. Under the old will in the event of his death, control of those shares was to pass to the head of U-Haul's in-house insurance company, a man whom Sam had once trusted but who was now one of the Golden Five and could be expected to vote the shares with Joe. He changed the provision so that Eva could vote his stock should he die.

For a moment he considered making this change in his circumstances known to U-Haul, but he was so angry with what was going on that he decided against it; for him it was a private decision.

Eva left for Norway with the children, accompanied by Aase. Sam joined her later for three weeks in July. Eva was elated throughout the trip. With Bente now ten years old and Esben seven, they could be left in a hotel room for short periods while Eva and Aase went out.

Aase, who attended college on the East Coast, considered herself fortunate to be observing the Shoen fight at a distance. From time to time her mother told Aase the latest antics. Aase left the trip early and planned to visit her mother in Telluride soon after Sam and Eva returned. The day she said good-bye to her mother in Larvik, Eva was standing on a balcony on the second story with a field of wild Norwegian flowers behind her. She smiled radiantly, and Aase paused in the doorway for a final look at her mother.

In late July Sam and Eva returned to Telluride and a few days later attended one of the frequent evening socials that friends in their circle held. Eileen McGinley, who had lived in Telluride several years after escaping big-city life in the East, met Eva and Sam there for the first time. McGinley and her partner operated a specialized public relations firm, and she chatted casually with Sam about it.

In Las Vegas L.S. was deeply hurt by Colwell's firing. She was very unhappy, and he thought it would be good for her to become friends with Eva. He suggested that Colwell accompany Eva to a dog show that week in Santa Barbara, California. As the women drove to the show, Eva knitted Sam a Christmas sweater. After one of Eva's dogs cowered before a judge, Colwell offered to keep the dog with her in Durango, Colorado, where she was living temporarily in one of L.S.'s RTC houses. But Eva missed the dog so much that when she drove to Durango to pick Sam up at the airport on Thursday, August 2, 1990, she took the dog back to Telluride with them.

Sam's stay at home was short. He was due back in Phoenix on Tuesday, August 7, and had an airplane reservation but on Saturday decided to drive down the next day so he could make a separate presentation on Monday. He had become comfortable in their time in Telluride. The danger lay in Phoenix. When he said good-bye to Eva and climbed into his car, he left his wife with no sense of apprehension.

That day Bente asked if a ten-year-old friend could sleep over, and Eva readily agreed. That evening the dogs refused to be silenced outside. The neighbors had complained they had been behaving badly for weeks. Eva brought the dogs into the house, but they still refused to obey her. They ran to the windows and barked uncontrollably, so finally she placed them in the mud room, where they finally quieted and lapsed into sleep.

Around midnight, after the children were in bed, Eva finished a cup of tea, read a book for a short time in her upstairs bedroom, then turned out the light and fell asleep. Outside, the air stirred and rocked the Aspen with a hush.

CHAPTER SIXTEEN

"PLEASE SEND SOMEBODY"

Bente was up early Monday morning and turned on the television. When her mother did not awaken at the usual hour, Bente first let the dogs outside, then turned them loose in the house. At 7:00 A.M. she decided to tell her mother about a funny trick one of the dogs had performed. At the top of the stairs Bente spotted her mother lying on her back on the landing, her legs splayed down the stairs. There was blood on the sheet in which she was partially wrapped, and she was pale white.

Bente screamed, and Esben and their guest came to her. The girls did not know how to perform CPR but knew of it and tried to breathe air into Eva's body. They pressed on her chest rhythmically as blood oozed from her body, spreading itself over their hands and arms.

Bente ran to the telephone in the bedroom to call the San Miguel County sheriff's office in nearby Telluride. The bed was drenched in blood. "Excuse me," Bente said. "My mom . . . I woke up. She's dead on the staircase." Her voice was high-pitched and breathless.

"She's sick?" the dispatcher asked.

"She's dead on the staircase! There's blood, OK?" Bente could barely control herself.

"What is your name?"

"Bente Shoen. I live in the Ski ranches—in a big log house. There was blood on the bed. Please send somebody."

"OK. You said she's not alive now?"

"I can't tell," Bente sobbed into the telephone. "Please send someone." Her voice rose to a high peak, and her plea was a cry of desperation.

Up and across the road Jeanne Josie looked outside her house to get a sense of how cold it was that morning. She had sold Sam and Eva their house and was a close friend of the family's. Josie was surprised to spot the Shoen children outdoors, still wearing nightclothes and without shoes. The dogs were running loose. She went out and heard Bente yelling for her, over and over, "Jeanne Josie! Jeanne Josie! Jeanne Josie!" Then Josie heard Bente scream, "Mommy's dead! Mommy's dead!" Josie ran down the road. The children took her hand and pulled her into the house, where she found Eva lying at the top of the stairs, her arms extended, her palms raised as if in supplication. Her open eyes, devoid of any life, stared at the ceiling.

Bente said they had tried CPR, "but Mommy was cold and hard." Josie bent down and could detect no pulse. The girls had called the parents of the girl staying overnight. Just then the telephone rang, and Josie picked it up.

Telluride County Sheriff Bill Masters had returned the night before from a trip to the East and was due at his office at 9:00 A.M. He was thirty-eight years old, had been reared in Tarzana, California, and attended Northern Arizona University in Flagstaff, Arizona. After obtaining a degree in police science, he drove to Telluride, where he had skied many times, thinking to stay with a friend for the summer before applying to the Los Angeles Police Department. His friend was gone, so Masters took a room and landed a job with the company that operated the ski lifts. His Volkswagen was crushed in a rock slide, and the spring of 1975 Masters was hitch-hiking to Telluride when the town marshal picked him up. Following a short conversation he offered Masters a job.

The Telluride marshal's office was responsible for policing the town proper, and at that time it had no uniforms and just one aging car. Law enforcement was decidedly informal. Masters was later appointed marshal, then in 1979 joined the sheriff's office as undersheriff. The next year the sheriff resigned, and the Board of

Supervisors appointed Masters to replace him. In 1982 and again in 1986 he was elected sheriff in his own right. The fall of 1990 he was running unopposed for his third elected term while at the same time he was getting divorced.

The Telluride County sheriff's office had twelve employees, nine of them deputies, to police a county that was approximately fifteen miles wide and a hundred miles long with a total permanent population of just four thousand. One of the deputies was the undersheriff who performed administrative duties, and two were based at Norwood, a hundred miles away. There was one undercover officer and one matron. That left a sergeant and three deputies for the rest of the county, including the area around Telluride.

There was also a deputy who had just completed training to teach an antidrug program to students and had taken the first course of John Reed & Associates, a Chicago-based and nationally recognized training center for interrogation techniques. His name was Kim Pound, and he was the only deputy not assigned to patrol duty that day.

Masters did not fit in with the largely liberal-thinking Telluride populace. He was very conservative and in 1981 had conducted a large-scale drug investigation using wiretaps that netted ninety pounds of cocaine along with the arrests of several local young men. Many people in San Miguel County opposed any kind of drug enforcement, and his first election in 1982 had been bitter. A number of people still considered him too uncompromising, but by 1990 he was accepted as a fair and able sheriff.

On Monday, August 6, 1990, Masters was outside his house, preparing to mount his racing bicycle for a workout, when he remembered he did not have his pager. As he went into the house, the telephone rang. It was his dispatcher. "I got this really strange call," she began, then told him what Bente Shoen had reported. Masters had never heard of the Shoen family and had no idea where in the Ski Ranch estates the house was located. Within minutes he was en route, hoping this was a mistake. It was a beautiful Colorado Rockies summer morning, he was in fine spirits, and he wanted nothing to spoil it.

*   *   *

In the middle of the night the telephone had rung at Sam's Paradise Valley house and awakened him, but when his house sitter answered it, the caller hung up.

Just after 7:00 A.M. the house sitter called Sam to the telephone. The father of the girl who had stayed the night with Bente was on the phone from Telluride. He told Sam there had been an accident. Eva had been discovered by the children lying on the stairs. He understood there was blood. He didn't know if she was dead or not. Sam called his house, and Josie answered.

"Jeanne, what's going on? Is Eva alive?" Sam asked desperately.

"No, Sam. I'm sorry," she said. After a few moments the house sitter removed the telephone from Sam's hand. He was unable to speak.

Masters received directions over the radio, then the news that Josie had seen the body. There was no longer any doubt that someone was dead. It had crossed his mind that the woman might have fallen and been unconscious. He found himself searching for an explanation that would make this no more than an ambulance call and not a law enforcement matter.

As he approached Lawson Hill, where the estates were located, he started looking for anything unusual. Only with difficulty did he find the house. An ambulance had already arrived, and one of the attendants approached Masters. "I think she's really dead," he said. "Jeanne's inside."

Masters met Josie at the doorway. "She's dead," she told him. "It looks like she's fallen." Masters entered the living room, then went up the wooden stairs to the landing. Blood had coagulated almost precisely in the center of Eva's forehead. Masters checked for a pulse, eased cautiously around the body, and looked into the bedroom, where he spotted a glint of metal on the floor. When he bent down, he observed the spent casing of a .25 caliber shell. He went back downstairs and ushered the attendants and Josie out the door. At his car he called the dispatcher. "I have a crime scene here," he told her. "I need evidence kits." He asked for the county coroner and more officers and then called Kim Pound, who was fast asleep. "Kim, I need you now."

Hearing Masters's tone of voice, Pound said, "It's a homicide, isn't it?"

"Yes," Masters said grimly, then gave his deputy directions.

Robert Dempsey, the coroner, worked primarily as a Realtor and stockbroker. He had, in fact, sold the land to the developer who built the Shoen residence. Averaging six deaths each year, all from natural causes, San Miguel County had not had a homicide in eleven years. The coroner was paid twenty-five dollars a body. Dempsey called Dave Erickson, his deputy (no relation to Don Erickson), who ran the local hardware store, and the two men drove out together. Sam Shoen was a hardware nut who could spend hours loitering in Erickson's store, so the men knew each other.

At the house they asked if anyone was seeing to the children, then went in to view Eva. It was obvious from Masters's demeanor that this was not a normal death. "We've got a weird scene here," he told them, then cautioned the men not to touch anything. They looked at the body and at the bedroom. Dempsey spotted the blood on Eva's forehead and decided she had been shot there.

Outside, beside the road, Masters located a pair of sunglasses. He asked the men if they belonged to them. They shook their heads. Neither of the men was trained for the job—Erickson had never so much as witnessed an autopsy—but they were called on to decide the cause of death, and in this case, even without an autopsy, that cause was clear enough: Eva Shoen had been shot to death.

When Pound arrived a few minutes later, Masters told him, "It looks like we have a homicide." Pound said nothing, only nodded, and the pair went inside. Pound, who was thirty-five years old, was originally from Maine, and traces of his New England accent were still apparent. He had attended Unity College on a basketball scholarship, worked a time for the Gallo brothers in central California, then joined the Durango, Colorado, police. During his seven years there he had assisted three homicide investigations before joining the San Miguel County sheriff's office.

A few minutes after he arrived, the undersheriff, Sky Walters, drove up along with the sergeant and a deputy. Masters dispatched his deputies to question everyone on the estate. Dogs were requested to search for scents. Masters told Pound to go up the hill and speak to the children.

In Las Vegas L.S. was up early on Monday and was preparing to go to one of his rental units to repair a clothes dryer. Sam telephoned from Arizona and in a voice that was barely audible told his father Eva was dead. Sam was chartering a plane and would be leaving at once for Telluride. Before hanging up, he told his father that he blamed himself for not having been there.

L.S. made a series of calls. He reached Paul and asked him to notify the family in Phoenix, then called Cecilia, Mary Anna, and Mike, who was vacationing in Germany with his family. Cecilia told her father that she had talked to Eva just that night. L.S. said he didn't know how Eva had died, but Cecilia's first thought was crystal clear. "She was murdered," she told her father. Not for an instant did she suspect Eva's death had been natural. What she didn't say was that, without any evidence to support her conclusion, she also suspected that the death "was related to Joe...." She immediately caught a plane and en route tried to convince herself that it was an accident but to no avail.

Though very shaken by the news, L.S. spent the next five hours repairing the rental's dryer. In Paradise Valley Sam was now informed that Eva had been shot to death. It was obvious to him who had done this. He reached Carol just before going to the airport and gave her the news. He was so broken up she could scarcely hear him mutter, "They've ripped my heart out."

When L.S. returned to the house, Carol told him that Eva was not just dead but had been killed. "No," L.S. said, shaking his head. "No."

Mike was shocked by the tragic news but even more disturbed because earlier his wife, Christa, had told him about a dream she'd had that night. In it Christa had been in Telluride, arranging china on a table with the owner of a secondhand store. Eva came into the store and said, "It's OK to sell these things. They used to be mine, but I don't need them anymore." Bente and Esben remained with Christa as Eva climbed into a suburban vehicle with a dirty blond-haired man Christa did not know.

Several hours after the first call L.S. telephoned Mike and told him the details. Eva had been shot in the back, murdered. Mike screamed.

Eva's daughter Aase had also talked to her mother the day before. Eva had regaled her with fresh Shoen stories, turning family conduct into amusing anecdotes. That morning Sam called to tell her that her mother had been murdered. Aase was stunned. "Sam," she asked after a moment, "do you think this is because of U-Haul?"

"Yes. I do," he told her in the whisper that had become his speaking voice.

Kim Pound gathered the three distraught children around him and quietly asked questions about Eva, the events of the previous night and of the morning. Pound had never met the victim, nor did he know who the Shoens were. Bente told Pound about the lawsuits and the fighting that had been going on in the family. As she used the name U-Haul several times, Pound realized that if this was part of the family that owned the company, there would be a great deal of money at stake here.

Pound called police in Phoenix, who confirmed that the name of the family owning U-Haul was Shoen, that the company was headquartered there, and that recent newspaper articles suggested a history of violence as well as a bitter dispute for control of the company.

After spending an hour with the children, Pound rose to leave and brief Masters on what he had learned. Seven-year-old Esben took his sleeve into his hand and asked, "You will find who killed my mom, won't you?" Pound assured him that he would do his best. With that promise on his mind he walked back to the Shoen residence.

When he reached the house, two crime scene technicians had arrived from the Colorado Bureau of Investigation. While the agents for the bureau were held in generally low esteem by

Colorado law enforcement people, the technicians were considered first-rate. They began meticulously working the area.

This was Masters's first homicide investigation, and from the moment he arrived at the house he had worked it as he would any crime scene. The evidence kits his deputies had brought up earlier were standard police issue, and from a physical evidence point of view this was similar to working a suicide, an area in which Masters had considerable experience. There had been nothing he could do about the damage already done to evidence by the dogs running about the house or the girls giving the victim CPR. But he had secured the scene at the earliest possible moment and was satisfied his team was discovering what physical evidence was to be found.

Pound worked his way through the documents in the house until Masters called him to help with Eva's body. They placed her carefully into a body bag, then with equal care carried her down the stairs to a truck on which she was to be transported to Montrose, where the pathologist would perform the autopsy. Masters's choices for an officer to head the investigation were limited, so Pound was not surprised to be told the case was assigned to him.

Both Masters and Pound knew the stark reality of murder. The victim usually knew the killer, and the murderer was more often than not someone close to her or him. No suspect could be ruled out, but at this moment a principal one was Eva's husband, Sam.

Sam arrived in Telluride late that morning and went straight to his children, whom he held fiercely in his arms as all of them cried. When Bente was able to speak, she told her father that she was certain her mother had been shot. Sam asked a family friend to call Dr. Day in Tucson, the psychologist he had come to trust, and learn precisely how he and others were to treat the children. In this moment of the loss of his wife, Sam was experiencing once again the horrible emptiness, a deep numbing that ran through him to his core, that he had felt when his mother, Anna Mary, had died. His vision of his murdered wife was mixed with that of his dead mother. But for all he was suffering at the moment he also understood what his children were experiencing, and he was going to do whatever it took to minimize the pain.

Pound came up to the house and asked to talk to Sam. The men stood in the graveled driveway as Pound explained that Eva had been shot, she had not been raped, and there was no evidence of robbery. Sam asked Pound if there was a chance this had been a paid killing. Pound paused, then said quietly, "A chance." He wanted to conduct an interview, and Sam was to understand that for now he was a suspect. Sam said he would talk to Pound, and he would not need a lawyer though he asked if they could speak the next day. He was in no shape for an interview at the moment, and his children needed him. Cecilia arrived early that afternoon, and Sam was immensely relieved to have a family member there for his children.

Masters returned to the tiny San Miguel County sheriff's office, where already the media attention had begun. Telluride had two weeklies, and each had sent a reporter to take a statement, as had the local radio station. The switchboard was flooded with telephone calls as word spread, and there were calls from newspapers in Norway, one of the British tabloids, the usual major American newspapers, and the dailies in Arizona. Masters had written a short statement, which he read in the squad room because he had no office, before he conducted an informal press conference.

He confirmed that Eva Shoen had been murdered and that his office was exploring every possible lead. When asked, he acknowledged that it was possible the murder could be connected to the long-standing U-Haul feud. There was no evidence of sexual assault or robbery. They were not certain, but it was possible a silencer had been used since no one reported being disturbed by a sharp report. Pressed for details, Masters said the murder might have been a "quasi-professional hit."

"Something is involved here," he said to explain himself, "that isn't readily apparent, and that's why I say 'quasi-professional.' It seems to be motiveless as far as what occurred at the crime scene itself."

* * *

L.S. asked Carol to arrange for them to go to Telluride, then wrote in his journal: "Appears to me that had Sam been at his Telluride home he would have been killed. He is fearful for his life and that of his children."

The day of the killing a lawyer and a senior executive from U-Haul arrived in Telluride and asked to speak to Masters. The sheriff was surprised by their abrupt manner and the threadbare suit the executive wore. They told him that there was a potential for adverse publicity against the company, and they hoped he would be sensitive to that concern. They asked if the Shoen family in general was in any danger, and Masters said he did not know but it was a possibility. They said they wanted a speedy resolution to the investigation, and for that purpose U-Haul was retaining private investigators, who would be arriving in the area any day. They expected him to cooperate with these investigators.

There were rough edges to these men that did not fit the image that usually went with a nationally known corporation. One of the investigators at the scene suggested they were more like truckers or teamster officials than slick three-piece-suit types. The investigation was to encounter a number of people like them working for U-Haul.

Aase called her father, Don Erickson, in hysterics. He had already received word of his former wife's murder. Aase flew at once to Phoenix, and by then Erickson had decided to travel with her to Telluride.

Tuesday L.S. awoke at 4:00 A.M., took a Xanax, and was able to sleep another three hours before getting up. The telephone rang ceaselessly as published accounts of the murder appeared nationwide. L.S. called Sam, who had not slept that night. His eldest son repeated that he believed his life was in danger, and he asked his father to assist in locating a safe place for the children and him.

A reporter from the Denver *Post* reached L.S., who declined comment. He then wrote his children:

DEAR LOVED ONES:

Your brother Sam's wife Eva, was assaulted in her Telluride home about 2 A.M. on Monday August 6 while asleep in her bed. A single bullet fired at close range entered her back, pierced her heart and exited her breast.* She managed to get out of bed and stumble a few feet before dying.... I am asking for your prayers for her, for Sam, her children and for the perpetrators of this heinous crime.

With love and respect,
Your dad,
LEONARD S. SHOEN

For three hours that morning Pound questioned Sam at the sheriff's office. Sam dealt with the many very sensitive questions Pound asked in a direct manner, accepting Pound's suspicions as reasonable. He told Pound the U-Haul story, summarized the history of the family, the fight for control of the company, and told him of the threats and violence. His manner was highly controlled, and he was able to hold tight the horrible emotions that raged inside him.

After the interview Masters asked Pound what he thought. "I don't know," Pound said, not certain what to make of Sam's ability to be in control of himself, "but I think we better check his alibi out."

Also on Tuesday morning, Dr. Thomas M. Canfield, a forensic pathologist, began Eva's autopsy at Montrose Memorial Hospital. The .25 caliber bullet had perforated her right lung and the right part of her heart, then lodged against the inside of her chest cavity. Eva had died when nearly all the blood had been pumped out of her damaged heart and filled her lungs.

The sergeant with the sheriff's office was closely watching the examination when he spotted something peculiar near Eva's breast. Dr. Canfield examined the spot microscopically and discovered a needle puncture consistent with an injection. Checking her other

*The bullet did not leave Eva's body.

breast, he observed a second needle puncture. Someone had used a large-bore needle on Eva in the moments before she was murdered. The doctor took samples and directed a full toxicology scan to determine what substance had been injected.

Otherwise the autopsy determined that Eva had been a remarkably fit woman. Before writing his report, Dr. Canfield examined the crime scene then concluded:

A) CAUSE OF DEATH: This 44 year old Caucasian female bled to death secondary to a gunshot wound to her back.

B) MANNER OF DEATH: Homicide.

The autopsy had largely stated the self-evident for Masters and Pound. It confirmed that Eva had not been raped, and though there was some bruising, suggesting a struggle, it had not been prolonged. Her fingernails had been clear of tissue or other foreign substances, indicating she had not scratched anyone. Only the needle marks had been completely unexpected. Why two single punctures in the same position beside each breast? Why had a large veterinarian-size needle been used? And what drug had been injected?

The men decided to withhold this information, the sunglasses, and other facts from the public. Though under Colorado law the autopsy report was a public record, Dempsey kept it at his home office and released it to no one.

The entire sheriff's office had canvassed the Ski Ranch estates and the businesses in town since Masters and Pound were focusing first on the usual suspects in a murder. That weekend Telluride had been filled with strangers attending a jazz festival. Possible suspects included any of them. Someone might have spotted Eva in town, become obsessed, followed her home, seen her husband leave, then returned that night. If that were the case, though, there would have been some evidence of a sexual assault. Yet Eva's panties were undisturbed on her body, and the autopsy confirmed there had been no penetration or intercourse. Valuable jewelry had been left on her hands, and nothing was missing from the house or bedroom, so robbery had also not been the motive.

If Eva had been the target of a contract killing, Masters and Pound were prepared to accept that the motive could lie anywhere in her life. But the local investigation revealed no affairs, no ugly secrets between husband and wife, no enemies. In Telluride Eva had been popular and without a threat.

Then one of the deputies brought back interesting information. An employee at a downtown business reported that a man had asked directions to the Ski Ranch estates the day of the killing. When the employee asked which house he wanted, the man had answered evasively, "I'm just looking for a residence." The man had said he was from Pine, Arizona. Arrangements were made to prepare a drawing of the suspect. Next Masters learned there had been a strange vehicle in the estates, a white four-wheel-drive Jeep Cherokee.

Sam had moved his children to a remote location that was a closely held secret. Security guards were hired to walk the forest and keep a vigilant eye with pump shotguns under their arms. Family and friends began arriving from across the country. A service was scheduled for Friday, and Sam instructed that the members of the inside group be informed they were not welcome. As one family member said, "Why should he have them spit in his eye?"

Mary Anna had moved into a hotel upon learning of Eva's murder, and she did not sleep the night before she left for Telluride. When she arrived on Wednesday, she was startled to see Sam. He had not slept since that phone call Monday morning. He had in fact sobbed throughout the first night, and the fatigue and grief were readily apparent. More striking were the fresh bandages on his head and forehead where he had slammed his head repeatedly against a wall in a nearly primeval display of anger, guilt, and grief.

Mary Anna knew how acutely the children were suffering, and Sam, in a voice that was hardly more than a whisper, told her she must help with them. She assured him of her permanent commitment to him and his family, and he was greatly relieved.

L.S. and Carol also arrived on Wednesday. L.S. was untypically subdued, but when he did speak, it was to solicit the name of the one behind the murder. There was no doubt in his mind what had caused Eva's murder. But time and again he was told this was not the time or place. "Shut up," Mary Anna snapped at one point. "That's not what this is about."

By now the media were demanding a statement, and Mary Anna was not the only one present who feared someone would blurt out a heartfelt accusation on national television. A television reporter was already waiting. Sam mentioned Eileen McGinley, and it was decided to bring her public relations firm in to advise them and serve as liaison with the media.

On Thursday the local weekly newspapers were published, and Telluride learned for the first time that Eva Shoen had been shot to death. Murder was so alien to the community there was nearly an audible gasp at the news. McGinley's reaction was typical. She had been suspicious of the first rumor that Eva had died of a heart attack but was unprepared for the truth. The fear of murder or at the least concern for it had been one of the motives for her and others like her to move here. One local couple told a reporter, "People are moving here with their big-city wealth and their big-city problems."

On Thursday McGinley received a telephone call from the friend who had hosted the previous week's social gathering. "I'm sorry to be so secretive, but can you come talk to Sam Shoen?" McGinley agreed and followed complicated instructions that led her to the place where Sam and his family were in hiding.

Mike had flown in from Germany but not before cautioning his family about their safety. If Eva's murder was connected to the family struggle, there was no telling how far it went. As he drove up to the house, he spotted the guards and did not consider it an overreaction in the least. He planned to buy a weapon as soon as he returned home.

McGinley arrived and spoke with Mike, Mary Anna, L.S., Cecilia, and Cecilia's husband. Bente and Esben were crying almost continually, and at times with no immediate provocation one of the adults would break down and sob. McGinley had never before witnessed such grief. When she saw Sam, she was shocked at his wretched appearance. When he thanked her for coming, she was startled by what she saw in his eyes—rage of such an intensity it frightened her.

McGinley was uncertain why she had been called but soon realized the group was asking for direction. She asked what they wanted to accomplish, and they told her they wanted to contribute to solving the murder. They had already decided to offer a one-million-dollar reward for information leading to the apprehension and conviction of those responsible.

McGinley cautioned against such a huge amount because it would bring out every weirdo in the country. Usually rewards in murders were approximately $10,000 or $20,000. The group compromised by offering $250,000 and reserved the option of raising it in the future to create additional publicity if the case remained unsolved.

McGinley suggested that there be a single spokesperson and that the focus of any comments be kept on the reward and the need to solve the murder. Mike agreed to do the speaking for the family. Because the public's cooperation was necessary it had to be reminded of the heinousness of the crime: that a loving mother had been brutally taken from her children. The media would want to cover the family's suffering, and that was to be turned to the family's advantage. McGinley designed a reward poster to be distributed at once. It carried a photograph of Eva and the amount of the reward prominently across the top. It read:

> The friends of Eva Berg Shoen are offering the sum of $250,000 for information leading to the arrest and conviction of the person or persons responsible for her brutal murder.
>
> On the morning of August 6, 1990, Eva's 10-year-old daughter awoke and found her slain mother's body in an upstairs bedroom of their home near Telluride, Colorado. . . . Eva had been shot with a 25 cal. handgun by an unknown assailant while her children slept.
>
> No motive has been determined. However, the murder may have been committed by a contract killer. Authorities are exploring any and all possible motives and persons.
>
> Eva was a happily devoted mother and wife, a lover of the outdoors and of animals, especially. Her constant good cheer and gentleness will be missed by all who knew her. . . .

The poster concluded with telephone numbers and the assurance of anonymity.

Mike found the murder a profoundly disturbing experience that dredged up long-suppressed memories. That afternoon he stood on the landing of the house where they were staying and spoke at length to Mary Anna about his life and shared those memories with her. Awkwardly he told her about his eighth-grade year, when Sam had been a freshman at boarding school and Suzanne had taken him to her bed, how he had lain there, willing himself to be small, growing cold in his fear.

Mary Anna told him not to be bothered by it. He wasn't alone. Sam had once told her a very similar story involving Suzanne.

By Tuesday afternoon Harry DeShong, Jr., speaking for U-Haul, was already fencing with Masters. "The police reference to the family feud," he said, "was ridiculous and very irresponsible." He claimed that members of the family in the inside group "are pretty devastated. We all feel very, very badly about it. Eva was very well liked by all the family members. She was quite a lady."

U-Haul had added security to the towers on Monday, and DeShong said that Shoen family members in Phoenix were concerned about their well-being "since we don't know what the circumstances [behind the slaying] are." Still, he suggested, in a strange interpretation of the murder's consequences, that the brothers "felt relatively certain that this incident would bring the family closer together."

A reporter asked Masters to clarify his earlier statement, and he said, "A lot of people are asking if this is related to the feud going on over the U-Haul business. We have no way of knowing." Pressed to narrow the list of suspects, he added, "All I can say is that most of the people of China are not suspects."

The focus of media coverage was on the feud, and even in the absence of hard evidence suggesting a connection, it was being made every day in the public eye. Reluctantly Masters was forced to acknowledge he suspected some relationship to U-Haul. The reality was he couldn't explain the murder in any normal way. "There's something else going on here," he told *The Wall Street*

Journal two days after first seeing Eva's body. "This doesn't appear to be a local issue."

As one example, on Thursday KUSA-TV, the ABC affiliate in Denver, opened its 9:00 P.M. news this way: "A hit man may have been contracted to kill a Telluride woman because of a family dispute. That's what the police are saying now. Eva Berg Shoen was found dead on Monday at the family home. She was shot between the eyes.* The mountaintop home was reported being guarded by several watchdogs when the shooting took place. Shoen's husband is involved in a family fight over the parent company of the truck rental company U-Haul...."

If the outside group was struggling to maintain a perspective, at least publicly, its Phoenix attorney, Marvin Johnson, had no such difficulty. He told the *Rocky Mountain News* reporter, "[The killer] would have known exactly were Sam was all the time. Whoever it was went after his wife because they knew how that would have hurt Sam." Johnson unabashedly told the Telluride *Times-Journal*, "I certainly think [the murder] was connected to the dispute."

The psychological report Dr. Day had prepared years before was leaked to the press, and an enterprising reporter reached the psychologist in Tucson, Arizona. "I don't have any idea about what may or may not have happened," he said, "because I have no ongoing connection with the family. Yes, I worked with them eleven years ago, but right now I'm just a shocked citizen like the rest of us."

Apprehension and paranoia spread through Telluride and San Miguel County. Masters acknowledged that his office was stretched thin for now, that the crime scene was consuming a lot of man-hours, and that Eva's murder was his number one priority. But he was quick to reassure the populace. "It doesn't appear to be a local case," he told them. "I do believe it to be a specific act of violence against that particular person and not a random-violence act.... [W]e don't have someone going around murdering

---

*A number of early media accounts made a similar misstatement, apparently based on the coroner's observation of Eva's body, not on the results of the autopsy.

people indiscriminantly [*sic*] in Ski Ranch, and I know there's a lot of fear of that."

Masters knew his community and in this regard had his finger on the pulse. Doors were now locked, and at night curtains were drawn across windows. Strangers were greeted with less friendliness or not at all.

On Thursday afternoon two private investigators with the Capitol Detective Agency arrived on a private U-Haul plane. They went straight to the sheriff's office and met with Masters to inform him that they had been retained by U-Haul to solve the murder. They offered their assistance to the sheriff.

Masters told them that he was concerned because they had been retained by only one side of the family when there was an open feud taking place between the family members. He told them that he was working for the victim, Eva Shoen, and would not be releasing any information to them since it would go to just one side.

The character of the ensuing U-Haul murder investigation was established that evening, when one of the private investigators took a call in a local bar from a "psychic" in Arizona. The man said an Israeli had flown in from Tel Aviv and killed Eva. Sam had met him in New York City and paid him $225,000 to kill his wife, with another $175,000 due after the fact. The killer was a handsome man who had gone into town and picked up a local woman, then spent the night with her. Now he was in Aspen, fishing.

The next morning the pair met with Masters again, and this time he gave them perfunctory information about what they knew, not much more than had already appeared in the press. Then one of the investigators enthusiastically related what they had learned from the "psychic" and urged Masters to follow up on it.

The coroner, Robert Dempsey, declined to release Eva's body for a funeral since tests were still ongoing, and Sam had been cautioned against an open casket funeral in any event. A friend of the family made arrangements, and a memorial service was scheduled for Friday, August 10, 1990, at Christ Presbyterian Church at 1:00 P.M.

Kim Pound met with L.S. that morning and conducted a three-hour interview during which L.S. talked virtually nonstop in one of his classic running stream-of-consciousness diatribes. He told Pound what he had been keeping to himself almost since learning Eva had been murdered. L.S. was certain that either Joe or Mark or at least someone very close to them had hired the killers. There was no doubt in his mind that Sam had been the target. There were men close to Joe and Mark who advocated violence as a way to solve business disputes, and from L.S.'s perspective, that had taken place here.

The afternoon was a blustery, overcast day, and throughout the service it thundered outside. The U-Haul investigators, who had arrived early, feverishly wrote down the license plate numbers of those in attendance. Afterward they scanned the crowd for clues, making special note that this was a "New Age" funeral service.

An empty urn was on display, and there were photographs of Eva inside the church. A singer rendered "Blowin' in the Wind," and the crowd sang "Morning Has Broken." The sobbing was audible throughout the crammed church. Don Erickson, Eva's first husband, realized that he was not present just for his daughter's sake. He wanted to be here. Erickson had never remarried. The service struck him much harder than he had anticipated, and he was moved by the pain of the family. As he cried, he also realized he had never stopped loving Eva.

Dr. Rick Melde, a close friend of Sam's, rose to speak. "We have gathered here to mourn the death of Eva Shoen, who was brutally murdered in the dark of night, while her husband was away and her children slept. She was found in the morning by her young children, who attempted heroically, but in vain, to revive their dead mother . . . for this had been a coldly calculated assassination by cowardly evil perpetrators.

"Robbed now are these children of their mother's love and affection, affirmation, and guidance early in their life. Robbed also is Sam, her husband, of a rare and special love. . . ."

"Hear me now, Sam! This is not an end. For life has mystery which is not easily understood; be reassured that you will be united again with Eva....

"To you now Eva, a final toast—Skoal, Eva. May your soul soar on the gossamer wings of Eternal Life.

"As it has been promised. So be it."

A reception was held downstairs immediately after the service. The pain was so palpable across Sam's face it was unbearable to watch.

Outside, L.S. spoke with a reporter. "She was assassinated," he said. "It was a professional job."

Pound took Don Erickson aside for a short interview, and afterward Erickson drove with Aase back to the secure location where the family was hiding. Once Bente had learned a bullet could pierce a window, she refused to go near one. Both children cried nearly constantly. They had slept with Sam every night since their mother's murder, and he passed the hours of darkness, weeping softly, cooing gently into the ears of his frightened children, reassuring them that they were safe with him. So fearful were the children that for weeks neither Bente nor Esben could be alone, both even insisting adults accompany them into the bathroom.

U-Haul's investigators were working to obtain a copy of the autopsy and were clearly frustrated when told it would not be made available to them. They interviewed someone who had attended the memorial service and recorded his comments when he said it didn't look to him as if Sam were grieving.

On Sunday the *Arizona Republic* splashed the U-Haul story across its pages with a story entitled "Death in a House Divided." Written by Charles Kelly and Randy Collier, it stripped the last vestige of local privacy from the Shoen family. Sam was reported to be in hiding. "He's in terror of his own life," L.S. told the reporters. The long, sordid history of boardroom brawls and family beatings was played out in excruciating detail. The article reported the reward and ran the telephone number for those with information. "We're trying to make sure that the maximum is done to bring to justice the person who paid for this professional execution," Mike was quoted as saying, carefully avoiding any mention of a connection between the murder and U-Haul.

* * *

Masters was distressed at the direction in which the murder investigation was going. His entire budget was less than seven hundred thousand dollars, and he could see that the turns this case was taking meant it was going to be very expensive. He met with the San Miguel county commissioners to request additional funds and was surprised when they expressed their displeasure with him for failing to brief them privately on the details of his celebrated murder investigation. He told them that if his office was unable to develop a suspect, the investigation was going to cost at least fifty thousand dollars. If his office was able to uncover a suspect, the cost would rise to two hundred thousand dollars. Unless the case took an unexpected twist at this point and proved very easy to solve, they should be prepared for a major trial, and the total cost, including the prosecution, would rise dramatically.

The commissioners, visibly agitated, started shouting and swearing at him. They made it known they did not intend to spend that kind of money. One scowled and said, "I don't give a damn who did it!" Masters told them that when it snowed, the commissioners never asked how much it was going to cost to clear the roads, they just cleared the roads. Murder was the same. But the commissioners refused to appropriate further funds, or as one observer said, "They didn't stand and be counted."

L.S. had watched Masters and Pound with suspicion and had in fact quizzed Pound during his interview to determine his competency to conduct a murder investigation. Pound had told him that one criminal investigation was like another, there was no magic in it. The crime scene had been sealed as effectively as the circumstances allowed, the sheriff's office along with the CBI technicians had developed every piece of physical evidence to be found, and the autopsy had been first-rate. Now it was a question of conducting interviews and following leads, tasks any experienced detective was qualified to perform.

L.S. was mollified but knew that when it came to money, the sheriff's office was working on a shoestring. The entire budget for criminal investigations for the year was less than eight hundred dollars. He wrote the county commissioners, offering fifty thousand dollars to help fund the investigation. The commissioners were thrilled, but Masters was very upset at the offer. San Miguel County was affluent, and this was not a question of lacking the money, only of being unwilling to spend it. He explained to the commissioners that accepting money from L.S. meant that one side of a feud was funding an investigation, and while even L.S. himself was a suspect, if they made an arrest on the other side, it would appear L.S. had purchased the result. It brought into question the integrity of his office, and a defense lawyer would have a field day in court with such an argument, both at the trial level and on appeal. "Don't take the money," he told them categorically. But they did.

The composite drawing had been completed but was withheld from the media. It depicted a nondescript white man, forty to fifty years old, with short brown hair, regular features, and a pale complexion.

On August 14 U-Haul's investigators met with Undersheriff Walters, who informed them that persons the pair had interviewed were reporting to the sheriff's office that the private investigators were claiming to be from the FBI and the Arizona attorney general's office. Walters expressed his displeasure with their conduct and told them that some members of the Shoen family thought that U-Haul investigators questioning witnesses was like "having the fox investigate the chicken coop." He told them he found their behavior "a strange way to cooperate."

Walters cautioned them that the Shoen residence was still marked off as a crime scene, and they were not to violate it. Once it was no longer a crime scene, it would remain private property, and the men had better have Sam Shoen's permission to be on it.

Watching this pair in operation since their arrival, Masters wondered if they were in Telluride to help or hinder.

By Tuesday L.S. and Carol were back in Las Vegas, and L.S. was now focusing his full attention on his daughter-in-law's murder. In his journal he wrote: "[The] best information is that this was a botched kidnapping. [Sam] tells me that [U-Haul] has two detectives and the FBI* doing a separate investigation in Phoenix. I can not help but believe that this [the hiring of detectives] is a political maneuver by my son, Joe, and company. . . . *I am getting suspicious . . . of Harry DeShong, Jr.* [emphasis in original] relative to Eva's death. He has a lot to lose were management to change. . . ."†

The same day L.S. wrote his children and asked each of them to contribute a hundred thousand dollars toward financing the investigation. "I have make [*sic*] a serious research and evaluation as to the appropriateness and competency of these people to conduct and coordinate this project. If it can be done they will do it."‡

In fact, Cecilia had already wired Sam two hundred thousand dollars. She had no idea how long he and his children would be in hiding, and she knew his financial resources would be stretched. Other members of the outside group had also offered him money.

McGinley called L.S. to explain how the media operated and to give him advice as well as words of caution. She had watched him closely in Telluride and believed him to be a fundamentally honest man who had built U-Haul and never given serious thought to the dynamics of his family. She also wanted the tenacity she saw in him directed in a positive manner.

She told L.S. that the media wanted him to say how he felt and to connect Eva's death to the struggle for control of U-Haul. They would press for him to name names, and he must not be drawn into that. She cautioned that his statements would have an impact on the company and that he must consider that in light of the chance that control of U-Haul could still change hands. She told him it would not be possible to separate the company from Eva's death because the media would not allow it. He must not play their game, and she said it was best for him to stall reporters for now and refer them to her.

* * *

---

*An FBI agent did assist U-Haul's private investigators for a short time under circumstannces that were never fully explained and that later developed were not official.
†No one has been charged in the murder and there has been no public disclosure of evidence linking Harry DeShong, Jr., or anyone else to it.
‡No one associated with the inside group made a contribution.

On August 15 L.S. wrote Joe: "...Eva's murder is the most difficult thing I have had to deal with in my life....As I see it my family is under a cloud until we can bring the perpetrators of this crime to justice. This will hang over our heads like a sword held by a thread. Please know that I love you...."

The same day Joe called his father and talked to him at some length about Patty Lee's declining physical condition. Then he told L.S. of *The Wall Street Journal* article and the Sunday piece in the *Arizona Republic*. Joe accused his father, Mike, and Marvin Johnson of saying that he and Mark were behind Eva's death. L.S. replied that neither he nor Mike had said any such thing and that he would like to see the articles quoting them as making such an accusation.

Joe told him the company's bankers were forced to deal with all the adverse publicity. L.S. replied he understood that and was doing his best to avoid hurting U-Haul. He told Joe that he was accusing no one, to reread his letter of August 8 asking for the help of all his sons and daughters. Joe said that he would reply to that in time but that L.S. would get his help only when he stopped talking to reporters; otherwise all his father would get from Joe was— At this point he uttered an obscenity.

Joe claimed he had sent lawyers and investigators to Telluride in response to the accusations he claimed L.S. was making. L.S. tried to convince Joe that this was counterproductive. They all should join together to support Sheriff Masters and solve the murder.

Joe dismissed the suggestion and instead resumed accusing his father. He denied ever beating Mike, and L.S. expressed his incredulity. He told his son that he had seen the assault for himself. How could Joe deny it? He urged Joe to read Dr. Day's report to gain some insight into his own behavior, and almost immediately Joe broke off the conversation.

L.S. was confused about why Joe would call him about Patty Lee when his son knew his father was in frequent communication with her. "Why not confront the fact that Eva was murdered[?]. That is what concerns all of us," he wrote in his journal. "...I can not help feeling sadness for [Joe] and Mark. The finger is pointing at them. These are the facts as they appear to others...."

But who really knows[?] I think it is in his and Mark's best interest that we get to the bottom of this crime."

Later that day L.S. received a call from Martha Groves, a reporter with the Los Angeles *Times,* who told him she had spent the afternoon interviewing Harry DeShong, Jr., and Mark about the murder and "battle" for control of U-Haul. When she repeated them to L.S., he found little truth in DeShong's comments and decided Joe's earlier call was intended to stop him from talking to this reporter. "This is stressful for me," he wrote after speaking to her. "I refused to comment on my thoughts as to whether relatives of mine were involved in Eva's murder."

The next day Paul called and said that "Joe was in bad shape." Mark and Sophia were in hiding, and he hoped L.S. would urge the family to stop talking to reporters. L.S. took this to be so much more of the "party line" and dismissed the comments because Paul had told him up front he was calling from his house, the same telephone line he had warned L.S. he believed was tapped.

The same day Joe wrote he would not be giving any money to the cause since he understood the sheriff did not want donations. "As I told you on the phone, I remain convinced that you, Mike and Sam have misdirected the San Miguel police [*sic*] to focus on the split in the Shoen family." Joe said he knew L.S. and none of the others had said anything publicly, but Marvin Johnson had, and "I am heavily influenced... by the absence of a categorical denial by any of you that the slaying is related...." He said he paid his taxes, and that was a sufficient contribution to the police. "In regard to investigative efforts undertaken by [U-Haul], I believe these were taken because of the clear innuendo created that somehow the insider Shoens had escalated from ruthless beatings to professional assassinations. Both allegations are totally false."

Joe closed his letter with this: "I share your grief on Eva's death. My heart goes out to her children, Esben and Bente. I can only imagine the extent of the grief that Sam must feel. Eva's death highlights my own mortality and the disfunctionality [*sic*] of continued disputes among the descendants of L. S. Shoen. Sincerely, Joe."

The only children mentioned in the letter were those of Sam. Joe said nothing about Aase.

Also on the same day, August 16, Mark, currently the president of U-Haul International, formally announced in a statement to the media that the company had hired detectives to investigate the murder. "All the necessary resources of this corporation are being used to help solve this crime.... People who kill Shoens are going to be apprehended and that goes for the person who killed Eva Shoen...."

Mark had more to say, and that something more seemed to be what this public statement was really about:

> The loose talk seeking to implicate the Shoens who are running the company to the slaying severely damages the public trust and is detrimental to employees, company operators, customers and shareholders.
>
> My concern of course is that the longer the water is muddied with conjecture and speculation the more difficult it becomes to apprehend the murderer. The preposterous notion that some member of the Shoen family is responsible only keeps police from focusing in on the perpetrator of this crime.... Eva's death is unrelated to the U-Haul business.... When the facts of this case come to light, I believe those who have been maligned in the press will be owed an apology by those who have made the irresponsible accusations.

He added that speculation that the controlling faction of U-Haul was connected to the murder was "the kind of thing we [have] come to expect from our litigious siblings." In fact, Mark's statement was the first published or disseminated comment by any Shoen suggesting a link between the murder and U-Haul.

DeShong confirmed that as many as eight investigators were working on the case. "We're trying to ensure that things that have been insinuated are being dealt with by us in a proactive way," he told reporters.

An underground network of communication had existed in U-Haul Towers since Joe had taken control. Newspaper clippings were slipped into plain folders, then left on desks for review and to be passed along. Management forbade any mention of the murder, but the folders were scattered throughout the buildings. The violence in Reno just months before had increased speculation that more violence was to follow, so when word of Eva's murder hit the newspapers, there was little surprise in many quarters. The only aspect that was unexpected was that Eva was the victim. Throughout the towers there was a sense of deep sorrow for "Doc Sam," for his affection for Eva and the closeness of their marriage were common knowledge.

When employees did speak of the murder, it was in hushed voices. "God, you don't think they would go that far, do you?" one asked. Another had been watching the news when word aired. She turned to a companion and explained that the killer had missed Sam and murdered Eva in error. Another employee dared to ask openly in the towers,* "Do you think Joe and Mark did it?" and the day after the murder received twelve telephone calls from co-workers suggesting the pair were responsible, not one to speak in their defense.

Orders by management to say nothing about the murder struck some employees as odd. There was also no official announcement of the killing, no memo. As one employee explained later in describing the environment in the towers, "Fear ran the company."

Fear was also dictating some of the behavior of members of the family. L.S. bought a .38 caliber revolver, which he placed beside his living-room chair. Mike bought a shotgun, which he slid under his bed along with a baseball bat, and for several weeks after returning to Washington State, he rigged trip wires throughout his house before he went to bed. Other family members were being very cautious or had alerted their local police to keep a special eye on their homes.

On August 17 a press release was sent to Martha Groves, the reporter with the Los Angeles *Times* who was covering the murder.

---

*He was fired a few months later.

The phantom release had no identifiable author. In bold print it was entitled "Dr. Pitts: U-Haul Founder Needs Treatment." It began:

> A source close to the founding family of U-Haul said today that company founder "L. S." Shoen suffers from manic-depression and needs treatment.
> The source, a prominent California psychologist, claimed that the reason he was willing to come forth with this information was due to the fact that Mark Shoen broke with family policy this week and issued a statement to the press about family matters. The source also said that he felt the Shoen family now in charge of U-Haul's daily operation had tried to keep this part of the family history quiet for so long out of respect to their father that it actually has hurt them deeply.

The strange press release claimed Dr. Pitts had diagnosed and treated L.S. in 1978. It said U-Haul's deteriorating condition was due in large part to L.S.'s declining mental state:

> L. S. Shoen sided with sons Sam and Mike, but the struggle for control of the company has been fueled by distortions and aberrant behavior on the father's part, including his working day and night at his word processor and incessantly mailing bizarre letters to his 12 children. This has progressed to the point of L.S. trying to convince the family that the chairman of the board, Joe Shoen, is the "devil" and behind so massive a series of manipulations that such charges defy both the logic and energy of anyone except a man driven by manic-depression. . . . The recent implication that family members were responsible for the murder of Eva Berg Shoen was seen by knowledgeable sources as further evidence of the father's mental disorders. . . .

It concluded by claiming Dr. Pitts thought L.S. should "be brought in for treatment."

In fact, Dr. Pitts had made no statement and had not issued a press release. The blatant attempt to label L.S. mentally ill was a familiar theme in the family, and those who had been arguing it were well known. So, too, was the often used attempt to cast Joe as victim. U-Haul refused comment on the bogus statement. And while the release argued that L.S. and others allied with him were publicly linking U-Haul and Joe and Mark Shoen to Eva's murder, in fact, they had not.

It later developed that Joe's high school friend who was the putative owner of Form Builders had discussed the press release with Mark and that drafts of the release had been faxed between his office and Joe's and Mark's. Once the text was settled on, the friend then faxed it anonymously to the newspaper.

Around this time the sheriff's office received an anonymous telephone call claiming to be from Phoenix. This was not unusual. Since word of the murder had broken, the sheriff's office had been flooded with calls from Phoenix, mostly from disgruntled former employees. It was evident that Joe and Mark Shoen were not well liked by many people. This call, however, had a different ring. The source claimed that a relative who owned a bar in Phoenix had seen "one of the Shoens" passing cash across a table in a back room before the murder. A few days later, after the murder, the relative said he was going to the airport to pick up a man who had "just done a job." Masters had the call traced to a pay telephone in Phoenix outside the bar the caller had named.

By this time the leads in Telluride, such as they had been, were exhausted. The investigation had to move to Arizona, and that week Pound and Masters flew there. They drove past the U-Haul Towers they had heard so much about, and Masters, who had been thinking in terms of downtown Los Angeles, commented, "That's the twin towers?" He was decidedly unimpressed. The men spotted an overweight security guard, cruised casually through the parking garage without being challenged and cracked a joke about the increased security they had heard so much about.

The next morning Masters and Pound were to meet a U-Haul secretary at a coffee shop, intending to gather general background on the company and senior management; they had made these arrangements by telephone with the secretary at her office. The secretary pulled up just behind them, but almost at the same instant Harry DeShong, Jr., arrived, accompanied by another of the Golden Five. The men told the officers they were there to let them know that they didn't have to make such arrangements with employees like this to obtain U-Haul's cooperation. But, DeShong told the men, they also needed to understand that U-Haul was a very aggressive corporation. DeShong and his companion left, but the subsequent interview was worthless because the secretary was shaken by the experience. The officers suspected that the real message was intended for the employee, and it was very different from the one delivered.

The two Colorado lawmen had also scheduled an interview with Joe for that morning and drove to the towers. As they walked up to the entrance, Masters wondered aloud if they should wear their clip-on badges. Pound said he thought they should: "My impression is he doesn't respect authority."

The officers were taken into Joe's eleventh-floor office, where they were greeted by Joe's lawyer. Masters and Pound approached the CEO in a friendly manner and said they would like to speak with Mark as well after they were finished. But Joe was already puffed up in indignation and anger, ready apparently to take the pair on, almost before the formalities were done. He had no interest in telling them where he had been at the time of the murder and made that clear.

"No, you can't talk to Mark," he then said.

"Do you make all the decisions for Mark?" they asked.

"While Mark works here, I make all the decisions for him and do his thinking," Joe responded haughtily, then exploded. He told them they could not interview any employee. He paid for the air and the air conditioning in the building, and the officers were not permitted to do anything in it. Joe shouted that all Masters and Pound were interested in was one side of the story, and there was no sense in wasting his time with them.

Joe was livid and nearly screaming at the officers, who had uttered hardly a word. Pound decided Joe thought he could intimidate two small-town deputies with such tactics. In less than five minutes they were escorted from the building.

Masters was stunned by what had just occurred. This was a murder investigation, and people usually cooperated in such cases. He had arrived anticipating some measure of support. "It's hard to believe that this is a billion-dollar company," one of them said, or that they had just met the CEO. As they went to the car, Pound added, "For someone who says he's not involved, he's being awfully uncooperative and vague as to where he was at the time of the murder."*

Ninety minutes after the confrontation with Joe, his attorney paged the officers. When they spoke, he said that Mark had agreed to be interviewed, so the men returned to the towers. Mark was joined in his office by a lawyer and one of the private investigators. Masters asked most of the questions while Pound took notes.

Part of Pound's training with John Reed & Associates was to ask questions intended to test a subject's general response to crime. This was helpful in pinpointing suspects. For instance, if the investigator asked, "What do you think should be done to murderers?" a normal response was that they should be imprisoned for life or executed or even that they should be helped. Other kinds of answers were red flags.

Mark's manner was not overtly aggressive, at least not against the officers, but at one point the private investigator made a comment, and Mark turned to him and said savagely, "You work for me, God damn it, and you do what I say!"

The officers asked Mark why he thought anyone would want to kill Eva. Mark's response was a nonchalant "Shit happens all the time."

Helping Bente and Esben through this tragedy placed a nearly unbearable burden on their father. They were sleeping in the same bed because the children refused to be any farther away from him.

---

*In the fall of 1992 Masters appeared on *Unsolved Mysteries* and commented on this interview. "One of the most frustrating parts of the case was the U-Haul corporate reaction to our investigation. We had troubles with the U-Haul president Joe Shoen and Mark Shoen in obtaining proper interviews. Joe Shoen himself was very hostile towards us when we tried to interview him. Claimed that he was going to interview us and that we weren't going to be allowed to interview him because he was paying for the air conditioning in the office building. These kinds of statements made it almost impossible for us to conduct proper interviews of people that we thought might have some knowledge of people that might cause Eva Berg Shoen harm."

Repeatedly throughout the night they would awaken him to be reassured that he was alive.

During the day the children coped by telling and retelling the story of discovering the body, their efforts at CPR, and the blood and horror of the experience. The adults with them in hiding found it difficult to hear the story again and again, but for Sam it was torture, and at times he was forced to leave the room. The children frantically described how pale Eva had been, not at all like their living mother, and how stiff her body was when they tried to move her. This exorcism of horror, prescribed as therapeutic by Dr. Day, could occur only if the children were free to speak, for to silence it meant burying the trauma—perhaps with long-term consequences.

Almost out of his mind with grief from bearing the emotional burden of his children, Sam asked again and again, "Why would someone do this? What does it mean?" When he spoke of his wife, he called her "my dear, sweet Eva." He had always taken many photographs and clutched a photo album with pictures of her and the family to him.

The scheme lawsuit initiated by U-Haul against Sam, Mary Anna, and Mike was scheduled to begin in Phoenix in early September 1990. In arguing for a continuance, Marvin Johnson said, "When this case started, I knew someone was going to get killed." As a direct result of Eva's murder, the court rescheduled the trial for February 1991. Sam was too emotionally battered to participate in his defense.

On August 19 L.S. heard from Paul that Patty Lee had died the previous night in her sleep. L.S. made the funeral arrangements. Then a longtime and very trusted U-Haul employee called L.S. and said she had decided that someone needed to tell him what was going on in the towers. She asked that he not tape-record the conversation or relate it to anyone.

She had been watching Joe, Mark, and DeShong before and since Eva's murder. DeShong was an arrogant man, filled with grandiose ideas and seemingly intoxicated with his power and big office. Rumors said he was not saving any of the sizable salary he was being paid, and there was really no likelihood he could earn it working anywhere else. For some time there had been the sense in the towers that Joe and Mark were going to lose control of U-Haul at any time, and then where would Harry DeShong, Jr., be?

DeShong mocked Mark in private; it was really DeShong who was in charge of the U-Haul investigators, not Mark. Some felt that months DeShong had been the real power in U-Haul, and Mark was now taking direction from him.

Mark had appeared stunned since the murder and was walking around the towers saying to people, "I know they think I did it, but I didn't do it, and I am willing to take a lie detector test or any other thing to prove it."

That night L.S. wrote in his journal: "I had eliminated Mark as a suspect right from the beginning. He is simply too open. Too spontaneous. If Mark wanted Sam killed he would do it himself. In fact I do not believe he would kill Sam. He would fight him but he would not kill him. Mark instinctively is a good person. No subterfuge about him. . . . "

The next day, August 20, L.S. wrote Masters and expressed his suspicions about DeShong. He gave a history of DeShong and his family's involvement with U-Haul, then wrote, " . . . Sophia and Paul recently told Joe and Mark that they would not resign the Voting Trust in January 1991," which was contrary to their earlier decision. "[Their intention to do so before] has been instrumental in precipitating the murder in my opinion. . . . "

Several pages later L.S. concluded:

At the moment I am persuaded that Joe did no more than create an environment in the "Corporation" conducive to this type of behavior. That another, Harry DeShong, Jr., or someone like him, took it upon himself to do this for personal power and money.* However I know that Joe personally experienced the ease and frustration of the professional murder of a witness to arson who was to testify the next morning. This witness was a key to "getting" the man, Dennis Saban, who had conned my

---

*This is only one theory of the murder. No one has been charged in the murder and there has been no public disclosure of evidence linking Edward J. "Joe" Shoen, Harry DeShong, Jr., or anyone else to it.

son, Mark, out of $700,000. Joe must have discussed this experience with Harry DeShong, Jr.

With Love and Respect,
LEONARD S. SHOEN

Masters spoke to Sam and suggested he bring in a medical examiner to conduct a private autopsy. Sam agreed, and on August 23, Dr. Michael M. Baden, director of the New York State Forensic Science Unit, performed a second autopsy on Eva.

For three hours he meticulously retraced the county medical examiner's steps. Portions of Eva's body were examined microscopically, and specimens were taken for further testing. Particular emphasis was placed on the two injection marks. Dr. Baden was then escorted to the murder scene to conduct an examination. But his written report provided no new information.

With Mark's public statements and the U-Haul press release attacking those in the outside group there was now less reason for them to stand mute on the almost daily speculation in the media that there was a connection between Eva's murder and the struggle for control of U-Haul.

Mike, who was still the primary spokesman for the group, told a reporter that Joe and Mark were blaming the outsiders for suggesting they were behind the killing but that Masters and others had come to that conclusion on their own.

"The possibility that they might be involved is a logical conclusion that all sorts of people have made without the help of Sam or myself," Mike said. "It has to do with their past misconduct." He added that whoever paid for the killing required access to a large amount of untraceable cash, and Joe and Mark had such access. "I hope my brothers had nothing to do with it, but it is a possibility."

Sam received a call that the U-Haul detectives were in the process of trying to gain access to Eva's body. He spoke with the funeral director, who cautioned it was possible they might find some legal device by which to do it. This would have been the ultimate violation. The director recommended immediate cremation since the coroner had now released the body to him. Sam gave the go-ahead to keep her out of U-Haul's clutches and remained upset over the incident for months.

Joe called his father in Las Vegas to share some of the "dope" his investigators had developed. According to his sources, the killing was the result of "some sort of shakedown for money" that had gone awry. His investigators told him that Eva had one injection mark, "maybe several," on her body, that there were signs of a struggle, that men were known to have been watching the house for hours before the killing, and most important, that Masters *knew* the killing was a bungled extortion attempt but was letting L.S. torture himself with false suspicions about his family's culpability.

L.S. was having none of it. If kidnapping was what this was about, he countered, why go after a "tiger" like Eva when either of the children was available?

"I don't have any idea," Joe said. "It makes more sense to me than ... someone coming in and shooting her out of spite or something."

L.S. fired back, "I think they were in there to shoot Sam."

Joe urged his father to talk to Masters about the needle marks, about the men outside the house. "None of your children were involved in this," he assured him. "I know your children, and while you may have difficulty remembering about them and their character, I know a lot about them.... There's nobody in our family going about intimidating, bullyboying, let alone physically harming anybody.... That is just simply ridiculous."

L.S. confronted Joe with his belief that Eva's murder "came out of the towers," a proposition Joe discounted. L.S. pressed his son, asking him loaded questions that would help the murder investigation, but Joe was suspicious. "You're running a tape on me, Pop," he told his father as he dodged the inquiries.

Shortly after receiving his wife's ashes, Sam went to her gravesite just outside Telluride and privately buried them. He wanted a marker that would be special and was uncertain how to proceed. He was recommended to a sculptor and drove for several hours with the children to meet him and discuss the project. He told the sculptor that he wanted a portrayal of the Madonna, a marker that would be more than an object of beauty, to inspire nonviolence, and a stone on which visitors to the cemetery could sit and find peace. The sculptor took the job, and Sam put the matter out of his mind.

Toward the end of August, accompanied by Aase, Sam drove his children to the East Coast, seeking to distance himself from the tragedy and to find a safe haven for them for a few weeks. He usually enjoyed driving but this time put himself behind the wheel with such an intensity it seemed he was using the experience to force recent memories from him. Along the interstate Bente and Esben told and retold the horror of finding their mother again. Tears ran down Sam's face, and with regularity he stopped the vehicle without explanation, found a place of privacy, and sobbed.

One day Esben spoke of Christmas and said that all he wanted was to find a big box under the tree and for his mother to be there for him. Sam was unable to drive farther that day.

L.S. had at last decided that he should no longer remain silent about his suspicions. He was contacted by an Associated Press reporter a few days after his last conversation with Joe, and this time L.S. said what had been in his thoughts for the past two weeks: that he believed Joe and Mark were mentally ill and that he suspected they were indirectly connected to the slaying. His comments ran in newspapers nationwide.

L.S. now began a relentless barrage of letters to both Masters and Pound. On August 25 he included past letters to his children, then said, "...Joe programs himself and others to do and say whatever he thinks is necessary to accomplish his objectives...." On August 26: "I need to tell you that my son, Edward Joe, attacks and is violent at times...." Enclosed was a summary of Joe's life behavior. On August 30 he sent cassette tapes of telephone conversations with Joe: "[B]oth these tapes reveal the extent to which Joe disliked Sam [and] Joe's denial of reality...."

Neither Masters nor Pound had ever seen anything like it. Masters was too controlled and polite to say what others in the community voiced. "We realize that Eva's death really has nothing at all to do with Telluride," one said. "It's just about the crazy Shoen family."

CHAPTER SEVENTEEN

FORTRESS AGAINST THE WORLD

On August 30, 1990, Capitol Detective Agency delivered its "confidential memorandum" to Mark at U-Haul, for technically he was its client. It was apparent that the thrust of its inquiry was not to solve the murder of Eva Shoen but rather to dig up dirt about her and find some scenario whereby Sam could be implicated in her killing.

The report castigated Masters for refusing to work with the private investigators. "He maintains that he will solve the case by himself," they claimed. They had questioned Erickson in Phoenix but had eliminated him as a suspect when his alibi that he had been in Texas at the time of the killing checked out. They had researched Dennis Saban's court records and reported he had "38 or 39 files in the court with thousands of pages" they were still evaluating.

But the real focus of the report was the victim, not her assailant. "We know we have to conduct a thorough background check on Eva Shoen," the report said. "It still must be done, both in Telluride, Phoenix and in her native country of Norway." It listed five reasons. "Eva could have been communicating with one of her friends in Norway and telling her all about what she was doing in America, including her sex life." It speculated perhaps Eva had left a diary in Norway the detectives should get their hands on. "She could have mentioned a love affair with a Ski Instructor, or someone else. We know Sam traveled. . . . Who knows what problems they may have been experiencing in their marriage? We must find this out...."

The report took exception to Eva's solid character. "Every newspaper article, T.V. editorial, every person that has been interviewed in Telluride says what about Eva Shoen? She was a princess on a white horse and could do no wrong. I never met a perfect person.... She may have developed a secret lover who was jealous and killed her. Right now, Masters is trying to tie the murder to you Mark and to Joe, and the U-Haul Corporation. He could be dangerous in his plot to solve the murder."

The memorandum attacked Masters for having a "BIG MOUTH" (emphasis in original) and presented a litany of pressures to which it claimed Masters was being subjected: He was going through a divorce; he was facing reelection; this was his first homicide, and he wasn't formally trained for that kind of work; he had refused to accept help from the FBI or the Colorado Bureau of Investigations,* and finally, the county commissioners had accepted fifty thousand dollars against Masters's wishes. "MORE PRESSURE" (emphasis in original), the report screamed repeatedly.

It also talked about Sam, urging the agency to do more to learn if he was having an affair on the road. "Maybe Eva has had her affairs as well," it suggested hopefully.

The report recommended that U-Haul pay Capitol to do a great deal more work. The head of the agency was traveling that month to Britain and wanted permission to make a side trip to Norway "to talk to Eva's parents, brother, friends and some of her employers." He never made the trip, but this was not the end of efforts to dig up dirt on Eva and suggest that Sam was responsible for her murder.

Also at this time U-Haul retained Jon Sellers, a local private investigator and part-time country music singer. In 1978 he had

---

*Masters requested FBI assistance, and the bureau at first refused. Much later it did begin assisting. Masters had requested CBI assistance the day of the murder, and two of its technicians scoured the crime scene for two days. It is true he refused to turn over the investigation to the CBI's investigators, who had no special experience with homicides.

retired from the Phoenix Police Department, where he had earned a solid reputation his last years as a homicide detective. He worked for the Arizona attorney general's office for three years, then became a private investigator. He now wore flamboyant western-style clothes, and in the years since his departure from official law enforcement his reputation had diminished.

Sellers was given the Capitol Detective Agency reports and told that he was to serve as liaison between U-Haul and the San Miguel County sheriff's office. U-Haul anticipated that Masters and Pound would be wanting to interview a number of its employees, and part of Sellers's job was to keep them off the premises and to be present during interviews. He later testified that he was told to conduct his own investigation of the murder of Eva Shoen, and he performed at least one electronic sweep of the U-Haul offices.

Almost his first meeting was with Suzanne, L.S.'s second wife. The years had not been kind to her. She was now overweight and had developed a pronounced matronly appearance. She told Sellers that L.S. was mentally ill and described what she called his drug addiction.

There was no doubt of her loyalty. "Joe is a very brilliant kid," she told a reporter, "and I've supported him ever since he was duly elected chairman of the board."

On September 5, almost one month to the day of Eva's murder, L.S. wrote to Pound to report a story coming from U-Haul that Sam was one of his prime suspects. However, Pound was satisfied that Eva was not murdered by her husband, at least on the basis of the evidence to date. When Pound first interviewed Sam, he was struck by the man's remarkable control over his emotions. His reaction had been more restrained than Pound expected for someone whose wife had just been killed. But Sam's alibi had checked out, and Pound now saw his grief and burning anger.

U-Haul's desire to cast suspicion on Sam continued to manifest itself. Mike had informed L.S. that Jon Sellers had called him and claimed that Sam was one of the suspects in the murder. Asked about it, Sam had replied, "My wife gets murdered, and her bloody body gets left for my kids to find, and these people try to imply that I killed her. That's the level these folks operate on." L.S. was very concerned that something might be done to frame his eldest son, and he expressed his fear to Pound.

The same day Paul called his father. He wanted to make it clear that he was disgusted by Joe and Mark's behavior since the killing, but despite that, he did not believe either of them was involved. It was true his brothers were convinced that everything would be fine in the family and in U-Haul with Sam out of the picture, but Paul did not believe they would resort to killing their brother or his wife.

He told his father that the U-Haul detectives were involved to learn what the San Miguel County sheriff's office was uncovering. Paul said that he did not know who had had Eva killed, but if it turned out to be anyone in the family, then the others would just have to take the consequences of being under scrutiny.

Paul also urged L.S. not to go public with his suspicions. L.S. told him that he disagreed, that only national publicity would "smoke out the killers in the near future." For that reason he would be appearing on *Hard Copy*.

Paul told his father that he believed that someone in U-Haul management "either made the hit or hired the killers." The thought of working every day with a killer gave him an eerie feeling. He asked his father if he had ever heard of the play *Murder in the Cathedral*. In the play the king complains about a rival, and finally one of his aides decides to help the king by killing the rival. The result is the destruction of the king.

L.S. asked if Paul thought anyone else in the family was in danger, and his son said no. This had been a botched attempt, and there was now simply too much heat for anyone to attempt to kill another Shoen.

The well-trusted U-Haul employee who had called L.S. on August 19 to express her concerns over DeShong called him again on September 7. Now that Masters had announced the murder investigation was centered in Phoenix, the towers were simmering with speculation and rumors. The fear was intense. Rank-and-file employees generally suspected that someone in management was involved.

Immediately after Eva's murder, she said, Joe and Mark had appeared devastated, and this had lasted for two weeks. They appeared nearly unable to function at work, and it seemed possible that they were not involved in the murder. Mark was controlling Joe with Mark's relentless temper tantrums and reportedly taking sedatives. At one recent meeting he took seven pills, one by one, before he was able to conduct it.

Paul had told her that Joe's house had been broken into without force; nothing had been taken, but his personal effects had been disturbed. Joe was very frightened of his wife, Heidi. The caller told L.S. she was frightened as well and he must tell no one that she had talked to him.

Pound was finally able to schedule an interview with DeShong after some weeks. DeShong's office was gaudily decorated and Pound spotted a heavyset man wearing a cowboy hat off to the side behaving as if he were just passing the time. After the introductions to DeShong, Pound asked who the cowboy was.

"He's a friend of mine," DeShong replied. "You don't need to know his name." Pound asked the man his name.

"Rick" was the answer Jon Sellers gave.

"What's your last name?" Pound asked.

"That's none of your business."

"It is, too. Now what's your last name?"

"I'm a friend who used to be a cop" was the only answer he was to get.

Pound proceeded with the interview. He was working at a disadvantage because his Colorado investigation had no subpoena authority in Arizona, and for now the federal authorities were refusing to get involved, considering this a local case. Pound was therefore required to finesse these interviews.

DeShong was noticeably nervous, and his mouth seemed dry, as he carefully responded to the questions, taking frequent sips of a soft drink. Still, he managed to brag about himself and wised off more than once. Following the pattern he was setting with his key interviews, Pound asked DeShong, "Harry, what do you think should happen to someone who kills someone else?"

DeShong was immediately accusatory and evasive. "That's a

stupid question. I don't think I should have to answer a question like that." And he didn't.

When Pound asked the key question, where DeShong had been when Eva Shoen was murdered, DeShong cautiously responded that he had been home with his wife.

But Patti DeShong told Pound she would not confirm if her husband had been home with her as he claimed. Her attorney had instructed her not to talk to him or to answer any other question for that matter.

On Friday, September 8, 1990, *A Current Affair* featured Eva's murder. Masters described her death as "a very vicious crime," explaining that it was especially callous because the killer or killers had left her body for the small children to find the next morning. No suspects had been ruled out. Mike went on camera and cautiously suggested that her death had been a "murder for hire."

Then Jon Sellers was interviewed in his wide white western hat, the one he preferred to wear when on television. He argued that his days-old investigation disclosed that all Shoens were in danger and that this had been a kidnap-hostage attempt that went awry. What he did not say on camera was that he had never been to Telluride and that his "theory" was based on admittedly second-hand information Masters had already determined to be incorrect.

Around the towers it was DeShong claiming credit for the kidnap-hostage theory. If the police bought it, the investigation would be steered away from U-Haul.

The large reward produced a blizzard of telephone calls and letters to the sheriff's office in Telluride, a surprising number from convicts looking to trade alleged information for money and a release from prison. The technique Masters and Pound developed was to learn how much interest in the money the caller had. People with real information evidenced no desire for it—they just wanted to see justice done—but most callers were keenly interested.

Pound wasted countless valuable hours running down bogus leads. Every one was investigated to exhaustion, and many had nothing to do with U-Haul. One man who called from Los Angeles was making perfect sense with his story until asked where he had received his information. "From my dog" came the response. Another insisted he speak directly to Masters because he had valuable information about the murder. Once he had the sheriff on the line, he said he had received what he knew from space aliens who had invaded his body.

A tape recording received by one of the newspapers in Telluride was brought to Masters by a reporter, shaken by what she had heard. Someone had recorded from one of the television shows Bente's call to the office the morning she discovered her mother's body and had superimposed a singsong voice that was taking obvious delight in the little girl's anguish.

Sellers was interviewed and spouted his story of extortion, stating again as fact events Masters knew had never taken place. He complained that Masters was falsely focusing the investigation on U-Haul. "In my opinion, the sheriff's office is a paid, private investigative unit for L. S. Shoen," he said. "I just wonder what would happen if one of those guys [the outside group] became a suspect.... All they seem to want to do is investigate Shoens."

Once Sellers was in place, interviews with U-Haul employees came to an end. Sellers later acknowledged that he reported directly to Joe in clearing such requests. Masters and Pound considered Sellers a hindrance to the process, not a facilitator. U-Haul seemed to behave as if they did not want the murder solved.

Masters found Sellers bizarre. In the mail he received tapes of Sellers singing country and western songs. Sellers went on national television with some bogus theory about the murder. "He needs to go back and consult his Ouija board again. It's a completely off-the-wall comment.... The whole scenario is just ludicrous," Masters told a reporter. "Sellers has really caused us to lose a lot of ground in our investigation... and apparently for no reason other than to get some headlines. I can't think of what else the motivation is, unless he's trying to screw up the investigation for his clients."

With practiced indignation Sellers retorted, "That's total bullshit. No one buys me."

By now the story of Eva's murder and the struggle for control of U-Haul had appeared in every major national newspaper and on television shows across the nation. Even the *Star,* one of the weekly supermarket tabloids, carried the tale between a story entitled "Davee, Davy Crockett: Coward of the Wild Frontier" and "New Miracle 'Tree of Life' Drug Could Save Thousands of Children Dying of AIDS."

In September Masters again accompanied Pound to Phoenix, and they attempted further interviews at the towers without success. Joe told them that if they ever came back on the premises, he would have them arrested, then ordered their photographs posted in the lobby as if they were criminals. Employees were instructed to call the Phoenix Police Department if they saw either man on the premises.

Interviews with employees occurred at their homes or at neutral locations, but word of who had seen the officers occasionally reached U-Haul. More than one dozen employees lost their jobs shortly after they were interviewed; neither Masters nor Pound was able to establish for a fact that their cooperation in the investigation, rather than coincidence, had been the cause. Regardless, it had a sobering impact on other employees and made the inquiry that much more difficult.

On September 15 Mike was quoted in the *Arizona Republic:* "They [Joe Shoen and others] dearly want to develop other suspects and draw public attention off them because to my knowledge, they have been the focus of interest [by the sheriff]...."

That day Joe called his father and spoke for two and a half hours. In an even, modulated voice, classic "Joe-speak," quoting from reports Capitol Detective Agency had given him, he tried to convince L.S. that Eva had been killed as part of a bungled "extortion" attempt. Joe also claimed the reports said there had been a struggle, repeated that Eva had been injected, that at least two men had done it and had waited outside for hours. He claimed that Sam had called that night when the men were in the house, that there was a footprint, and that Masters had found two types of blood at the scene.

Joe said that Masters wanted to create a news event because he couldn't solve the murder and publicity would advance his career. After all, he was an elected official. "He's a loose cannon," Joe insisted, "wanders around like ... a small-town Columbo. ... "

The younger Shoen told his father that someone had also broken into his house, and he accused Masters. Joe tried to convince L.S. that Marvin Johnson stood to profit from the murder, but L.S. had great difficulty following the logic. "Who has talked murder, guns and drugs from the start?" Joe asked before answering his own question. "Marvin Johnson. ... "*

L.S. was unconvinced by Joe's arguments, even less so because he had watched Sellers pitching part of the same line the previous Friday on *A Current Affair*. He asked just whom Sellers reported to at U-Haul, and Joe claimed he reported to no one.

Then Joe said, "I've heard people say Sam killed Eva, too. You know that's trash talk. I don't like it. It's the same cocksuckers who say I killed her. That's trash talk."

Joe told his father that L.S. was manic-depressive. Joe also said in part that his father wanted to see him in jail and wanted him to commit suicide. L.S. assured his son that was not at all the case, that both Joe and Mark were sick and needed treatment for their mental condition. Joe was suffering from a "postconcussion personality disorder" caused by his automobile accident in 1969, and Mark's from his bout with encephalitis. He urged Joe to go with him to the "best mental health clinic in the world," and the two of them would be cured.

"I appreciate your concern," Joe replied. "It flatters me as it would flatter any child to know that their parent was concerned about them. It flatters me. I am flattered. ... I'd like you to know that I'm very concerned about your health at the same time though I'm the guy who canceled the payments under your contract. You know, it's all the same person."

L.S. laughed without humor about Joe's attempt to force him to admit he suffered from a mental illness in order to have the payments restored. "The only way I could figure justifying paying you," Joe said, "was that you were off your rocker."

"You didn't think maybe it might even be OK to pay me that just because I worked for forty-two years?"

---

*As noted earlier, no one has been charged in the murder and there has been no public disclosure of evidence linking Marvin Johnson or anyone else to it.

Joe repeated he would pay only if his father was disabled. L.S. countered with "If you still think I'm manic-depressive, why don't you pay me anyway?"

Joe now turned angry and began attacking. "... You got this stuff so goddamn fucking public...." He had "fucking people all up my ass ... that's how fucking public it is."

L.S. explained that publicity was the only way the murder would be solved. People had to know about Eva's death and the quarter-million-dollar reward. How else were they going to learn who did it?

"We're not, unfortunately," Joe said. "That's the fucking rub. We're not gonna."

The next day L.S. wrote his "Dear, beloved son" Joe to emphasize what he had said over the telephone, then ended the letter: "[I]t is my belief that the death of Eva emanated from the Shoen feud. I believe Sam was the intended victim, not Eva. That an environment was created by your belief and that of others in your group that Sam was the person who is responsible for the conflict between members of my family. That if Sam were out of the picture all would be well. I believe that the killers were hired by someone close to the top in the [U-Haul] organization. Someone who believed he had too much to lose should management change. Someone who believed he had everything to lose...."

Also on September 16 L.S. wrote the U-Haul Board of Directors:

You can not but realize that Sam was to be murdered. That Eva was not to be the victim. Further you must realize that this murder had its impetus from the environment created by those in control of [U-Haul] who held the belief that if Sam were out of the picture all would be well. Each of you were [sic] a part of that environment much as you may want to deny this.

... The Amerco Family companies and my family have been and are being destroyed. *Is that so difficult to understand* [emphasis in original]? Some of you have been participating in this for three and one-half years. Is this the way you want to live your life?

... Eva's murder should be ample evidence that a power & profit oriented organization (such as how Joe operates U-Haul) destroys rather than creates. What more do you need?

... I am requesting the following:

1) That [U-Haul]'s detectives and you look for the person who arranged Eva's (Sam's) murder in the top echelons of [U-Haul].

2) That the Shareholder's meeting be moved from Tonopah to Las Vegas or Phoenix.

3) That voting on the proposed Shareholder's resolutions be postponed until after the Voting Trust between my sons, Edward [Joe], Mark, Paul, James and my daughter, Sophia, expires in January 1991. You know that both Paul and Sophia have clearly expressed their desire to be permitted to vote their own shares.

With Love and Respect,
LEONARD S. SHOEN

In September L.S. sat at his word processor in his office at his home in Las Vegas and began working on a project he entitled "Dense." Over the next year he wrote, rewrote, and added to the material until it reached book length. It was an examination of his life and an attempt to insert meaning into the events of the past four years. It began:

L. S. SHOEN'S THEORY THAT EDWARD "JOE" SHOENS "CONCUSSION" ON 6/6/69 AS A RESULT OF AN AUTO ACCIDENT ACCOUNTS FOR WHAT LSS BELIEVES IS JOE'S CHANGED PERSONALITY AND CONFUSING BE-HAVIOR ... [emphasis in original].

(Note: The same theory applies to Mark's behavior. Mark had encephalitis? when a baby, became very dehydrated and suffered brain damage which was not diagnosed until he was 12. *See pages 13 & 14 herein & my diary for 1962.* His personality has always been very aggressive and volatile.) ...

DIAGNOSIS AS EXTRACTED FROM CONSULTATION & MEDICAL LITERATURE BY L. S. SHOEN. *(NOTE: I KNOW THAT I AM NOT QUALIFIED TO MAKE THIS DIAGNOSIS.)*

L.S. then analyzed Joe's behavior and concluded that he suffered from a personality disorder and from denial. He quoted extracts from his journal beginning in 1965, followed by his analysis. It was a remarkable effort on his part to seek understanding, and he threw himself into the project with the same zeal he had always demonstrated for business.

He called the work "Dense" because for so many years he had been dense in perceiving what was taking place, and as a result, he believed, Eva was dead. He bore his guilt for her murder in his soul and in his own eccentric way was seeking release through understanding because, he believed, if he understood how he had caused this, he could find some way to set matters right.

There were those who believed that the impetus behind Eva's murder had been fear on the part of some senior U-Haul managers that the company was about to lose its injunction case, which was on appeal in Arizona. That and the defection of Paul and Sophia, which could take place the following January, were taken to be the end of Joe's reign over U-Haul.

A similar case had recently been decided in Delaware. There the court had granted the injunction and ordered an expedited trial so the status of the newly issued stock that kept the existing board in place could be determined before the next shareholders' meeting. Management had been forbidden to engage in any entrenching measures prior to the trial.

On September 18, 1990, the long-awaited decision of the Arizona Court of Appeals on the U-Haul case was handed down. The court held that the outside group had failed to prove that it obtained majority control of the corporation on July 24. It adopted the lower court's decision that the directors had acted primarily in the company's interest by preventing a possible sale of U-Haul by the outside group had they obtained control of the company.

The court referred to the outside group as "dissident stockholders" and stated that the company had acted correctly to forestall "a hostile takeover." In doing so, the court ignored the fact that the outsiders were not a hostile force; they were existing shareholders who had sought to exercise their rights under the rules of the company and the laws that governed it.

M&A and Corporate Governance Law Reporter was adamant in its condemnation of the ruling. "Had this action been brought in Delaware," it wrote, "the court probably would not have treated it like a hostile takeover situation. In an internal control struggle ... the principle of majority rule should be closely guarded."

While the decision made an interesting footnote in the evolution of the law concerning a change in control of corporations, the outcome was devastating to the outside group. There seemed little prospect of success in appealing to the Arizona State Supreme Court, and the only remaining course of action was to press for a trial on the lawsuit. All the while Joe and his supporters would continue in power and retain the vast resources of U-Haul to fund their every action.

This was no small matter. In one proceeding already Mike had appeared for the outside group assisted by a single attorney. Twenty-two lawyers standing in the courtroom had then logged their appearance on behalf of U-Haul.

On September 19 L.S. and his son Jimmie spoke by telephone. Jimmie told his father—whom he consistently called L.S. rather than Father or Dad—that if his father would simply get rid of his lawyers, the problems in the family would be resolved. It was as simple as that.

L.S. did not agree. He told Jimmie that it was imperative that L.S. and Joe go to a mental clinic for mutual treatment.

"Without you there would be no fight," Jimmie told his father, disagreeing with his assessment, "because it takes two to tango and you're always willing to tango. It's pretty easy to find somebody else to go at it. So the day you quit, guess what? *Voilà*, it's over.... You're real big on analyzing everybody else, but you won't do shit for yourself."

Later Jimmie said, "It's your big deal that you're going to tape everything and think you're Sherlock Holmes or something. ... After this particular telephone call, if you want to talk to me, don't hook up your tape recorder because I won't talk to you.... You personally, L.S., are destroying [U-Haul] and our family. You are the one who's responsible. You are the only one who can do anything about it.... As far as I'm concerned, this is going to go on for twenty or thirty years, and I'm prepared for that, and that's just fine by me. I don't have a problem with it."

His anger was beginning to rise. "You just quit fighting!" he nearly shouted at his father. "Go find somebody else to fight with that ain't related to you and doesn't work for U-Haul.... Go sue a fucking tenant or somebody. I don't care. Whatever it takes for you to get off of this shit. Do it!... It's so fucking easy...."

As the conversation ended, "You ain't man enough to handle the problem that you could do by yourself," Jimmie said, "just like you weren't man enough to tell your wife sixteen years ago that you had a son by a lady you weren't married to.... You're an idiot.... You're a fucking lunatic, L.S!"

The same day L.S. received another call from Joe, who assured his father he was cooperating with the police in the murder investigation. "I have bent over backwards trying to help the sheriff," he claimed. They rehashed Joe's ancient grievances against his father. L.S. told his son that he did not believe Joe was taking Eva's murder seriously and that Joe had created an environment at U-Haul in which people close to him believed all would be well if Sam were out of the picture. Joe told his father he would not attempt to dissuade him from such thoughts.

L.S. told his son that for three and a half years he had feared that someone in his family, probably Sam, might be killed. In fact, he had talked to Joe about this in 1987, and Joe had chosen to take his remarks as his father's threat against him.

Joe accused L.S. of falsifying evidence for the Reno Police Department that caused him to be charged with beating up Mike. L.S. told his son he had tapes of the beating in his possession. Nothing had been falsified. "I won't sit back and shut up anymore," he warned.

Joe replied, "I feel that I am being verbally beat on."

L.S. again tried to get Joe to go to a clinic with him with no success. "You stole from my children" was Joe's response, apparently meaning L.S. had caused the IRS Form Builders case that resulted in the substantial judgment against him.

"I know now that I am a good father," L.S. said. "I am being one now."

"You are like Muhammad Ali. Your brain is being affected.

You are old and have traveled too many hard miles.... What will make you, LSS, happy?"

L.S. said he would be happy if Joe would go with him for an evaluation. His son answered, "You have seen a lot of strange things. Maybe you have seen a UFO. I assure you that we will not talk again for a year."

"I have never been in an adversary position with you," L.S. said. "I love you. I want to help you." Joe hung up without a word.

At about this time Eileen McGinley issued a press release reporting that two members of U-Haul management's voting trust had said before the murder that they intended to leave. U-Haul's attorneys responded by claiming the release suggested Joe was responsible for the murder. McGinley hastily recalled the release as she had no wish to be sued. She had no idea who had murdered Eva or why, but from her perspective her job was done. Eva Shoen's murder and the reward for information leading to its solution were national and international news.

She withdrew from her role, but during those hectic weeks after the killing she had stumbled on a quotation for which she did not have an attribution. "These things," it said, "will destroy the human race. Politics without principle. Progress without compassion. Wealth without work." There was more, but she stopped with the last. "Wealth without work." How true. How very true.

Pound was now living almost full-time and on his own in Phoenix. The man from the Phoenix bar identified by the anonymous caller had taken and passed a lie detector test and been eliminated as a suspect. But by the time Pound had finished his first interviews a pattern was beginning to emerge. Back in Telluride, Pound met with Masters and reviewed what he had learned. With sinking hearts they realized that if, in fact, the murder had emanated from U-Haul Towers, this was going to be a complicated, long, and potentially frustrating investigation.

The Phoenix Police Department was very cooperative and provided Pound's initial office space. Most significantly it assigned its special operations group to help with a helicopter for surveillance of suspects. But it was the Arizona Department of Public Safety that provided the greatest assistance to the San Miguel County deputy, treating the murder investigation very much as if it were their own and opening its arms to Pound. Assigned to assist the Colorado deputy was a veteran narcotics officer, Randy Nations, a gregarious and shrewd investigator with widespread contacts in Arizona's crime underworld.

Nations was the officer who answered the telephone when the sheriff's office called, and he was assigned to work with Pound full-time. The selection of a narcotics investigator was no accident. Pound was receiving a steady flow of information that Joe and Mark were involved in drug trafficking and used U-Haul as a front to distribute drugs. It was an aspect of the case he and Nations followed vigorously in the early months, but eventually they were unable to develop any hard evidence linking Joe, Mark, DeShong, or U-Haul to drug traffic.

The sunglasses found at the murder scene proved to be a thirty-five-dollar pair of Pacific Eyes and T's sold in only twenty-four stores in California and Arizona. They appeared to have fallen from someone's pocket, and Pound found it interesting that they had shown up in Colorado at a murder site.

Pound understood that the role of the U-Haul detectives was to learn as much about the murder investigation as was possible, so every few days he changed hotels and checked regularly to see if he was being followed. Because of the reward, leads were flooding into the Telluride office. Almost all of them turned out to be useless, but the only way to be certain was to follow up on each of them. As a result, Pound and Nations worked fifteen-hour days, seven days a week. U-Haul's attitude and lack of cooperation led Pound to direct his inquiry at the company; but many leads pointed in other directions, and these were followed up as well. The investigators went to California, Texas, Nevada, Washington, D.C., and Oregon to check out leads.

Shortly after Nations joined the investigation, he and Sky Walters were informed that Joe would agree to be interviewed if Pound wasn't along. The men went, but the "interview" proved pointless as Joe went on the offensive and never allowed meaningful questioning. He made it clear that he would be asking the questions and did not intend to cooperate with the officers.

On September 23 Sam managed to speak of his wife's death to his father over the telephone. As he struggled to control his anger, in a soft-spoken voice he said, "I simply cannot let myself believe that Joe and Mark were behind the murder of Eva." His father argued that he must face the fact that they might be indirectly responsible. Sam could not yet comprehend so vile an act.

That fall's shareholders' meeting was set for 5:00 P.M. on September 28, 1990, and once again in Tonopah. The night before, L.S. gave the family's situation his deepest consideration and reached the decision that the "craziness" must come to an end. From now on he would not mince words.

This time a horde of reporters and television cameras were present in an attempt to film what was about to occur. The board refused entry to anyone who did not hold shares and refused to admit journalists given proxies to vote at the last second. Sellers screened everyone wishing to enter.

Katrina was asked by a reporter why the meeting had been scheduled for such a remote location. She said, "I really think it's to discourage us from coming, to discourage all shareholders... and to harass us."

L.S. said, "I don't have any idea what's going to happen in there. I never know."

Joe arrived by private plane and was chauffeured to the meeting hall. He hustled in, dodging cameras and reporters, refusing all comment, looking highly agitated. One of the men with him held his coat over his face as if he were on his way to appear before a grand jury. Again there was a guard present. Joe began by reading a short speech. L.S. called out from the floor to be recognized, but Joe steadfastly ignored him.

"Mr. Chairman. Wait a minute. Mr. Chairman, I am your father. I established this company. I have some points to make. I have never in the history of your life, in my relationship with you, ever prohibited you or stopped you from speaking your mind within a reasonable limit. The fact is I have never stopped you."

Joe continued without hesitation. His statement said in effect that the necessary votes to elect a board and adopt new measures for the company had already been cast. Without giving anyone an opportunity to speak, Joe bolted from the room with his small entourage and climbed into the waiting car, television cameras and reporters in hot pursuit. Joe had run from the meeting, one who was there said, as if he thought someone were about to shoot him.

Outside Katrina reported what had taken place in the meeting. Her brother had left so fast he had not taken their proxies. One of the minority shareholders commented that it was the shortest U-Haul meeting on record. Mary Anna said to a reporter, "They continued their campaign of oppression against the shareholders."

Overlooked in the anger over the unusual manner in which the meeting had been conducted was what had just taken place. The new measures further diluted the Shoen family stock, installed staggered, multiyear directors' terms, and imposed a two-thirds majority of shareholders' votes to change the board. Joe no longer needed to cling to his majority, and the board could not again be swept out of office at a single meeting.

On October 2, 1992, *Hard Copy* aired its U-Haul murder story nationwide. Its theme was "father accus[es] two of [his sons] of murder." L.S. went on camera to describe Eva's murder as "a family hit" and linked it to the feud for control of the company.

"I'm convinced it [the murderer] was someone that was close to either my son Joe or my son Mark," he said. " . . . [N]ow I know both these boys are sick. I'm convinced. I don't know. Obviously, I don't know this for a fact, but I am convinced that these sons, either one or both of them, directly or indirectly are responsible for this." He said, "My son Sam was to be hit. He was to be removed from the picture, and I think these two young men, my young sons, either programmed other people to believe this or else had done it themselves, that if Sam was out of the way, everything would be OK with the family and the business and everything would be great."*

On October 8 James Carty wrote his brother-in-law, L. S. Shoen:

DEAR LEONARD:

Damned is the one who destroys his offspring or sets one against another. The moral difference between such a person and the being who put six million Jews in the oven is, at best, a mere quibble.

The story of the U-Haul troubles ala the former emperor has made the *Vancouver Columbian.* . . . Your conduct has disgraced my sister [Anna Mary] . . . [and my family is] tarnished with the disgrace which you have brought upon the family and your suggestion that the murder may be laid at the hands of my sisters [*sic*] sons Joe and Mark. . . .

You have abused so many people and have broken so many financially that there must be a thousand out there who would not hesitate to murder a Shoen, any Shoen. . . . I do not forget what anyone does to or for me or my family.

Sincerely,
JAMES CARTY

PS Do you still have the letter Mom wrote you about your chasing every loose skirt in Portland almost before my sister was in the ground? I cannot remember where I have stored mine away.

On October 9 L.S. received a reply to his decision about going public. Joe and Mark sued him and their brother Mike for libel. The complaint alleged they had exposed Joe and Mark to "hatred, contempt, ridicule, or obloquy, had a tendency to cause [them] to be shunned or avoided, and had a tendency to injure [them] in [their] occupation[s]."†

---

*As a consequence of this and other similar statements, L.S. was sued by Joe and Mark for libel. The statements are offered here not as assertions of fact but to report the events as they occurred.

†At least three such lawsuits were filed in three different jurisdictions, sometimes with both Joe and Mark as plaintiffs, sometimes with them alone. The cases were ultimately dismissed or ended up in federal court in Phoenix. The language taken here is representative of the language in all of them.

Mike was seemingly caught in the crossfire. Typical of the supposedly damning comments Mike had made to the press was a statement to the Denver *Post*. "[I don't] know who killed Eva and I certainly hope it's not my brothers."

But L.S. refused to backpedal despite the suit. He said to a reporter that he believed Joe and Mark were mentally ill and that he continued to suspect that they were indirectly connected to the murder. He told another reporter, "I know that both these boys are sick. Joe at least is psychotic."

On October 10 L.S. wrote to tell his children of his conclusion that "Joe's behavior was and is at best psychotic." He cited some twenty-seven letters and documents that he believed helped lead to that conclusion. He concluded: "The litigation could be resolved in a mutually beneficial way. We could all know the truth. Jesus Christ has said that the truth will make us free. Isn't this what we all want?"

In response to the libel suit L.S. prepared a "press release" he had no intention of giving to the media. He sent it to James Carty, ostensibly to have him check it for libel, but he knew James would make it available to Joe and Mark. It gave L.S.'s reasons for having openly discussed his suspicions but more significantly said that he had placed his diaries, letters, and other documents in a secure, fireproof location. He wrote: "I believe that Joe & Co. might have my office and big shed 'torched' by a professional arsonist." He wanted them to know such an action would "not destroy my records relative to their behavior and Eva's murder."

That evening Sam called again, as he did nearly every night. He had been crying and spoke in a low, even voice. How different his response to the loss of his wife was from that of his father when Anna Mary had died. "Oh, God," Sam said, "everything I gave my life to is broken...." L.S. reminded him that he had his children. "I do. I'm doing my best for them.... Oh, God.... I hate to see them suffer...." He began to cry again.

"Just tell me how you feel," L.S. said gently.

"How I feel is..." Sam could scarcely be heard through the tears. "I'm sending you pictures because I want people to know what happened. I want them to know what's gone.... It's just, oh, God, just so goddamned wrong."

"Yes, it is."

"I know other tragedies occur all the time. I know this is just my world this time. But it was my entire world."

L.S. told his eldest son that he knew he had been taking a beating for others for a very long time. L.S. said he had been responsible for it.

"You're not responsible, Dad.... It's all these 'what ifs,' you know, and it goes on forever. You can 'what if' it to death. It's just so goddamn sad." Sam began crying again. "She sure didn't deserve it. And neither did I or the kids."

He told his father the platitudes he heard daily from caring friends. "It's not true. None of that stuff is true. I don't think these things make you a better person. They make you a lesser person. They take from you...." His crying resumed. "... The only thing that gives me any hope is the fact that Eva didn't die and that life continues and that she's still here." His voice broke. "But I can't believe it."

His children, who had been sleeping, called out for their father. "Yes, sweetheart," Sam said to them. "Right here. I'm right here. I'm coming. Right here, Bente. OK? Bente, I'm right here, sweetheart."

After he had put Bente back in bed, he told his father how damaging their mother's murder had been to both children. He also said how much he appreciated his father being there for him. Then he said, "... There's not a damn thing that's the same anymore.... My Eva's gone. Eva was my fortress against the world."

He told his father that he had finally decided whoever murdered his wife had meant to kill him and sedate her. L.S. agreed.

L.S. repeated that he was there for his son.

Sam said he appreciated that, but "The only thing I worry about calling you ... is that it prods you into doing foolish things, and I can't call you if it does that."

L.S. admitted he could do foolish things.

"I just don't want to be responsible for it, Dad," Sam said. L.S. offered words of encouragement. Life was worth living for its noble purposes. " . . . I've done that in the last couple years," Sam replied, "but it looks like it's going to cost me everything."

"Yes. I know. I know. . . . It's a big price to pay."

"I just ache, Dad. I ache and ache and ache. I don't want any more trouble." He told how he was tortured by his knowledge of what the killers had done to Eva before killing her. "She was such a gentle, sweet person"—his voice broke—"and everything has been so grotesque. . . . My God," he sobbed, "it's like they killed us all."

One of the developments that had come as a surprise to L.S. and others as a result of Eva's murder was to learn that Joe and Heidi had been separated for more than a year and that she had filed for divorce. Heidi and L.S. had never been particularly close before, but now they shared an adversary. On October 17 she spoke to him by telephone.

Heidi had been to court with Joe earlier that day and commented at how "greedy" he had looked. As they entered the courtroom, she had told him, "Joe, it looks like to me I finally do have your attention." His face flushed in vivid anger.

Heidi told her father-in-law that she wanted to be fair, but ". . . I want what's mine. Seems to me that's a U-Haul phrase. What is ours we want." She told L.S. she was proud of herself for having taken Joe on alone. "I don't have a cadre of brothers and sisters and fathers who are lawyers and smart and business people [to help]. . . ."

She pointed out how exposed she felt. "Do you realize what I'm up against if you reconcile with him for Christ's sake? The whole fucking family! Joe alone is enough. Joe, Mark, and Harry and that whole cadre I tell you is enough to scare me. Last night as I laid [sic] in my bed and I thought, you know, what happened to Eva, happened to her after, after Doc Sam told Joe he wanted to play hardball. Well, if I didn't send him the hardball message yesterday, I don't know what I did."

She said that Joe was furious that their divorce threatened his stock. "This is Joe's worst nightmare. . . ."

CHAPTER EIGHTEEN

THE SHOEN BIRTHRIGHT

That fall Pound interviewed Paul Shoen while Jon Sellers was present. The Colorado deputy explained the difficulty he had faced since bringing the investigation to Phoenix. Until then people had been extremely cooperative, "and then, when we ran into U-Haul, it was 'Don't talk to anybody. You're not allowed. We'll arrange all the meetings. We'll have all the attorneys there.'"

He asked where Paul had been when he learned of Eva's murder. Paul explained he had been at home in Phoenix when L.S. called, then asked him to relay the news to the family in the Phoenix area. When asked his feelings at the time, Paul said, "I was shocked. I was shocked...."

Asked to relate Joe's reaction when informed, Paul became evasive. "I'm trying to remember precisely, and I don't really remember. Like I say, I was kinda in shock...."

When questioned if Joe had said anything, Paul answered, "I don't know. He may have said something. I just don't remember exactly."

Pound asked who might have been behind Eva's murder. Paul stammered and rambled, then produced the name of the outside group's lawyer, Marvin Johnson.* "Did you come up with that

---

*There has never been the slightest suggestion that Marvin Johnson was a suspect in the murder.

feeling that day or did you talk to somebody?" Pound asked.

Paul said he had been "hanging out" in northern California and had been visiting with his uncle James Carty, who told him about all the crooks he knew from having been a prosecutor. Paul said he decided Johnson must know the same kind of people.

Asked where he had been the weekend of the murder, Paul replied he had visited with his aunt who had since died and spent time with his girl friend, in Phoenix. He had no problem with Pound's contacting the girl friend for confirmation.

"Paul," Pound asked, "why would someone kill Eva Shoen?"

"You got me. I mean, if it wasn't a random act, somebody had a reason, but it's not a reason I'd be aware of. My guess is Sam might know or her best girl friend might know, but Telluride is a long way from my circle, and I don't know her friends. I don't know what they were doing."

"Who do you think probably would be the most likely suspect?"

"You know, I really have no idea. I don't really suspect anybody. I mean, not seriously."

"What do you mean 'not seriously'?"

Paul suggested Marvin Johnson again, and almost at that moment a secretary entered the office and handed him a file of Johnson quotes about the murder. Paul had not appeared to summon anyone, yet there she was after Johnson's name had been spoken aloud.

Paul continued to dodge the question of whom else he suspected in the killing. "... I'm not real anxious to go around pointing the finger because if I'm fucking wrong, I was willing to send somebody up the river on the basis of bullshit, and you guys know how much I know about this. I know jack diddly squat.... I know fucking next to nothing."

"Paul, why wouldn't you be a suspect?"

"Because I didn't do it. I didn't have anything to do with it. I don't know why it was done...." He said he had no reason to kill anyone. "I believe in live and let live. If you got problems, you got problems, but I don't believe in fucking killing people and harm to people...."

Pound said he understood Paul had been intending to pull out of the voting trust. "Yeah, I didn't sign [a renewal], and it expires in January. I'm not signing it. It's not, I mean, it's not a big deal.

Compared to Eva being dead, it's not... You know, but how's it relate?"

"Is it a big deal to someone else?"

"Yeah, well, you know, it's a big deal to, huh, well, I think now it's not even a big deal to Mark and Joe, but, uh, at one point they, uh, it was important to them and they, uh, you know, gave me a hard time verbally over it, tried to convince me to sign up again, but they just, uh, they're getting the same thing, you know, they want, you know, they swore up a Board of Directors and, you know, keep them in power and go for it from there."

Pound asked if anyone in the company would lose his or her job or something very important if Joe and Mark were no longer in control of U-Haul.

"Yeah, yeah, well, uh, you know," Paul stammered, "there could be any number of people, uh, you know, I just say, uh, you know, I don't, you know, whenever you change your top executives, you get a change of some of your key players, you know."

"What about Harry [DeShong, Jr.]?"

"I think, uh, that L.S. hired him once. I'm not real high on Harry, you know, but Harry might lose his job, he might lose his job, I can't predict it, it might be a big thing to him or it might not be a big thing to him. I'm not really close enough to know."

Pound asked if DeShong had moved up fast since rejoining the company.

"Yeah, he's real fast. I'm not necessarily real high on it, but whatever..."

"Why aren't you high on it?"

"Harry's not my type of leader, OK? He's just a little, you know..."

"How does Harry lead?"

"Well, he's a little, kind of a little bit of a quarreling kind, you know. That's about it, you know, I mean..."

"Does he intimidate you?"

"Uh, uh, I guess he kinda tries, but you know, I don't know how many people take him seriously. He's just kinda a little bit of a bully. That's all, you know."

Paul explained that he did not see how killing Eva saved anybody's job in U-Haul. It could be argued her death could "break

Sam's ass," but it was just as likely to make him even more formidable.

Asked if he had anything to lose if L.S. and Sam returned to the company, Paul replied, "Oh, yeah. I got something to lose, I've got an appraised value of my stock that's about forty million dollars...." He said that in his opinion, he stood to lose no matter who ran the company. He would just as soon no Shoen was in control.

Pound asked what cars Paul owned. He answered, "I have a little blue Karmann-Ghia, a silver pickup, a Land Rover, a Volkswagen van, a green Range Rover, a red Jaguar, ... so I don't have or drive one like you're looking for." Pound asked how he knew what kind of car he was looking for. Paul said one of the U-Haul lawyers had let him know, then acknowledged they had also briefed him on what questions to prepare for.

"Paul," Pound said, "a lot of people think we're only looking at one side. I want to look at everybody. I want you to really know we are. Is there anybody in your family or within this company or people that you know who would be capable of doing something like that?"

After a long pause Paul said, "No."

Shortly after he began the investigation, Pound assembled everything that had been uncovered and sent copies to the FBI's Violent Criminal Apprehension Program, which performs highly scientific analyses of evidence and is able to reach conclusions that can narrow complex investigations such as the Shoen murder. Results trickled in excruciatingly slowly, but finally Pound had the FBI's opinion. The program said he was not searching for a transient. Whoever had killed Eva was familiar with the house. It provided other details Pound kept to himself. The analysis could not determine if the murder had been a professional killing or not.

In late October attorneys informed Pound that Joe, Mark, and DeShong were no longer available to be interviewed. Further, what interviews had taken place in the towers had been tape-recorded by U-Haul. It had refused Pound and Nations permission to tape for themselves, promising that a transcript of the interviews would be made available, but when Pound asked for them, the company refused to turn them over.

Katrina was considering entering an agreement with Paul and informed her father. On October 22 L.S. wrote her:

> In negotiating with Paul keep in mind that the principle exists and is prevalent that the cover up of atrocities, including murders in the USA, usually continues until the powers that be are out for one reason or another. I am not inclined to make any deal that does not result in Joe & Co. losing their power to shut up and cover up the killing of Eva.
>
> My primary motivation in working as I am and doing the things I am doing is to get to the bottom of Eva's murder. Otherwise this will hang over all of us including my great grandchildren. We can not begin to heal this wound until her murderers are at least identified. Leaving this question open is to create a myth or worse.

L.S. no longer believed it possible to sell out to Joe or to make any accommodation that would leave him in power in the company. Eva Shoen's murder had made that impossible. From L.S.'s perspective the outside group was locked in permanent combat with Joe, which would end only when one side prevailed. Mike and others in the group held a similar position.

On October 24 L.S. wrote his children concerning Joe and Mark's "mental health," calling them "sociopaths": "The other members of my family, . . . my other daughters and sons and their mates, must come to understand both Joe and Mark if we are to ever have any real peace outside [U-Haul]'s sale or bankruptcy. Further they are dangerous to our mental and physical health.* FOR GOD'S SAKE HELP ME WITH THIS. FOR CERTAIN I AM AT THEIR MERCY . . . [emphasis in original]."

U-Haul Towers had been receiving a series of anonymous letters directed primarily at Joe, all strikingly similar. One bore Joe's

---

*L.S. made similar statements in public that are the subject of libel suits.

picture, and under it was typed "#1 Suspect for ten weeks."* Beside his photograph was a copy of the reward poster in Eva's murder. Nearly the lower half of the page was filled with two words typed over and over. "Why Joe? Why Joe? Why Joe? Why Joe?"

Another read:

Word on the street—
Someone you thought you could trust implicitly has been talking Joe!!! The lid is coming off of your diabolic plot to commit the perfect murder! Your arrogance is only exceeded by your gutless, yellow-bellied cowardliness! You are without a doubt the lowest form of cowardly slime to crawl this earth! Everything you touch turns into something grotesque and hideous!...And now you are about to be indicted for murder!!! I wonder what life will be like for Edward J. Shoen in prison? I can only hope it will be the daily hell you so richly deserve!!!
Justice, sweet justice is about to descend upon you Joe!!!

Another said authorities had granted immunity to a source to testify against Joe. "Time is running out Joe!!!"

Then the anonymous letters added another target. It had Joe's photograph with the caption "#1 Suspect," a copy of the *Time* magazine article on the murder, and beside it Mark's picture with the caption "#2 Suspect." Below Mark was a quote about him taken from an earlier news account: "Mark Shoen 'knows how to get things done—that's his strong point.' "

Still another had a picture of a U-Haul trailer with the reward poster on the side in place of the usual gaudy picture. It said, "Put Your Hometown 'CLAIM TO FAME' on a U-Haul trailer! I will not rest until [Eva's] killers have been brought to justice!"

Finally, one was mailed to one of Joe's secretaries, addressing her by name. The message was typed in the corner of the reward poster: "If you have any information regarding this case, no matter how small or insignificant it may be, don't be afraid to come forward—Please contact the authorities immediately! 'And the truth shall set you free.' "

---

*As noted earlier, no one has been charged in the murder and there has been no public disclosure of evidence linking Edward J. "Joe" Shoen or anyone else to it.

* * *

It appeared to Pound that Dr. Canfield had been peeved when a second autopsy had been performed. When the results of Canfield's toxicology report were not made available to the law officer shortly after the first autopsy, Pound had called Dr. Canfield about them. The doctor put him off, and when Pound called back a few days later, Canfield was clearly miffed by the pressure. Pound couldn't understand the reaction. He was conducting a murder investigation, and the results of the test could be crucial to its direction. For three months he and Masters had speculated about what could have been injected into Eva. Finally, in November, Pound was informed that the test determined the only drug present in Eva's body was caffeine, which had come from the tea she had been drinking. No other substance the test checked for had been injected.

Pound had wanted to keep the existence of the needle marks quiet, but it was not possible to ask questions about drugs and injections without the information eventually surfacing. Although they were a mystery after he learned the results, Pound tentatively settled on a plausible explanation. If nothing had been injected, the needle marks were a diversion intended to direct the investigation away from the real killers. Many things could have been used to accomplish the same purpose, but in this case the needle marks were used to suggest a medical model for the killing. Since Eva's husband was a doctor, a sloppy or desperate investigation might have concluded that he had tried to kill his own wife in some clever way but that the attempt had been botched, so she had been shot dead. A large-bore needle had been used because its marks were more likely to be spotted or because one was conveniently available.

Masters and Pound had concluded that Eva was the intended victim. The physical evidence told them that the killers had watched the house for an extended time and there could have been absolutely no doubt that Sam was not home. Every window was exposed to view, making the house a "fishbowl," as Pound described it.

The purpose in killing Eva was to send a message. Sam had been spending a lot of time in Phoenix and was the leader of the outside group; killing his wife would push him into such grieving that he would be out of the picture for all practical reasons. In addition, anyone not playing ball in the company would be made to understand just what the danger was in switching sides.

With his knowledge of the physical evidence and the FBI analysis Pound constructed a reasonable description of the murder. The killers had driven to Telluride and spent a portion of the day in town. There had been at least two, more likely three men. Even before arriving, they had known indirectly from Sam's Paradise Valley house sitter that he would be away from Telluride. The decision to kill Eva had been made in advance and placed on hold for a time, then hastily implemented. After arriving, they had checked their escape route, then parked their four-wheel-drive vehicle in the estates at about 7:00 P.M. They walked in the dark to the house and took up positions to watch Eva and the children through the evening.

The sheriff's office had tested the dogs by walking up to the house at night and learned they barked no matter how carefully a man approached. But when they were placed in the mud room, they did not respond. So during the evening the killers had approached the house to cause the dogs to bark, knowing Eva would put them away.

Eva had turned out the lights in her room at about midnight. The medical examiner said she could have been killed as late as two in the morning. Pound believed one man remained with the vehicle and two men entered through the front door, which was unlocked. They went straight up the stairs, and once in the bedroom they wrestled with Eva only long enough to inject her to create the diversion. Then they pressed the small-caliber gun directly against her back to muffle the sound as they shot her. They went immediately out into the night and waited. If Eva had managed to reach a telephone, the killers would have seen a light go on.

Eva was scared, dazed, and weak. Afraid to scream because it would awaken her children and put them in danger, she managed to hobble to the top of the landing. Now well into shock, she fell or sat down at the top of the stairs. With her strength waning she leaned back on the landing as the blood drained from her body, and she quietly died.

After a few minutes, seeing no commotion or lights in the house, the killers went back inside the house to be certain Eva was dead. Then they walked to their vehicle, and one man stumbled, losing his sunglasses. They drove back to Phoenix.

In the final analysis, Pound suspected, whoever was responsible was not willing to kill a blood relative of the Shoen family. But Eva had married into the Shoens, and by the murder of Eva, Sam was made to suffer and his children to experience the grief and pain of losing their mother.

That was the theory. There was no way to know for certain. Maybe someone in or connected to the family had done it, but then maybe not. Pound kept an open mind and explored many leads that led away from the family dispute, but when those were exhausted, the leads that remained forced his attention back to the towers.

For one thing, Pound was suspicious of the fact that the U-Haul board met the Monday of the murder. A source had told him that there had been screaming and shouting behind the closed doors— before official word of the murder had reached the towers.

L.S. was spending long hours every day on his telephone speaking to former and current U-Haul employees to learn what was taking place in the company and to solicit information from them about whom they suspected in the murder. As he developed what he thought was new information, he passed it on to Pound by letter.

For nearly a year L.S. had been feuding with Marvin Johnson and his handling of the outside group's lawsuits. Before Eva's murder he had stopped an attempt by Johnson to have the group pay him and the attorney assisting him one million dollars each. The group had already paid him a quarter of a million dollars and had an agreement that he would be paid more only if they acquired control of U-Haul. Johnson disagreed with that assessment of their arrangement.

Johnson had written L.S. and told him to keep his "mouth shut," then criticized him when previously taped statements aired. L.S.

was offended by the tone of the letter. Writing back on November 3, he said that Johnson had not known the facts when the hearing for the injunction had been held the previous year. "We did not 'win' and this adverse ruling," L.S. wrote, "by Judge Hall has cost me and my family in excess of Two Billion dollars and the life of my son, Sam's wife, Eva."

L.S. concluded the letter with this: "Further that [this letter] will *not* cause you to pout. I realize that I might have written more succinctly. Like 'keep your mouth shut,' or 'take your head out of your ass.' . . . "

Several months later Johnson stepped aside as the outside group's lawyer by mutual agreement. He then filed a bill for $3.5 million and subsequently sued his clients for the money.

In the midst of this tragedy L.S. was trying desperately to be a normal parent and grandparent to his family, no matter which side of the feud they were on. On November 10, for example, he wrote a joint letter to Sophia, Theresa, and Katrina on their birthdays. "My memories are of children and young girls. Beings whom I could love unconditionally. Beings who were of no threat to me. Just cuddly, warm and trusting. Females that could not possibly break my heart. It was great while it lasted. Four girls in a row were something to inspire a father. To fill his life with joy. . . . *Hug, hug, kiss, kiss and happy birthday* . . . [emphasis in original]."

Late that same month he wrote to Joe's older son, who was named for Sam, on his thirteenth birthday. It made no mention of his troubles, the feud, or his difficulties with the boy's father. "Today I want to communicate to you that I love you. . . . I also love your mother and your father. They are both good people as you well know. Also that you have a joyful thirteenth year. Remember I am with you in my heart. That I am proud of you. Happy birthday. . . . "

Almost at the same time L.S. was deposed in the libel lawsuit his sons had brought against him. Asked directly if he believed Joe had hired any person to kill Eva, L.S. replied, "I think Joe is very capable of having done it." Asked if he thought any differently about the situation since he appeared on *Hard Copy*, L.S. said, "Yes. I'm firmer in my belief."

On December 30 James Carty wrote L.S. on the occasion of the pending new year: "The Holiday season is a time of good cheer and a proper time to reflect on both the future and the moments and times of the past.... It is a time of prayer and a word with God asking ... his eternal damnation upon those who seek to harm and damage [James's relatives]. So this will be my New Years [*sic*] greeting to you, you bastard...." He copied the letter to the *Arizona Republic* and the Jewish Holocaust Society.

Sam returned to Telluride in time for Bente and Esben to begin their school year, wanting to give them as much continuity in their lives as possible. He had nearly forgotten about the gravestone he had ordered when the sculptor called to tell him it was ready. Sam drove with his children to the studio. When they entered, Bente and Esben spotted the graceful Madonna holding an infant in her arms and eagerly ran ahead of him. The moment they reached the statue they climbed up and cuddled in its arms, all smiles. Watching them, Sam thought this might be the most therapeutic moment since the murder of their mother.

The statue was carved from a nearly iridescent marble and possessed the special quality Sam had hoped for. It was almost as if Eva were there in the room with them, and he was speechless. Some weeks later the marker was carefully laid over Eva's ashes in Telluride.

On January 5, 1991, L.S. wrote Pound:

> Today Heidi Shoen telephoned me from a telephone booth. Says she does not want to talk to me from her home nor does she want me to call her there....
>
> Says that [Joe] and Mark think they are the only ones who ever lost a mother. Says she knows that their uncle Jim [James Carty] has told them that I, LSS, killed their mother.
>
> *Says that I should seriously consider the idea that Eva was to be killed not Sam* [emphasis in original]. That there is a connection with killing Eva and the death of their mother....

Heidi had also told L.S. to stop analyzing Joe's mental state because he was not qualified and it tended to discredit his observations about Joe's behavior. L.S. told her he thought it was a little late for that. He had already told the world what he thought about his two sons.

On January 30, 1991, *Trial Watch* aired a segment on the murder of Eva. L.S. said, "I believe that the motivation behind this or the impetus behind this was either one of my two sons ... and I think that the killer came up here and didn't have any intention of killing Eva. I think he came up here to kill Sam." The major American newspapers picked up the quote, and fresh articles appeared nationwide.

The scheme lawsuit for sixty million dollars in damages had been rescheduled for February 5, 1991, in Phoenix before Maricopa County Judge Frederick Martone. At the final pretrial conference the week before Martone ruled that L. S. Shoen and Mike should be dismissed from the suit, leaving Sam and Mary Anna as defendants. He granted the inside group's motion that there be no mention of the murder of Eva Shoen during the trial because the information might prejudice the jury in Sam's favor.

The trial lasted for six weeks, during which the U-Haul lawyers attempted to prove that the defendants had breached their "fiduciary duties" by engaging in secret negotiations to take control of the company. Sam and Mary Anna had been receiving minimal U-Haul salaries at the time and were technically employed as consultants. Sam in particular, they claimed, had harmed the company by failing to disclose his negotiations with potential buyers. Finally Sam was accused of trying to engineer a leveraged buyout of the company and had given putative "confidential" information to certain junk bond specialists.

Joe took the stand and testified that the outside group's efforts during July 1988 had caused a hundred-million-dollar stock offering to be withdrawn, damaging the company. Throughout his testimony a stiff, even wooden Joe referred to Sam in nothing but terms of politeness, calling him "my brother, Dr. Shoen."

An attorney for the outside group drew testimony from Joe that an article in *Business Week* that described the feud in the family and the Reno beating were contributing factors in withdrawing the offering. Joe reluctantly conceded that none of his siblings had done anything illegal; indeed, the group had reported its actions to the U.S. Securities and Exchange Commission.

The star U-Haul witness was a consultant on whom the company had lavished a $350,000 fee. Testifying as an expert, he acknowledged that his appearance on the stand was costing U-Haul another $30,000 or $50,000. "So now you're the four-hundred-thousand-dollar witness," an outside group lawyer said.

The outsiders' lawyers argued that U-Haul suffered no damage as a result of their efforts and that they had behaved well within their rights as shareholders. The defense consisted almost entirely of Sam's testimony, assisted by some hastily drawn charts. Asked why he had left U-Haul, Sam testified to the burdensome board meetings and said, "I was peppered by brother Joe with what can only be described as obscene phone calls at home and at work numerous times. I just decided it wasn't worth it." He also testified that a number of factors had caused the failure of the offering, not the least of which was the issuance of the disputed 8,099 shares of stock.

The case went to the jury on March 19 and it returned a verdict in favor of Sam and Mary Anna within seventy minutes. One juror acknowledged afterward that they had actually made up their minds five minutes after sitting down in the jury room. U-Haul declined comment and immediately appealed the verdict.

During the trial Joe and Mark had appeared before a federal judge in Phoenix, arguing that he issue an immediate finding that they were being libeled by their father, whom they described as a "bitter and hate-filled man." Their lawyers argued that a swift ruling was essential to "tell L. S. Shoen that the law will not tolerate his statements to the national media and the national public that the plaintiffs are directly or indirectly responsible for the murder."

"L.S. never called his sons killers," L.S.'s lawyer told the press. L.S. explained, "I think that they misinterpret what I'm doing. I'm trying to get the word out, and that's all."

Joe and Mark's attorneys argued that their clients were not

public figures and indeed sought to avoid publicity. The court denied their request, and the lawsuit proceeded.*

L.S. had not been deterred by Joe's and Mark's libel suits. He believed that his daughter-in-law's murder would be solved only if the spotlight of attention were kept on the brutal slaying. He was convinced that there was a connection between her death and the struggle for control of U-Haul. That same March he appeared on the nationally broadcast *Exposé*.

"What do you think [Eva] was the victim of?" the interviewer asked.

L.S. answered from his heart: "Of being a member of my family and married to Sam."

"Hell of a price," the interviewer said.

"Yes, for her to pay, difficult for me to handle that."

"You somehow feel responsible?"

"Yes, I do. I definitely do."

He felt much more than that. With the killing of Sam's wife, L.S. had at long last thrown himself into a self-education campaign in search of understanding. He had dug his years-old journals out of storage, resurrected letters, read, reread, and studied Dr. Day's prophetic report. He believed that he now grasped what had led to this tragic state of affairs. From this and the numerous books he had read he had formed his oft-stated opinion that Joe and Mark were mentally ill.

Day had written that "L.S. should allow the full consequences of their behavior to befall Mark and Joe. They should not be protected from financial pain or boredom or unfulfillment or vocational limbo." L.S. recalled the special arrangement he had given them with Form Builders, his actions to extract them from the Saban incident, and many others. "I DID NOT DO," he scribbled in the margin in bold print.

* * *

*The federal court in Phoenix subsequently ruled that Joe and Mark Shoen were "arguably public figures," and a federal judge in California, where one of the three libel suits was originally filed, castigated Joe and Mark for accusing L.S. and Mike of going public with statements linking them to the murder when it had been Mark who had uttered the first such comments.

In late May Masters and Pound decided to go public with a photograph of the Pacific Eyes and T's sunglasses found at the murder scene and the composite drawing of the man who had asked for directions the day of the killing. Pound gave an interview in Phoenix. "People think we're just down here looking at U-Haul," he said, "but that's not the case. We're not pointing the finger at U-Haul."

Asked about the status of the investigation, a weary Pound acknowledged, "It's been an uphill struggle."

Pound returned to Telluride every few weeks only to do laundry and file reports with Masters. The sheriff had told him, "I don't want to overcontrol you, but sometimes I feel like I'm losing control of the investigation." Pound did his best to keep Masters apprized, but the truth was he was gathering so much information it was difficult to brief the sheriff on all of it.

Pound received telephone calls day and night. He had put his "heart and soul" into the investigation and was proud of his effort. He knew that some of his suspects in U-Haul management were intensely frustrated that the investigation had been so tenacious, that it had proved impossible to intimidate either Pound or Masters.

Pound had concluded that the Shoens were a highly atypical American family. He found it disconcerting that both sides in the feud for control of U-Haul used media consultants, and he thought it a peculiar reaction to a murder investigation. But as he came to understand the litigious family better, he understood why the Shoens were more comfortable dealing with this issue through representatives.

Pound had exhausted leads connecting the murder to the Mafia, the Mexican Mafia, and outlaw bikers. By the summer of 1991, as the anniversary of the murder approached, Pound was exhausted and keenly frustrated. His marriage had been troubled even before he'd drawn this assignment, and now he was in the middle of a divorce. He had no personal life to speak of, and he could see no end in sight. For a company whose managers proclaimed their innocence so aggressively, Pound could not find an alternative plausible reason for their lack of cooperation other than the one that was obvious and repeated to him by sources so often: If they were innocent, why did they act so guilty?

Sam was determined by this time to move on with his life especially now that the preparation and scheme trial were behind him. Bente and Esben were behaving nearly normally by now. The long months when they had slept in the same bed, then in the same room were starting to end. Bente no longer awakened her father while he slept to reassure herself that he was alive. Though they had stopped insisting someone accompany them into the bathroom, they still did not like being by themselves. They were occasionally frightened but no longer terrified.

Though every day Sam was reminded that his heart had been ripped out of him, he was somewhat improved as well. For six months after Eva's murder he had walked about in a fog, unable to concentrate. He would suddenly become aware of the world outside his grief but have no idea where he was or why he had gone there.

But the worst of that was behind him. Sam accepted a position with the U.S. Agency for International Development in the Africa bureau where he would use his medical degree and business experience to aid stricken African countries. He had once told the Christian Brothers that he wanted to be a doctor so that he could heal the sick of the world. Now that was what he was doing.*

Sam had given the events of the past several years a great deal of consideration during the long winter. He had decided that the single greatest error he had committed was his refusal of Joe's offer to buy his shares for ten cents on the dollar, or sixteen million dollars. Sam was not poor in his own right, and sixteen million was more money than he could have spent in a lifetime. It had been arrogance that had caused him to turn down the offer, arrogance he now believed had caused the murder of his wife.

Eva's murder had accomplished something all the harassment and lawsuits had failed to do. He was at long last "out of the picture." Since the killing of his wife he had been a nonplayer in

---

*Shortly after the Clinton administration took office, Sam was fired along with other Bush administration appointees.

the struggle for control of the company. He could not bear to speak of U-Haul, and for the most part the outside group was rudderless.

In June 1991 Sam packed a family vehicle and a twenty-six-foot U-Haul truck to make the move to Washington, D.C., where he would work. Before leaving Telluride, he granted one of his rare media interviews to the Denver *Post.*

"I can believe that someone was hired to kill me—and I wasn't home," he told the reporter. "The only scenario that doesn't assume that whoever did this was an idiot is the hired killer scenario."

Sam defended Masters staunchly. "The criticism of Bill Masters has come from one source, and only one source—U-Haul." Sam pointed out that if Eva had been murdered in nearly any major city, the investigation would have been dropped after two months.

Sam described the fight for control of U-Haul as "crazy, senseless, foolish, tragic." He did not mince words in placing blame: "There is no feud in my family. There is one person, my brother Joe. You can lay the whole mess at his doorstep. He is 100 percent accountable . . . and he will be held accountable."

On the afternoon of June 14 Randy Nations received a summons to U-Haul Towers, where Jon Sellers told him that Joe Shoen had information about the murder he wanted to pass along. Nations was ushered into a tenth-floor office where Joe, Mark, DeShong, and a U-Haul attorney sat. Sellers took a seat in the room as well. A tape recorder was running, but Nations was refused permission to make his own recording.

Joe claimed that he had received the name of a suspect from an attorney, who said the suspect had owned a Jeep Cherokee the year before and was molesting his own daughter, who had stolen a .25 caliber gun from her mother at about the time of the murder. The suspect reportedly had a criminal record for fraud and matched the composite drawing. Joe thought Nations might want this information. Pressed for details, Joe became ambiguous.

Then what appeared to be the real purpose of the meeting became obvious. Joe went on to say that he knew Nations recently had conducted an interview and asked questions that suggested

Joe was a suspect. Joe claimed Nations had asked if Dennis Saban and Mark had had a homosexual relationship. Nations asked what the point was in telling him information he already had, that Joe seemingly had nothing to offer other than to let Nations know he knew the contents of the interview. Then he said he had additional information that Nations might find interesting.

Joe reported he had gone to his stepmother Suzanne's house, where he met a man he thought was named Steve. This Steve said that he had information that Sam had been stopped by the Navajo Tribal Police speeding at about 2:30 A.M. on the Monday of Eva's murder. Sam had been drinking, and the officers had detained him for a time, given him coffee, then sent him on his way. They had taken a photograph of Sam in the car that Steve claimed a friend of his had seen.

Joe said he had no interest in this information and had scarcely paid attention to the man even though he was placing his brother at a location at a time that would make him a suspect in the murder of his wife. Joe did not know his name, nor for that matter was he even certain "Steve" was correct. This was surprising since Joe insisted that U-Haul was marshaling its resources to solve this murder. According to Joe, he had received this information and had not bothered to get the man's name or even refer the information to the police immediately.

At this moment Suzanne suddenly appeared in the room unannounced. Steve was supposed to be her friend, but she didn't know if that was his name. Joe pressed his point regardless, saying that if Sam had been arrested or stopped by the police at that time, this should be a matter of interest to Nations. He urged the detective to investigate it.

Joe and Mark had more information about planes mysteriously leaving Telluride the night of the killing and now being housed by the Ford Motor Company in Grand Rapids, Michigan, but it was very vague and sounded pointless. Then Joe and Mark launched into an attack on Pound and Masters, lambasting the sheriff's office for being incompetent and Pound for being unable to conduct a proper investigation. After a half hour they told Nations to leave because they had nothing more for him.

There had been a surreal quality to the meeting as if it had been orchestrated. Suzanne's mysterious entrance just after her name had come up only reinforced that impression. None of the information checked out, including that about the man who was molesting his own daughter. The Navajo Tribal Police had not stopped Sam or taken his photograph; it was just so much wasted effort and misdirection. In the end that was what this really had seemed: a blatant attempt by Joe to cast suspicion toward Sam.

A special report was aired over local television in Phoenix on the anniversary of Eva Shoen's murder, and nationally *Inside Edition* carried the story as a feature. Sam agreed that publicity was needed to advertise the quarter-of-a-million-dollar reward if the murder was to be solved, so he consented to interviews. On *Inside Edition* he was asked, "Do you have a lot of enemies?"

"No."

"Could you count them on one hand?"

With a controlled anger so profound it burned in his eyes Sam said, "I can count them on one finger."

For the first time Joe agreed to be interviewed as part of a short-lived company effort to counter the negative publicity. "I think that my brother Sam was caught up in preserving, basically under glass, what he perceives to be my father's legacy," Joe said in explaining the fight over U-Haul.

The interview turned to the murder. "Joe, did you in any way take part or orchestrate the killing of Eva?"

"No."

"You have no idea who may have committed that crime?"

Joe paused. "I have no idea whatsoever."

On the local show in Phoenix a stiff and apparently rehearsed Joe argued that he'd "be happy" to be interviewed by the FBI. "I would welcome them on this case." He dismissed Masters and Pound as "enthusiastic."

Joe was asked to respond to his father's public comments. He said, "I'm very sad that my father"—he smiled unconvincingly—"has made statements such as these, but they are illogical."

The reporter asked, "Did you kill Eva Shoen?"

Joe paused; his eyelids fluttered spasmodically; then he said, "No. It is illogical to say I did, and I think that if you have adequate information, you'd come to the same conclusion that it is illogical."

"Do you know who killed Eva?"

Again Joe's eyelids fluttered before he answered. "No, I do not. I have no idea." Then he added, "My father is a very unhappy man"—again Joe smiled at the mention of his father—"but he's still my father. I still love him very dearly."

"You've said you didn't kill Eva Shoen, that it would be illogical, but you have plotted to kill before, haven't you?"

Joe grinned condescendingly. "No, and if you have specific question about that, I'd like to get into that here today." He smiled broadly.

"Well, I'd love to get into that, and to do that, I'd like to play for you a piece of a telephone conversation that you had with your father."

A portion of L.S.'s tape recording of his conversation with Joe when he described sitting up all night to murder Suzanne was then played. It ended with, " 'Unfortunately [Suzanne] didn't come through the door.' "

" 'Thank God,' " L.S. said on the tape.

" 'Isn't that a bitch?' " Joe was heard saying.

Joe responded on television by arguing that the conversation with his father was the product of his dysfunctional family. He claimed that his father had overdosed on drugs and that his brother Sam had told him to kill Suzanne.

"But you still haven't answered my question," the reporter said. "Did you do [say] that?"

Joe smirked. "I did what I just told you I did."

"You did wait up with a gun, waiting to kill Suzanne?"

"Of course not, of course, I didn't do that. . . . We pretended in our codependent family that the problem was Suzanne's behavior, as my father and my brother Sam are now pretending that the problem is my behavior."

Throughout the interview Joe had trouble with his smile, never seeming to get it right or working at the appropriate times. It left a decidedly negative image.

As the summer heat in Phoenix rose, Pound found himself covering the same territory over and over. The only difference was new faces, but the theories and stories were familiar. He had interviewed both Ned and Dennis Saban. The senior Saban had suggested he speak to his daughter, Marcie, since she knew the Shoens and had, in fact, once dated L.S. It was a remote lead, and for months Pound carried her name on his list of persons to interview eventually.

As the first anniversary of Eva's murder arrived, Pound finally made arrangements to meet Marcie at the Velvet Turtle, a well-known restaurant in Phoenix near her house. Convinced this was a waste of time, he arrived with Randy Nations. What could a dowdy fiftyish ex–girl friend of L. S. Shoen's have to offer the investigation? Marcie was late, and Pound went to the entrance, thinking he should just call and cancel. Just then a stunningly beautiful woman in her late thirties, dressed in a white pantsuit, stepped from a white Porsche and walked through the door. Pound was transfixed by Marcie's looks as well as surprised by her youth. He had never before seen such an attractive woman and found himself gawking.

Marcie joined the officers, but as he expected, she had little to offer the investigation. What he did take away from the meeting was something personal. At one point, when the interview had turned casual, he responded to an issue by saying without thinking, "I'm going through a divorce right now. You know how women are."

Marcie had fixed her eyes on his and said, as if in a challenge, "The man who gets me is going to be lucky."

Within an instant Pound realized he was going to be that man. After Marcie had driven off, Pound asked Nations if he thought it would be unethical for him to take Marcie out. Nations said he saw no problem with it, so Pound paged her with just one more question: Would she go to dinner with him?

When they met, Pound explained that the murder investigation was consuming his life, and if they were going to see each other, there had to be one rule: They were not to talk about the case, the Shoens, the Sabans, any of it. Marcie laughed and agreed.

The prospects for a solution to the killing were dwindling with the passing time. Members of the family were coming to accept that just maybe the case would never be solved, that they might have to live out their lives knowing nothing more about what had taken place than they now knew. The experience had a different impact on family members though there seemed little doubt in the minds of some what this killing had been about.

Katrina had been in Africa on her honeymoon when word reached her a week after the murder. The caller first asked if she was sitting, then said to her husband, "Tell her Eva was killed a week ago."

"How?" he asked.

"She was shot."

"Katrina," he said to his wife, "Eva was killed."

A shiver ran through Katrina's body, followed by a violent spasm. She began to cry and was hysterical for days, during which she became fearful for her life and the rest of the family. In her mind there was absolutely not the slightest doubt who had murdered Eva and why. Her husband had told her a year earlier that he thought the family feud was going to lead to this, but she had not taken him seriously.

Mary Anna was deposed in one of the suits and asked, "Do you believe it's possible that your brother Joseph Shoen hired someone to commit the murder of Eva Berg Shoen?"

"Yes," she answered, "I believe that's a possibility."*

"What do you base that belief . . . on?"

"My lifelong relationship with my brother Joe, and the fact that the police investigation continues to center around Phoenix, Arizona, and the [U-Haul] Towers."

"Anything else?"

"The circumstances of her death as well."

She was asked to explain her answer. "Joe wants what he wants," she said, "and he will lay in wait for what he wants, and I believe he wanted my brother Sam out of the picture."

She was asked what Joe wanted. "What it is that he wants is complete control and to be in power of the [U-Haul] company,

---

*As noted earlier, no one has been charged in the murder and there has been no public disclosure of evidence linking Edward J. "Joe" Shoen or anyone else to it.

and I believe that he has done and will continue to do whatever is necessary to maintain his control."

"So you believe," the attorney asked, "that because your brother wishes to remain in control of [U-Haul] . . . he might have gone as far as to hire someone to commit the murder of Eva Berg Shoen? . . ."

"Yes."

Mary Anna added that Joe had "infinite patience to obtain and maintain power."

She was asked the basis for this comment. "One thing that comes to mind," she answered, "is Joe having told me when he originally seized control that my brother Sam should go on a, quote, long vacation, and the manner in which he said that frightened me somewhat." He had told her much the same thing at the airport in Las Vegas later, she said.

"And you interpreted that to mean that he wanted Sam dead?"

"No," Mary Anna said. "I don't think he wanted Sam dead. I think he wanted him out of the picture."

She was asked if she had expressed this belief about Joe to others in the outside group. "I've expressed it to all of my siblings, Mike, Sam, L.S., Cecilia, Katrina, and actually I don't know that I've spoke with Theresa about it. I can't recall."

"And what was their response to your statement that you believed your brother Joseph Shoen could possibly have been involved?"

"I believe they agree with me."

Mary Anna had watched Joe on a videotape denying any knowledge of Eva's murder. "And your comment to Cecilia was that you thought Joe looked dishonest on the tape?"

"Guilty as sin is another way of putting it."

"Guilty of what?"

"Only Joe knows."

Mike had been deposed as well and was asked if his brother Joe Shoen was responsible for the murder.

"Possibly," he answered.

"Is your brother Mark Shoen responsible for the murder of Eva Shoen?"

"Possibly."

"What do you base your assertion that Joe Shoen may possibly be responsible for the murder of Eva Shoen on?"

"My knowledge of Joe."

" . . . Do you believe that Joe Shoen possibly was involved in the murder of Eva Shoen?"

"Yes."

Cecilia in her deposition was asked, "Do you know who murdered Eva Berg Shoen?"

"No."

" . . . Do you believe that your brother Mark Shoen murdered Eva Shoen?"

"No."

"Do you believe that your brother Edward Joseph Shoen murdered Eva Shoen?"

"No."

"Do you believe that your brother Edward Joseph Shoen hired someone to commit that murder?"

"Yes."*

"You do believe that?"

"Yes." When she had heard the news, she said, " . . . My first thought was that she was murdered and it was related to Joe before I even knew that she was murdered."

One of the husbands was asked, "Has anyone ever told you that Edward Joseph Shoen was involved in the murder of Eva Shoen?"

"Not unequivocally, no." He was asked to explain himself. "A lot of people have said they thought or felt that both Edward and Mark were either directly or indirectly involved. . . . "

"Who are these people that have told you?"

" . . . Every family member, every Shoen family member, and every person that I have discussed this with has come to the same conclusion."

Mark's deposition was quite different in tone and content. He was asked if he was going to give money to help in the murder

---

*As noted earlier, no one has been charged in the murder and there has been no public disclosure of evidence linking Edward J. "Joe" Shoen or anyone else to it.

investigation. "... I am not going to give up my money," he testified. "The police have their money to go find murderers...."

He acknowledged that Masters had requested a lie detector test
from him. Asked if he had taken it, Mark said, "No, I didn't."
He explained his lawyer had told him not to, and he didn't think
they were reliable anyway.

"... The people who know you well," he was asked, "do they
suspect [you of murder]?"

"Hard to tell, isn't it?" Mark answered.

The experience had taught some members of the family important
lessons. Mary Anna believed that Eva's murder and the aftermath
had caused her to "straighten out" her values. She lost her arrogance and developed a sense of fallibility. She was more humble,
more self-reliant as a result, and more in control of her life.

Mike had a similar experience. He, too, was stripped of his
arrogance and saw his life's priorities with greater clarity. His wife
was "a gift from God," and he believed Eva's death in a strange
way had strengthened his own marriage.

For Katrina the experience had been a coming-of-age. It had
started when she refused to invite Joe to her wedding. She had
faced the reality that she must punish people for being wrong. "If
someone is ruining your life," she said, "you don't act as if they
aren't."

There was a sadder side to the changes, however. As a consequence of the feud, she was estranged from her mother, Suzanne,
and from her sister Sophia. Her faith in God was restored, and
she prayed now as part of her daily life. She hoped that all the
family members had learned from this.

When Katrina looked at Joe and Mark, she saw that they had
money and power but were very unhappy. No one respected them.
While others in the family were getting on with their lives, Joe and
Mark were locked in a trap.

In fact, a year after Eva's murder Mark had taken a high school
friend to the Sunflower ranch. The friend had been shocked to see
it was stocked like an arsenal, with food and weapons everywhere.
Mark had said this was where he planned to hole up if the IRS or
anyone else ever came for him.

*   *   *

Since his first date with Marcie Saban, Pound saw her nearly every day. For ten furious weeks they courted, then on October 19, 1991, were married in a lavish wedding. The news struck the Shoen family like a thunderbolt since they had not known the two even knew each other. Pound realized how it looked, but what was he to do? He loved Marcie.

In November Pound drove to Denver in one more attempt to interest the FBI. He believed he had more than enough evidence to suggest that Eva's murder had been planned and executed across state lines. The meeting went well, and a few days later an agent arrived in Telluride. He spent four days reading Pound's files and told the deputy that he could not imagine how he had managed to accomplish so much in so short a time. The FBI finally opened a file on the case.

On December 17, 1991, Pound learned that Joe was trying to have the records of his divorce proceedings with Heidi sealed. At a similar proceeding Joe had complained to the judge that he was the "number one suspect" in the murder of Eva Shoen. Pound and Nations decided to sit in on part of the hearing. Joe got up from the table and spotted Pound. His face turned bright red, and he walked stiffly down the aisle as if to go into the outer hallway. Just as he reached the doors, he suddenly spun on his heel, returned to where Pound sat, and slid on the bench beside him, pressing himself against Pound, his arm wrapped across his shoulders.

"Kim, are you practicing safe sex?" he whispered hoarsely into Pound's ear.

"I sure am, Joe. I'm glad you're concerned," Pound answered.

"Why don't you suck my cock?" Joe said fiercely.

Pound was stunned. "I'm glad we're having this conversation," he said.

Now Joe's voice turned threatening. "You better watch yourself in Arizona."

"Are you threatening a police officer, Joe?"

"You're not a police officer in this state," Joe said.

"I am in Colorado. Why don't you come up and visit me there sometime?"

"You'll never make it to Colorado," Joe said.

Nations had heard some of this and asked Pound, "What's he saying?" Pound repeated it.

Nations leaned across Pound and said, "Joe, I am a police officer here. Don't push your luck."

"Can I talk to you outside?" Joe said. In the hallway Joe told Nations how upset he was about his marriage and that he believed Pound was not out to solve the murder but on a vendetta to put Joe Shoen in jail.

A few days later Pound was served with a subpoena by Joe in one of his lawsuits. Mark was present at the deposition as Pound refused to provide any information about his investigation. During a break, while the attention of those in the room was elsewhere, Mark suddenly said to Pound, "You're next."

"Mark, you're not making a threat, are you?" Pound said.

Just then his lawyer jumped in and led Mark away. He came back to explain that his client meant only he intended to sue Pound.*

Since his marriage to Marcie, Pound had given his personal situation a great deal of thought. He could see no end to the investigation. It could be solved any day; then again it might never be solved. He still remembered vividly little Esben's taking his hand and saying, "You will find who killed my mom, won't you?" That moment had motivated Pound a thousand times when he was near exhaustion, but it could not keep him going indefinitely.

He was proud of the work he had done, and his was not an easy decision. He had never wanted to believe that because people had money and power, they could go into a small town and the local police would be too incompetent to solve the murder.

Pound wasn't certain if this investigation had cost him his previous marriage, but he knew it had done it no good. From Joe's

*No suit was filed.

and Mark's comments they seemed prepared to make his marriage to Marcie part of the investigation. He was not going to let that happen. He informed Masters that he was resigning and moving permanently to Phoenix, where he would take a job with Ned Saban.*

Before the change took effect, Pound had one final lead to follow. In late December 1991 he received a call from the Payson Police Department in Arizona, not far from the Sunflower ranch. He met with an officer who had worked narcotics the year before. The officer said that in July 1990 a reliable informant told him that there was a cache of drugs at the Shoen ranch. The narcotics officer recorded the information, intending to follow up, but before he did, he heard of the murder of Eva Shoen. He asked his informant if this was the same family and was told that it was. The man claimed now to have seen the drugs and said he had just been in the bunkhouse, where he spotted a handgun as well. When someone reported that the informant had been nosing around, one of the men in charge challenged him and ran him off.

Pound asked why he hadn't received this information at the time. Since this was a reliable source the narcotics officer had used before, he could have obtained a warrant and searched the ranch. The murder could possibly have been solved within days of the killing. The narcotics officer was surprised by the question. He *had* called the Colorado Bureau of Investigation and reported the information immediately, but nothing had happened. He had been wondering for more than a year why no one from Colorado had followed up. That was why he was contacting Pound now.

Pound had never been given the information.

Pound's resignation took effect on February 19, 1992, though Masters retained him as a reserve officer to use as necessary. He was no longer investigating Eva's murder, but not a day passed that he did not think of it and his promise to Esben. Masters was now responsible for the investigation and maintained a file though the San Miguel County sheriff's office did not have an investigator in Arizona. As the third anniversary of Eva Shoen's murder ap-

---

*In 1993 Pound took a position with the Apache Junction Police Department in Arizona.

proached, Masters no longer responded to informants with information that might link the case to U-Haul.

Real homicide investigations aren't like those in the movies or in most books. Sometimes people really do get away with murder.

Joe was virtually alone by now. He had lost his wife and his sons. He had driven his father out of his life by engaging in treacherous conduct. He was richer than he had ever been, but it is not likely he was any richer than he would have been had he left the company in the hands of his father and Sam.

There was irony in what had taken place. Joe and Mark had placed the wealth of Form Builders into their children's names and controlled the money and the company through their roles as conservators. But someday their children will be of age. And they have learned from their fathers how a child treats his father in matters of business.

Some time after the murder of Eva, Dr. Samuel Shoen sat in a Phoenix hotel lobby and with tears in his eyes described the horrifying events since the loss of his wife. What would Anna Mary, his long-dead mother, have done if she were alive? Without hesitation he said that she would march up to U-Haul Towers, tell her sons there that what they were doing was wrong, and throw them out.

How was all this to end? he was asked. Surely the bad guys had won, hadn't they?

Sam was suddenly angry and shook his head in disagreement. "The bad guys never win," he said firmly. "The more they seem to win, the unhappier they are. How can you win by crucifying your father? The worst thing that could ever have happened was for Joe to gain control of U-Haul. Now he has it, and it is destroying him."

Anna Mary, dead now for more than thirty-five years, had told L.S. shortly before her death that the success he enjoyed with U-Haul was how God meant for life to be for them. L.S. had not believed her. He remembered the nights around the campfires in the Willamette Valley of Oregon when his father had told his children that someday he would make them rich. His father had not managed to accomplish it, but L.S. had. None of his children had wanted for a single material thing in the world.

There had been another message those nights by the fire. Life existed as it had in the Old Testament: years of good luck, followed by an equal number of bad. If there was success in life, L.S. believed to his core, there was a price to be paid that could not be avoided.

When Anna Mary had died so tragically, L.S. thought he had paid that price. Now he knew he hadn't.

What L.S. saw when he watched Joe was James Carty destroying the Carty family farm. Whether he knew it or not, that was what Joe's reign in U-Haul was all about, and it wouldn't end until he was ousted from power or the company went under.

In Las Vegas L.S. wrote his endless letters while the cancer of murder ate at his soul and he watched his life's work being slowly destroyed in his final years. Yet another generation must pass into adulthood without a mother. There was no peace and no happiness for him.

L.S. had examined his life and reached the conclusion that he should never have spent it building U-Haul. At the age of seventy-six he had it in his mind that he alone was the cause of all this sorrow, and his guilt weighed heavily on him. He could not remake the past, but there was one final legacy he could give his family: He could do everything in his power to right this wrong with what remained of his days.

By this time there appeared to be no end to the interminable lawsuits. L.S., by training, if not practice, a lawyer himself, sitting in his office in Las Vegas, had concluded he would not live to see the end of them. Only if the murder of his daughter-in-law were solved would control of U-Haul change, he believed. Only then.

But the murder of Eva Berg Shoen remains unsolved and may in fact never be officially resolved. Despite the suspicions or beliefs of members of the Shoen family and of current or former employees of U-Haul, no evidence has been published that links any member of the family or of U-Haul management to her death. While investigators acknowledge that the murder may have been motivated in some measure by the family feud, they also make clear that it is possible there is no connection whatsoever. The reality is we may never know.

For the family as a whole it seems to make little difference. The sides are solidly drawn at last. For those who still care for one another the family is irretrievably split. There will be no more happy Christmas holidays together. All that is finished.

"How," one of the children asked, "can I celebrate Christmas with them after all that has happened?"

This in the end has become the Shoen birthright.

If the police and the courts have not solved the murder of Eva Shoen, that, too, makes little difference to the children of L. S. Shoen. In their hearts many of them have their answer.

SANTA FE

Following *Unsolved Mysteries'* rebroadcast of Eva's murder on April 21, 1993, a caller from New Mexico, Kelly Lemons, contacted the San Miguel County Sheriff's Office. He claimed his brother-in-law, Frank Emer Marquis, age thirty-eight, had bragged that he had murdered Eva Shoen. Lemons said that several weeks after Eva's murder Marquis told him he had been burglarizing a house. When a woman arrived at the home, surprising him, he shot her in the back. Marquis had been on parole in 1990 after serving eight years in the New Mexico Penitentiary for two counts of criminal sexual penetration—i.e., rape.

A friend of Marquis, Jeff Beale, said he had been in Telluride with Marquis the weekend of the murder. He recalled that Marquis had had a .22- or .25-caliber automatic handgun in his possession; he had also been missing one of the nights they were there. Another friend, Jared Ward, with whom Marquis worked as a car salesman, claimed he had loaned the gun to Marquis for that weekend trip. A different co-worker said Ward had been upset when Marquis returned the gun because it had been fired. Questioned, Marquis said he had "shot a dog" with the gun. In relating the story, Ward, however, did not remember that the gun had been fired or that he had been upset when it was returned.

At 5 P.M. on July 20, 1993, a San Miguel County deputy and others arrested Marquis, who had been housesitting for a friend in Santa Fe, New Mexico. When Marquis learned he was being charged with homicide, he turned to the friend and said, "I've never had anything to do with a homicide in my life." The day after his arrest he met with his public defender assigned for the extradition proceeding and said, "I know that everyone always tells you they're not guilty. But I'm not guilty." When he had been arrested in 1980 he had acknowledged his guilt and implicated himself in several other rapes as well.

From his home on the east coast, Sam told reporters, "I hope they have caught the person who did it. . . . I very much hope this is the man. My children and I will sleep easier."

Jon Sellers was exuberant. "I think they did a magnificent job following up. This helps exonerate the U-Haul family name, which I said would happen all along."

Kim Pound told the press, "This is a big relief to me," but privately he was disturbed. Sheriff Masters had always assured Pound that he would be there to make the arrest with him in what was the biggest case of both their careers. Instead Masters had told neither Pound nor Randy Nations that an arrest was about to be made. Also, uncharacteristically, Masters had left on a vacation to Boston shortly before Marquis was taken into custody and had avoided public comment afterward. As an elected official, Masters might have been expected to call a press conference and bask in the glory. After reviewing the case details Pound admitted, "I have very serious doubts that this is the right person."

He wasn't the only one. In Las Vegas, L.S. heard that Masters was claiming that sexual assault and burglary had been the motives for the attack on his daughter-in-law by her lone assailant and that the murder was not connected to the struggle for control of U-Haul. "I don't think they have the killer," L.S. told reporters bluntly. "I think this is a smoke screen." He said that he believed Marquis had been arrested within weeks of the publication of *Birthright* to divert attention from the work.

As details of Masters's case appeared in the press, Sam was having doubts himself. Reading that Lemons claimed Marquis had shot Eva when she interrupted him during a burglary, he said, "If that quote reflects what this guy really said, then either he's lying or he's not the killer."

Masters had said repeatedly that burglary and sexual assault did not appear to be motives in the killing, yet here he was attributing both of them to Marquis. It appeared that he was doing so based on Marquis's prior arrest history, not based upon the facts.

Additionally, on July 16 Masters had obtained Ward's .25-caliber Lorcin handgun, and the CBI compared it to the shell casing found at the murder scene and to the bullet taken from Eva. The gun was "similar in class characteristics," but not a match. Hundreds, if not thousands, of guns fit that standard.

Indeed, Marquis's arrest raised more questions than it answered. Beale, for example, was not certain if the pair had returned to Santa Fe on Sunday, prior to Eva's murder, or on Monday. Lemons, who acknowledged his interest in the $250,000 reward, had been instructed by police to obtain Marquis's admission that he had murdered the woman on tape. When he called Marquis, however, and attempted to have him repeat the alleged statements, Marquis said nothing about killing anyone.

Finally, there were major unresolved issues. Although investigators remained certain that more than one killer had been involved, Marquis's alleged version of the event was that he had acted alone. In addition, though sexual assault was purported to have been Marquis's motive in part, Eva's panties and nightgown had been undisturbed.

And there were the needle marks. Masters had no explanation of their significance if Marquis was the killer. Indeed, the search warrant issued listed many items the sheriff hoped to find in Marquis's effects that would connect him to the murder, but not needles. Marquis's passport, sandpaper, and a screwdriver were all that was seized.

U-Haul issued an unusual press release: "According to U-Haul International Executive Vice President Harry DeShong, 'At U-Haul International we certainly understand the importance of gathering the best personnel, identifying a goal and establishing a strategy for success in achieving that goal. We're always pleased to offer positive comment on the accomplishments of the law enforcement community. U-Haul International is proud of their efforts, and apparent success in arresting a suspect in the Eva Shoen murder case.' "

The reward offer of $250,000, to be paid by Eva Berg Shoen's loved ones to any person who provides information that leads to the arrest and conviction of those responsible for her murder, remains outstanding. Information should be forwarded to:

Sheriff Bill Masters
San Miguel County
P.O. Box 455
Telluride, Colorado 81435
303-728-3081
or
Sheriff Joe Arpaio
Maricopa County
102 W. Madison
Phoenix, Arizona 85003
602-256-1000

INDEX

412